THE ENCYCLOPÆDIA OF FONTS

THE ENCYCLOPÆDIA OF FONTS

THE ENCYCLOPÆDIA OF FONTS

THE ENCYCLOPÆDIA OF FONTS

THE ENCYCLOPÆDIA OF FONTS

THE ENCYCLOPÆDIA OF FONTS

THE ENCYCLOPÆDIA OF FONTS

GWYN HEADLEY

"Fonts are the clothes words wear."

CAROLINE ARCHER

For Yvonne. Thank you for telling me.

First published in Great Britain in 2005 by Cassell Illustrated,
a division of Octopus Publishing Group Limited
2-4 Heron Quays, London E14 4JP

ISBN 13: 9781844032068
ISBN-10: 1 84403 206 X

CONTENTS

INTRODUCTION

The first rule to remember is that there are rules. That's how type was set. That's how music is notated. Silence and white space lie at the heart of good music, speech and typography. A great blues guitarist pays just as much attention to the gaps as to the notes, just as comic timing depends on the critical pause, and good typography sits comfortably on the page, as invisible as silence.

WHAT IS A FONT?

What is a typeface, and what is a font? The names are seemingly interchangeable, but it is time to offer a definition. Typefaces are hot metal, fonts are digital. This is an abrupt division, but all revolutions are abrupt. For 530 years typefaces were made from an alloy of lead (large point sizes were carved out of wood). In the past 30 years the change to digital has been total, though as recently as 2002 the Encyclopaedia Britannica dismissed computer-generated fonts with "The electronically created letter that lives out its

A FOUNT OF BULMER MT REGULAR 12PT

—	&	[	*thin*	(	j		'	'	?	!		;	1	2	3	4	5	6	7	8	9	0
æ				e										£	ff	A	B	C	D	E	F	G
	v	c	d		i		s		f	g												
ffi														fl	fi							
k														*thick space*	*nut space*	H	I	K	L	M	N	O
	l	m	n	h	o	y	p	,		w												
hairs																						
z								q	:					*em quad*		P	Y	R	S	T	U	W
	v	u	t	*middle*	a		r															
x								.	-							X	Q	Z	Æ	Œ	V	J

brief life while moving across the face of a signboard or a cathode-ray tube is not a typographic item."

Typefaces emerged from the heat of furnaces, the clang of punches, vats of molten metal, the shouts of sweaty, burly men, a distant cry from the measured serenity of the drawing office. By contrast fonts are created with no more noise or discomfort than the agreeable hum of a contented air conditioner.

Hand-set metal type used to be stored in large wooden trays called Cases, divided into smaller compartments which held all the letters and figures in a particular typeface. The largest compartment held the commonest letter, the lowercase 'e', while the smallest compartments held rarities such as the 'ct–' ligature. One tray held all the characters of one point size, and this collection was called a Fount.

English being the perverse and glorious language it is, this was pronounced Font. Distaste for the English love of the U led the Americans to favour the non-U, leaving us with the word font, which was used with blithe disregard for the word's proud heritage and definition as the basin in a church which holds baptismal water. Speaking of the compilation of an Encyclopaedia of Fonts produces a markedly different response from a cleric or architectural historian than from a typographer. There was no such confusion with typefaces. The most evocative description is an observation by type guru Caroline Archer:–

"Fonts are the clothes words wear."

THE NIGHTMARE OF FONT MANAGEMENT

Because anybody can create a font, too many people do. One tiny error in the code and a rogue font will crash your system. There are font management programs to help try and overcome this; the market leader is Extensis's Suitcase, used in the preparation of this book. It is far from perfect – transferring data from a desktop to a laptop so they worked in synchronicity was close to impossible. Try and buy fonts from reputable foundries. The right people get rewarded for

their work, you're paying an honest rate for honest toil – and believe me, creating a good font is genuine toil – and the fonts will have been rigorously tested so as to minimise the risk of conflicts on your computer.

There are unfortunately too many rogue foundries, rip-off fonts and unabashed thieves out there, and by buying their products you do your own little part to benefit the world of crime. So if you see a font called Jabot Display which looks just like Peignot – one of the most original and distinctive typefaces of the twentieth century – it isn't Peignot; someone has simply stolen the design. Don't buy it. It could also crash your computer. One of these unsavoury foundries was run by a guy who ordained himself and is currently spending time in gaol for sex offences, perhaps not the best person to be sending money to. Plenty of good independent small foundries exist, producing original new font designs of serene beauty and startling innovation, and their fonts are created with care and devotion. Use them as much as you can, and continue to buy the classic fonts from the original classic foundries.

FONT CREATION

One example will serve for the danger of font creation. Good art student gets job, achieves a degree of recognition for his work, gets married, they have a baby, baby becomes toddler, toddler grasps a pen from daddy's desk and attempts to copy Daddy working, and daddy (for it is always he), entranced, enraptured and besotted with his own creation, creates a font based on his daughter's handwriting (for it is always her). Now at this stage in the days of hot metal type the designer's dream would be interrupted by the ridicule of his colleagues, the disdain of his managing director, the incomprehension of the company accountant and the impossibility of taking his dream from hot metal into cold type. Now, alas, the editorial control has been stripped away and the font, in all its gory frightfulness, can be on the market within hours. And worse still, there are a few people – a very few, mind you – who persuade themselves to pay good money for these creations.

It is difficult to allocate correct credit to the designers of typefaces before the 1960s. In an age when the account of the Charge of the Light Brigade was simply credited "From Our Own Correspondent" the modesty of anonymity was shared by the majority of type designers, credit going to the foundry. Many typographical historians have carried out remarkable and valuable research, discovering the lettering artists working in foundries from staff records and salary slips, but attribution is the preserve of the scholar, not the compiler. The publisher would be grateful to learn of any corrections or emendations for future editions.

FONT NAMES

Giving different fonts the same name is a quick and easy way of getting your computer to crash. Never be tempted to change the name of a legally purchased font. If it turns out to be the cause of your crashing computer, you have an avenue of complaint. Font names used to be descriptive, e.g. Old Style No. 7, then the designer's name began to be attached to them – Goudy Old Style – then the foundries wanted their credit – Linotype Inagur. This has led to a certain degree of confusion in the finding of fonts, at least when searching alphabetically. The nomenclature of fonts follows the fine example of the Welsh language in often mutating the beginning of the name rather than the end, thus making some fonts nigh impossible to find. Take Triumvirate Condensed. You know where you are, don't you? You look under T. But it's not there. Aha! Dimly recalling the font was marketed by Computer Graphics you search for CGTriumvirate and luckily you find it and install it on your computer. But when you come to create your layout using Triumvirate, you find it's vanished. Nothing under Triumvirate, nothing under CGTriumvirate. That's because you forgot to look under ATTriumvirate, which is where your InDesign or Quark program will have filed it.

No, I don't know why. Live with it.

We are told daily by politicians that educational standards are constantly rising. Exam results are improving, top grades are everywhere. Rodrigo Cavazos designed a font called Peregrine. It is sold by CA Partners as Perrigrine. There are enough examples of such sloppy editing in font names to please the most finicky pedant.

FONT FORMATS

One of the reasons for the plethora of font formats is the natural reluctance to be dominated by one proprietary system; another is the tremendous advance in computing speeds and processing power. TrueType was developed to combat the hegemony of Adobe's PostScript Type 1, while Adobe and Microsoft have since joined forces to promote OpenType, which has been enthusiastically embraced by Apple. However this is not the place to discuss the relative merits and problems of various font formats, because they are discussed in far greater detail and clarity than we could offer here on Luc Devroye's home page at http://jeff.cs.mcgill.ca/~luc/fonts.html, an extraordinary site, which is a shrine to typography.

BLACKLETTER, ITALIC, ROMAN, SANS SERIF AND SUITES

A useful text font usually has a minimum of four weights: roman (or regular), italic, bold and bold italic. Please throw away the bold italic. Italics actually come in three varieties: an entirely separate font, italic, and oblique or slanted Roman. This partly explains the appearance of some apparent text fonts under the Display heading – only one weight is available – and conversely some single weight text fonts such as Poliphilus have an associated italic under a different name, such as Blado, an entirely separate font. The use of oblique or slanted Roman is unprofessional and deprecated.

The first printed book was set in Blackletter, a replica of fifteenth century Middle European monastic script. It is still occasionally used in Germany, although associating it with the Nazis and fascism is completely wrong: for some bizarre reason the Nazis associated Blackletter with Judaism, and banned the style in 1940. The serif Roman faces in which the great majority of books are set today originated in Italy in the late fifteenth century, as did Italic. It took some time for italic fonts to take their place as an expected weight in font design, and we have recently begun to witness a quiet revolution in font marketing, one that is every bit as significant as the move from hot metal to digital.

When a new text font is designed today, there is a strong possibility that it will be presented by the foundry as a suite. The serif roman version of the font may be Humanist, Garalde, Transitional or Didone in its basic style, but there will also be a Slab serif version, a Lineale and even a monospaced derivation, in dozens or even hundreds of weights. Typographers can use one basic font to fill every print or web requirement. Although there had been several earlier attempts to create such conglomerations, it was the introduction of Agfa Rotis in 1989 that swept the market and inspired many imitators. Rotis became the corporate font of the 1990s, used by banks, book publishers and building societies. Sadly the designer Otl Aichl never lived to see the worldwide success of his creation.

TYPE CLASSIFICATIONS

The core division is between Text and Display. Type classification came into its own in the twentieth century, when the making of lists reached its zenith and became a discipline in its own right. Up until the latter half of the last century, designers competed in a never-ending quest to create the perfect, most legible font. Now the standards have shifted, and the prize will be to the first to produce a totally illegible font. We have nearly achieved this, as you will see from the examples in this encyclopaedia. Type classifications were created in order to arrange the fundamental styles of legible type. Civilisation having

apparently progressed beyond the necessity for legibility, these classifications are approaching redundancy but nonetheless they will linger for as long as there is a demand by someone to read music, hieroglyphs or books.

As described above, the typographic trend that marks the dawn of the new millennium is the rise of the font suite: a range of similar looking text fonts appearing in serif, sans serif, slab serif and script or display formats. These will be designed from the drawing board up to fulfil stringent demands of clarity and legibility for corporate users, both in print and for web use. Strange that one half of the type world is striving towards the ever more perfect letter form while the other half steers ever closer to illegibility. This is the first book to group these font suites together as complete families rather than splitting them among their respective styles.

Given the limitless possibilities for font creation, it seems overambitious to divide the exploding Display category into any but the broadest systematics – but of course we had to try. The following table demonstrates the divisions within this encyclopaedia and their direct comparisons with the best-known type classifications.

GUTENBERG AND THE WONDERFUL WORLD OF INSECTS

Everyone interested in the printed word is aware of Gutenberg's Bible, the first book to be printed from movable type and recognised as the most valuable book in the world. What few of us realise is that 99.9% of books published today trace their ancestry back, not to Gutenberg's Bible, but to a forgotten title by Albro T Gaul, first published by Rinehart in New York in 1953 and titled The Wonderful World of Insects. It was the first book to be photoset, and so from our definition it was the first book to use fonts rather than typefaces. Buried at the back of the book is this modest paragraph: "The Wonderful World of Insects derives added significance from the manner in which

THE CLASSIFICATIONS OF TYPE as arranged in this Encyclopædia and elsewhere

2002 This book	1991 Adobe	1988 Linotype	1986 Bitstream	1971 Alexander Lawson	1967 British 2961
TEXT					
UNCIAL					
BLACKLETTER Lombardic Chancery Fraktur English Lineale	BLACKLETTER	BLACKLETTER BROKEN	BLACKLETTER	BLACKLETTER Rotunda Gothic Antique Bastarda Text	MEDIOEVALI
SERIFS Humanist Garalde Transitional Didone Slab Glyphic Misc Engravers	Venetian Oldstyle Garalde Oldstyle Transitional Didone (Modern) Slab Serif Glyphic	Old Face Transitional Modern Face Slab Serif	SERIFS Oldstyle Transitional Modern Clarendon Slabserif Engravers	SERIFS Oldstyle–Venetian Oldstyle–Aldine French Oldstyle–Dutch English Transitional Modern Square Serif	SERIFS Humanist Garalde Transitional Didone Slab Serif Glyphic
LINEALES Grotesques Neo Grotesques Geometrics Humanist Misc	SANS SERIF	SANS SERIF	SANSERIF	SANS SERIF Gothic Geometric Humanist	LINEALE
MISC Faux Fonts Suites Monospace	MONOSPACED				
SCRIPTS Formal Calligraphic Handwriting Poster Kid Misc	SCRIPT	SCRIPT & BRUSH	SCRIPT	SCRIPT CURSIVE	SCRIPT
DISPLAY Script Lineale Serif Other Woodcut / Western Grunge Moderne Curly Cutouts Dot / OCR / Computer Graphic Psychedelic Stencil	DECORATIVE & DISPLAY Computer Related Hand tooled, inline, outline, Stencil Capitals, Swash, Expert Collection	DECORATIVE & DISPLAY Exotic / Freeform	DECORATED Computer Stencil	DISPLAY DECORATIVE	GRAPHIC

1964 German DIN	1961 ATypI	1957 Aldo Novarese	1954 Maximilien Vox	1925 British 20C	1921 Thibaudeau
	Lapidari				
GEBROCHENE SCHRIFTEN	**FRACTURA**	**MEDIOEVALI**	**FRACTURE**	**BLACKLETTER**	**GOTHIQUE**
Rotunda					
Barok-Fraktur					
Schwabacher	Fraktur				
Textura	Schwabacher				
	Textura / Gothic		Gothique		
SERIFS	**SERIFS**	**SERIFS**	**SERIFS**	**SERIFS**	**SERIFS**
Venezianische Renaissance-Antiqua	Humane	Veneziani	Humane	Venetian	Elzevir
Französische Renaissance-Antiqua	Garalde		Garalde	Old Face	
Barock-Antiqua	Réale	Transizionali	Réale	Transitional	
Klassizistische Antiqua	Didone	Bodoniani	Didone	Modern	Didot
					Égyptienne anglaise
	Mécane	Egiziani	Mécane	Egyptian	Égyptienne
	Incise		Incise		Helléniques
	LINÉALE	**LINEARI**	**LINÉALE**	**SANS-SERIF**	**ANTIQUE**
	Grotesque	Grotesques			
	Neo Grotesque	Neo-Grotesques			
	Geométric	Geométricas			
	Humanist	Humanistas	Linéale Humaniste		
SCHREIBSCHRIFTEN	**SCRIPTE**	**SCRITTI**	**SCRIPTE**	**SCRIPT**	**CURSIVE**
	Manuaire		Manuaire		
		FANTASIE	**FORMES ÉTRANGÈRES**	**DISPLAY**	
		Ornati			

it was composed. It is the first volume composed with the revolutionary Higonnet-Moyroud photographic type-composing machine. Absolutely no type, in the conventional sense, was used in the preparation of this book." And what was the first photoset text font to be used? That old Monotype Didone stand-by, Scotch Roman.

USING THE ENCYCLOPAEDIA OF FONTS

This book is intended as a successor to Jaspert Berry and Johnson's Encyclopaedia of Typefaces, published by Blandford Press, an ancestral company of Cassell Illustrated, over half a century ago. That classic book, like other compendiums before and since, divided its typefaces into accepted classifications – Venetian, Old Face, Modern, Sans serif &c – then listed them alphabetically. It worked, but a book that listed fonts by style was needed. It wasn't so much of a problem when there were relatively few hot metal foundries and therefore fewer types, but in the early 21st century when 664 fonts could be listed as Transitional Serif alone, this writer felt it was past time to rearrange the lists. The concept of this book is to list fonts visually, to show them as they have evolved chronologically and stylistically.

CLASSIFICATION OF FONTS

Therefore after the divisions between Text and Display, and the subdivisions of Serif, Script, Sans and so on as listed in the table of type classifications above, the fonts are primarily arranged by date; however where two or more fonts show marked similarities they are grouped together, with the earliest design coming first. For the benefit of abcderians, there is also an alphabetical index, and an index of font designers.

The encyclopædia is designed to be used in conjunction with commercial font catalogues which will show examples of the variety of weights available. Without these, it is designed to be the only font book you'll ever need.

Many typefaces have achieved huge success, often due to the assiduous marketing of the foundries, but some, like Frank Heine's Remedy, have simply captured the zeitgeist and spawned a host of imitators. In this book we can see the inspirations and the derivations, the (Latin alphabet) world-shaking fonts such as Garamond, Caslon, Baskerville, Bodoni, the Grotesques, Futura, Gill Sans, Times New Roman, Helvetica and Agfa Rotis, along with their ancestors and descendants.

FONT WEIGHTS

There are many more individually designed fonts displayed in this book than in any other single volume font compendium. To pack in as many separate fonts as we possibly could, we have only shown the one weight, often called Roman, Book, Regular, Medium, Normal or some similar calming, middle-of-the-matrix name. Using a logarithmic rule, we have indicated the number of available weights in each font family, which is an essential guide to its versatility. The Berlin foundry FontFont inclines towards producing a staggering number of weights for each family and dividing them into 'paying weights' and 'free weights' – when a font is purchased it may arrive with a plethora of additional free weights with special characters, ligatures. Their 'Fago' already has 256 weights and counting, while at the furthest extreme font designer Alessio Leonardi is presently working on a font with over 600 weights. In a computer driven age, creating a range of weights is relatively easy; back in hot metal days the designs of different weights were often substantially altered, as indeed were the designs for point sizes. 72 point was completely distinct from 6 point, a fine point which has eluded many modern digital foundries, with the honourable exception of a few designers such as the late Justin Howes with his Founder's Caslon range. Gill Sans Light is not just a lighter version of Gill Sans; though recognisably similar, it has an entirely separate personality, like siblings in a large family.

Where another font weight has produced a completely different design, vide Futura and Futura Black, as against a thickened, extended, condensed or slenderised version of the core design, we have tried to show the two.

SELECTING THE FONTS

How difficult can it be to produce a book like this? You choose the fonts, you put them in order, and that's about it. Yes, but … Look at it like this. You know those wonderful tins of coloured crayons made by Lakeland or Faber-Castell? When high streets had art shops I used to press my nose against the windows salivating at the rainbow – more than the rainbow – of colours. I could probably just about afford a box of twelve, but there were boxes of 36, and 72, and it was rumoured (but only rumoured) that at the back of Green & Stone somebody had actually seen a box of 256 different coloured crayons. Wow. Imagine 256 different colours! Far out, as we used to say at the time. OK, now fast-forward forty years. I'm asked to compile the Encyclopædia of Fonts. I've been a fontoholic for years. It's a privilege and an honour. I jump at the chance.

Now think back on those crayons again. You have a house full of them, more than you ever imagined. There are in fact over 18,000 colours. And you've spilt them all on the floor, every imaginable different colour, and you have to arrange them all sequentially. The Germans have a word for it – Albtraum. But because you've only got physical space for two and a half thousand or so, you have to look at all the colours to decide which ones you're going to throw out. And I mean you have to look at them closely. Of course you can't pick them up and study them microscopically, because – didn't I mention this? – you can't actually touch any of them. Oh, and the maker's name can't be seen on most of them. You have to sort them not just by the colour but by the date they were manufactured, and find out if they were made in Sweden or Germany or the Netherlands or America. Who made them? Who did they make them for? Why did

they give them those strange names: Viridian, Reseda, Alizarin Crimson, Chrome Yellow? Or, in this case, Banshee, Zennor, Boberia? Because all these fantasy colours are fonts, thousands of them, dateless and anonymous in the majority of cases, yet all sharing 36 items of common heritage – the Latin alphabet and the Arabic numerals. What I have striven to do in this book is to arrange a small selection of the available fonts in a chromatic scale. And as with all publishing projects, we are also constrained by cost and utility: it is not feasible to publish a book of 2,000+ pages (it would be too unwieldy to use) nor would it be financially viable for the publisher.

This book is like a fine wine; it will improve with age and revision. Inevitably there will be omissions and protestations – "why isn't Furtwangler Extended included?" You now know the reason; there simply aren't enough pages.

FONT SAMPLES

Font samples are usually marvellous examples of sententiousness, homilies and boredom, and after Jack Nicholson in "The Shining", the thought of 2000 repetitions of 'the quick brown fox jumps over the lazy dog' is reason enough to start slaughtering wife and family and claiming justifiable homicide. So in this book we have used the widest variety of pangrams we could find, and in a few cases thrown in some light-hearted (we hope) definitions of the font's name to ensure this properly lives up to the title of The Encyclopaedia of Fonts.

Gwyn Headley

Gwyn Headley
Harlech & London, 2005

Fonts are listed in the book firstly by classification, then by date, then by style. For each font we show the name, the designer, his or her nationality, the date the design first appeared, the foundries in the order in which they introduced the typeface or font, the credit for the recutting or digitising, and the number of weights. The logarithmic bar underneath each font sample gives a quick visual indication of the number of weights available.

Neue Hammer Unziale

Designer	Victor Hammer
Nationality	AT
Date Designed	1953
Foundries	Klingspor Linotype Adobe
Number of weights	1

ABCDEFGHIJKLMNOPQRSTUVWXYZ
abcdefghijklmnopqrstuvwxyz1234567890
We promptly judged antique ivory buckles for the next prize.

American Uncial

Designer	Victor Hammer
Nationality	AT
Date Designed	1953
Foundries	Linotype Elsner+Flake URW++
Number of weights	1

abcdefghijklmnopqrstuvwxyz
abcdefghijklmnopqrstuvwxyz1234567890
may jo equal the fine record by solving six puzzles a week?

Uncial

Designer	Miles Inc
Nationality	US
Date Designed	1993
Foundries	Creative Alliance
Number of weights	1

ABCDEFGHIJKLMNOPQRSTUVWXYZ
abcdefghijklmnopqrstuvwxyz1234567890
My help squeezed back in again and joined the weavers after six.

Omnia

Designer	Karlgeorg Hoefer
Nationality	DE
Date Designed	1990
Foundries	Linotype Adobe
Number of weights	1

abcdefghijklmnopqrstuvwxyz
abcdefghijklmnopqrstuvwxyz1234567890
the risque gown maked a very brazen exposure of juicy flesh.

Benedikt

Designer	Bo Berndal
Nationality	SE
Date Designed	1991
Foundries	Monotype
Number of weights	1

ABCDEFGHIJKLMNOPQRSTUVWXYZ
ABCDEFGHIJKLMNOPQRSTUVWXYZ1234567890
WEST QUICKLY GAVE BERT HANDSOME PRIZES FOR
SIX JUICY PLUMS.

Lukrezia

Designer	Jürgen Brinckmann
Nationality	DE
Date Designed	1993
Foundries	FontFont
Number of weights	1

ABCDEFÇHIJKLMNOPQRSTUVWXYZ
ABCDEFÇHIJKLMNOPQRSTUVWXYZ1234567890
ZWEEDSE EX-VIP, BEHOORLIJK ÇEK OP QUANTUMFYSICA.

Uncia

Designer	Julius de Goede
Nationality	NL
Date Designed	1998
Foundries	Monotype
Number of weights	1

ABCDEFGHIJKLMNOPQRSTUVWXYZ
ABCDEFGHIJKLMNOPQRSTUVWXYZ1234567890
LLANFAIRPWLLGWYNGYLLGOGERYCHWYRNDROBWLLLLAN
TYSILIOGOGOGOCH.

Benedict Uncial

Designer	Philip Bouwsma
Nationality	US
Date Designed	1994
Foundries	Monotype
Number of weights	1

ABCDEFGHIJKLMNOPQRSTUVWXYZ
ABCDEFGHIJKLMNOPQRSTUVWXYZ1234567890
FRED SPECIALIZED IN THE JOB OF MAKING VERY
QUAINT WAX TOYS.

Colmcille

Designer	Monotype
Nationality	UK
Date Designed	1991
Foundries	Monotype
Number of weights	1

ABCDEFGHIJKLMNOPQRSTUVWXYZ
abcdefghijklmnopqrstuvwxyz1234567890
Just keep examining every low bid quoted for
zinc etchings.

Carolus Magnus

Designer	Manfred Klein
Nationality	DE
Date Designed	1991
Foundries	FontFont
Number of weights	1

abcdefghijklmnopqrstuvwxyz

abcdefghijklmnopqrſtuvwxyz1234567890

freight to me ſixty dozen quart jarſand twelve black panſ.

Studz

Designer	Michael Harvey
Nationality	UK
Date Designed	1996
Foundries	Adobe Linotype
Number of weights	1

ABCDEFGHIJKLMNOPQRSTUVWXYZ

ABCDEFGHIJKLMNOPQRSTUVWXYZ1234567890

QUIXOTIC CONSERVATIVES VET FIRST KEY ZERO-GROWTH JEREMIAD.

Simplex

Designer	S H De Roos
Nationality	NL
Date Designed	1939
Foundries	Amsterdam Monotype Type Revivals
Number of weights	1

ABCDEFGHIJKLMNOPQRSTUVWXYZ

abcdefghijklmnopqrstuvwxyz1234567890

Lazy movers quit hard-packing of papier-mache jewellery boxes.

Eirinn

Designer	Norbert Reiners
Nationality	DE
Date Designed	1994
Foundries	Linotype
Number of weights	1

abcdefghijklmnopqrstuvwxyz

abcdefghijklmnopqnrtuvwxyz1234567890

Céad Míle Fáilte!

Korigan

Designer	Thierry Puyfoulhoux
Nationality	FR
Date Designed	1995
Foundries	ITC Linotype Monotype
Number of weights	1

ABCDEFGHIJKLMNOPQRSTUVWXYZ

ABCDEFGHIJKLMNOPQRSTUVWXYZ1234567890

Moi, je veux quinze clubs a golf et du whisky pur.

Abbot Uncial

Designer	Richard Yeend
Nationality	UK
Date Designed	1996
Foundries	Monotype
Number of weights	1

ABCDEFGHIJKLMNOPQRSTUVWXYZ

ABCDEFGHIJKLMNOPQRSTUVWXYZ1234567890

BREEZILY JANGLING £3,416,857,209 WISE ADVERTISER AMBLES TO THE BANK, HIS EXCHEQUER AMPLIFIED.

Iona

Designer	Gerard Mariscalchi
Nationality	CA
Date Designed	1998
Foundries	Monotype
Number of weights	1

ABCDEFGHIJKLMNOPQRSTUVWXYZ

ABCDEFGHIJKLMNOPQRSTUVWXYZ1234567890

Iona Jones moved from Nefyn to Harlech.

Forkbeard

Designer	Michael Gills
Nationality	UK
Date Designed	1998
Foundries	ITC Linotype Monotype
Number of weights	1

ABCDEFGHIJKLMNOPQRSTUVWXYZ

ABCDEFGHIJKLMNOPQRSTUVWXYZ1234567890

Jeb quickly drove a few extra miles on the glazed pavement.

Vadstenakursive

Designer	Bo Berndal
Nationality	SE
Date Designed	1989
Foundries	Monotype
Number of weights	1

ABCDEFGHIJKLMNOPQRSTUVWXYZ

abcdefghijklmnopqrstuvwxyz1234567890

Quixotic Conservatives vet first key zero-growth jeremiad.

Madonna

Designer	Jürgen Brinckmann
Nationality	DE
Date Designed	1993
Foundries	FontFont
Number of weights	1

ABCDEFGHIJKLMNOPQRSTUVWXYZ

abcdefghijklmnopqrstuvwxyz1234567890

Zwei Boxkämpfer jagen Eva quer durch Sylt.

Francesca Gothic

Designer	Philip Bouwsma
Nationality	US
Date Designed	1994
Foundries	Creative Alliance
Number of weights	1

ABCDEFGHIJKLMNOPQRSTUVWXYZ

abcdefghijklmnopqrstuvwxyz1234567890

A quick movement of the enemy will jeopardize six gunboats.

Hrabanus

Designer	Philip Bouwsma
Nationality	US
Date Designed	1994
Foundries	Monotype
Number of weights	1

ABCDEFGHIJKLMNOPQRSTUVWXYZ

abcdefghijklmnopqrstuvwxyz1234567890

All questions asked by five watch experts amazed the judge.

Frances Uncial

Designer	Michael Gills
Nationality	UK
Date Designed	1995
Foundries	Creative Alliance Letraset ITC
Number of weights	1

abcdefghijkLmnopqrstuvwxyz

abcdefghijkLmnopqrstuvwxyz1234567890

jay visited back home and gazed upon a brown fox and quail.

Percolator

Designer	Adam Roe
Nationality	US
Date Designed	1996
Foundries	CA Partners
Number of weights	1

ABCDEFGHIJKLMNOPQRSTUVWXYZ

ABCDEFGHIJKLMNOPQRSTUVWXYZ1234567890

back in june we delivered oxygen equipment of the same size.

Humanistika

Designer	Hellmut G Bomm
Nationality	DE
Date Designed	1997
Foundries	Linotype
Number of weights	1

ABCDEFGHIJKLMNOPQRSTUVWXYZ

ABCDEFGHIJKLMNOPQRSTUVWXYZ1234567890

Jail zesty vixen who grabbed pay from quack.

Uppsala

Designer	Paul Shaw, Garrett Boge
Nationality	US
Date Designed	1998
Foundries	LetterPerfect
Number of weights	1

ABCDEFGHIJKLMNOPQRSTUVWXYZ
ABCDEFGHIJKLMNOPQRSTUVWXYZ1234567890
Astronaut Quincy B. Zack defies gravity with six jet fuel pumps.

Minska

Designer	Carl Crossgrove
Nationality	US
Date Designed	1996
Foundries	ITC Linotype Creative Alliance Fontek
Number of weights	1

ABCDEFGHIJKLMNOPQRSTUVWXYZ
ABCDEFGHIJKLMNOPQRSTUVWXYZ1234567890
Vie promptly judged antique ivory buckles for the next prize.

Aquitaine Initials

Designer	Steven Albert
Nationality	FR
Date Designed	1987
Foundries	Linotype ITC
Number of weights	1

ABCDEFGHIJKLMNOPQRSTUVWXYZ
ABCDEFGHIJKLMNOPQRSTUVWXYZ1234567890
...BUT NOT AN UNCIAL.

Irish Text

Designer	Torsten Weisheit
Nationality	DE
Date Designed	1997
Foundries	Linotype
Number of weights	1

ABCDEFGHIJKLMNOPQRSTUVWXYZ
ABCDEFGHIJKLMNOPQRSTUVWXYZ1234567890
The exodus of jazzy pigeons is craved by squeamish walkers.

Skreech

Designer	Jim Marcus
Nationality	US
Date Designed	1994
Foundries	T-26 Creative Alliance
Number of weights	1

ABCDEFGHIJKLMNOPQRSTUVWXYZ
ABCDEFGHIJKLMNOPQRSTUVWXYZ1234567890
While jauntily waxing parquet decks, Suez sailors vomit abaft.

Textur Lombardic

Designer	Linotype
Nationality	DE
Date Designed	1990
Foundries	Linotype
Number of weights	1

ABCDEFGHIJKLMNOPQRSTUVWXYZ
abcdefghijklmnopqrsfuvwxyz1234567890
My grandfather picks up quartz and valuable onyx jewels.

Averoigne

Designer	David F Nalle
Nationality	US
Date Designed	1993
Foundries	Scriptorium
Number of weights	1

ABCDEFGHIJKLMNOPQRSTUVWXYZ?
ABCDEFGHIJKLMNOPQRSTUVWXYZ?
CLARK ASHTON SMITH INVENTED THIS FICTIONAL
REGION OF FRANCE.

Blackmoor

Designer	David Quay
Nationality	UK
Date Designed	1993
Foundries	Monotype ITC
Number of weights	1

ABCDEFGHIJKLMNOPQRSTUVWXYZ
abcdefghijklmnopqrstuvwxyz1234567890
Five big quacking zephyrs jolt my wax bed.

Albany Telegram

Designer	Jim Marcus
Nationality	US
Date Designed	1997
Foundries	ITC
Number of weights	1

abcdefghijklmnopqrstuvwxyz?
abcdefghijklmnopqrstuvwxyz1234567890?
The five boxing wizards jump quickly.

Duc de Berry

Designer	Gottfried Pott
Nationality	FR
Date Designed	1990
Foundries	Linotype Adobe
Number of weights	2

ABCDEFGHIJKLMNOPQRSTUVWXYZ
abcdefghijklmnopqrstuvwxyz1234567890
Owner of the fabulous manuscript Les Tres Riches Heures

Chancery

Bastarda

Designer	Foundry
Nationality	US
Date Designed	2000
Foundries	Foundry
Number of weights	1

ABCDEFGHIJKLMNOPQRSTUVWXYZ

abcdefghijklmnopqrstuvwxyz1234567890

A poor imitation of Cancellaresca Bastarda.

Bollatica

Designer	Philip Bouwsma
Nationality	US
Date Designed	1999
Foundries	Monotype
Number of weights	1

ABCDEFGHIJKLMNOPQRSTUVWXYZ

abcdefghijklmnopqrstuvwxyz1234567890

Breezily jangling £3,416,857,209, wise advertiser ambles to the bank, his exchequer amplified.

Castiglione

Designer	David F Nalle
Nationality	US
Date Designed	1992
Foundries	Scriptorium
Number of weights	1

ABCDEFGHIJKLMNOPQRSTUVWXYZ?
abcdefghijklmnopqrstuvwxyz1234567890?

Chestnut ice-cream.

Clairvaux

Designer	Linotype
Nationality	FR
Date Designed	1991
Foundries	Adobe Linotype
Number of weights	2

ABCDEFGHIJKLMNOPQRSTUVWXYZ

abcdefghijklmnopqrstuvwxyz1234567890

Dumpy kibitzer jingles as exchequer overflows.

San Marco

Designer	Karlgeorg Hoefer
Nationality	DE
Date Designed	1990
Foundries	Linotype Monotype
Number of weights	1

ABCDEFGHIJKLMNOPQRSTUVWXYZ

abcdefghijklmnopqrstuvwxyz1234567890

The vixen jumped quickly on her foe barking with zeal.

Linotype Sangue

Designer	Gabriele Laubinger
Nationality	DE
Date Designed	1997
Foundries	Linotype
Number of weights	1

ABCDEFGHIJKLMNOPQRSTUVWXYZ
abcdefghijklmnopqrstuvwxyz1234567890
Five or six big jet planes zoomed quietly by the tower.

Koberger

Designer	Manfred Klein
Nationality	DE
Date Designed	1991
Foundries	FontFont
Number of weights	2

ABCDEFGHIJKLMNOPQRSTUVWXYZ
abcdefghijklmnopqrstuvwxyz1234567890
How quickly daft jumping zebras vex.

Schoensperger

Designer	Manfred Klein
Nationality	DE
Date Designed	1991
Foundries	FontFont
Number of weights	2

ABCDEFGHIJKLMNOPQRSTUVWXYZ
abcdefghijklmnopqrstuvwxyz1234567890
Waltz, nymph, for quick jigs vex Bud.

Johannes G

Designer	Manfred Klein
Nationality	DE
Date Designed	1991
Foundries	FontFont
Number of weights	2

ABCDEFGHIJKLMNOPQRSTUVWXYZ
abcdefghijklmnopqrstuvwxyz1234567890
Quick zephyrs blow, vexing daft Jim.

Johabu

Designer	Bo Berndal
Nationality	SE
Date Designed	1990
Foundries	Monotype
Number of weights	1

ABCDEFGHIJKLMNOPQRSTUVWXYZ
abcdefghijklmnopqrstuvwxyz1234567890
Martin J. Hixeypozer quickly began his first word.

Luthersche Fraktur

Designer	Linotype
Nationality	DE
Date Designed	1970
Foundries	Linotype Elsner+Flake
	Bitstream
Number of weights	2

ABCDEFGHIJKLMNOPQRSTUVWXYZ
abcdefghijklmnopqrstuvwxyz1234567890
Many big jackdaws quickly zipped over the fox pen.

Lucida Blackletter

Designer	Kris Holmes
Nationality	US
Date Designed	1989
Foundries	Bigelow & Holmes
Number of weights	1

ABCDEFGHIJKLMNOPQRSTUVWXYZ
abcdefghijklmnopqrstuvwxyz1234567890
Part of the Lucida suite of fonts.

Buckingham Fraktur

Designer	Linotype
Nationality	DE
Date Designed	1990
Foundries	Linotype
Number of weights	2

ABCDEFGHIJKLMNOPQRSTUVWXYZ
abcdefghijklmnopqrstuvwxyz1234567890
Not the capital of Buckinghamshire.

Textur Gotisch

Designer	Linotype
Nationality	DE
Date Designed	1990
Foundries	Linotype
Number of weights	2

ABCDEFGHIJKLMNOPQRSTUVWXYZ
abcdefghijklmnopqrstuvwxyz1234567890
Crazy Fredericka bought many very exquisite opal jewels.

Wilhelm Klingspor Gotisch

Designer	Rudolf Koch
Nationality	DE
Date Designed	1925
Foundries	Linotype Adobe
Number of weights	1

ABCDEFGHIJKLMNOPQRSTUVWXYZ
abcdefghijklmnopqrstuvwxyz1234567890
How razorback-jumping frogs can level six piqued gymnasts!

Alte Schwabacher

Designer	Genzsch & Heyse
Nationality	DE
Date Designed	1835
Foundries	URW++
Number of weights	1

ABCDEFGHIJKLMNOPQRSTUVWXYZ

abcdefghijklmnopqrstuvwxyz1234567890

Jackdaws love my big sphinx of quartz.

Weiss Rundgotisch

Designer	Emile Rudolf Weiss
Nationality	DE
Date Designed	1936
Foundries	Bauer URW++
Number of weights	1

ABCDEFGHIJKLMNOPQRSTUVWXYZ

abcdefghijklmnopqrstuvwxyz1234567890

Six crazy kings vowed to abolish my quite pitiful jousts.

Wittenberger Fraktur

Designer	Monotype
Nationality	DE
Date Designed	1906
Foundries	Monotype Adobe
Number of weights	4

ABCDEFGHIJKLMNOPQRSTUVWXYZ

abcdefghijklmnopqrstuvwxyz1234567890

Sixty zippers were quickly picked from the woven jute bag.

Rudolph

Designer	CA Partners
Nationality	UK
Date Designed	1990
Foundries	CA Partners
Number of weights	1

ABCDEFGHIJKLMNOPQRSTUVWXYZ

abcdefghijklmnopqrstuvwxyz1234567890

Rudolph the Red knows rain, dear.

Fette Fraktur

Designer	Johannes Wagner
Nationality	DE
Date Designed	1875
Foundries	URW++ Linotype Adobe
Number of weights	2

ABCDEFGHIJKLMNOPQRSTUVWXYZ

abcdefghijklmnopqrstuvwxyz1234567890

Viewing quizzical abstracts mixed up hefty jocks.

Brokenscript

Designer	Just van Rossum
Nationality	NL
Date Designed	1994
Foundries	FontFont
Number of weights	4

ABCDEFGHIJKLMNOPQRSTUVWXYZ

abcdefghijklmnopqrstuvwxyz1234567890

Sexy qua lijf, doch bang voor het zwempak.

Amherst Gothic

Designer	Richard Yeend
Nationality	UK
Date Designed	2003
Foundries	Linotype
Number of weights	3

ABCDEFGHIJKLMNOPQRSTUVWXYZ

abcdefghijklmnopqrstuvwxyz1234567890

New farm hand (picking just six quinces) proves strong but lazy.

Ophelia

Designer	Jürgen Brinckmann
Nationality	DE
Date Designed	1993
Foundries	FontFont
Number of weights	2

ABCDEFGHIJKLMNOPQRSTUVWXYZ

abcdefghijklmnopqrstuvwxyz1234567890

Sexy qua lijf, doch bang voor het zwempak.

Bamberg

Designer	DTF
Nationality	US
Date Designed	1991
Foundries	DTF
Number of weights	2

ABCDEFGHIJKLMNOPQRSTUVWXYZ

abcdefghijklmnopqrstuvwxyz1234567890

A UNESCO world heritage city in Germany

Dala LT

Designer	Linotype
Nationality	DE
Date Designed	1995
Foundries	Linotype
Number of weights	1

ABCDEFGHIJKLMNOPQRSTUVWXYZ

abcdefghijklmnopqrstuvwxyz1234567890

Turgid saxophones blew over Mick's jazzy quiff.

Linotype Richmond

Designer	Linotype
Nationality	UK
Date Designed	1990
Foundries	Linotype
Number of weights	6

ABCDEFGHIJKLMNOPQRSTUVWXYZ
abcdefghijklmnopqrstuvwxyz1234567890
Six big devils from Japan quickly forgot how to waltz.

Hoyerswerda Fraktur

Designer	Richard Yeend
Nationality	UK
Date Designed	1998
Foundries	Monotype
Number of weights	2

ABCDEFGHIJKLMNOPQRSTUVWXYZ
abcdefghijklmnopqrstuvwxyz1234567890
William Jex quickly caught five dozen Conservatives.

Clemente Rotunda

Designer	Philip Bouwsma
Nationality	US
Date Designed	1997
Foundries	Monotype
Number of weights	1

ABCDEFGHIJKLMNOPQRSTUVWXYZ
abcdefghijklmnopqrstuvwxyz1234567890
Jail zesty vixen who grabbed pay from quack.

Agincourt

Designer	David Quay
Nationality	UK
Date Designed	1983
Foundries	Letraset ITC
Number of weights	1

ABCDEFGHIJKLMNOPQRSTUVWXYZ
abcdefghijklmnopqrstuvwxyz1234567890
A village in France where England won a notable battle against the French in 1322.

Linotext

Designer	Morris Fuller Benton
Nationality	US
Date Designed	1901
Foundries	Linotype Adobe Monotype
Number of weights	2

ABCDEFGHIJKLMNOPQRSTUVWXYZ
abcdefghijklmnopqrstuvwxyz1234567890
Elite Kanzlei with D. Stempel AG, Comtesse with C.F. Rühl, etc.

Wedding Text

Designer	Morris Fuller Benton
Nationality	US
Date Designed	1901
Foundries	CA Partners Linotext Bitstream Adobe Monotype
Recut/Digitised by	Agfa, 1999
Number of weights	2

ABCDEFGHIJKLMNOPQRSTUVWXYZ

abcdefghijklmnopqrstuvwxyz1234567890

The job of waxing linoleum frequently peeves chintzy kids.

Engravers' Old English

Designer	Bitstream
Nationality	US
Date Designed	1980
Foundries	Bitstream Monotype
Number of weights	1

ABCDEFGHIJKLMNOPQRSTUVWXYZ

abcdefghijklmnopqrstuvwxyz1234567890

Brawny gods flocked up just to quiz and vex him.

Mariage Antique

Designer	URW++
Nationality	FR
Date Designed	1990
Foundries	URW++
Number of weights	2

ABCDEFGHIJKLMNOPQRSTUVWXYZ

abcdefghijklmnopqrstuvwxyz1234567890

A large fawn jumped quickly over white zinc boxes.

Crusader

Designer	Ian Patterson
Nationality	UK
Date Designed	1995
Foundries	Monotype
Number of weights	1

ABCDEFGHIJKLMNOPQRSTUVWXYZ

abcdefghijklmnopqrstuvwxyz1234567890

Many-wived Jack laughs at probes of sex quiz.

Gothique

Designer	Mecanorma
Nationality	FR
Date Designed	1990
Foundries	Mecanorma
Number of weights	1

ABCDEFGHIJKLMNOPQRSTUVWXYZ

abcdefghijklmnopqrstuvwxyz1234567890

Playing jazz vibe chords quickly excites my wife.

Notre Dame

Designer	Karlgeorg Hoefer
Nationality	DE
Date Designed	1993
Foundries	Adobe
Number of weights	3

ABCDEFGHIJKLMNOPQRSTUVWXYZ
abcdefghijklmnopqrstuvwxyz1234567890
Sphinx of black quartz judge my vow.

Goudy Text

Designer	Frederic W Goudy
Nationality	US
Date Designed	1918
Foundries	Monotype Adobe Castle
Number of weights	1

ABCDEFGHIJKLMNOPQRSTUVWXYZ
abcdefghijklmnopqrstuvwxyz1234567890
Jim just quit and packed extra bags for Liz Owen.

Old English Text

Designer	Morris Fuller Benton
Nationality	US
Date Designed	1901
Foundries	Monotype
Number of weights	1

ABCDEFGHIJKLMNOPQRSTUVWXYZ
abcdefghijklmnopqrstuvwxyz1234567890
Exquisite farm wench gives body jolt to prize stinker.

Old English

Designer	Monotype Design Staff
Nationality	UK
Date Designed	1935
Foundries	Letraset ITC Monotype URW++
Number of weights	2

ABCDEFGHIJKLMNOPQRSTUVWXYZ
abcdefghijklmnopqrstuvwxyz1234567890
Compare the B with Old English Text.

Basque

Designer	CA Partners
Nationality	FR
Date Designed	1990
Foundries	CA Partners
Number of weights	1

ABCDEFGHIJKLMNOPQRSTUUWXYZ
abcdefghijklmnopqrstuvwxyz1234567890
Exquisite farm wench gives body jolt to prize stinker.

Lineale

Auferstehung

Designer Johannes Plass
Nationality DE
Date Designed 1997
Foundries Linotype
Number of weights 1

ABCDEFGHIJKLMNOPQRSTUVWXYZ
abcdefghijklmnopqrstuuwxyz1234567890
Mr. Jork, IU quiz Ph.D., bags few lynx.

Gotharda

Designer Milo Dominik Ivir
Nationality DE
Date Designed 1997
Foundries Linotype
Number of weights 1

ABCDEFGHIJKLMNOPQRSTUVWXYZ
abcdefghijklmnopqrstuvwxyz1234567890
Five wine experts jokingly quizzed sample Chablis.

Airam

Designer Maria Martina Schmitt
Nationality AT
Date Designed 2003
Foundries Linotype
Number of weights 1

ABCDEFGHIJKLMNOPQRSTUVWXYZ
abcdefghijklmnopqrstuvwxyz1234567890
Pack my box with five dozen liquor jugs.

Amherst Fraktur

Designer Richard Yeend
Nationality UK
Date Designed 2003
Foundries Linotype
Number of weights 3

ABCDEFGHIJKLMNOPQRSTUVWXYZ
abcdefghijklmnopqrstuvwxyz1234567890
Sympathizing would fix Quaker objectives.

Jenson Classico

Designer Nicolas Jenson, L de Arrighi
Nationality FR
Date Designed 1470
Foundries Linotype
Recut/Digitised by Franco Luin, 1993
Number of weights 5

ABCDEFGHIJKLMNOPQRSTUVWXYZ
abcdefghijklmnopqrstuvwxyz1234567890
Many big jackdaws quickly zipped over the fox pen.

Griffo Classico

Designer	Francesco Griffo
Nationality	IT
Date Designed	1495
Foundries	Linotype
Recut/Digitised by	Franko Luin
Number of weights	5

ABCDEFGHIJKLMNOPQRSTUVWXYZ
abcdefghijklmnopqrstuvwxyz1234567890
Quick zephyrs blow, vexing daft Jim.

Tiffany

Designer	MacKellar, Smiths & Jordan
Nationality	US
Date Designed	1884
Foundries	ITC Bitstream Adobe Elsner+Flake Linotype URW++
Recut/Digitised by	Ed Benguiat, 1974
Number of weights	8

ABCDEFGHIJKLMNOPQRSTUVWXYZ
abcdefghijklmnopqrstuvwxyz1234567890
The sex life of the woodchuck is a provocative question for most vertebrate zoology majors.

Golden Type

Designer	William Morris
Nationality	UK
Date Designed	1890
Foundries	Kelmscott Press Linotype
Recut/Digitised by	Sigrid Engelman, Helga Jorgensen, Andrew Newton, 1989
Number of weights	5

ABCDEFGHIJKLMNOPQRSTUVWXYZ
abcdefghijklmnopqrstuvwxyz1234567890
Designed by the great artist craftsman for his Kelmscott Press.

Clearface

Designer	Morris Fuller Benton
Nationality	US
Date Designed	1907
Foundries	ATF ITC Monotype
Recut/Digitised by	Victor Caruso, 1979
Number of weights	8

ABCDEFGHIJKLMNOPQRSTUVWXYZ
abcdefghijklmnopqrstuvwxyz1234567890
Sympathizing would fix Quaker objectives.

Belwe

Designer	George Belwe
Nationality	DE
Date Designed	1913
Foundries	Schelter & Giesecke Bitstream
Number of weights	4

ABCDEFGHIJKLMNOPQRSTUVWXYZ
abcdefghijklmnopqrstuvwxyz1234567890
Sympathizing would fix Quaker objectives.

Centaur

Designer	Bruce Rogers
Nationality	US
Date Designed	1914
Foundries	Monotype
Number of weights	15

ABCDEFGHIJKLMNOPQRSTUVWXYZ
abcdefghijklmnopqrstuvwxyz1234567890

One of the finest Venetian faces of the C20.

Souvenir

Designer	Morris Fuller Benton
Nationality	US
Date Designed	1914
Foundries	ITC Adobe Bitstream Elsner+Flake Linotype URW++
Recut/Digitised by	Ed Benguiat
Number of weights	8

ABCDEFGHIJKLMNOPQRSTUVWXYZ
abcdefghijklmnopqrstuvwxyz1234567890

Desperately over-used in the 1970s.

Horley Old Style

Designer	Monotype
Nationality	UK
Date Designed	1925
Foundries	Monotype Adobe
Recut/Digitised by	Robert Norton, 1977
Number of weights	8

ABCDEFGHIJKLMNOPQRSTUVWXYZ
abcdefghijklmnopqrstuvwxyz1234567890

Horley is a town near Monotype's UK headquarters.

Worcester

Designer	Adrian Williams
Nationality	UK
Date Designed	1974
Foundries	ATF
Number of weights	4

ABCDEFGHIJKLMNOPQRSTUVWXYZ
abcdefghijklmnopqrstuvwxyz1234567890

A large fawn jumped quickly over white zinc boxes.

Pastonchi

Designer	Francesco Pastonchi, E. Cotti
Nationality	IT
Date Designed	1927
Foundries	Monotype
Number of weights	12

ABCDEFGHIJKLMNOPQRSTUVWXYZ
abcdefghijklmnopqrstuvwxyz1234567890

Poet, type designer, journalist and childrens' book author.

Schneidler Amalthea

Designer	Friedrich Hermann Ernst Schneidler
Nationality	DE
Date Designed	1936
Foundries	Linotype
Number of weights	5

ABCDEFGHIJKLMNOPQRSTUVWXYZ

abcdefghijklmnopqrstuvwxyz1234567890

Was Amalthea the nymph who nursed Jupiter with goat's milk¿

Schneidler Mediaeval

Designer	Friedrich Hermann Ernst Schneidler
Nationality	DE
Date Designed	1936
Foundries	Linotype
Number of weights	5

ABCDEFGHIJKLMNOPQRSTUVWXYZ

abcdefghijklmnopqrstuvwxyz1234567890

Was F H Ernst Schneidler born in Berlin¿

Stempel Schneidler

Designer	Stempel
Nationality	DE
Date Designed	1936
Foundries	Fundición Tipográfica Bauer Adobe
Number of weights	10

ABCDEFGHIJKLMNOPQRSTUVWXYZ

abcdefghijklmnopqrstuvwxyz1234567890

Have we just quoted on nine dozen boxes of gray lamp wicks¿

Berkeley Oldstyle

Designer	Frederic W Goudy
Nationality	US
Date Designed	1938
Foundries	ITC Linotype Bitstream
Recut/Digitised by	Tony Stan, 1983
Number of weights	6

ABCDEFGHIJKLMNOPQRSTUVWXYZ

abcdefghijklmnopqrstuvwxyz1234567890

Originally known as University of California Old Style.

Trajanus

Designer	Warren Chappell
Nationality	US
Date Designed	1940
Foundries	Stempel Linotype
Number of weights	6

ABCDEFGHIJKLMNOPQRSTUVWXYZ

abcdefghijklmnopqrstuvwxyz1234567890

Trajan's Column in Rome is acknowledged to show Roman lettering at its finest.

Scripps College Old Style MT

Designer Frederic W Goudy
Nationality US
Date Designed 1941
Foundries Scripps College
Recut/Digitised by Sumner Stone, 1997
Number of weights 3

ABCDEFGHIJKLMNOPQRSTUVWXYZ
abcdefghijklmnopqrstuvwxyz1234567890
How vexing a fumble to drop a jolly zucchini in the quicksand.

Vendôme

Designer François Ganeau
Nationality FR
Date Designed 1952
Foundries Olive URW++
Number of weights 6

ABCDEFGHIJKLMNOPQRSTUVWXYZ
abcdefghijklmnopqrstuvwxyz1234567890
Place Vendôme in Paris is a very smart address, named after a town in the Loir-et-Cher.

Benguiat

Designer Ed Benguiat
Nationality US
Date Designed 1977
Foundries ITC bit
Number of weights 6

ABCDEFGHIJKLMNOPQRSTUVWXYZ
abcdefghijklmnopqrstuvwxyz1234567890
Designer's name.

Benguiat Condensed

Designer Ed Benguiat
Nationality US
Date Designed 1977
Foundries ITC
Number of weights 6

ABCDEFGHIJKLMNOPQRSTUVWXYZ
abcdefghijklmnopqrstuvwxyz1234567890
Pack my box with five dozen liquor jugs.

Brighton

Designer Alan Bright
Nationality UK
Date Designed 1979
Foundries ITC Letraset
Number of weights 3

ABCDEFGHIJKLMNOPQRSTUVWXYZ
abcdefghijklmnopqrstuvwxyz1234567890
The vixen jumped quickly on her foe barking with zeal.

Weidemann

Designer	Kurt Weidemann
Nationality	DE
Date Designed	1983
Foundries	ITC Bitstream
Number of weights	8

ABCDEFGHIJKLMNOPQRSTUVWXYZ

abcdefghijklmnopqrstuvwxyz1234567890

Originally named BIBLICA and designed for an ecumenical Catholic/Protestant Bible.

Esprit

Designer	Jovica Veljovic
Nationality	YU
Date Designed	1985
Foundries	ITC Adobe
Number of weights	8

ABCDEFGHIJKLMNOPQRSTUVWXYZ

abcdefghijklmnopqrstuvwxyz1234567890

Pack my box with five dozen liquor jugs.

Cantoria

Designer	Ron Carpenter
Nationality	US
Date Designed	1986
Foundries	Linotype Adobe Monotype
Number of weights	10

ABCDEFGHIJKLMNOPQRSTUVWXYZ

abcdefghijklmnopqrstuvwxyz1234567890

Originally named Ehmcke and designed by F H Ehmcke.

Guardi

Designer	Reinhard Haus
Nationality	DE
Date Designed	1986
Foundries	Adobe
Recut/Digitised by	Linotype
Number of weights	6

ABCDEFGHIJKLMNOPQRSTUVWXYZ

abcdefghijklmnopqrstuvwxyz1234567890

An inspired calligrapher can create pages of beauty using stick ink, quill, brush, pick-axe, buzz saw, or even strawberry jam.

Hollandse

Designer	CG
Nationality	NL
Date Designed	1989
Foundries	CG
Number of weights	1

ABCDEFGHIJKLMNOPQRSTUVWXYZ

abcdefghijklmnopqrstuvwxyz1234567890

When we go back to Juarez, Mexico, do we fly over picturesque Arizona?

Legacy Serif

Designer Ronald Arnholm
Nationality SE
Date Designed 1992
Foundries ITC Elsner+Flake Monotype
Adobe Linotype
Number of weights 7

ABCDEFGHIJKLMNOPQRSTUVWXYZ
abcdefghijklmnopqrstuvwxyz1234567890

Puzzled women bequeath jerks very exotic gifts.

Visage

Designer Garrett Boge
Nationality US
Date Designed 1993
Foundries Monotype
Number of weights 10

ABCDEFGHIJKLMNOPQRSTUVWXYZ
abcdefghijklmnopqrstuvwxyz1234567890

My help squeezed back in again and joined the weavers after six.

Winchester New ITC

Designer ITC
Nationality UK
Date Designed 1995
Foundries ITC
Number of weights 12

ABCDEFGHIJKLMNOPQRSTUVWXYZ
abcdefghijklmnopqrstuvwxyz1234567890

A city in Hampshire, formerly the capital of England.

Kallos

Designer Phill Grimshaw
Nationality UK
Date Designed 1996
Foundries Linotype Monotype ITC
Number of weights 6

ABCDEFGHIJKLMNOPQRSTUVWXYZ
abcdefghijklmnopqrstuvwxyz1234567890

Zweedse ex-VIP, behoorlijk gek op quantumfysica.

Obelisk ITC

Designer Phill Grimshaw
Nationality UK
Date Designed 1996
Foundries Linotype ITC
Number of weights 5

ABCDEFGHIJKLMNOPQRSTUVWXYZ
abcdefghijklmnopqrstuvwxyz1234567890

A Greek word for what the ancient Egyptians called a tekhen.

Garalde

Sabellicus

Designer	Bo Berndal
Nationality	SE
Date Designed	1998
Foundries	CA Exclusives
Number of weights	4

ABCDEFGHIJKLMNOPQRSTUVWXYZ
abcdefghijklmnopqrstuvwxyz1234567890
Marcus Antonio Coccio Sabellicus (1436-1506) was a Venetian historian.

Bembo

Designer	Francesco Griffo
Nationality	IT
Date Designed	1495
Foundries	Aldus Manutius Adobe Monotype
Number of weights	24

ABCDEFGHIJKLMNOPQRSTUVWXYZ
abcdefghijklmnopqrstuvwxyz1234567890
How quickly daft jumping zebras vex.

Poliphilus

Designer	Francesco Griffo
Nationality	IT
Date Designed	1498
Foundries	Monotype
Number of weights	1

ABCDEFGHIJKLMNOPQRSTUVWXYZ
abcdefghijklmnopqrstuvwxyz1234567890
Back in June we delivered oxygen equipment of the same size.

Blado

Designer	detto Vincentino
Nationality	IT
Date Designed	1499
Foundries	Monotype
Number of weights	1

ABCDEFGHIJKLMNOPQRSTUVWXYZ
abcdefghijklmnopqrstuvwxyz1234567890
When italics were standalone fonts, Blado partnered Poliphilus.

Garamond

Designer	Claude Garamond
Nationality	FR
Date Designed	1532
Foundries	Garamond Monotype Adobe
Number of weights	1

ABCDEFGHIJKLMNOPQRSTUVWXYZ
abcdefghijklmnopqrstuvwxyz1234567890
Jail zesty vixen who grabbed pay from quack.

CG Garamond No. 3

Designer	Claude Garamond
Nationality	FR
Date Designed	1532
Foundries	CA Partners
Number of weights	4

ABCDEFGHIJKLMNOPQRSTUVWXYZ
abcdefghijklmnopqrstuvwxyz1234567890
Verily the dark ex-Jew quit Zionism, preferring the cabala.

Garamond 3

Designer	Claude Garamond
Nationality	FR
Date Designed	1532
Foundries	Linotype Adobe
Number of weights	8

ABCDEFGHIJKLMNOPQRSTUVWXYZ
abcdefghijklmnopqrstuvwxyz1234567890
Moi, je veux quinze clubs a golf et du whisky pur.

Garamond Handtooled

Designer	Claude Garamond
Nationality	FR
Date Designed	1532
Foundries	ITC
Number of weights	1

ABCDEFGHIJKLMNOPQRSTUVWXYZ
abcdefghijklmnopqrstuvwxyz1234567890
Portez ce vieux whisky au juge blond qui fume.

Simoncini Garamond

Designer	Claude Garamond
Nationality	FR
Date Designed	1532
Foundries	Adobe Linotype
Number of weights	3

ABCDEFGHIJKLMNOPQRSTUVWXYZ
abcdefghijklmnopqrstuvwxyz1234567890
Jim just quit and packed extra bags for Liz Owen.

Stempel Garamond

Designer	Claude Garamond
Nationality	FR
Date Designed	1532
Foundries	Adobe Linotype
Number of weights	13

ABCDEFGHIJKLMNOPQRSTUVWXYZ
abcdefghijklmnopqrstuvwxyz1234567890
Five or six big jet planes zoomed quickly by the tower.

Garamond Classico

Designer	Claude Garamond
Nationality	FR
Date Designed	1532
Foundries	Linotype
Number of weights	5

ABCDEFGHIJKLMNOPQRSTUVWXYZ
abcdefghijklmnopqrstuvwxyz1234567890
Many-wived Jack laughs at probes of sex quiz.

Adobe Garamond

Designer	Claude Garamond
Nationality	FR
Date Designed	1532
Foundries	Monotype Linotype Adobe
Number of weights	21

ABCDEFGHIJKLMNOPQRSTUVWXYZ
abcdefghijklmnopqrstuvwxyz1234567890
For only €49, jolly housewives made inexpensive meals using quick-frozen vegetables.

Granjon

Designer	Claude Garamond
Nationality	US
Date Designed	1535
Foundries	Mergenthaler Linotype Adobe
Recut/Digitised by	George W. Jones, 1928
Number of weights	6

ABCDEFGHIJKLMNOPQRSTUVWXYZ
abcdefghijklmnopqrstuvwxyz1234567890
Mix Zapf with Veljovic and get quirky Beziers.

Van Dijck

Designer	Christoffel Van Dijck
Nationality	NL
Date Designed	1650
Foundries	Monotype
Recut/Digitised by	Jan van Krimpen
Number of weights	8

ABCDEFGHIJKLMNOPQRSTUVWXYZ
abcdefghijklmnopqrstuvwxyz1234567890
William said that everything about his jacket was in quite good condition except for the zipper.

Janson

Designer	Nicholas Kis
Nationality	HU
Date Designed	1690
Foundries	Monotype
Recut/Digitised by	Horst Heiderhoff, Adrian Frutiger
Number of weights	8

ABCDEFGHIJKLMNOPQRSTUVWXYZ
abcdefghijklmnopqrstuvwxyz1234567890
Dumpy kibitzer jingles as exchequer overflows.

Janson Text

Designer	Nicholas Kis
Nationality	HU
Date Designed	1690
Foundries	Linotype Adobe Mergenthaler Linotype URW++
Number of weights	12

ABCDEFGHIJKLMNOPQRSTUVWXYZ

abcdefghijklmnopqrstuvwxyz1234567890

Crisper, blacker and wider than the more faithful Monotype Janson.

Kis Classico

Designer	Nicholas Kis
Nationality	HU
Date Designed	1690
Foundries	Linotype
Recut/Digitised by	Franco Luin, 1993
Number of weights	5

ABCDEFGHIJKLMNOPQRSTUVWXYZ

abcdefghijklmnopqrstuvwxyz1234567890

How razorback-jumping frogs can level six piqued gymnasts!

Ehrhardt

Designer	Ehrhardt
Nationality	DE
Date Designed	1691
Foundries	Ehrhardt Monotype Adobe
Recut/Digitised by	Monotype 1937
Number of weights	4

ABCDEFGHIJKLMNOPQRSTUVWXYZ

abcdefghijklmnopqrstuvwxyz1234567890

The quick brown fox jumps over the lazy dog.

Plantin

Designer	Robert Granjon
Nationality	BE
Date Designed	1700
Foundries	Plantin Monotype
Recut/Digitised by	F H Pierpont, 1913
Number of weights	20

ABCDEFGHIJKLMNOPQRSTUVWXYZ

abcdefghijklmnopqrstuvwxyz1234567890

We promptly judged antique ivory buckles for the next prize.

News Plantin

Designer	Robert Granjon
Nationality	BE
Date Designed	1700
Foundries	Monotype
Number of weights	4

ABCDEFGHIJKLMNOPQRSTUVWXYZ

abcdefghijklmnopqrstuvwxyz1234567890

Questions of a zealous nature have become by degrees petty waxen jokes.

Plantin Schoolbook

Designer	Robert Granjon
Nationality	BE
Date Designed	1700
Foundries	Plantin Monotype
Number of weights	4

ABCDEFGHIJKLMNOPQRSTUVWXYZ
abcdefghijklmnopqrstuvwxyz1234567890
We promptly judged antique ivory buckles for the next prize.

Founder's Caslon 12

Designer	William Caslon
Nationality	UK
Date Designed	1720
Foundries	ITC H W Caslon
Recut/Digitised by	Justin Howes, 1998
Number of weights	3

ABCDEFGHIJKLMNOPQRSTUVWXYZ
abcdefghijklmnopqrstuvwxyz 1234567890
Here's a curiosity—a copy of an original typeface in its varying point sizes
with all its original faults and imperfections, rather than a redrawing.

Caslon No. 224

Designer	William Caslon
Nationality	UK
Date Designed	1725
Foundries	ITC Bitstream
Recut/Digitised by	Edward Benguiat, 1982
Number of weights	8

ABCDEFGHIJKLMNOPQRSTUVWXYZ
abcdefghijklmnopqrstuvwxyz1234567890
Quick wafting zephyrs vex bold Jim.

TF Caslon Display

Designer	Joseph D Treacy
Nationality	US
Date Designed	1725
Foundries	Treacyfaces
Number of weights	4

ABCDEFGHIJKLMNOPQRSTUVWXYZ
abcdefghijklmnopqrstuvwxyz1234567890
Jaded reader with fabled roving eye seized by quickened impulse to
expand budget.

Caslon 3

Designer	William Caslon
Nationality	UK
Date Designed	1725
Foundries	Monotype Adobe
Number of weights	4

ABCDEFGHIJKLMNOPQRSTUVWXYZ
abcdefghijklmnopqrstuvwxyz1234567890
Hark! Toxic jungle water vipers quietly drop on zebras for meals!

Caslon 540

Designer	William Caslon
Nationality	UK
Date Designed	1725
Foundries	Monotype Linotype URW++
Number of weights	4

ABCDEFGHIJKLMNOPQRSTUVWXYZ

abcdefghijklmnopqrstuvwxyz1234567890

Six big juicy steaks sizzled in a pan as five workmen left the quarry.

Caslon Antique

Designer	William Caslon
Nationality	UK
Date Designed	1725
Foundries	Linotype URW++
Number of weights	1

ABCDEFGHIJKLMNOPQRSTUVWXYZ

abcdefghijklmnopqrstuvwxyz1234567890

No relation to Caslon.

Caslon Classico

Designer	William Caslon
Nationality	UK
Date Designed	1725
Foundries	Linotype
Recut/Digitised by	Franko Luin
Number of weights	5

ABCDEFGHIJKLMNOPQRSTUVWXYZ

abcdefghijklmnopqrstuvwxyz1234567890

Will Major Douglas be expected to take this true-false quiz very soon?

Founder's Caslon 30

Designer	William Caslon
Nationality	UK
Date Designed	1725
Foundries	ITC Linotype Monotype
Recut/Digitised by	Justin Howes, 1998
Number of weights	3

ABCDEFGHIJKLMNOPQRSTUVWXYZ

abcdefghijklmnopqrstuvwxyz1234567890

The juke box music puzzled a gentle visitor from a quaint valley town.

Caslon Italic

Designer	William Caslon
Nationality	UK
Date Designed	1725
Foundries	Linotype Letraset
Recut/Digitised by	Ed Benguiat
Number of weights	1

ABCDEFGHIJKLMNOPQRSTUVWXYZ

abcdefghijklmnopqrstuvwxyz1234567890

Just work for improved basic techniques to maximize your typing skill.

Adobe Caslon

Designer	William Caslon
Nationality	UK
Date Designed	1725
Foundries	Adobe Linotype Monotype
Recut/Digitised by	Carol Twombly
Number of weights	28

ABCDEFGHIJKLMNOPQRSTUVWXYZ

abcdefghijklmnopqrstuvwxyz1234567890

When we go back to Juarez, Mexico, do we fly over picturesque Arizona?

Big Caslon

Designer	William Caslon
Nationality	UK
Date Designed	1725
Foundries	Font Bureau
Recut/Digitised by	Matthew Carter
Number of weights	1

ABCDEFGHIJKLMNOPQRSTUVWXYZ

abcdefghijklmnopqrstuvwxyz1234567890

Questions of a zealous nature have become by degrees petty waxen jokes.

Founder's Caslon 42

Designer	William Caslon
Nationality	UK
Date Designed	1725
Foundries	ITC Linotype Monotype
Recut/Digitised by	Justin Howes, 1998
Number of weights	4

ABCDEFGHIJKLMNOPQRSTUVWXYZ

abcdefghijklmnopqrstuvwxyz1234567890

Lazy movers quit hard-packing of papier-mache jewellery boxes.

Caslon Ten Eighty TF

Designer	William Caslon
Nationality	UK
Date Designed	1725
Foundries	Treacy Faces
Recut/Digitised by	Joseph Treacy
Number of weights	1

ABCDEFGHIJKLMNOPQRSTUVWXYZ

abcdefghijklmnopqrstuvwxyz1234567890

Now is the time for all brown dogs to jump over the lazy lynx.

Binny Old Style

Designer	Binny & Ronaldson
Nationality	US
Date Designed	1863
Foundries	Lanston Monotype Monotype
Number of weights	2

ABCDEFGHIJKLMNOPQRSTUVWXYZ

abcdefghijklmnopqrstuvwxyz1234567890

Lazy movers quit hard-packing of papier-mache jewellery boxes.

Cheltenham Old Style

Designer	Morris Fuller Benton, Bertram Goodhue
Nationality	US
Date Designed	1900
Foundries	URW++
Recut/Digitised by	18.0
Number of weights	16

ABCDEFGHIJKLMNOPQRSTUVWXYZ
abcdefghijklmnopqrstuvwxyz1234567890
Jail zesty vixen who grabbed pay from quack.

Cheltenham Old Style No 2

Designer	Morris Fuller Benton, Bertram Goodhue
Nationality	US
Date Designed	1900
Foundries	URW++
Number of weights	7

ABCDEFGHIJKLMNOPQRSTUVWXYZ
abcdefghijklmnopqrstuvwxyz1234567890
The quick brown fox jumps over the lazy dog.

Old Style 7

Designer	Miller & Richard
Nationality	UK
Date Designed	1902
Foundries	Linotype Adobe
Recut/Digitised by	LIN
Number of weights	4

ABCDEFGHIJKLMNOPQRSTUVWXYZ
abcdefghijklmnopqrstuvwxyz1234567890
Mix Zapf with Veljovic and get quirky Beziers.

Century Old Style

Designer	Morris Fuller Benton
Nationality	US
Date Designed	1904
Foundries	Bitstream Kingsley ATF Monotype URW
Number of weights	3

ABCDEFGHIJKLMNOPQRSTUVWXYZ
abcdefghijklmnopqrstuvwxyz1234567890
Many big jackdaws quickly zipped over the fox pen.

Imprint

Designer	Monotype Design Staff (Gerard Meynell, Edward Johnston, J H Mason, Ernest Jackson)
Nationality	UK
Date Designed	1913
Foundries	Monotype
Number of weights	8

ABCDEFGHIJKLMNOPQRSTUVWXYZ
abcdefghijklmnopqrstuvwxyz1234567890
Imprint Shadow is one of the most popular inline serif fonts.

Goudy Old Style

Designer	Frederic W Goudy
Nationality	US
Date Designed	1915
Foundries	ATF Bitstream DTP Monotype
Number of weights	1

ABCDEFGHIJKLMNOPQRSTUVWXYZ

abcdefghijklmnopqrstuvwxyz1234567890

And Jamshyd's Sev'n-ring'd Cup where no one knows;

Goudy Catalogue

Designer	Morris Fuller Benton
Nationality	US
Date Designed	1916
Foundries	ATF Bitstream Elsner+Flake Monotype URW++
Number of weights	2

ABCDEFGHIJKLMNOPQRSTUVWXYZ

abcdefghijklmnopqrstuvwxyz1234567890

Jail zesty vixen who grabbed pay from quack.

Gill Facia

Designer	Eric Gill
Nationality	UK
Date Designed	1923
Foundries	Monotype
Number of weights	8

ABCDEFGHIJKLMNOPQRSTUVWXYZ

abcdefghijklmnopqrstuvwxyz1234567890

West quickly gave Bert handsome prizes for six juicy plums.

Italian Old Style

Designer	Monotype
Nationality	US
Date Designed	1924
Foundries	Monotype
Number of weights	4

ABCDEFGHIJKLMNOPQRSTUVWXYZ

abcdefghijklmnopqrstuvwxyz1234567890

For only €49, jolly housewives made inexpensive meals using quick-frozen vegetables.

Golden Cockerel Type

Designer	Eric Gill
Nationality	UK
Date Designed	1929
Foundries	ITC
Recut/Digitised by	Dave Farey, Richard Dawson 1996
Number of weights	3

ABCDEFGHIJKLMNOPQRSTUVWXYZ

abcdefghijklmnopqrstuvwxyz1234567890

Jeb quickly drove a few extra miles on the glazed pavement.

Truesdell

Designer	Frederic W Goudy
Nationality	US
Date Designed	1930
Foundries	Monotype
Recut/Digitised by	Steve Matteson, 1994
Number of weights	9

ABCDEFGHIJKLMNOPQRSTUVWXYZ

abcdefghijklmnopqrstuvwxyz1234567890

About sixty codfish eggs will make a quarter pound of very fizzy jelly.

Figural

Designer	Oldrich Menhart
Nationality	CZ
Date Designed	1940
Foundries	Grafotechna Linotype Monotype ITC
Recut/Digitised by	Michael Gills, 1992
Number of weights	5

ABCDEFGHIJKLMNOPQRSTUVWXYZ

abcdefghijklmnopqrstuvwxyz1234567890

The five boxing wizards jump quickly.

Book Antiqua

Designer	Hermann Zapf
Nationality	DE
Date Designed	1950
Foundries	Monotype
Number of weights	4

ABCDEFGHIJKLMNOPQRSTUVWXYZ

abcdefghijklmnopqrstuvwxyz1234567890

Chosen as a core font for Microsoft Windows & OS X.

Berling

Designer	Karl-Erik Forsberg
Nationality	DE
Date Designed	1951
Foundries	Berling URW++
Number of weights	4

ABCDEFGHIJKLMNOPQRSTUVWXYZ

abcdefghijklmnopqrstuvwxyz1234567890

Grumpy wizards make toxic brew for the evil Queen and Jack.

Aldus

Designer	Hermann Zapf
Nationality	DE
Date Designed	1954
Foundries	Stempel Adobe
Number of weights	4

ABCDEFGHIJKLMNOPQRSTUVWXYZ

abcdefghijklmnopqrstuvwxyz1234567890

Jazzy saxophones blew over Mick's turgid quiff.

Dante

Designer	Giovanni Mardersteig
Nationality	CH
Date Designed	1954
Foundries	Bodoni Adobe
Number of weights	25

ABCDEFGHIJKLMNOPQRSTUVWXYZ

abcdefghijklmnopqrstuvwxyz1234567890

Breezily jangling €3,416,857,209 wise advertiser ambles to the bank, his exchequer amplified.

Trump Mediaeval

Designer	Georg Trump
Nationality	DE
Date Designed	1954
Foundries	Weber CG
Number of weights	8

ABCDEFGHIJKLMNOPQRSTUVWXYZ

abcdefghijklmnopqrstuvwxyz1234567890

Pavilions of Splendour's preferred text font.

Antiqua

Designer	Arno Drescher
Nationality	DE
Date Designed	1956
Foundries	J. Wagner URW++
Number of weights	58

ABCDEFGHIJKLMNOPQRSTUVWXYZ

abcdefghijklmnopqrstuvwxyz1234567890

Big July earthquakes confound zany experimental vow.

New Aster

Designer	Francesco Simoncini
Nationality	IT
Date Designed	1958
Foundries	Simoncini Linotype Adobe
Recut/Digitised by	Linotype 1982
Number of weights	8

ABCDEFGHIJKLMNOPQRSTUVWXYZ

abcdefghijklmnopqrstuvwxyz1234567890

The juke box music puzzled a gentle visitor from a quaint valley town.

Sabon

Designer	Jan Tschischold
Nationality	NL
Date Designed	1964
Foundries	Monotype Linotype Adobe
Number of weights	9

ABCDEFGHIJKLMNOPQRSTUVWXYZ

abcdefghijklmnopqrstuvwxyz1234567890

Sexy qua lijf, doch bang voor het zwempak.

Sabon Next

Designer	Jan Tschichold
Nationality	NL
Date Designed	1964
Foundries	Linotype
Recut/Digitised by	Jean-François Porchez, 2002
Number of weights	8

ABCDEFGHIJKLMNOPQRSTUVWXYZ
abcdefghijklmnopqrstuvwxyz1234567890

Sexy qua lijf, doch bang voor het zwempak.

Cartier

Designer	Carl Dair
Nationality	CA
Date Designed	1967
Foundries	Mono Lino
Number of weights	9

ABCDEFGHIJKLMNOPQRSTUVWXYZ
abcdefghijklmnopqrstuvwxyz1234567890

Designed for the 1967 Montreal World's Fair and the Canadian Centennial.

Raleigh

Designer	Robert Norton, Carl Dair, Adrian Williams, David Anderson
Nationality	UK, CA
Date Designed	1967
Foundries	Typsettra Bitstream URW++
Number of weights	4

ABCDEFGHIJKLMNOPQRSTUVWXYZ
abcdefghijklmnopqrstuvwxyz1234567890

Based on Cartier by Carl Dair for the Canadian Centennial.

Olympian

Designer	Matthew Carter
Nationality	UK
Date Designed	1970
Foundries	Mergenthaler Linotype Adobe
Number of weights	4

ABCDEFGHIJKLMNOPQRSTUVWXYZ
abcdefghijklmnopqrstuvwxyz1234567890

How razorback-jumping frogs can level six piqued gymnasts!

CG Holland Seminar

Designer	Hollis Holland
Nationality	US
Date Designed	1973
Foundries	CA Partners
Number of weights	2

ABCDEFGHIJKLMNOPQRSTUVWXYZ
abcdefghijklmnopqrstuvwxyz1234567890

Breezily jangling $3,416,857,209,wise advertiser ambles to the bank, his exchequer amplified.

Garth Graphic

Designer	Constance Blanchard, Renée le Winter
Nationality	US
Date Designed	1979
Foundries	Adobe Monotype
Number of weights	16

ABCDEFGHIJKLMNOPQRSTUVWXYZ
abcdefghijklmnopqrstuvwxyz1234567890
How razorback-jumping frogs can level six piqued gymnasts!

Novarese

Designer	Aldo Novarese
Nationality	IT
Date Designed	1979
Foundries	ITC
Number of weights	7

ABCDEFGHIJKLMNOPQRSTUVWXYZ
abcdefghijklmnopqrstuvwxyz1234567890
Lazy movers quit hard-packing of papier-mache jewellery boxes.

Galliard

Designer	Matthew Carter
Nationality	UK
Date Designed	1979
Foundries	ITC Bitstream Adobe
Number of weights	8

ABCDEFGHIJKLMNOPQRSTUVWXYZ
abcdefghijklmnopqrstuvwxyz1234567890
Crazy Fredericka bought many very exquisite opal jewels.

Footlight

Designer	Monotype
Nationality	UK
Date Designed	1980
Foundries	Monotype
Number of weights	8

ABCDEFGHIJKLMNOPQRSTUVWXYZ
abcdefghijklmnopqrstuvwxyz1234567890
But still the Vine her ancient Ruby yields,

Caxton

Designer	Leslie Usherwood
Nationality	CA
Date Designed	1981
Foundries	ITC
Number of weights	6

ABCDEFGHIJKLMNOPQRSTUVWXYZ
abcdefghijklmnopqrstuvwxyz1234567890
Many big jackdaws quickly zipped over the fox pen.

Administer

Designer Les Usherwood
Nationality CA
Date Designed 1981
Foundries Monotype Red Rooster
Number of weights 5

ABCDEFGHIJKLMNOPQRSTUVWXYZ
abcdefghijklmnopqrstuvwxyz1234567890
Sphinx of black quartz judge my vow.

Usherwood

Designer Les Usherwood
Nationality CA
Date Designed 1984
Foundries ITC Adobe
Number of weights 8

ABCDEFGHIJKLMNOPQRSTUVWXYZ
abcdefghijklmnopqrstuvwxyz1234567890
The job of waxing linoleum frequently peeves chintzy kids.

Column

Designer Adrian Williams
Nationality UK
Date Designed 1985
Foundries Monotype
Number of weights 5

ABCDEFGHIJKLMNOPQRSTUVWXYZ
abcdefghijklmnopqrstuvwxyz1234567890
Will Major Douglas be expected to take this true-false quiz very soon?

Leawood

Designer Leslie Usherwood
Nationality CA
Date Designed 1985
Foundries ITC Linotype Adobe
Elsner+Flake Bitstream Monotype
Number of weights 8

ABCDEFGHIJKLMNOPQRSTUVWXYZ
abcdefghijklmnopqrstuvwxyz1234567890
Quixotic Conservatives vet first key zero-growth jeremiad.

Calisto

Designer Ron Carpenter
Nationality UK
Date Designed 1987
Foundries Monotype
Number of weights 4

ABCDEFGHIJKLMNOPQRSTUVWXYZ
abcdefghijklmnopqrstuvwxyz1234567890
And still a Garden by the Water blows.

Giovanni

Designer	Robert Slimbach
Nationality	US
Date Designed	1989
Foundries	Adobe ITC
Number of weights	6

ABCDEFGHIJKLMNOPQRSTUVWXYZ
abcdefghijklmnopqrstuvwxyz1234567890
Verily the dark ex-Jew quit Zionism, preferring the cabala.

Economist

Designer	Gunnlauger Briem
Nationality	IS
Date Designed	1989
Foundries	Economist
Recut/Digitised by	A Patel
Number of weights	7

ABCDEFGHIJKLMNOPQRSTUVWXYZ
abcdefghijklmnopqrstuvwxyz1234567890
Jaded zombies acted quaintly but kept driving their oxen forward.

Galena

Designer	Jean-Renaud Cuaz
Nationality	FR
Date Designed	1990
Foundries	Monotype
Number of weights	13

ABCDEFGHIJKLMNOPQRSTUVWXYZ
abcdefghijklmnopqrstuvwxyz1234567890
Quixotic Conservatives vet first key zero-growth jeremiad.

Palladio

Designer	Hermann Zapf
Nationality	DE
Date Designed	1990
Foundries	URW++
Number of weights	6

ABCDEFGHIJKLMNOPQRSTUVWXYZ
abcdefghijklmnopqrstuvwxyz1234567890
Perhaps President Clinton's amazing sax skills will be judged quite favourably.

Agfa Wile Roman

Designer	Cynthia Hollandsworth
Nationality	US
Date Designed	1990
Foundries	Monotype
Number of weights	8

ABCDEFGHIJKLMNOPQRSTUVWXYZ
abcdefghijklmnopqrstuvwxyz1234567890
Waltz, nymph, for quick jigs vex Bud.

Scala

Designer	Martin Majoor
Nationality	NL
Date Designed	1990-1998
Foundries	FontFont
Number of weights	63

ABCDEFGHIJKLMNOPQRSTUVWXYZ

abcdefghijklmnopqrstuvwxyz1234567890

A huge family of serif and sans in 63 weights and styles.

Columbus

Designer	Patricia Saunders
Nationality	UK
Date Designed	1992
Foundries	Monotype
Number of weights	14

ABCDEFGHIJKLMNOPQRSTUVWXYZ

abcdefghijklmnopqrstuvwxyz1234567890

Six big juicy steaks sizzled in a pan as five workmen left the quarry.

Nordik

Designer	Bo Berndal
Nationality	SE
Date Designed	1992
Foundries	Monotype
Number of weights	4

ABCDEFGHIJKLMNOPQRSTUVWXYZ

abcdefghijklmnopqrstuvwxyz1234567890

Back in June we delivered oxygen equipment of the same size.

Birka

Designer	Franko Luin
Nationality	SL
Date Designed	1992
Foundries	Linotype
Number of weights	7

ABCDEFGHIJKLMNOPQRSTUVWXYZ

abcdefghijklmnopqrstuvwxyz1234567890

About sixty codfish eggs will make a quarter pound of very fizzy jelly.

Carniola

Designer	Franko Luin
Nationality	SL
Date Designed	1993
Foundries	Linotype
Number of weights	7

ABCDEFGHIJKLMNOPQRSTUVWXYZ

abcdefghijklmnopqrstuvwxyz1234567890

Sexy qua lijf, doch bang voor het zwempak.

Marco Polo

Designer	Franko Luin
Nationality	SL
Date Designed	1993
Foundries	Linotype
Number of weights	3

ABCDEFGHIJKLMNOPQRSTUVWXYZ
abcdefghijklmnopqrstuvwxyz1234567890
Now is the time for all brown dogs to jump over the lazy lynx.

TF Habitat

Designer	Joseph D Treacy
Nationality	US
Date Designed	1985
Foundries	TreacyFonts Monotype
Number of weights	19

ABCDEFGHIJKLMNOPQRSTUVWXYZ
abcdefghijklmnopqrstuvwxyz1234567890
May Jo equal the fine record by solving six puzzles a week?

Regent

Designer	AB Vista Company
Nationality	SE
Date Designed	1995
Foundries	FontHaus Creative Alliance
Number of weights	1

ABCDEFGHIJKLMNOPQRSTUVWXYZ
abcdefghijklmnopqrstuvwxyz1234567890
Waltz, nymph, for quick jigs vex Bud.

Carré Noir

Designer	Albert Boton
Nationality	FR
Date Designed	1996
Foundries	Monotype
Number of weights	10

ABCDEFGHIJKLMNOPQRSTUVWXYZ
abcdefghijklmnopqrstuvwxyz1234567890
Grumpy wizards make toxic brew for the evil Queen and Jack.

Origami

Designer	Carl Crossgrove
Nationality	US
Date Designed	1996
Foundries	CA Partners Monotype Adobe
Number of weights	8

ABCDEFGHIJKLMNOPQRSTUVWXYZ
abcdefghijklmnopqrstuvwxyz1234567890
Verbatim reports were quickly given by Jim Fox to his amazed audience.

Paradigm

Designer	Nick Shinn
Nationality	UK
Date Designed	1996
Foundries	Monotype
Number of weights	9

ABCDEFGHIJKLMNOPQRSTUVWXYZ

abcdefghijklmnopqrstuvwxyz1234567890

Was there a quorum of able whizzkids gravely exciting the jaded fish at ATypI?

Pompei

Designer	Albert Boton
Nationality	FR
Date Designed	1996
Foundries	CA Exclusives
Number of weights	8

ABCDEFGHIJKLMNOPQRSTUVWXYZ

abcdefghijklmnopqrstuvwxyz1234567890

Quick wafting zephyrs vex bold Jim.

Rowena

Designer	Gustav Andrejs Grinbergs
Nationality	LV
Date Designed	1996
Foundries	Linotype
Number of weights	6

ABCDEFGHIJKLMNOPQRSTUVWXYZ

abcdefghijklmnopqrstuvwxyz 1234567890

Will Major Douglas be expected to take this true-false quiz very soon?

Loire

Designer	Jean Lochu
Nationality	FR
Date Designed	1997
Foundries	Monotype
Number of weights	8

ABCDEFGHIJKLMNOPQRSTUVWXYZ

abcdefghijklmnopqrstuvwxyz1234567890

Martin J. Hixeypozer quickly began his first word.

Buccardi

Designer	Bo Berndal
Nationality	SE
Date Designed	1998
Foundries	Monotype
Number of weights	6

ABCDEFGHIJKLMNOPQRSTUVWXYZ

abcdefghijklmnopqrstuvwxyz1234567890

Sixty zippers were quickly picked from the woven jute bag.

Old Claude

Designer	Paul Shaw
Nationality	US
Date Designed	1998
Foundries	Monotype Letterperfect Adobe
Number of weights	2

ABCDEFGHIJKLMNOPQRSTUVWXYZ
abcdefghijklmnopqrstuvwxyz1234567890
Jaded zombies acted quaintly but kept driving their oxen forward.

Clifford Eighteen

Designer	Akiro Kobayashi
Nationality	JP
Date Designed	1999
Foundries	FontFont
Number of weights	10

ABCDEFGHIJKLMNOPQRSTUVWXYZ
abcdefghijklmnopqrstuvwxyz1234567890
Jail zesty vixen who grabbed pay from quack.

Biblon

Designer	Frantisek Storm
Nationality	CZ
Date Designed	2000
Foundries	Storm
Number of weights	8

ABCDEFGHIJKLMNOPQRSTUVWXYZ
abcdefghijklmnopqrstuvwxyz1234567890
Back in June we delivered oxygen equipment of the same size.

Berndal

Designer	Bo Berndal
Nationality	SE
Date Designed	2003
Foundries	Linotype
Number of weights	5

ABCDEFGHIJKLMNOPQRSTUVWXYZ
abcdefghijklmnopqrstuvwxyz1234567890
And David's Lips are lock't; but in divine.

Burgstädt Antiqua

Designer	Richard Yeend
Nationality	UK
Date Designed	2003
Foundries	Linotype
Number of weights	2

ABCDEFGHIJKLMNOPQRSTUVWXYZ
abcdefghijklmnopqrstuvwxyz1234567890
High piping Pelevi, with "Wine! Wine! Wine!

Cajoun

Designer	Hans Jurgen Ellenberger
Nationality	DE
Date Designed	2003
Foundries	Linotype
Number of weights	1

ABCDEFGHIJKLMNOPQRSTUVWXYZ

abcdefghijklmnopqrstuvwxyz1234567890

Red Wine!"— the Nightingale cries to the Rose.

Whitenights

Designer	Lars Bergquist
Nationality	SE
Date Designed	2003
Foundries	Linotype
Number of weights	12

ABCDEFGHIJKLMNOPQRSTUVWXYZ

abcdefghijklmnopqrstuvwxyz1234567890

That yellow Cheek of hers to'incarnadine.

Angkoon

Designer	Xavier Dupré
Nationality	FR
Date Designed	2003
Foundries	FontFont
Number of weights	82

ABCDEFGHIJKLMNOPQRSTUVWXYZ

abcdefghijklmnopqrstuvwxyz1234567890

Fred specialized in the job of making very quaint wax toys.

Fournier

Designer	P S Fournier
Nationality	FR
Date Designed	1742
Foundries	Fournier Monotype Adobe
Number of weights	9

ABCDEFGHIJKLMNOPQRSTUVWXYZ

abcdefghijklmnopqrstuvwxyz1234567890

Moi, je veux quinze clubs a golf et du whisky pur.

Baskerville Old Face

Designer	John Baskerville
Nationality	UK
Date Designed	1750
Foundries	Elsner+Flake
Number of weights	3

ABCDEFGHIJKLMNOPQRSTUVWXYZ

abcdefghijklmnopqrstuvwxyz1234567890

Murky haze enveloped a city as jarring quakes broke forty-six windows.

Transitional

Baskerville

Designer	John Baskerville
Nationality	UK
Date Designed	1750
Foundries	Baskerville Monotype Adobe Bitstream
Number of weights	12

ABCDEFGHIJKLMNOPQRSTUVWXYZ
abcdefghijklmnopqrstuvwxyz1234567890
Sphinx of black quartz judge my vow.

Baskerville Classico

Designer	John Baskerville
Nationality	UK
Date Designed	1750
Foundries	Omnibus
Recut/Digitised by	Franko Luin, 1995
Number of weights	5

ABCDEFGHIJKLMNOPQRSTUVWXYZ
abcdefghijklmnopqrstuvwxyz1234567890
Zweedse ex-VIP, behoorlijk gek op quantumfysica.

New Baskerville

Designer	John Baskerville
Nationality	UK
Date Designed	1750
Foundries	ITC
Recut/Digitised by	Linotype, 1974
Number of weights	8

ABCDEFGHIJKLMNOPQRSTUVWXYZ
abcdefghijklmnopqrstuvwxyz1234567890
Viewing quizzical abstracts mixed up hefty jocks.

Bell MT

Designer	Richard Austin
Nationality	UK
Date Designed	1788
Foundries	Bell & Stephenson Monotype Adobe URW++
Number of weights	15

ABCDEFGHIJKLMNOPQRSTUVWXYZ
abcdefghijklmnopqrstuvwxyz1234567890
Come, fill the Cup, and in the Fire of Spring.

Bulmer

Designer	William Martin
Nationality	UK
Date Designed	1790
Foundries	Shakespeare Press Monotype Adobe Bitstream
Number of weights	12

ABCDEFGHIJKLMNOPQRSTUVWXYZ
abcdefghijklmnopqrstuvwxyz1234567890
The International Magazine of Follies, Grottoes and Garden Buildings.

Century

Designer Linn Boyd Benton & T. L. De Vinne
Nationality US
Date Designed 1894
Foundries ATF ITC Bitstream
Recut/Digitised by Tony Stan, 1975
Number of weights 18

ABCDEFGHIJKLMNOPQRSTUVWXYZ
abcdefghijklmnopqrstuvwxyz1234567890

CenturyFB digitised by Greg Thompson; Century Nova designed by Charles Hughes.

Cheltenham

Designer Bertram G. Goodhue
Nationality US
Date Designed 1896
Foundries ATF Adobe Bitstream ITC
Recut/Digitised by Tony Stan, 1975
Number of weights 18

ABCDEFGHIJKLMNOPQRSTUVWXYZ
abcdefghijklmnopqrstuvwxyz1234567890

Mr. Jock, TV quiz Ph.D., bags few lynx.

Cochin

Designer Charles Malin, Georges Peignot
Nationality FR
Date Designed 1912
Foundries Deberny & Peignot Adobe
Number of weights 4

ABCDEFGHIJKLMNOPQRSTUVWXYZ
abcdefghijklmnopqrstuvwxyz1234567890

The July sun caused a fragment of black pine wax to ooze on the velvet quilt.

Goudy

Designer Frederic W Goudy
Nationality US
Date Designed 1916
Foundries Adobe URW++ Linotype
Number of weights 13

ABCDEFGHIJKLMNOPQRSTUVWXYZ
abcdefghijklmnopqrstuvwxyz1234567890

The vixen jumped quickly on her foe barking with zeal.

Century Schoolbook

Designer Morris Fuller Benton
Nationality US
Date Designed 1918
Foundries Bitstream DTP URW++
Number of weights 4

ABCDEFGHIJKLMNOPQRSTUVWXYZ
abcdefghijklmnopqrstuvwxyz1234567890

The Winter Garment of Repentance fling:?

Goudy Modern MT

Designer	Frederic W Goudy
Nationality	US
Date Designed	1918
Foundries	Adobe
Recut/Digitised by	Franko Luin, 1994
Number of weights	2

ABCDEFGHIJKLMNOPQRSTUVWXYZ
abcdefghijklmnopqrstuvwxyz1234567890
Portez ce vieux whisky au juge blond qui fume.

Perpetua

Designer	Eric Gill
Nationality	UK
Date Designed	1928
Foundries	Monotype
Number of weights	12

ABCDEFGHIJKLMNOPQRSTUVWXYZ
abcdefghijklmnopqrstuvwxyz1234567890
Big July earthquakes confound zany experimental vow.

Weiss Roman

Designer	Emil Rudolf Weiss
Nationality	DE
Date Designed	1928
Foundries	Bauer Linotype Bitstream Adobe Monotype
Number of weights	4

ABCDEFGHIJKLMNOPQRSTUVWXYZ
abcdefghijklmnopqrstuvwxyz1234567890
Martin J. Hixeypozer quickly began his first word.

Minister

Designer	M Fahrenwaldt
Nationality	DE
Date Designed	1929
Foundries	Schriftguss Adobe URW++
Number of weights	8

ABCDEFGHIJKLMNOPQRSTUVWXYZ
abcdefghijklmnopqrstuvwxyz1234567890
Playing jazz vibe chords quickly excites my wife.

Times

Designer	Stanley Morison
Nationality	UK
Date Designed	1931
Foundries	Monotype
Number of weights	10

ABCDEFGHIJKLMNOPQRSTUVWXYZ
abcdefghijklmnopqrstuvwxyz1234567890
Now the commonest serif font in the world.

Times New Roman

Designer	Stanley Morison, Victor Lardent
Nationality	UK
Date Designed	1931
Foundries	Monotype
Number of weights	7

ABCDEFGHIJKLMNOPQRSTUVWXYZ
abcdefghijklmnopqrstuvwxyz1234567890

Designed in 1931 as a text face for The Times, then England's leading newspaper. Probably the most famous font.

Times Eighteen

Designer	Stanley Morison
Nationality	UK
Date Designed	1935
Foundries	Monotype
Number of weights	4

ABCDEFGHIJKLMNOPQRSTUVWXYZ
abcdefghijklmnopqrstuvwxyz1234567890

West quickly gave Bert handsome prizes for six juicy plums.

Times Ten

Designer	Stanley Morison
Nationality	UK
Date Designed	1935
Foundries	Monotype
Number of weights	9

ABCDEFGHIJKLMNOPQRSTUVWXYZ
abcdefghijklmnopqrstuvwxyz1234567890

Breezily jangling $3,416,857,209,wise advertiser ambles to the bank, his exchequer amplified.

Times Europa

Designer	Walter Tracy
Nationality	UK
Date Designed	1971
Foundries	Monotype
Recut/Digitised by	Walter Tracy, 1972
Number of weights	6

ABCDEFGHIJKLMNOPQRSTUVWXYZ
abcdefghijklmnopqrstuvwxyz1234567890

Commissioned by The Times to replace Times New Roman.

Electra

Designer	W A Dwiggins
Nationality	US
Date Designed	1935
Foundries	Nacional Linotype Adobe Monotype
Recut/Digitised by	Linotype, 1994
Number of weights	14

ABCDEFGHIJKLMNOPQRSTUVWXYZ
abcdefghijklmnopqrstuvwxyz1234567890

Zwei Boxkämpfer jagen Eva quer durch Sylt.

Pilgrim

Designer	Eric Gill
Nationality	UK
Date Designed	1935
Foundries	Linotype
Number of weights	2

ABCDEFGHIJKLMNOPQRSTUVWXYZ
abcdefghijklmnopqrstuvwxyz1234567890
The exodus of jazzy pigeons is craved by squeamish walkers.

Bernhard Modern

Designer	Lucian Bernhard
Nationality	AT
Date Designed	1937
Foundries	Bitstream
Number of weights	4

ABCDEFGHIJKLMNOPQRSTUVWXYZ
abcdefghijklmnopqrstuvwxyz1234567890
My grandfather picks up quartz and valuable onyx jewels.

Haarlemmer

Designer	Jan van Krimpen
Nationality	NL
Date Designed	1938
Foundries	Monotype DTL
Recut/Digitised by	Frank E. Blockland, 2002
Number of weights	7

ABCDEFGHIJKLMNOPQRSTUVWXYZ
abcdefghijklmnopqrstuvwxyz1234567890
Zweedse ex-VIP, behoorlijk gek op quantumfysica.

New Caledonia

Designer	W A Dwiggins
Nationality	US
Date Designed	1939
Foundries	Linotype
Recut/Digitised by	John Quaranta, 1978
Number of weights	12

ABCDEFGHIJKLMNOPQRSTUVWXYZ
abcdefghijklmnopqrstuvwxyz1234567890
A mad boxer shot a quick, gloved jab to the jaw of his dizzy opponent.

Corona

Designer	Chauncey H Griffith
Nationality	US
Date Designed	1941
Foundries	Mergenthaler Linotype Adobe
Number of weights	3

ABCDEFGHIJKLMNOPQRSTUVWXYZ
abcdefghijklmnopqrstuvwxyz1234567890
For only €4, jolly housewives made inexpensive meals using quick-frozen vegetables.

Palatino

Designer Hermann Zapf
Nationality DE
Date Designed 1950
Foundries Stempel Linotype Adobe Monotype Apple
Number of weights 14

ABCDEFGHIJKLMNOPQRSTUVWXYZ
abcdefghijklmnopqrstuvwxyz1234567890

Chosen as a core font for Microsoft Windows & OS X

Spectrum

Designer Jan Van Krimpen
Nationality NL
Date Designed 1952
Foundries Enschedé Monotype MCL Adobe Linotype
Number of weights 9

ABCDEFGHIJKLMNOPQRSTUVWXYZ
abcdefghijklmnopqrstuvwxyz1234567890

Zweedse ex-VIP, behoorlijk gek op quantumfysica.

Gazette

Designer E W Shaar
Nationality US
Date Designed 1954
Foundries Adobe Monotype
Number of weights 3

ABCDEFGHIJKLMNOPQRSTUVWXYZ
abcdefghijklmnopqrstuvwxyz1234567890

For only €49, jolly housewives made inexpensive meals using quick-frozen vegetables.

Meridien

Designer Adrian Frutiger
Nationality CH
Date Designed 1957
Foundries Deberny & Peignot Adobe
Number of weights 6

ABCDEFGHIJKLMNOPQRSTUVWXYZ
abcdefghijklmnopqrstuvwxyz1234567890

Fred specialized in the job of making very quaint wax toys.

AT News No 2

Designer Jackson Burke
Nationality US
Date Designed 1960
Foundries CA Partners
Number of weights 3

ABCDEFGHIJKLMNOPQRSTUVWXYZ
abcdefghijklmnopqrstuvwxyz1234567890

When we go back to Juarez, Mexico, do we fly over picturesque Arizona?

Octavian

Designer	Will Carter, David Kindersley
Nationality	UK
Date Designed	1961
Foundries	Monotype
Number of weights	6

ABCDEFGHIJKLMNOPQRSTUVWXYZ

abcdefghijklmnopqrstuvwxyz1234567890

Quixotic Conservatives vet first key zero-growth jeremiad.

Apollo

Designer	Adrian Frutiger
Nationality	CH
Date Designed	1962
Foundries	Monotype Adobe
Number of weights	9

ABCDEFGHIJKLMNOPQRSTUVWXYZ

abcdefghijklmnopqrstuvwxyz1234567890

Sympathizing would fix Quaker objectives.

Life

Designer	W Bilz, F Simoncini
Nationality	US
Date Designed	1964
Foundries	Simoncini Rastignano Ludwig & Mayer Linotype Bitstream Elsner+Flake URW++ Adobe Monotype
Number of weights	3

ABCDEFGHIJKLMNOPQRSTUVWXYZ

abcdefghijklmnopqrstuvwxyz1234567890

Puzzled women bequeath jerks very exotic gifts.

Rotation

Designer	Arthur Ritzel
Nationality	DE
Date Designed	1971
Foundries	Linotype
Number of weights	4

ABCDEFGHIJKLMNOPQRSTUVWXYZ

abcdefghijklmnopqrstuvwxyz1234567890

West quickly gave Bert handsome prizes for six juicy plums.

Photina

Designer	José Mendoza y Almeida
Nationality	ES
Date Designed	1972
Foundries	Monotype
Number of weights	8

ABCDEFGHIJKLMNOPQRSTUVWXYZ

abcdefghijklmnopqrstuvwxyz1234567890

William said that everything about his jacket was in quite good condition except for the zipper.

Zapf International

Designer Hermann Zapf
Nationality DE
Date Designed 1977
Foundries ITC URW++ Bitstream
Elsner+Flake Linotype
Number of weights 8

ABCDEFGHIJKLMNOPQRSTUVWXYZ
abcdefghijklmnopqrstuvwxyz1234567890
Martin J. Hixeypozer quickly began his first word.

Adroit

Designer Phil Martin
Nationality US
Date Designed 1981
Foundries URW++ CA Partners
Number of weights 4

ABCDEFGHIJKLMNOPQRSTUVWXYZ
abcdefghijklmnopqrstuvwxyz1234567890
How quickly daft jumping zebras vex.

Else NPL

Designer Robert Norton
Nationality UK
Date Designed 1982
Foundries Adobe
Number of weights 4

ABCDEFGHIJKLMNOPQRSTUVWXYZ
abcdefghijklmnopqrstuvwxyz1234567890
The juke box music puzzled a gentle visitor from a quaint valley town.

Timeless

Designer Typoart
Nationality DE
Date Designed 1982
Foundries Linotype URW++
Number of weights 3

ABCDEFGHIJKLMNOPQRSTUVWXYZ
abcdefghijklmnopqrstuvwxyz1234567890
May Jo equal the fine record by solving six puzzles a week?

Versailles

Designer Adrian Frutiger
Nationality CH
Date Designed 1984
Foundries Adobe
Number of weights 8

ABCDEFGHIJKLMNOPQRSTUVWXYZ
abcdefghijklmnopqrstuvwxyz1234567890
Lazy movers quit hard-packing of papier-mache jewellery boxes.

Gamma

Designer	Jovica Veljovic
Nationality	YU
Date Designed	1986
Foundries	ITC Linotype
Number of weights	10

ABCDEFGHIJKLMNOPQRSTUVWXYZ
abcdefghijklmnopqrstuvwxyz1234567890
Jail zesty vixen who grabbed pay from quack.

Hiroshige

Designer	Cynthia Hollandsworth
Nationality	US
Date Designed	1986
Foundries	Adobe URW++
Number of weights	8

ABCDEFGHIJKLMNOPQRSTUVWXYZ
abcdefghijklmnopqrstuvwxyz1234567890
Five or six big jet planes zoomed quickly by the tower.

Slimbach

Designer	Robert Slimbach
Nationality	US
Date Designed	1987
Foundries	ITC Adobe Elsner+Flake Linotype URW++
Number of weights	8

ABCDEFGHIJKLMNOPQRSTUVWXYZ
abcdefghijklmnopqrstuvwxyz1234567890
Sixty zippers were quickly picked from the woven jute bag.

Jamille

Designer	Mark Jamra
Nationality	CH
Date Designed	1988
Foundries	URW++ ITC Linotype AGP Elsner+Flake
Number of weights	8

ABCDEFGHIJKLMNOPQRSTUVWXYZ
abcdefghijklmnopqrstuvwxyz1234567890
Martin J. Hixeypozer quickly began his first word.

Wilke

Designer	Martin Wilke
Nationality	DE
Date Designed	1988
Foundries	Linotype
Number of weights	6

ABCDEFGHIJKLMNOPQRSTUVWXYZ
abcdefghijklmnopqrstuvwxyz1234567890
The juke box music puzzled a gentle visitor from a quaint valley town.

Utopia

Designer	Robert Slimbach
Nationality	US
Date Designed	1989
Foundries	Adobe
Number of weights	24

ABCDEFGHIJKLMNOPQRSTUVWXYZ

abcdefghijklmnopqrstuvwxyz1234567890

Grumpy wizards make toxic brew for the evil Queen and Jack.

Ellington

Designer	Michael Harvey
Nationality	UK
Date Designed	1990
Foundries	Monotype Adobe
Number of weights	8

ABCDEFGHIJKLMNOPQRSTUVWXYZ
abcdefghijklmnopqrstuvwxyz1234567890
Will Major Douglas be expected to take this true-false quiz very soon?

Minion

Designer	Robert Slimbach
Nationality	US
Date Designed	1990
Foundries	Adobe Linotype
Number of weights	31

ABCDEFGHIJKLMNOPQRSTUVWXYZ
abcdefghijklmnopqrstuvwxyz1234567890
We have just quoted on nine dozen boxes of gray lamp wicks.

Monkton

Designer	Adrian Williams
Nationality	UK
Date Designed	1990
Foundries	Monotype
Number of weights	8

ABCDEFGHIJKLMNOPQRSTUVWXYZ
abcdefghijklmnopqrstuvwxyz1234567890
West quickly gave Bert handsome prizes for six juicy plums.

Thorndale

Designer	Galiad Computers
Nationality	UK
Date Designed	1991
Foundries	Monotype
Number of weights	4

ABCDEFGHIJKLMNOPQRSTUVWXYZ
abcdefghijklmnopqrstuvwxyz1234567890
Back in June we delivered oxygen equipment of the same size.

Emona

Designer	Franko Luin
Nationality	SL
Date Designed	1992
Foundries	Linotype
Number of weights	11

ABCDEFGHIJKLMNOPQRSTUVWXYZ
abcdefghijklmnopqrstuvwxyz1234567890

New farm hand (picking just six quinces) proves strong but lazy.

Res Publica

Designer	Franko Luin
Nationality	SL
Date Designed	1992
Foundries	Omnibus
Number of weights	9

ABCDEFGHIJKLMNOPQRSTUVWXYZ
abcdefghijklmnopqrstuvwxyz1234567890

Astronaut Quincy B. Zack defies gravity with six jet fuel pumps.

Charter

Designer	Matthew Carter
Nationality	US
Date Designed	1993
Foundries	Bitstream ITC Monotype
Number of weights	14

ABCDEFGHIJKLMNOPQRSTUVWXYZ
abcdefghijklmnopqrstuvwxyz1234567890

Charter CX Precision

Euclides

Designer	Bo Berndal
Nationality	SE
Date Designed	1990
Foundries	Monotype
Number of weights	4

ABCDEFGHIJKLMNOPQRSTUVWXYZ
abcdefghijklmnopqrstuvwxyz1234567890

Five big quacking zephyrs jolt my wax bed.

Isolde

Designer	Franko Luin
Nationality	SL
Date Designed	1993
Foundries	Linotype
Number of weights	5

ABCDEFGHIJKLMNOPQRSTUVWXYZ
abcdefghijklmnopqrstuvwxyz1234567890

Playing jazz vibe chords quickly excites my wife.

Jante Antiqua

Designer	Poul Søgren
Nationality	DK
Date Designed	1993
Foundries	Monotype
Number of weights	4

ABCDEFGHIJKLMNOPQRSTUVWXYZ
abcdefghijklmnopqrstuvwxyz1234567890

Perhaps President Clinton's amazing sax skills will be judged
quite favourably.

Kalix

Designer	Franko Luin
Nationality	SL
Date Designed	1993
Foundries	Linotype
Number of weights	7

ABCDEFGHIJKLMNOPQRSTUVWXYZ
abcdefghijklmnopqrstuvwxyz1234567890

Six big devils from Japan quickly forgot how to waltz.

Läckö

Designer	Bo Berndal
Nationality	SE
Date Designed	1993
Foundries	Monotype
Number of weights	4

ABCDEFGHIJKLMNOPQRSTUVWXYZ
abcdefghijklmnopqrstuvwxyz1234567890

Jail zesty vixen who grabbed pay from quack.

Miramar

Designer	Franko Luin
Nationality	SL
Date Designed	1993
Foundries	Linotype
Number of weights	5

ABCDEFGHIJKLMNOPQRSTUVWXYZ
abcdefghijklmnopqrstuvwxyz1234567890

Jimmy and Zack, the police explained, were last seen diving into a field
of buttered quahogs.

Omnibus

Designer	Franko Luin
Nationality	SL
Date Designed	1993
Foundries	Linotype
Recut/Digitised by	Omnibus
Number of weights	7

ABCDEFGHIJKLMNOPQRSTUVWXYZ
abcdefghijklmnopqrstuvwxyz1234567890

Jazzy saxophones blew over Mick's turgid quiff.

Ragnar

Designer	Franko Luin
Nationality	SL
Date Designed	1993
Foundries	Omnibus Linotype
Number of weights	7

ABCDEFGHIJKLMNOPQRSTUVWXYZ
abcdefghijklmnopqrstuvwxyz1234567890
Quick wafting zephyrs vex bold Jim.

TF Ardent

Designer	Joseph D Treacy
Nationality	US
Date Designed	1990
Foundries	Monotype
Number of weights	4

ABCDEFGHIJKLMNOPQRSTUVWXYZ
abcdefghijklmnopqrstuvwxyz1234567890
Six big devils from Japan quickly forgot how to waltz.

TF Arrow

Designer	Joseph D Treacy
Nationality	US
Date Designed	1995
Foundries	Treacyfaces
Number of weights	5

ABCDEFGHIJKLMNOPQRSTUVWXYZ
abcdefghijklmnopqrstuvwxyz1234567890
A font with vestigial serifs.

Hoefler Text

Designer	Jonathan Hoefler
Nationality	US
Date Designed	1995
Foundries	Hoefler Type Foundry
Number of weights	1

ABCDEFGHIJKLMNOPQRSTUVWXYZ
abcdefghijklmnopqrstuvwxyz1234567890
The Bird of Time has but a little way

Esquisse

Designer	Alexis Merlaut
Nationality	FR
Date Designed	1996
Foundries	Monotype
Number of weights	4

ABCDEFGHIJKLMNOPQRSTUVWXYZ
abcdefghijklmnopqrstuvwxyz1234567890
Sympathizing would fix Quaker objectives.

Georgia

Designer	Matthew Carter
Nationality	UK
Date Designed	1996
Foundries	Microsoft Apple
Number of weights	1

ABCDEFGHIJKLMNOPQRSTUVWXYZ
abcdefghijklmnopqrstuvwxyz1234567890

Chosen as a core font for Microsoft Windows.

Plantagenet

Designer	Ross Mills
Nationality	CA
Date Designed	1996
Foundries	CA Exclusives
Number of weights	12

ABCDEFGHIJKLMNOPQRSTUVWXYZ
abcdefghijklmnopqrstuvwxyz1234567890

An inspired calligrapher can create pages of beauty using stick ink, quill, brush, pick-axe, buzz saw, or even strawberry jam.

Pocketype

Designer	Bo Berndal
Nationality	SE
Date Designed	1994
Foundries	Monotype
Number of weights	5

ABCDEFGHIJKLMNOPQRSTUVWXYZ
abcdefghijklmnopqrstuvwxyz1234567890

Jack amazed a few girls by dropping the antique onyx vase!

Promemoria

Designer	Bo Berndal
Nationality	SE
Date Designed	1996
Foundries	Monotype
Number of weights	3

ABCDEFGHIJKLMNOPQRSTUVWXYZ
abcdefghijklmnopqrstuvwxyz1234567890

Quick wafting zephyrs vex bold Jim.

Pavane

Designer	Lars Bergquist
Nationality	SE
Date Designed	1997
Foundries	Timberwolf CA Exclusives
Number of weights	2

ABCDEFGHIJKLMNOPQRSTUVWXYZ
abcdefghijklmnopqrstuvwxyz1234567890

Martin J. Hixeypozer quickly began his first word.

Monteverdi

Designer	Lars Bergquist
Nationality	SE
Date Designed	1997
Foundries	CA Exclusives
Number of weights	4

ABCDEFGHIJKLMNOPQRSTUVWXYZ

abcdefghijklmnopqrstuvwxyz1234567890

Perhaps President Clinton's amazing sax skills will be judged quite favourably.

Maxime

Designer	Eric de Berranger
Nationality	FR
Date Designed	1999
Foundries	Monotype
Number of weights	14

ABCDEFGHIJKLMNOPQRSTUVWXYZ

abcdefghijklmnopqrstuvwxyz1234567890

Portez ce vieux whisky au juge blond qui fume.

Oneleigh

Designer	Nick Shinn
Nationality	UK
Date Designed	1999
Foundries	FontFont
Number of weights	14

ABCDEFGHIJKLMNOPQRSTUVWXYZ

abcdefghijklmnopqrstuvwxyz1234567890

Brawny gods just flocked up to quiz and vex him.

Reminga

Designer	Xavier Dupré
Nationality	FR
Date Designed	2001
Foundries	FontFont
Number of weights	23

ABCDEFGHIJKLMNOPQRSTUVWXYZ

abcdefghijklmnopqrstuvwxyz1234567890

Crazy Fredericka bought many very exquisite opal jewels.

Atma

Designer	Alan Greene
Nationality	UK
Date Designed	2002
Foundries	FontFont
Number of weights	94

ABCDEFGHIJKLMNOPQRSTUVWXYZ

abcdefghijklmnopqrstuvwxyz1234567890

Fred specialized in the job of making very quaint wax toys.

Breughel

Designer	Adrian Frutiger
Nationality	CH
Date Designed	1981
Foundries	URW++ Linotype
Number of weights	8

ABCDEFGHIJKLMNOPQRSTUVWXYZ
abcdefghijklmnopqrstuvwxyz1234567890

No kidding, Lorenzo called off his trip to visit Mexico City just because they told him the conquistadores were extinct.

Tibere

Designer	Albert Boton
Nationality	FR
Date Designed	2003
Foundries	FontFont
Number of weights	26

ABCDEFGHIJKLMNOPQRSTUVWXYZ
abcdefghijklmnopqrstuvwxyz1234567890

How vexing a fumble to drop a jolly zucchini in the quicksand.

Didot

Designer	Firmin Didot
Nationality	FR
Date Designed	1784
Foundries	Didot Hoefler
Recut/Digitised by	Adrian Frutiger, 1991
Number of weights	12

ABCDEFGHIJKLMNOPQRSTUVWXYZ
abcdefghijklmnopqrstuvwxyz1234567890

Portez ce vieux whisky au juge blond qui fume?

Linotype Didot

Designer	Firmin Didot
Nationality	FR
Date Designed	1784
Foundries	Linotype
Recut/Digitised by	Adrian Frutiger, 1992
Number of weights	12

ABCDEFGHIJKLMNOPQRSTUVWXYZ
abcdefghijklmnopqrstuvwxyz1234567890

Sympathizing would fix Quaker objectives.

Bodoni

Designer	Giambattista Bodoni
Nationality	IT
Date Designed	1788
Foundries	Bodoni Monotype Adobe Bauer
Number of weights	7

ABCDEFGHIJKLMNOPQRSTUVWXYZ
abcdefghijklmnopqrstuvwxyz1234567890

Waltz, nymph, for quick jigs vex Bud.

Didone

Bauer Bodoni

Designer Giambattista Bodoni
Nationality IT
Date Designed 1788
Foundries Elsner+Flake Monotype Bauer
Recut/Digitised by Heinrich Jost, Louis Höll, 1926
Number of weights 13

ABCDEFGHIJKLMNOPQRSTUVWXYZ
abcdefghijklmnopqrstuvwxyz1234567890
Six big devils from Japan quickly forgot how to waltz.

Bodoni Antiqua

Designer Giambattista Bodoni
Nationality IT
Date Designed 1788
Foundries URW++
Number of weights 12

ABCDEFGHIJKLMNOPQRSTUVWXYZ
abcdefghijklmnopqrstuvwxyz1234567890
Puzzled women bequeath jerks very exotic gifts.

Bodoni Classic

Designer Giambattista Bodoni
Nationality IT
Date Designed 1788
Foundries FontFont
Recut/Digitised by Gert Wiescher, 1994
Number of weights 23

ABCDEFGHIJKLMNOPQRSTUVWXYZ
abcdefghijklmnopqrstuvwxyz1234567890
Jazzy saxophones blew over Mick's turgid quiff.

Bodoni Six

Designer Giambattista Bodoni
Nationality IT
Date Designed 1788
Foundries ITC Linotype Monotype
Recut/Digitised by Janice Fishman, Holly Goldsmith, Jim Parkinson, Sumner Stone 1994
Number of weights 9

ABCDEFGHIJKLMNOPQRSTUVWXYZ
abcdefghijklmnopqrstuvwxyz1234567890
Ebenezer unexpectedly bagged two tranquil aardvarks with his jiffy vacuum cleaner.

Bodoni Twelve

Designer Giambattista Bodoni
Nationality IT
Date Designed 1788
Foundries ITC Linotype Monotype
Recut/Digitised by Janice Fishman, Holly Goldsmith, Jim Parkinson, Sumner Stone 1994
Number of weights 9

ABCDEFGHIJKLMNOPQRSTUVWXYZ
abcdefghijklmnopqrstuvwxyz1234567890
Jaded reader with fabled roving eye seized by quickened impulse to expand budget.

Bodoni Seventy-Two

Designer	Giambattista Bodoni
Nationality	IT
Date Designed	1788
Foundries	ITC Elsner+Flake Lino. Mono.
Recut/Digitised by	Janice Fishman, Holly Goldsmith, Jim Parkinson, Sumner Stone 1994
Number of weights	11

ABCDEFGHIJKLMNOPQRSTUVWXYZ
abcdefghijklmnopqrstuvwxyz1234567890

For only $49, jolly housewives made inexpensive meals using quick-frozen vegetables.

Bodoni Classico

Designer	Giambattista Bodoni
Nationality	IT
Date Designed	1788
Foundries	Linotype
Recut/Digitised by	Franko Luin, 1995
Number of weights	5

ABCDEFGHIJKLMNOPQRSTUVWXYZ
abcdefghijklmnopqrstuvwxyz1234567890

Brawny gods just flocked up to quiz and vex him.

Bodoni IBM

Designer	Giambattista Bodoni
Nationality	IT
Date Designed	1788
Foundries	URW++
Number of weights	3

ABCDEFGHIJKLMNOPQRSTUVWXYZ
abcdefghijklmnopqrstuvwxyz1234567890

Jim just quit and packed extra bags for Liz Owen.

WTC Our Bodoni

Designer	Giambattista Bodoni
Nationality	IT
Date Designed	1788
Foundries	CA Partners
Recut/Digitised by	Tom Carnase, Massimo Vignelli, 1989
Number of weights	6

ABCDEFGHIJKLMNOPQRSTUVWXYZ
abcdefghijklmnopqrstuvwxyz1234567890

Will Major Douglas be expected to take this true-false quiz very soon?

Bodoni No 2

Designer	Giambattista Bodoni
Nationality	IT
Date Designed	1788
Foundries	Elsner+Flake URW
Number of weights	2

ABCDEFGHIJKLMNOPQRSTUVWXYZ
abcdefghijklmnopqrstuvwxyz1234567890

Viewing quizzical abstracts mixed up hefty jocks.

Walbaum

Designer J E Walbaum
Nationality DE
Date Designed 1800
Foundries Berthold Linotype Monotype URW++ Storm
Number of weights 9

ABCDEFGHIJKLMNOPQRSTUVWXYZ

abcdefghijklmnopqrstuvwxyz1234567890

Forsaking monastic tradition, twelve jovial friars gave up their vocation for a questionable existence on the flying trapeze.

Scotch Roman MT

Designer A D Farmer
Nationality UK
Date Designed 1904
Foundries Linotype Monotype Adobe Miller & Richard
Number of weights 2

ABCDEFGHIJKLMNOPQRSTUVWXYZ

abcdefghijklmnopqrstuvwxyz1234567890

Sympathizing would fix Quaker objectives.

Modern No. 20

Designer Monotype
Nationality UK
Date Designed 1850
Foundries Monotype Letraset Bitstream
Number of weights 1

ABCDEFGHIJKLMNOPQRSTUVWXYZ

abcdefghijklmnopqrstuvwxyz1234567890

Quick wafting zephyrs vex bold Jim.

Monotype Modern

Designer Monotype Design
Nationality UK
Date Designed 1880
Foundries Monotype
Number of weights 8

ABCDEFGHIJKLMNOPQRSTUVWXYZ
abcdefghijklmnopqrstuvwxyz1234567890

Jaded zombies acted quaintly but kept driving their oxen forward.

Modern No. 216

Designer Monotype
Nationality UK
Date Designed 1900
Foundries ITC Linotype Bitstream
Recut/Digitised by Edward Benguiat, 1982
Number of weights 8

ABCDEFGHIJKLMNOPQRSTUVWXYZ
abcdefghijklmnopqrstuvwxyz1234567890

Jazzy saxophones blew over Mick's turgid quiff.

Solid Antique Roman

Designer	Monotype
Nationality	UK
Date Designed	1900
Foundries	Monotype
Number of weights	1

ABCDEFGHIJKLMNOPQRSTUVWXYZ

abcdefghijklmnopqrstuvwxyz1234567890

Five or six big jet planes zoomed quickly by the tower.

Carlton

Designer	F H Emcke
Nationality	DE
Date Designed	1908 / 1929
Foundries	Amsterdam
Recut/Digitised by	1994.0
Number of weights	1

ABCDEFGHIJKLMNOPQRSTUVWXYZ

abcdefghijklmnopqrstuvwxyz1234567890

Quick wafting zephyrs vex bold Jim.

Tiemann

Designer	Walter Tiemann
Nationality	DE
Date Designed	1923
Foundries	Klingspor Linotype
Number of weights	2

ABCDEFGHIJKLMNOPQRSTUVWXYZ
abcdefghijklmnopqrstuvwxyz1234567890

The sex life of the woodchuck is a provocative question for most vertebrate zoology majors.

Elante

Designer	W A Dwiggins
Nationality	US
Date Designed	1935
Foundries	Monotype
Number of weights	4

ABCDEFGHIJKLMNOPQRSTUVWXYZ
abcdefghijklmnopqrstuvwxyz1234567890

Sphinx of black quartz judge my vow.

Bernhard Modern Roman

Designer	Lucian Bernhard
Nationality	AT
Date Designed	1937
Foundries	Monotype
Number of weights	4

ABCDEFGHIJKLMNOPQRSTUVWXYZ
abcdefghijklmnopqrstuvwxyz1234567890

Quixotic Conservatives vet first key zero-growth jeremiad.

Caledonia

Designer	W A Dwiggins
Nationality	US
Date Designed	1938
Foundries	Mergenthaler Linotype Linotype
Number of weights	8

ABCDEFGHIJKLMNOPQRSTUVWXYZ
abcdefghijklmnopqrstuvwxyz1234567890
Will Major Douglas be expected to take this true-false quiz very soon?

Fairfield

Designer	Rudolph Ruzicka
Nationality	CZ
Date Designed	1939
Foundries	Mergenthaler Linotype Adobe Monotype
Recut/Digitised by	Alex Kaczun, 1991
Number of weights	20

ABCDEFGHIJKLMNOPQRSTUVWXYZ
abcdefghijklmnopqrstuvwxyz1234567890
Sphinx of black quartz judge my vow.

AT Athenaeum

Designer	Alessandro Butti, Aldo Novarese
Nationality	IT
Date Designed	1945
Foundries	Monotype
Number of weights	5

ABCDEFGHIJKLMNOPQRSTUVWXYZ
abcdefghijklmnopqrstuvwxyz1234567890
Now is the time for all brown dogs to jump over the lazy lynx.

Diotima

Designer	Gudrun Zapfvon Hesse
Nationality	DE
Date Designed	1952
Foundries	Stempel Adobe Linotype
Number of weights	5

ABCDEFGHIJKLMNOPQRSTUVWXYZ
abcdefghijklmnopqrstuvwxyz1234567890
Sphinx of black quartz judge my vow.

Americana

Designer	Richard Isbell
Nationality	US
Date Designed	1965
Foundries	ATF Bitstream URW++
Number of weights	4

ABCDEFGHIJKLMNOPQRSTUVWXYZ
abcdefghijklmnopqrstuvwxyz1234567890
One of the last hot metal typefaces.

Maximus LT

Designer	Walter Tracy
Nationality	UK
Date Designed	1967
Foundries	Linotype Adobe
Number of weights	1

ABCDEFGHIJKLMNOPQRSTUVWXYZ
abcdefghijklmnopqrstuvwxyz1234567890
Big July earthquakes confound zany experiment.

Zapf Book

Designer	Hermann Zapf
Nationality	DE
Date Designed	1976
Foundries	ITC Franklin Bitstream
	Elsner+Flake Linotype
Number of weights	8

ABCDEFGHIJKLMNOPQRSTUVWXYZ
abcdefghijklmnopqrstuvwxyz1234567890
Mix Zapf with Veljovic and get quirky Beziers.

Fenice

Designer	Aldo Novarese
Nationality	IT
Date Designed	1977-1980
Foundries	Nebbiolo ITC Adobe Bitstream
Number of weights	8

ABCDEFGHIJKLMNOPQRSTUVWXYZ
abcdefghijklmnopqrstuvwxyz1234567890
Quick wafting zephyrs vex bold Jim.

Basilia

Designer	André Gürtler
Nationality	CH
Date Designed	1978
Foundries	Monotype Linotype
Number of weights	6

ABCDEFGHIJKLMNOPQRSTUVWXYZ
abcdefghijklmnopqrstuvwxyz1234567890
Waltz, nymph, for quick jigs vex Bud.

AT Basilia

Designer	André Gürtler
Nationality	CH
Date Designed	1978
Foundries	Monotype
Number of weights	6

ABCDEFGHIJKLMNOPQRSTUVWXYZ
abcdefghijklmnopqrstuvwxyz1234567890
Will Major Douglas be expected to take this true-false quiz very soon?

Veljovic

Designer	Jovica Veljovic
Nationality	YU
Date Designed	1984
Foundries	ITC Adobe
Number of weights	8

ABCDEFGHIJKLMNOPQRSTUVWXYZ
abcdefghijklmnopqrstuvwxyz1234567890
Mix Zapf with Veljovic and get quirky Beziers.

Centennial

Designer	Adrian Frutiger
Nationality	CH
Date Designed	1986
Foundries	Linotype Monotype
Number of weights	17

ABCDEFGHIJKLMNOPQRSTUVWXYZ
abcdefghijklmnopqrstuvwxyz1234567890
Sixty zippers were quickly picked from the woven jute bag.

Arepo

Designer	Sumner Stone
Nationality	US
Date Designed	1988
Foundries	Monotype
Number of weights	4

ABCDEFGHIJKLMNOPQRSTUVWXYZ
abcdefghijklmnopqrstuvwxyz1234567890
The vixen jumped quickly on her foe barking with zeal.

Charlotte

Designer	Michael Gills
Nationality	UK
Date Designed	1992
Foundries	Linotype ITC
Number of weights	5

ABCDEFGHIJKLMNOPQRSTUVWXYZ
abcdefghijklmnopqrstuvwxyz1234567890
While waxing parquet decks, jaunty Suez sailors vomit abaft.

Esperanto

Designer	Franko Luin
Nationality	SL
Date Designed	1992
Foundries	Omnibus Linotype
Number of weights	12

ABCDEFGHIJKLMNOPQRSTUVWXYZ
abcdefghijklmnopqrstuvwxyz1234567890
Jaded zombies acted quaintly but kept driving their oxen forward.

Boberia

Designer	Bo Berndal
Nationality	SE
Date Designed	1994
Foundries	Linotype
Number of weights	3

ABCDEFGHIJKLMNOPQRSTUVWXYZ

abcdefghijklmnopqrstuvwxyz1234567890

Was there a quorum of able whizzkids gravely exciting the jaded fish at ATypI?

Throhand

Designer	David Berlow
Nationality	US
Date Designed	1995
Foundries	Font Bureau
Number of weights	12

ABCDEFGHIJKLMNOPQRSTUVWXYZ

abcdefghijklmnopqrstuvwxyz1234567890

The designer thinks it's a C16 Garamond

Celeste

Designer	Christopher Burke
Nationality	UK
Date Designed	1995
Foundries	FontFont
Number of weights	32

ABCDEFGHIJKLMNOPQRSTUVWXYZ

abcdefghijklmnopqrstuvwxyz1234567890

Quick wafting zephyrs vex bold Jim.

Pax

Designer	Franko Luin
Nationality	SL
Date Designed	1995
Foundries	Linotype
Number of weights	12

ABCDEFGHIJKLMNOPQRSTUVWXYZ

abcdefghijklmnopqrstuvwxyz1234567890

Many big jackdaws quickly zipped over the fox pen.

Pax #2

Designer	Franko Luin
Nationality	SL
Date Designed	1995
Foundries	Linotype
Number of weights	7

ABCDEFGHIJKLMNOPQRSTUVWXYZ

abcdefghijklmnopqrstuvwxyz1234567890

A large fawn jumped quickly over white zinc boxes.

Acanthus

Designer	Akira Kobayashi
Nationality	JP
Date Designed	1998
Foundries	FontFont
Number of weights	38

ABCDEFGHIJKLMNOPQRSTUVWXYZ

abcdefghijklmnopqrstuvwxyz1234567890

A Mediterranean plant whose leaves form the architectural decoration on the Corinthian capital

Moorbacka

Designer	Bo Berndal
Nationality	SE
Date Designed	1998
Foundries	Monotype
Number of weights	4

ABCDEFGHIJKLMNOPQRSTUVWXYZ

abcdefghijklmnopqrstuvwxyz1234567890

Verily the dark ex-Jew quit Zionism, preferring the cabala.

Stancia

Designer	Jean-Renaud Cuaz
Nationality	FR
Date Designed	1998
Foundries	Monotype
Number of weights	6

ABCDEFGHIJKLMNOPQRSTUVWXYZ

abcdefghijklmnopqrstuvwxyz1234567890

All questions asked by five watch experts amazed the judge.

Stancia Lyrica

Designer	Jean-Renaud Cuaz
Nationality	FR
Date Designed	1998
Foundries	Monotype
Number of weights	6

ABCDEFGHIJKLMNOPQRSTUVWXYZ

abcdefghijklmnopqrstuvwxyz1234567890

How razorback-jumping frogs can level six piqued gymnasts!

Gianotten

Designer	Antonio Pace
Nationality	IT
Date Designed	1999
Foundries	Linotype
Number of weights	12

ABCDEFGHIJKLMNOPQRSTUVWXYZ

abcdefghijklmnopqrstuvwxyz1234567890

Jaded reader with fabled roving eye seized by quickened impulse to expand budget.

Twinkle

Designer	Tomi Haaparaanta
Nationality	FI
Date Designed	1999
Foundries	Creative Alliance
Number of weights	2

ABCDEFGHIJKLMNOPQRSTUVWXYZ

abcdefghijklmnopqrstuvwxyz1234567890

An inspired calligrapher can create pages of beauty using stick ink, quill, brush, pick-axe, buzz saw, or even strawberry jam.

Danubia

Designer	Viktor Solt-Bittner
Nationality	AT
Date Designed	2002
Foundries	FontFont
Number of weights	12

ABCDEFGHIJKLMNOPQRSTUVWXYZ

abcdefghijklmnopqrstuvwxyz1234567890

Jay visited back home and gazed upon a brown fox and quail.

Cellini

Designer	Albert Boton
Nationality	FR
Date Designed	2003
Foundries	FontFont
Number of weights	20

ABCDEFGHIJKLMNOPQRSTUVWXYZ

abcdefghijklmnopqrstuvwxyz1234567890

Verily the dark ex-Jew quit Zionism, preferring the cabala.

Clarendon

Designer	R Besley
Nationality	UK
Date Designed	1845
Foundries	Fann Street Foundry Bitstream URW++
Number of weights	4

ABCDEFGHIJKLMNOPQRSTUVWXYZ

abcdefghijklmnopqrstuvwxyz1234567890

Pack my box with five dozen liquor jugs.

Bookman

Designer	A C Phemister
Nationality	UK
Date Designed	1860
Foundries	Ludlow ITC Bitstream Adobe
Recut/Digitised by	Edward Benguiat, 1975
Number of weights	8

ABCDEFGHIJKLMNOPQRSTUVWXYZ

abcdefghijklmnopqrstuvwxyz1234567890

The five boxing wizards jump quickly.

Slab

Clarion

Designer	Monotype
Nationality	UK
Date Designed	1860
Foundries	Monotype
Number of weights	3

ABCDEFGHIJKLMNOPQRSTUVWXYZ
abcdefghijklmnopqrstuvwxyz1234567890
The risque gown marked a brazen exposure of very juicy flesh.

Egyptian 72

Designer	Monotype
Nationality	UK
Date Designed	1860
Foundries	Monotype
Number of weights	1

ABCDEFGHIJKLMNOPQRSTUVWXYZ
abcdefghijklmnopqrstuvwxyz1234567890
Freight to me sixty dozen quart jars and twelve black pans.

Cushing

Designer	J Stearns Cushing
Nationality	US
Date Designed	1897-1901
Foundries	ITC ATF Adobe Lanston Monotype Bitstream
Recut/Digitised by	Vincent Pacella, 1982
Number of weights	8

ABCDEFGHIJKLMNOPQRSTUVWXYZ
abcdefghijklmnopqrstuvwxyz1234567890
Five big quacking zephyrs jolt my wax bed.

Century Expanded

Designer	Morris Fuller Benton
Nationality	US
Date Designed	1904
Foundries	FC URW++
Number of weights	4

ABCDEFGHIJKLMNOPQRSTUVWXYZ
abcdefghijklmnopqrstuvwxyz1234567890
King Alexander was partly overcome just after quizzing Diogenes in his tub.

Gloucester Old Style MT

Designer	Monotype
Nationality	UK
Date Designed	1905
Foundries	Monotype
Number of weights	5

ABCDEFGHIJKLMNOPQRSTUVWXYZ
abcdefghijklmnopqrstuvwxyz1234567890
Jelly-like above the high wire, six quaking pachyderms kept the climax of the extravaganza in a dazzling state of flux.

Venus Egyptienne

Designer Bauer
Nationality DE
Date Designed 1910
Foundries Bauer Linotype
Number of weights 2

ABCDEFGHIJKLMNOPQRSTUVWXYZ

abcdefghijklmnopqrstuvwxyz1234567890

Jack amazed a few girls by dropping the antique onyx vase!

New Century Schoolbook

Designer Morris Fuller Benton
Nationality US
Date Designed 1919
Foundries Linotype-Hell
Number of weights 4

ABCDEFGHIJKLMNOPQRSTUVWXYZ

abcdefghijklmnopqrstuvwxyz1234567890

Verbatim reports were quickly given by Jim Fox to his amazed audience.

Ionic

Designer Chauncey H Griffith
Nationality US
Date Designed 1925
Foundries Mergenthaler Linotype Monotype
Number of weights 3

ABCDEFGHIJKLMNOPQRSTUVWXYZ

abcdefghijklmnopqrstuvwxyz1234567890

Playing jazz vibe chords quickly excites my wife.

Bookman Old Style

Designer Ludlow
Nationality US
Date Designed 1925
Foundries Ludlow ITC Bitstream Monotype
Number of weights 4

ABCDEFGHIJKLMNOPQRSTUVWXYZ

abcdefghijklmnopqrstuvwxyz1234567890

Used as a core font in Microsoft Windows.

Belwe Roman

Designer Georg Belwe
Nationality DE
Date Designed 1926
Foundries Schelter & Giesecke Bitstream
Number of weights 4

ABCDEFGHIJKLMNOPQRSTUVWXYZ

abcdefghijklmnopqrstuvwxyz1234567890

Quick zephyrs blow, vexing daft Jim.

Belwe Mono

Designer	George Belwe, Alan Meeks
Nationality	US
Date Designed	1989
Foundries	Linotype ITC
Number of weights	2

ABCDEFGHIJKLMNOPQRSTUVWXYZ

abcdefghijklmnopqrstuvwxyz1234567890

The vixen jumped quickly on her foe barking with zeal.

Joanna

Designer	Eric Gill
Nationality	UK
Date Designed	1930
Foundries	Hague & Gill Adobe Linotype
Number of weights	14

ABCDEFGHIJKLMNOPQRSTUVWXYZ

abcdefghijklmnopqrstuvwxyz1234567890

The most elegant slab serif font ever drawn.

Memphis

Designer	Rudolf Weiss
Nationality	DE
Date Designed	1929
Foundries	Stempel Linotype URW++ Adobe
Number of weights	7

ABCDEFGHIJKLMNOPQRSTUVWXYZ

abcdefghijklmnopqrstuvwxyz1234567890

Brawny gods just flocked up to quiz and vex him.

Stymie

Designer	Morris Fuller Benton
Nationality	US
Date Designed	1931
Foundries	URW++ Bitstream Letraset Franklin Elsner+Flake Linotype
Recut/Digitised by	Mathew Carter
Number of weights	10

ABCDEFGHIJKLMNOPQRSTUVWXYZ

abcdefghijklmnopqrstuvwxyz1234567890

The golf equivalent of a snooker.

Beton

Designer	Heinrick Jost
Nationality	DE
Date Designed	1931
Foundries	Bauer Linotype Elsner+Flake Monotype URW++
Number of weights	1

ABCDEFGHIJKLMNOPQRSTUVWXYZ

abcdefghijklmnopqrstuvwxyz1234567890

Extra Bold is popular.

Rockwell

Designer Monotype Design Staff

Nationality UK

Date Designed 1934

Foundries Monotype Adobe

Number of weights 9

ABCDEFGHIJKLMNOPQRSTUVWXYZ

abcdefghijklmnopqrstuvwxyz1234567890

Five wine experts jokingly quizzed sample chablis.

Eden

Designer R Hunter Middleton

Nationality US

Date Designed 1934

Foundries CastleType

Recut/Digitised by Jason Castle

Number of weights 2

ABCDEFGHIJKLMNOPQRSTUVWXYZ

abcdefghijklmnopqrstuvwxyz1234567890

Forsaking monastic tradition, twelve jovial friars gave up their vocation for a questionable existence on the flying trapeze.

Candida

Designer Jakob Erbar

Nationality DE

Date Designed 1936

Foundries Ludwig & Mayer Bitstream
Fundacion Bauer URW++

Number of weights 4

ABCDEFGHIJKLMNOPQRSTUVWXYZ

abcdefghijklmnopqrstuvwxyz1234567890

Jackdaws love my big sphinx of quartz.

Melior

Designer Hermann Zapf

Nationality DE

Date Designed 1952

Foundries Stempel Adobe

Number of weights 4

ABCDEFGHIJKLMNOPQRSTUVWXYZ

abcdefghijklmnopqrstuvwxyz1234567890

Jazzy saxophones blew over Mick's turgid quiff.

Egizio

Designer Aldo Novarese

Nationality IT

Date Designed 1955

Foundries Nebiolo URW++

Number of weights 1

ABCDEFGHIJKLMNOPQRSTUVWXYZ

abcdefghijklmnopqrstuvwxyz1234567890

Portez ce vieux whisky au juge blond qui fume.

Egyptienne

Designer	Adrian Frutiger
Nationality	CH
Date Designed	1955
Foundries	URW++ Linotype
Number of weights	4

ABCDEFGHIJKLMNOPQRSTUVWXYZ
abcdefghijklmnopqrstuvwxyz1234567890

Six big juicy steaks sizzled in a pan as five workmen left the quarry.

Volta

Designer	K F Bauer, Walter Baum
Nationality	DE
Date Designed	1955
Foundries	Bauer Elsner+Flake Linotype URW++
Number of weights	5

ABCDEFGHIJKLMNOPQRSTUVWXYZ
abcdefghijklmnopqrstuvwxyz1234567890

Back in my quaint garden jaunty zinnias vie with flaunting phlox.

Tyfa

Designer	Josef Tyfa
Nationality	CZ
Date Designed	1959
Foundries	Typoart
Recut/Digitised by	Frantisek Storm, 1998
Number of weights	6

ABCDEFGHIJKLMNOPQRSTUVWXYZ
abcdefghijklmnopqrstuvwxyz1234567890

Jimmy and Zack, the police explained, were last seen diving into a field of buttered quahogs.

New Clarendon

Designer	Monotype
Nationality	UK
Date Designed	1960
Foundries	Monotype
Number of weights	5

ABCDEFGHIJKLMNOPQRSTUVWXYZ
abcdefghijklmnopqrstuvwxyz1234567890

Based on the face cut by R. Besley & Co., Fann Street Foundry, 1845

Impressum

Designer	K F Bauer, Walter Baum
Nationality	DE
Date Designed	1962
Foundries	Bauer Adobe URW++
Number of weights	3

ABCDEFGHIJKLMNOPQRSTUVWXYZ
abcdefghijklmnopqrstuvwxyz1234567890

Many-wived Jack laughs at probes of sex quiz.

Egyptian 505

Designer	André Gürtler
Nationality	CH
Date Designed	1966
Foundries	Bitstream
Number of weights	4

ABCDEFGHIJKLMNOPQRSTUVWXYZ
abcdefghijklmnopqrstuvwxyz1234567890
Quick wafting zephyrs vex bold Jim.

Serifa

Designer	Adrian Frutiger
Nationality	CH
Date Designed	1967
Foundries	Bauer ITC Bitstream URW++
Number of weights	6

ABCDEFGHIJKLMNOPQRSTUVWXYZ
abcdefghijklmnopqrstuvwxyz1234567890
Univers with serifs.

Digi Antiqua

Designer	Dr Rudolf Hell
Nationality	DE
Date Designed	1970
Foundries	Linotype
Number of weights	1

ABCDEFGHIJKLMNOPQRSTUVWXYZ
abcdefghijklmnopqrstuvwxyz1234567890
Jack amazed a few girls by dropping the antique onyx vase!

Lubalin Graph

Designer	Herb Lubalin
Nationality	US
Date Designed	1974
Foundries	ITC Linotype Elsner+Flake Bitstream Monotype Adobe
Recut/Digitised by	Ed Benguiat, 1981
Number of weights	10

ABCDEFGHIJKLMNOPQRSTUVWXYZ
abcdefghijklmnopqrstuvwxyz1234567890
Dumpy kibitzer jingles as exchequer overflows.

Italia

Designer	Colin Brignall
Nationality	UK
Date Designed	1977
Foundries	Letraset Bitstream ITC
Number of weights	3

ABCDEFGHIJKLMNOPQRSTUVWXYZ
abcdefghijklmnopqrstuvwxyz1234567890
Mix Zapf with Veljovic and get quirky Beziers.

Renault

Designer	Wolff Olins Agency
Nationality	UK
Date Designed	1978
Foundries	Linotype URW++ Elsner+Flake
Number of weights	4

ABCDEFGHIJKLMNOPQRSTUVWXYZ
abcdefghijklmnopqrstuvwxyz1234567890

Fernando Alonso drives for Renault.

Accolade

Designer	Chew Loon
Nationality	MY
Date Designed	1979
Foundries	URW++ Font Company
Number of weights	4

ABCDEFGHIJKLMNOPQRSTUVWXYZ
abcdefghijklmnopqrstuvwxyz1234567890

Sphinx of black quartz judge my vow.

Glypha

Designer	Adrian Frutiger
Nationality	CH
Date Designed	1979
Foundries	Adobe
Number of weights	6

ABCDEFGHIJKLMNOPQRSTUVWXYZ
abcdefghijklmnopqrstuvwxyz1234567890

55 Oblique is a slanted Roman; if it was a real italic it would be 56

Bramley

Designer	Alan Meeks
Nationality	UK
Date Designed	1980
Foundries	Letraset Linotype
Number of weights	4

ABCDEFGHIJKLMNOPQRSTUVWXYZ
abcdefghijklmnopqrstuvwxyz1234567890

My help squeezed back in again and joined the weavers after six.

Nimrod

Designer	Robin Nicholas
Nationality	UK
Date Designed	1980
Foundries	Monotype
Number of weights	7

ABCDEFGHIJKLMNOPQRSTUVWXYZ
abcdefghijklmnopqrstuvwxyz1234567890

About sixty codfish eggs will make a quarter pound of very fizzy jelly.

Boldface

Designer	URW++
Nationality	DE
Date Designed	1990
Foundries	URW++
Number of weights	1

ABCDEFGHIJKLMNOPQRSTUVWXYZ

abcdefghijklmnopqrstuvwxyz1234567890

Breezily jangling $3,416,857,209 wise advertiser ambles to the bank, his exchequer amplified.

Poseidon

Designer	Adrian Williams
Nationality	UK
Date Designed	1991
Foundries	Monotype
Number of weights	6

ABCDEFGHIJKLMNOPQRSTUVWXYZ

abcdefghijklmnopqrstuvwxyz1234567890

Zweedse ex-VIP, behoorlijk gek op quantumfysica.

PMN Caecilia

Designer	Peter Matthias Noordzij
Nationality	NL
Date Designed	1991
Foundries	Linotype
Number of weights	24

ABCDEFGHIJKLMNOPQRSTUVWXYZ

abcdefghijklmnopqrstuvwxyz1234567890

Jimmy and Zack, the police explained, were last seen diving into a field of buttered quahogs.

Calvert

Designer	Margaret Calvert
Nationality	ZA
Date Designed	1992
Foundries	Monotype Linotype Adobe
Number of weights	3

ABCDEFGHIJKLMNOPQRSTUVWXYZ

abcdefghijklmnopqrstuvwxyz1234567890

Designer with Jock Kinnear of Britain's road signage.

Elysium

Designer	Michael Gills
Nationality	UK
Date Designed	1992
Foundries	Linotype Monotype ITC
Number of weights	5

ABCDEFGHIJKLMNOPQRSTUVWXYZ

abcdefghijklmnopqrstuvwxyz1234567890

Slab serifs face bracketed serifs.

LinoLetter

Designer	Reinhard Haus, André Gürtler
Nationality	DE
Date Designed	1992
Foundries	Linotype Adobe Monotype
Number of weights	20

ABCDEFGHIJKLMNOPQRSTUVWXYZ
abcdefghijklmnopqrstuvwxyz1234567890
Six crazy kings vowed to abolish my quite pitiful jousts.

Scriptek

Designer	David Quay
Nationality	UK
Date Designed	1992
Foundries	Letraset Monotype ITC
Number of weights	2

ABCDEFGHIJKLMNOPQRSTUVWXYZ
abcdefghijklmnopqrstuvwxyz1234567890
Mix Zapf with Veljovic and get quirky Beziers.

Silica

Designer	Sumner Stone
Nationality	US
Date Designed	1993
Foundries	Monotype
Number of weights	6

ABCDEFGHIJKLMNOPQRSTUVWXYZ
abcdefghijklmnopqrstuvwxyz1234567890
Playing jazz vibe chords quickly excites my wife.

Jeunesse Slab

Designer	Johannes Birkenbach
Nationality	DE
Date Designed	1993
Foundries	Monotype
Number of weights	2

ABCDEFGHIJKLMNOPQRSTUVWXYZ
abcdefghijklmnopqrstuvwxyz1234567890
Quick zephyrs blow, vexing daft Jim.

Devin

Designer	Franko Luin
Nationality	SL
Date Designed	1994
Foundries	Linotype
Number of weights	7

ABCDEFGHIJKLMNOPQRSTUVWXYZ
abcdefghijklmnopqrstuvwxyz1234567890
Six crazy kings vowed to abolish my quite pitiful jousts.

HoTom

Designer	Thomas Hofman
Nationality	DE
Date Designed	1996
Foundries	Linotype
Number of weights	1

ABCDEFGHIJKLMNOPQRSTUVWXYZ
abcdefghijklmnopqrstuvwxyz1234567890
Five big quacking zephyrs jolt my wax bed.

Sheriff

Designer	Peter Verheul
Nationality	NL
Date Designed	1996
Foundries	FontFont
Number of weights	16

ABCDEFGHIJKLMNOPQRSTUVWXYZ
abcdefghijklmnopqrstuvwxyz1234567890
Sexy qua lijf, doch bang voor het zwempak.

Linotype Conrad

Designer	Akira Kobayashi
Nationality	JP
Date Designed	1999
Foundries	Linotype
Number of weights	4

ABCDEFGHIJKLMNOPQRSTUVWXYZ
abcdefghijklmnopqrstuvwxyz1234567890
Brawny gods just flocked up to quiz and vex him.

Avance

Designer	Evert Bloemsma
Nationality	NL
Date Designed	2000
Foundries	FontFont
Number of weights	12

ABCDEFGHIJKLMNOPQRSTUVWXYZ
abcdefghijklmnopqrstuvwxyz1234567890
Assymetrical serifs.

Napoleone Slab ITC

Designer	Silvio Napoleone
Nationality	CA
Date Designed	2001
Foundries	ITC Monotype
Number of weights	6

ABCDEFGHIJKLMNOPQRSTUVWXYZ
abcdefghijklmnopqrstuvwxyz1234567890
Playing jazz vibe chords quickly excites my wife.

Olsen

Designer	Morten Rostgaard Olsen
Nationality	DK
Date Designed	2001
Foundries	FontFont
Number of weights	49

ABCDEFGHIJKLMNOPQRSTUVWXYZ
abcdefghijklmnopqrstuvwxyz1234567890
Martin J. Hixeypozer quickly began his first word.

Siseriff

Designer	Bo Berndal
Nationality	SE
Date Designed	2003
Foundries	Linotype
Number of weights	9

ABCDEFGHIJKLMNOPQRSTUVWXYZ
abcdefghijklmnopqrstuvwxyz1234567890
To fly—and Lo! the Bird is on the Wing.

Romana

Designer	Théophile Baudoire
Nationality	FR
Date Designed	1860
Foundries	J. Wagner
Number of weights	1

ABCDEFGHIJKLMNOPQRSTUVWXYZ
abcdefghijklmnopqrstuvwxyz1234567890
Ain't dat absurd! I always heard
the little wings was on the bird.

Excelsior

Designer	Chauncey H Griffith
Nationality	US
Date Designed	1931
Foundries	Mergenthaler Linotype Adobe
Number of weights	1

ABCDEFGHIJKLMNOPQRSTUVWXYZ
abcdefghijklmnopqrstuvwxyz1234567890
Quick wafting zephyrs vex bold Jim.

Albertus

Designer	Berthold Wolpe
Nationality	DE
Date Designed	1932
Foundries	Monotype
Number of weights	1

ABCDEFGHIJKLMNOPQRSTUVWXYZ
abcdefghijklmnopqrstuvwxyz1234567890
Dumpy kibitzer jingles as exchequer overflows.

Friz Quadrata

Designer Ernst Friz
Nationality CH
Date Designed 1965
Foundries VGC Bitstream ITC
Recut/Digitised by Victor Caruso, 1974
Number of weights 1

ABCDEFGHIJKLMNOPQRSTUVWXYZ
abcdefghijklmnopqrstuvwxyz1234567890
Pavilions of Splendour.

Baker Signet

Designer Arthur Baker
Nationality US
Date Designed 1965
Foundries Linotype
Number of weights 1

ABCDEFGHIJKLMNOPQRSTUVWXYZ
abcdefghijklmnopqrstuvwxyz1234567890
Five wine experts jokingly quizzed sample chablis.

CG Signature

Designer Arthur Baker
Nationality US
Date Designed 1965
Foundries Bitstream
Number of weights 1

ABCDEFGHIJKLMNOPQRSTUVWXYZ
abcdefghijklmnopqrstuvwxyz1234567890
Questions of a zealous nature have become by degrees petty
waxen jokes.

Serpentine Serif

Designer Dick Jensen
Nationality US
Date Designed 1972
Foundries Elsner+Flake Linotype Adobe
Monotype URW++
Number of weights 1

ABCDEFGHIJKLMNOPQRSTUVWXYZ
abcdefghijklmnopqrstuvwxyz1234567890
Jimmy and Zack, the police explained, were last seen
diving into a field of buttered quahogs.

Korinna

Designer Antonio DiSpigna, Edward
Benguiat
Nationality IT
Date Designed 1974
Foundries Berthold ITC Bitstream
Number of weights 1

ABCDEFGHIJKLMNOPQRSTUVWXYZ
abcdefghijklmnopqrstuvwxyz1234567890
My grandfather picks up quartz and valuable onyx jewels.

Newtext

Designer	Ray Baker
Nationality	UK
Date Designed	1974
Foundries	Bitstream ITC
Number of weights	1

ABCDEFGHIJKLMNOPQRSTUVWXYZ
abcdefghijklmnopqrstuvwxyz1234567890
Quick zephyrs blow, vexing daft Jim.

Pasquale

Designer	Tony Stan
Nationality	US
Date Designed	1975
Foundries	Monotype
Number of weights	8

ABCDEFGHIJKLMNOPQRSTUVWXYZ
abcdefghijklmnopqrstuvwxyz1234567890
Jaded reader with fabled roving eye seized by quickened impulse to expand budget.

Quorum

Designer	Ray Baker
Nationality	UK
Date Designed	1977
Foundries	ITC Bitstream Adobe Elsner+Flake Linotype Monotype Typography URW++
Number of weights	5

ABCDEFGHIJKLMNOPQRSTUVWXYZ
abcdefghijklmnopqrstuvwxyz1234567890
Six crazy kings vowed to abolish my quite pitiful jousts.

Claridge

Designer	Adrian Williams
Nationality	UK
Date Designed	1979
Foundries	Monotype CG
Number of weights	1

ABCDEFGHIJKLMNOPQRSTUVWXYZ
abcdefghijklmnopqrstuvwxyz1234567890
We promptly judged antique ivory buckles for the next prize.

Icone

Designer	Adrian Frutiger
Nationality	CH
Date Designed	1980
Foundries	Linotype
Number of weights	1

ABCDEFGHIJKLMNOPQRSTUVWXYZ
abcdefghijklmnopqrstuvwxyz1234567890
How razorback-jumping frogs can level six piqued gymnasts!

Barcelona

Designer	Edward Benguiat
Nationality	US
Date Designed	1981
Foundries	ITC Linotype
Number of weights	8

ABCDEFGHIJKLMNOPQRSTUVWXYZ

abcdefghijklmnopqrstuvwxyz1234567890

Jackdaws love my big sphinx of quartz.

Isbell

Designer	Richard Isbell, Jerry Campbell
Nationality	US
Date Designed	1981
Foundries	ITC Bitstream AGP Franklin Elsner+Flake
Number of weights	1

ABCDEFGHIJKLMNOPQRSTUVWXYZ

abcdefghijklmnopqrstuvwxyz1234567890

Mix Zapf with Veljovic and get quirky Beziers.

Grafiko

Designer	Linotype
Nationality	DE
Date Designed	1981
Foundries	Linotype
Number of weights	1

ABCDEFGHIJKLMNOPQRSTUVWXYZ

abcdefghijklmnopqrstuvwxyz1234567890

Zwei Boxkämpfer jagen Eva quer durch Sylt.

Symbol

Designer	Aldo Novarese
Nationality	IT
Date Designed	1984
Foundries	ITC URW++ Adobe Bitstream Elsner+Flake Linotype
Number of weights	1

ABCDEFGHIJKLMNOPQRSTUVWXYZ

abcdefghijklmnopqrstuvwxyz1234567890

Note the strangely distorted g. The Symbol font on your computer is the Greek alphabet version of Times New Roman.

Elan

Designer	Albert Boton
Nationality	FR
Date Designed	1985
Foundries	ITC Linotype
Number of weights	8

ABCDEFGHIJKLMNOPQRSTUVWXYZ

abcdefghijklmnopqrstuvwxyz1234567890

Moi, je veux quinze clubs a golf et du whisky pur.

Tiepolo

Designer Cynthia Hollandsworth, Arthur Baker
Nationality US
Date Designed 1987
Foundries ITC Adobe Elsner+Flake URW
Number of weights 6

ABCDEFGHIJKLMNOPQRSTUVWXYZ
abcdefghijklmnopqrstuvwxyz1234567890
AlphaOmega Typography Designers described it as a sans serif
with serifs.

Pacella

Designer Vincent Pacella
Nationality US
Date Designed 1987
Foundries ITC Linotype Elsner+Flake Monotype
Number of weights 1

ABCDEFGHIJKLMNOPQRSTUVWXYZ
abcdefghijklmnopqrstuvwxyz1234567890
Five wine experts jokingly quizzed sample chablis.

Memo

Designer Albert Boton
Nationality FR
Date Designed 1988
Foundries Monotype
Number of weights 8

ABCDEFGHIJKLMNOPQRSTUVWXYZ
abcdefghijklmnopqrstuvwxyz1234567890
A mad boxer shot a quick, gloved jab to the jaw of his dizzy opponent.

Angie

Designer Jean-François Porchez
Nationality FR
Date Designed 1989
Foundries FontFont
Number of weights 1

ABCDEFGHIJKLMNOPQRSTUVWXYZ
abcdefghijklmnopqrstuvwxyz1234567890
Moi, je veux quinze clubs a golf et du whisky pur.

Latienne

Designer Mark Jamra
Nationality CH
Date Designed 1991
Foundries Linotype Elsner+Flake URW++
Number of weights 1

ABCDEFGHIJKLMNOPQRSTUVWXYZ
abcdefghijklmnopqrstuvwxyz1234567890
Many-wived Jack laughs at probes of sex quiz.

Mendoza

Designer José Mendoza
Nationality FR
Date Designed 1991
Foundries Linotype ITC Adobe
Number of weights 1

ABCDEFGHIJKLMNOPQRSTUVWXYZ
abcdefghijklmnopqrstuvwxyz1234567890
Quixotic Conservatives vet first key zero-growth jeremiad.

Saga

Designer Franko Luin
Nationality SL
Date Designed 1992
Foundries Linotype
Number of weights 7

ABCDEFGHIJKLMNOPQRSTUVWXYZ
abcdefghijklmnopqrstuvwxyz 1234567890
Sexy qua lijf, doch bang voor het zwempak.

Barbedor

Designer Hans Eduard Meier
Nationality CH
Date Designed 1992
Foundries Linotype URW
Number of weights 1

ABCDEFGHIJKLMNOPQRSTUVWXYZ
abcdefghijklmnopqrstuvwxyz 1234567890
A large fawn jumped quickly over white zinc boxes.

Syndor

Designer Hans-Eduard Meier
Nationality CH
Date Designed 1992
Foundries ITC URW++ Elsner+Flake
Monotype
Number of weights 1

ABCDEFGHIJKLMNOPQRSTUVWXYZ
abcdefghijklmnopqrstuvwxyz1234567890
William Jex quickly caught five dozen Conservatives.

Beowolf

Designer Erik van Blokland, Just van Rossum
Nationality NL
Date Designed 1993
Foundries FontFont Font Bureau
Number of weights 1

ABCDEFGHIJKLMNOPQRSTUVWXYZ
abcdefghijklmnopqrstuvwxyz1234567890
Marketed as the first RandomFont; it changes its shape every time it gets printed.

Exlibris

Designer	Bo Berndal
Nationality	SE
Date Designed	1993
Foundries	Monotype
Number of weights	1

ABCDEFGHIJKLMNOPQRSTUVWXYZ
abcdefghijklmnopqrstuvwxyz1234567890
Many-wived Jack laughs at probes of sex quiz.

Jeunesse

Designer	Johannes Birkenbach
Nationality	DE
Date Designed	1993
Foundries	Monotype
Number of weights	4

ABCDEFGHIJKLMNOPQRSTUVWXYZ
abcdefghijklmnopqrstuvwxyz1234567890
Many big jackdaws quickly zipped over the fox pen.

Semper

Designer	Franko Luin
Nationality	SL
Date Designed	1993
Foundries	Linotype
Number of weights	1

ABCDEFGHIJKLMNOPQRSTUVWXYZ
abcdefghijklmnopqrstuvwxyz1234567890
Jane Ellis was responsible for this book.

Memento

Designer	Franko Luin
Nationality	SL
Date Designed	1993
Foundries	Linotype
Number of weights	1

ABCDEFGHIJKLMNOPQRSTUVWXYZ
abcdefghijklmnopqrstuvwxyz1234567890
Just work for improved basic techniques to maximize your typing skill.

Perrywood MT

Designer	Johannes Birkenbach
Nationality	DE
Date Designed	1993
Foundries	Monotype
Number of weights	1

ABCDEFGHIJKLMNOPQRSTUVWXYZ
abcdefghijklmnopqrstuvwxyz1234567890
Big July earthquakes confound zany experimental vow.

Gilgamesh

Designer	Michael Gills
Nationality	UK
Date Designed	1994
Foundries	Linotype Monotype ITC
Number of weights	1

ABCDEFGHIJKLMNOPQRSTUVWXYZ

abcdefghijklmnopqrstuvwxyz1234567890

Breezily jangling €3,416,857,209 wise advertiser ambles to the bank, his exchequer amplified.

Alcuin

Designer	Gudrun Zapf von Hesse
Nationality	DE
Date Designed	1994
Foundries	URW++
Number of weights	1

ABCDEFGHIJKLMNOPQRSTUVWXYZ

abcdefghijklmnopqrstuvwxyz1234567890

Sphinx of black quartz judge my vow.

LuMarc

Designer	Marc Lubbers
Nationality	NL
Date Designed	1994
Foundries	Linotype
Number of weights	1

ABCDEFGHIJKLMNOPQRSTUVWXYZ

abcdefghijklmnopqrstuvwxyz1234567890

Sexy qua lijf, doch bang voor het zwempak.

Vega

Designer	Franko Luin
Nationality	SL
Date Designed	1994
Foundries	Linotype
Number of weights	1

ABCDEFGHIJKLMNOPQRSTUVWXYZ

abcdefghijklmnopqrstuvwxyz1234567890

Five big quacking zephyrs jolt my wax bed.

Cicero

Designer	Thierry Puyfoulhoux
Nationality	FR
Date Designed	1995
Foundries	Presence
Number of weights	1

ABCDEFGHIJKLMNOPQRSTUVWXYZ

abcdefghijklmnopqrstuvwxyz1234567890

Alfredo just must bring very exciting news to the plaza quickly.

Crane

Designer	Lennart Hansson
Nationality	SE
Date Designed	1995
Foundries	Monotype
Number of weights	1

ABCDEFGHIJKLMNOPQRSTUVWXYZ

abcdefghijklmnopqrstuvwxyz1234567890

The July sun caused a fragment of black pine wax to ooze on the velvet quilt.

Grantofte

Designer	Bo Berndal
Nationality	SE
Date Designed	1995
Foundries	Monotype
Number of weights	1

ABCDEFGHIJKLMNOPQRSTUVWXYZ

abcdefghijklmnopqrstuvwxyz1234567890

The risque gown marked a brazen exposure of very juicy flesh.

Runa Serif

Designer	Lennart Hansson
Nationality	SE
Date Designed	1995
Foundries	Miles
Number of weights	1

ABCDEFGHIJKLMNOPQRSTUVWXYZ

abcdefghijklmnopqrstuvwxyz1234567890

Puzzled women bequeath jerks very exotic gifts.

Scherzo

Designer	Albert Boton
Nationality	FR
Date Designed	1995
Foundries	CA Partners
Number of weights	6

ABCDEFGHIJKLMNOPQRSTUVWXYZ

abcdefghijklmnopqrstuvwxyz1234567890

A large fawn jumped quickly over white zinc boxes.

Maverick

Designer	Christopher Kalscheuer
Nationality	DE
Date Designed	1995
Foundries	FontFont
Number of weights	1

ABCDEFGHIJKLMNOPQRSTUVWXYZ

abcdefghijklmnopqrstuvwxyz1234567890

Six big juicy steaks sizzled in a pan as five workmen left the quarry.

Rustika

Designer Franko Luin
Nationality SL
Date Designed 1995
Foundries Linotype
Number of weights 1

ABCDEFGHIJKLMNOPQRSTUVWXYZ
abcdefghijklmnopqrstuvwxyz1234567890
When we go back to Juarez, Mexico, do we fly over picturesque Arizona?

Binary

Designer Mauricio Reyes
Nationality ES
Date Designed 1997
Foundries ITC Linotype
Number of weights 1

ABCDEFGHIJKLMNOPQRSTUVWXYZ
abcdefghijklmnopqrstuvwxyz1234567890
Many-wived Jack laughs at probes of sex quiz.

Central

Designer Bayer
Nationality DE
Date Designed 1998
Foundries Monotype
Number of weights 2

ABCDEFGHIJKLMNOPQRSTUVWXYZ
abcdefghijklmnopqrstuvwxyz1234567890
The risque gown marked a brazen exposure of very juicy flesh.

Magellan

Designer Bo Berndal
Nationality SE
Date Designed 1998
Foundries Monotype
Number of weights 1

ABCDEFGHIJKLMNOPQRSTUVWXYZ
abcdefghijklmnopqrstuvwxyz1234567890
Many big jackdaws quickly zipped over the fox pen.

Stockholm

Designer Paul Shaw, Garrett Boge
Nationality US
Date Designed 1998
Foundries Monotype
Number of weights 1

ABCDEFGHIJKLMNOPQRSTUVWXYZ
abcdefghijklmnopqrstuvwxyz1234567890
The exodus of jazzy pigeons is craved by squeamish walkers.

Eureka

Designer	Peter Bilak
Nationality	SK
Date Designed	1998
Foundries	FontFont
Number of weights	1

ABCDEFGHIJKLMNOPQRSTUVWXYZ

abcdefghijklmnopqrstuvwxyz1234567890

Hark! Toxic jungle water vipers quietly drop on zebras for meals!

Tresillian

Designer	Philip Bouwsma
Nationality	US
Date Designed	1998
Foundries	Monotype
Number of weights	1

ABCDEFGHIJKLMNOPQRSTUVWXYZ

abcdefghijklmnopqrstuvwxyz1234567890

No kidding, Lorenzo called off his trip to visit Mexico City just because they told him the conquistadores were extinct.

Selune

Designer	Jean Lochu
Nationality	FR
Date Designed	1999
Foundries	CA Partners
Number of weights	1

ABCDEFGHIJKLMNOPQRSTUVWXYZ

abcdefghijklmnopqrstuvwxyz1234567890

For only $49, jolly housewives made inexpensive meals using quick–frozen vegetables.

Oldrichium ITC

Designer	George Thompson
Nationality	US
Date Designed	2000
Foundries	ITC
Number of weights	8

ABCDEFGHIJKLMNOPQRSTUVWXYZ

abcdefghijklmnopqrstuvwxyz1234567890

Based on a design by Czech typographer Oldrich Menhart.

Parango

Designer	Xavier Dupré
Nationality	FR
Date Designed	2000
Foundries	FontFont
Number of weights	1

ABCDEFGHIJKLMNOPQRSTUVWXYZ

abcdefghijklmnopqrstuvwxyz1234567890

Just keep examining every low bid quoted for zinc etchings.

Parable

Designer	Christopher Burke
Nationality	UK
Date Designed	2002
Foundries	FontFont
Number of weights	30

ABCDEFGHIJKLMNOPQRSTUVWXYZ
abcdefghijklmnopqrstuvwxyz1234567890
Fred specialized in the job of making very quaint wax toys.

Hawkhurst

Designer	Richard Yeend
Nationality	UK
Date Designed	2003
Foundries	Linotype
Number of weights	1

ABCDEFGHIJKLMNOPQRSTUVWXYZ
abcdefghijklmnopqrstuvwxyz1234567890
Woke—and a thousand scatter'd into Clay:

Auriol

Designer	Georges Auriol
Nationality	FR
Date Designed	1901
Foundries	Deberny & Peignot Linotype
Number of weights	9

ABCDEFGHIJKLMNOPQRSTUVWXYZ
abcdefghijklmnopqrstuvwxyz1234567890
The British Mah-Jong Association.

Harrington

Designer	anon
Nationality	US
Date Designed	1910
Foundries	Dover
Recut/Digitised by	Dan X Solo
Number of weights	1

ABCDEFGHIJKLMNOPQRSTUVWXYZ
abcdefghijklmnopqrstuvwxyz1234567890
The July sun caused a fragment of black pine wax to ooze on the velvet quilt.

Locarno

Designer	Rudolf Koch
Nationality	DE
Date Designed	1922
Foundries	Klingspor Bitstream Letraset Linotype Monotype ITC
Recut/Digitised by	Alan Meeks, 1985
Number of weights	2

ABCDEFGHIJKLMNOPQRSTUVWXYZ
abcdefghijklmnopqrstuvwxyz1234567890
A Swiss lakeside resort.

Misc

CG Bernhardt

Designer	Lucian Bernhard
Nationality	AT
Date Designed	1929
Foundries	CA Partners
Number of weights	3

ABCDEFGHIJKLMNOPQRSTUVWXYZ
abcdefghijklmnopqrstuvwxyz1234567890
About sixty codfish eggs will make a quarter pound of very fizzy jelly.

Koch Antiqua

Designer	Rudolf Koch
Nationality	DE
Date Designed	1933
Foundries	Linotype Spiece Graphics
Number of weights	1

ABCDEFGHIJKLMNOPQRSTUVWXYZ
abcdefghijklmnopqrstuvwxyz1234567890
Jail zesty vixen who grabbed pay from quack.

Athenaeum

Designer	Alessandro Butti
Nationality	IT
Date Designed	1945
Foundries	Nebiolo Monotype
Number of weights	1

ABCDEFGHIJKLMNOPQRSTUVWXYZ
abcdefghijklmnopqrstuvwxyz1234567890
Greek seat of the gods

CG Musketeer

Designer	Tony Geddes
Nationality	UK
Date Designed	1968
Foundries	Miles Monotype
Number of weights	1

ABCDEFGHIJKLMNOPQRSTUVWXYZ
abcdefghijklmnopqrstuvwxyz1234567890
Good to use if you want a text version of Windsor.

Serif Gothic

Designer	Antonio DiSpigna, Herb Lubalin
Nationality	IT
Date Designed	1974
Foundries	ITC Bitstream Adobe Franklin Linotype Monotype
Number of weights	6

ABCDEFGHIJKLMNOPQRSTUVWXYZ
abcdefghijklmnopqrstuvwxyz1234567890
How razorback-jumping frogs can level six piqued gymnasts!

Delphin

Designer	Georg Trump
Nationality	DE
Date Designed	1951
Foundries	Weber Adobe
Number of weights	1

ABCDEFGHIJKLMNOPQRSTUVWXYZ

abcdefghijklmnopqrstuvwxyz1234567890

William said that everything about his jacket was in quite good condition except for the zipper.

Roman Script

Designer	Bob McGrath
Nationality	UK
Date Designed	1979
Foundries	URW++
Number of weights	2

ABCDEFGHIJKLMNOPQRSTUVWXYZ

abcdefghijklmnopqrstuvwxyz1234567890

Questions of a zealous nature have become by degrees petty waxen jokes.

Sully Jonquières

Designer	José Mendoza
Nationality	FR
Date Designed	1980
Foundries	Mecanorma
Number of weights	1

ABCDEFGHIJKLMNOPQRSTUVWXYZ

abcdefghijklmnopqrstuvwxyz1234567890

Lazy movers quit hard-packing of papier-mache jewellery boxes.

Kursivschrift

Designer	Linotype Library
Nationality	DE
Date Designed	1985
Foundries	Linotype
Recut/Digitised by	Linotype Library
Number of weights	5

ABCDEFGHIJKLMNOPQRSTUVWXYZ

abcdefghijklmnopqrstuvwxyz1234567890

Fred specialized in the job of making very quaint wax toys.

Aquinas

Designer	David Quay
Nationality	UK
Date Designed	1989
Foundries	Linotype Letraset ITC
Number of weights	1

ABCDEFGHIJKLMNOPQRSTUVWXYZ

abcdefghijklmnopqrstuvwxyz1234567890

Five big quacking zephyrs jolt my wax bed.

Marigold

Designer	Arthur Baker
Nationality	US
Date Designed	1989
Foundries	Adobe Glyph
Number of weights	1

ABCDEFGHIJKLMNOPQRSTUVWXYZ

abcdefghijklmnopqrstuvwxyz1234567890

A golden yellow flower, Calendula officinalis.

Oxford

Designer	Arthur Baker
Nationality	US
Date Designed	1989
Foundries	Adobe Alpha Omega
Number of weights	1

ABCDEFGHIJKLMNOPQRSTUVWXYZ

abcdefghijklmnopqrstuvwxyz1234567890

Sphinx of black quartz judge my vow.

Elegante

Designer	Ray Cruz
Nationality	US
Date Designed	1990
Foundries	CA Exclusives
Number of weights	1

ABCDEFGHIJKLMNOPQRSTUVWXYZ

abcdefghijklmnopqrstuvwxyz1234567890

Quick zephyrs blow, vexing daft Jim.

Cerigo

Designer	Jean-Renaud Cuaz
Nationality	FR
Date Designed	1993
Foundries	ITC
Number of weights	6

ABCDEFGHIJKLMNOPQRSTUVWXYZ

abcdefghijklmnopqrstuvwxyz1234567890

The quick brown fox jumps over the lazy dog.

Tarquinius

Designer	Norbert Reiners
Nationality	DE
Date Designed	1996
Foundries	FontFont
Number of weights	1

ABCDEFGHIJKLMNOPQRSTUVWXYZ

abcdefghijklmnopqrstuvwxyz1234567890

The July sun caused a fragment of black pine wax to ooze on the velvet quilt.

Compendio

Designer	Christian Bauer
Nationality	DE
Date Designed	1997
Foundries	Linotype
Number of weights	2

ABCDEFGHIJKLMNOPQRSTUVWXYZ
abcdefghijklmnopqrstuvwxyz1234567890
Puzzled women bequeath jerks very exotic gifts.

Vineyard

Designer	Akira Kobayashi
Nationality	JP
Date Designed	1999
Foundries	ITC
Number of weights	1

ABCDEFGHIJKLMNOPQRSTUVWXYZ
abcdefghijklmnopqrstuvwxyz1234567890
The quick brown fox jumps over the lazy dog.

Oxalis

Designer	Franck Jalleau
Nationality	FR
Date Designed	1996
Foundries	Monotype
Number of weights	9

ABCDEFGHIJKLMNOPQRSTUVWXYZ
abcdefghijklmnopqrstuvwxyz1234567890
The yellow-flowering wood sorrel.

Equilibre Gauche

Designer	Alexis Merlaut
Nationality	FR
Date Designed	1997
Foundries	Monotype
Number of weights	1

ABCDEFGHIJKLMNOPQRSTUVWXYZ
abcdefghijklmnopqrstuvwxyz1234567890
Mr. Jock, TV quiz Ph.D., bags few lynx.

Page Serif

Designer	Albert Boton
Nationality	FR
Date Designed	2003
Foundries	FontFont
Number of weights	28

ABCDEFGHIJKLMNOPQRSTUVWXYZ
abcdefghijklmnopqrstuvwxyz1234567890
Back in my quaint garden jaunty zinnias vie with flaunting phlox.

Engravers

Designer	Robert Wiebking
Nationality	US
Date Designed	1899
Foundries	Linotype URW++
Number of weights	1

ABCDEFGHIJKLMNOPQRSTUVWXYZ
ABCDEFGHIJKLMNOPQRSTUVWXYZ1234567890
HOW QUICKLY DAFT JUMPING ZEBRAS VEX.

Engravers Bold Face #9

Designer	Robert Wiebking
Nationality	US
Date Designed	1899
Foundries	Adobe
Number of weights	1

ABCDEFGHIJKLMNOPQRSTUVWXYZ
ABCDEFGHIJKLMNOPQRSTUVWXYZ1234567890
A MAD BOXER SHOT A QUICK, GLOVED JAB TO THE JAW OF HIS DIZZY OPPONENT.

Copperplate Gothic

Designer	Frederic W Goudy
Nationality	US
Date Designed	1901
Foundries	ATF Bitstream
Number of weights	9

ABCDEFGHIJKLMNOPQRSTUVWXYZ
ABCDEFGHIJKLMNOPQRSTUVWXYZ1234567890
JADED READER WITH FABLED ROVING EYE SEIZED BY QUICKENED IMPULSE TO EXPAND BUDGET.

Copperplate

Designer	Frederic W Goudy, Clarence Marder
Nationality	US
Date Designed	1905
Foundries	Elsner+Flake URW++
Number of weights	1

ABCDEFGHIJKLMNOPQRSTUVWXYZ
ABCDEFGHIJKLMNOPQRSTUVWXYZ1234567890
AND THIS FIRST SUMMER MONTH THAT BRINGS THE ROSE?

Engravure

Designer	Monotype
Nationality	UK
Date Designed	1920
Foundries	Monotype
Number of weights	1

ABCDEFGHIJKLMNOPQRSTUVWXYZ
ABCDEFGHIJKLMNOPQRSTUVWXYZ1234567890
WALTZ, NYMPH, FOR QUICK JIGS VEX BUD.

Barclay Open

Designer	Photo-Lettering
Nationality	UK
Date Designed	1920
Foundries	Monotype
Number of weights	1

ABCDEFGHIJKLMNOPQRSTUVWXYZ
abcdefghijklmnopqrstuvwxyz
1234567890
Big July earthquakes confound zany camels.

Burin Sans

Designer	Monotype
Nationality	FR
Date Designed	1925
Foundries	Monotype
Number of weights	2

ABCDEFGHIJKLMNOPQRSTUVWXYZ
abcdefghijklmnopqrstuvwxyz1234567890
Burin is the French for an engraving tool.

Burin Roman

Designer	Monotype
Nationality	FR
Date Designed	1930
Foundries	Monotype
Number of weights	2

ABCDEFGHIJKLMNOPQRSTUVWXYZ
abcdefghijklmnopqrstuvwxyz1234567890
Portez ce vieux whisky au juge blond qui fume.

Chevalier

Designer	Emil A Neukomm
Nationality	DE
Date Designed	1946
Foundries	Monotype URW
Number of weights	1

ABCDEFGHIJKLMNOPQRSTUVWXYZ
ABCDEFGHIJKLMNOPQRSTUVWXYZ
1234567890
THE JULY SUN CAUSED A FRAGMENT OF BLACK PINE.

Citation

Designer	Trevor Loane
Nationality	UK
Date Designed	1990
Foundries	Linotype ITC
Number of weights	1

ABCDEFGHIJKLMNOPQRSTUVWXYZ
ABCDEFGHIJKLMNOPQRSTUVWXYZ1234567890
THE EXODUS OF JAZZY PIGEONS IS CRAVED BY
SQUEAMISH WALKERS.

Orlando AT

Designer	Tim Rolands
Nationality	US
Date Designed	1996
Foundries	Tim Rolands Monotype
Number of weights	1

ABCDEFGHIJKLMNOPQRSTUVWXYZ
ABCDEFGHIJKLMNOPQRSTUVWXYZ1234567890
BASED ON A HOT METAL TYPEFACE CALLED OLIVER.

Blair

Designer	Jim Spiece
Nationality	US
Date Designed	1997
Foundries	Linotype ITC
Number of weights	3

ABCDEFGHIJKLMNOPQRSTUVWXYZ
ABCDEFGHIJKLMNOPQRSTUVWXYZ1234567890
DUMPY KIBITZER JINGLES AS EXCHEQUER OVERFLOWS.

Doric 12

Designer	Caslon
Nationality	UK
Date Designed	1830
Foundries	Stephenson Blake Linotype
Recut/Digitised by	Walter Tracy, 1972
Number of weights	1

ABCDEFGHIJKLMNOPQRSTUVWXYZ
abcdefghijklmnopqrstuvwxyz1234567890
Quick zephyrs blow, vexing daft Jim.

Grotesque

Designer	Thorowgood
Nationality	UK
Date Designed	1832
Foundries	Thorowgood Monotype URW++
Number of weights	1

ABCDEFGHIJKLMNOPQRSTUVWXYZ
abcdefghijklmnopqrstuvwxyz1234567890
How quickly daft jumping zebras vex.

Grotesque MT

Designer	Monotype
Nationality	UK
Date Designed	1890
Foundries	Monotype Linotype
Number of weights	11

ABCDEFGHIJKLMNOPQRSTUVWXYZ
abcdefghijklmnopqrstuvwxyz1234567890
Waltz, nymph, for quick jigs vex Bud.

Lineale Grotesques

Akzidenz-Grotesk

Designer Berthold
Nationality DE
Date Designed 1896
Foundries Berthold
Number of weights 33

ABCDEFGHIJKLMNOPQRSTUVWXYZ

abcdefghijklmnopqrstuvwxyz1234567890

Akzidenz Grotesk was based on British sans serif designs but given a legibility which made it the first usable text lineale.

Basic Commercial LT

Designer Berthold
Nationality US
Date Designed 1900
Foundries Berthold Linotype
Number of weights 8

ABCDEFGHIJKLMNOPQRSTUVWXYZ

abcdefghijklmnopqrstuvwxyz1234567890

Brawny gods just flocked up to quiz and vex him.

Alternate Gothic

Designer Morris Fuller Benton
Nationality US
Date Designed 1903
Foundries ATF Bitstream Eisner+Flake
Number of weights 3

ABCDEFGHIJKLMNOPQRSTUVWXYZ

abcdefghijklmnopqrstuvwxyz1234567890

The five boxing wizards jump quickly.

Franklin Gothic

Designer Morris Fuller Benton
Nationality US
Date Designed 1903
Foundries ATF Ludlow ITC
Recut/Digitised by Victor Caruso, 1980
Number of weights 18

ABCDEFGHIJKLMNOPQRSTUVWXYZ

abcdefghijklmnopqrstuvwxyz1234567890

Most often seen used in the **Condensed Demi weight** as a no-nonsense display sans.

Venus

Designer Wagner & Schmidt
Nationality DE
Date Designed 1907
Foundries Bauer Linotype
Number of weights 5

ABCDEFGHIJKLMNOPQRSTUVWXYZ

abcdefghijklmnopqrstuvwxyz1234567890

Mr. Jock, TV quiz Ph.D., bags few lynx.

Lightline Gothic

Designer	Morris Fuller Benton
Nationality	US
Date Designed	1908
Foundries	ATF Elsner+Flake Linotype Monotype
Number of weights	1

ABCDEFGHIJKLMNOPQRSTUVWXYZ

abcdefghijklmnopqrstuvwxyz1234567890

Pack my box with five dozen liquor jugs.

News Gothic

Designer	Morris Fuller Benton
Nationality	US
Date Designed	1908
Foundries	ATF
Number of weights	4

ABCDEFGHIJKLMNOPQRSTUVWXYZ

abcdefghijklmnopqrstuvwxyz1234567890

Sympathizing would fix Quaker objectives.

Erbar

Designer	J Erbar
Nationality	DE
Date Designed	1922
Foundries	Ludwig & Mayer Linotype
Number of weights	2

ABCDEFGHIJKLMNOPQRSTUVWXYZ

abcdefghijklmnopqrstuvwxyz1234567890

Five big quacking zephyrs jolt my wax bed.

DIN

Designer	Deutsche Industrie Normal
Nationality	DE
Date Designed	1923
Foundries	Stempel FontFont
Number of weights	1

ABCDEFGHIJKLMNOPQRSTUVWXYZ

abcdefghijklmnopqrstuvwxyz1234567890

Jail zesty vixen who grabbed pay from quack.

DIN 1451

Designer	Deutsche Industrie Normal
Nationality	DE
Date Designed	1925
Foundries	Linotype
Number of weights	4

ABCDEFGHIJKLMNOPQRSTUVWXYZ

abcdefghijklmnopqrstuvwxyz1234567890

Five or six big jet planes zoomed quickly by the tower.

DIN Mittelschrift

Designer	Deutsche Industrie Normal
Nationality	DE
Date Designed	1925
Foundries	Stempel Linotype
Number of weights	2

ABCDEFGHIJKLMNOPQRSTUVWXYZ

abcdefghijklmnopqrstuvwxyz1234567890

Many-wived Jack laughs at probes of sex quiz.

Neuzeit S

Designer	C W Pischner
Nationality	DE
Date Designed	1928
Foundries	Stempel Linotype
Recut/Digitised by	Linotype, 1966
Number of weights	2

ABCDEFGHIJKLMNOPQRSTUVWXYZ

abcdefghijklmnopqrstuvwxyz1234567890

Dumpy kibitzer jingles as exchequer overflows.

Bell Gothic

Designer	Chauncey H Griffith
Nationality	US
Date Designed	1938
Foundries	Mergenthaler Linotype
	Bitstream
Number of weights	3

ABCDEFGHIJKLMNOPQRSTUVWXYZ

abcdefghijklmnopqrstuvwxyz1234567890

Puzzled women bequeath jerks very exotic gifts.

Trade Gothic

Designer	Jackson Burke
Nationality	US
Date Designed	1948
Foundries	Mergenthaler Linotype Adobe
	Monotype
Number of weights	11

ABCDEFGHIJKLMNOPQRSTUVWXYZ

abcdefghijklmnopqrstuvwxyz1234567890

Turgid saxophones blew over Mick's jazzy quiff.

City Street Type Berlin East

Designer	anon
Nationality	DE
Date Designed	1950
Foundries	FontFont
Recut/Digitised by	Ole Schaefer, Verena Gerlach, 2000
Number of weights	12

ABCDEFGHIJKLMNOPQRSTUVWXYZ

abcdefghijklmnopqrstuvwxyz1234567890

From Unter den Linden to Alexanderplatz.

City Street Type Berlin West

Designer	anon
Nationality	DE
Date Designed	1950
Foundries	FontFont
Recut/Digitised by	Ole Schaefer, Verena Gerlach, 2000
Number of weights	12

ABCDEFGHIJKLMNOPQRSTUVWXYZ
abcdefghijklmnopqrstuvwxyz1234567890
15 Oldenburgallee, Charlottenburg, Berlin.

Folio

Designer	Konrad F Bauer, Walter Baum
Nationality	DE
Date Designed	1957
Foundries	Bauer URW++
Number of weights	7

ABCDEFGHIJKLMNOPQRSTUVWXYZ
abcdefghijklmnopqrstuvwxyz1234567890
Jim just quit and packed extra bags for Liz Owen.

Helvetica

Designer	Max Miedinger
Nationality	CH
Date Designed	1957
Foundries	Haas Stempel Linotype Adobe
Number of weights	36

ABCDEFGHIJKLMNOPQRSTUVWXYZ
abcdefghijklmnopqrstuvwxyz1234567890
The face of the mid twentieth century.

Univers

Designer	Adrian Frutiger
Nationality	CH
Date Designed	1957
Foundries	Deberny & Peignot Adobe Creative Alliance Linotype
Number of weights	28

ABCDEFGHIJKLMNOPQRSTUVWXYZ
abcdefghijklmnopqrstuvwxyz1234567890
Helvetica's nearest competitor.

Digi Grotesk

Designer	Linotype Hell
Nationality	DE
Date Designed	1968
Foundries	Linotype Hell
Number of weights	6

ABCDEFGHIJKLMNOPQRSTUVWXYZ
abcdefghijklmnopqrstuvwxyz1234567890
Six crazy kings vowed to abolish my quite pitiful jousts.

Linotype Syntax

Designer	Hans-Eduard Meier
Nationality	DE
Date Designed	1968
Foundries	Stempel Linotype Adobe Monotype URW++
Number of weights	5

ABCDEFGHIJKLMNOPQRSTUVWXYZ
abcdefghijklmnopqrstuvwxyz1234567890
How razorback-jumping frogs can level six piqued gymnasts!

CG Symphony

Designer	Bayer
Nationality	DE
Date Designed	1969
Foundries	Monotype
Number of weights	4

ABCDEFGHIJKLMNOPQRSTUVWXYZ
abcdefghijklmnopqrstuvwxyz1234567890
Hans Eduard Meir designed the near identical Syntax.

AG Old Face

Designer	Berthold
Nationality	DE
Date Designed	1972
Foundries	Berthold
Recut/Digitised by	Günter Gerhard Lange
Number of weights	6

ABCDEFGHIJKLMNOPQRSTUVWXYZ
abcdefghijklmnopqrstuvwxyz1234567890
Akzidenz Grotesk was based on British sans serif designs but given a legibility which made it the first usable text lineale.

VAG Rundschrift

Designer	Volkswagen Audi Group
Nationality	DE
Date Designed	1975
Foundries	Bitstream Linotype URW++
Number of weights	4

ABCDEFGHIJKLMNOPQRSTUVWXYZ
abcdefghijklmnopqrstuvwxyz1234567890
VAG Rounded in German. VAG stands for Volkswagen Audi Group.

Frutiger

Designer	Adrian Frutiger
Nationality	CH
Date Designed	1976
Foundries	Linotype Adobe
Number of weights	14

ABCDEFGHIJKLMNOPQRSTUVWXYZ
abcdefghijklmnopqrstuvwxyz1234567890
The job of waxing linoleum frequently peeves chintzy kids.

Bell Centennial

Designer	Matthew Carter
Nationality	UK
Date Designed	1978
Foundries	Bitstream
Number of weights	5

ABCDEFGHIJKLMNOPQRSTUVWXYZ

abcdefghijklmnopqrstuvwxyz1234567890

Five wine experts jokingly quizzed sample chablis.

CG Heldustry

Designer	Phil Martin
Nationality	US
Date Designed	1978
Foundries	CA Partners
Number of weights	4

ABCDEFGHIJKLMNOPQRSTUVWXYZ

abcdefghijklmnopqrstuvwxyz1234567890

Jack amazed a few girls by dropping the antique onyx vase!

CG Triumvirate

Designer	Monotype
Nationality	UK
Date Designed	1980
Foundries	Monotype
Number of weights	16

ABCDEFGHIJKLMNOPQRSTUVWXYZ

abcdefghijklmnopqrstuvwxyz1234567890

Sixty zippers were quickly picked from the woven jute bag.

Lexikos

Designer	Vince Whitlock
Nationality	UK
Date Designed	1980
Foundries	Letraset Linotype Monotype ITC
Number of weights	1

ABCDEFGHIJKLMNOPQRSTUVWXYZ

abcdefghijklmnopqrstuvwxyz1234567890

A quick movement of the enemy will jeopardize six gunboats.

Verdana

Designer	Matthew Carter
Nationality	UK
Date Designed	1980
Foundries	Apple Microsoft
Number of weights	4

ABCDEFGHIJKLMNOPQRSTUVWXYZ

abcdefghijklmnopqrstuvwxyz1234567890

We have just quoted on nine dozen boxes of gray lamp wicks.

Corinthian

Designer Colin Brignall
Nationality UK
Date Designed 1981
Foundries Letraset Linotype ITC
Number of weights 4

ABCDEFGHIJKLMNOPQRSTUVWXYZ
abcdefghijklmnopqrstuvwxyz1234567890

May Jo equal the fine record by solving six puzzles a week?

Arial

Designer Robin Nicholas, Patricia Saunders
Nationality UK
Date Designed 1982
Foundries Monotype Microsoft
Number of weights 24

ABCDEFGHIJKLMNOPQRSTUVWXYZ
abcdefghijklmnopqrstuvwxyz1234567890

Arial in Shakespeare's Tempest was a creature of the ether.

Neue Helvetica

Designer Max Miedinger
Nationality CH
Date Designed 1983
Foundries Haas, many others
Recut/Digitised by Linotype Design Studio, 1983
Number of weights 51

ABCDEFGHIJKLMNOPQRSTUVWXYZ
abcdefghijklmnopqrstuvwxyz1234567890

Quixotic Conservatives vet first key zero-growth jeremiad.

Lancé Condensed

Designer Joachim Müller-Lancé
Nationality DE
Date Designed 1983-1993
Foundries FontFont
Number of weights 3

ABCDEFGHIJKLMNOPQRSTUVWXYZ
abcdefghijklmnopqrstuvwxyz1234567890

William Jex quickly caught five dozen Conservatives.

Tahoma

Designer Matthew Carter
Nationality UK
Date Designed 1985
Foundries Microsoft
Number of weights 1

ABCDEFGHIJKLMNOPQRSTUVWXYZ
abcdefghijklmnopqrstuvwxyz1234567890

Freight to me sixty dozen quart jars and twelve black pans.

Abadi

Designer	Ong Chong Wah
Nationality	CN
Date Designed	1987
Foundries	Monotype
Number of weights	14

ABCDEFGHIJKLMNOPQRSTUVWXYZ

abcdefghijklmnopqrstuvwxyz1234567890

Verily the dark ex-Jew quit Zionism, preferring the cabala.

Formata

Designer	Bernd Möllenstadt
Nationality	DE
Date Designed	1988
Foundries	Berthold
Number of weights	34

ABCDEFGHIJKLMNOPQRSTUVWXYZ

abcdefghijklmnopqrstuvwxyz1234567890

Germany's favourite corporate font, used by Allianz, Postbank and VW Skoda.

Esseltube

Designer	Bo Berndal
Nationality	SE
Date Designed	1990
Foundries	CA Partners
Number of weights	1

ABCDEFGHIJKLMNOPQRSTUVWXYZ

abcdefghijklmnopqrstuvwxyz1234567890

While waxing parquet decks, Suez sailors vomit jauntily abaft.

Geneva

Designer	Susan Kare
Nationality	US
Date Designed	1990
Foundries	Apple
Number of weights	1

ABCDEFGHIJKLMNOPQRSTUVWXYZ

abcdefghijklmnopqrstuvwxyz1234567890

Jeb quickly drove a few extra miles on the glazed pavement.

SNV

Designer	Verein Schweizer Straßenfachmanner
Nationality	CH
Date Designed	1990
Foundries	URW++
Number of weights	3

ABCDEFGHIJKLMNOPQRSTUVWXYZ

abcdefghijklmnopqrstuvwxyz1234567890

SNV = Swiss Standards Association - equivalent to the German DIN.

Westerveldt

Designer	Photo-Lettering
Nationality	UK
Date Designed	1990
Foundries	Monotype
Number of weights	1

ABCDEFGHIJKLMNOPQRSTUVWXYZ
abcdefghijklmnopqrstuvwxyz1234567890

Jay visited back home and gazed upon a brown fox and quail.

Bosis

Designer	Bo Berndal
Nationality	SE
Date Designed	1991
Foundries	Creative Alliance
Number of weights	4

ABCDEFGHIJKLMNOPQRSTUVWXYZ
abcdefghijklmnopqrstuvwxyz1234567890

How vexing a fumble to drop a jolly zucchini in the quicksand.

Eurocrat

Designer	Adrian Williams
Nationality	UK
Date Designed	1991
Foundries	CA Partners
Number of weights	5

ABCDEFGHIJKLMNOPQRSTUVWXYZ
abcdefghijklmnopqrstuvwxyz1234567890

Grumpy wizards make toxic brew for the evil Queen and Jack.

Vectora

Designer	Adrian Frutiger
Nationality	CH
Date Designed	1991
Foundries	Adobe
Number of weights	8

ABCDEFGHIJKLMNOPQRSTUVWXYZ
abcdefghijklmnopqrstuvwxyz1234567890

The exodus of jazzy pigeons is craved by squeamish walkers.

Isonorm

Designer	Robert Kirchner
Nationality	DE
Date Designed	1993
Foundries	Mecanorma Monotype URW++
Number of weights	1

ABCDEFGHIJKLMNOPQRSTUVWXYZ
abcdefghijklmnopqrstuvwxyz1234567890

Lazy movers quit hard-packing of papier-mache jewellery boxes.

PL Brazilia 3 & 7

Designer Miles Inc
Nationality US
Date Designed 1993
Foundries Monotype
Number of weights 2

ABCDEFGHIJKLMNOPQRSTUVWXYZ
abcdefghijklmnopqrstuvwxyz1234567890
Back in June we delivered oxygen equipment of the same size.

Schulbuch Bayern

Designer Just van Rossum
Nationality NL
Date Designed 1993
Foundries FontFont
Number of weights 2

ABCDEFGHIJKLMNOPQRSTUVWXYZ
abcdefghijklmnopqrstuvwxyz1234567890
Bavarian schoolbook writing.

Schulbuch Nord

Designer Just van Rossum
Nationality NL
Date Designed 1993
Foundries FontFont
Number of weights 2

ABCDEFGHIJKLMNOPQRSTUVWXYZ
abcdefghijklmnopqrstuvwxyz1234567890
Northern German schoolbook writing.

Schulbuch Süd

Designer Just van Rossum
Nationality NL
Date Designed 1993
Foundries FontFont
Number of weights 2

ABCDEFGHJJKLMNOPQRSTUVWXYZ
abcdefghijklmnopqrstuvwxyz1234567890
Southern German schoolbook writing.

Case Study No. 1

Designer Linotype Library
Nationality DE
Date Designed 1995
Foundries Linotype
Number of weights 6

ABCDEFGHIJKLMNOPQRSTUVWXYZ
abcdefghijklmnopqrstuvwxyz1234567890
New farm hand [picking just six quinces] proves strong but lazy.

Charcoal

Designer	Apple
Nationality	US
Date Designed	1995
Foundries	Apple
Number of weights	1

ABCDEFGHIJKLMNOPQRSTUVWXYZ

abcdefghijklmnopqrstuvwxyz1234567890

Now is the time for all brown dogs to jump over the lazy lynx.

Info

Designer	Erik Spiekermann, Ole Schäfer
Nationality	DE
Date Designed	1996
Foundries	FontFont
Number of weights	60

ABCDEFGHIJKLMNOPQRSTUVWXYZ

abcdefghijklmnopqrstuvwxyz1234567890

Back in my quaint garden jaunty zinnias vie with flaunting phlox.

Letter Gothic Text

Designer	Albert Pinggera
Nationality	IT
Date Designed	1996
Foundries	FontFont
Number of weights	5

ABCDEFGHIJKLMNOPQRSTUVWXYZ

abcdefghijklmnopqrstuvwxyz1234567890

Many big jackdaws quickly zipped over the fox pen.

Trebuchet

Designer	Vincent Connare
Nationality	US
Date Designed	1996
Foundries	Microsoft
Number of weights	1

ABCDEFGHIJKLMNOPQRSTUVWXYZ

abcdefghijklmnopqrstuvwxyz1234567890

Alfredo just must bring very exciting news to the plaza quickly.

Mundo Sans

Designer	Estudio Mariscali
Nationality	IT
Date Designed	1996
Foundries	Type-o-Tones
Number of weights	1

ABCDEFGHIJKLMNOPQRSTUVWXYZ

abcdefghijklmnopqrstuvwxyz1234567890

All questions asked by five watch experts amazed the judge.

Veto

Designer	Hartmut Schaarschmidt
Nationality	DE
Date Designed	1996
Foundries	Linotype
Number of weights	7

ABCDEFGHIJKLMNOPQRSTUVWXYZ
abcdefghijklmnopqrstuvwxyz1234567890
Martin J. Hixeypozer quickly began his first word.

Conduit ITC

Designer	Mark van Bronkhurst
Nationality	NL
Date Designed	1997
Foundries	Linotype ITC
Number of weights	6

ABCDEFGHIJKLMNOPQRSTUVWXYZ
abcdefghijklmnopqrstuvwxyz1234567890
Jaded zombies acted quaintly but kept driving their oxen forward.

Spitz

Designer	Oliver Brentzel
Nationality	DE
Date Designed	1997
Foundries	Linotype
Number of weights	5

ABCDEFGHIJKLMNOPQRSTUVWXYZ
abcdefghijklmnopqrstuvwxyz1234567890
Hark! Toxic jungle water vipers quietly drop on zebras for meals!

Linotype Ordinar

Designer	Lutz Baar
Nationality	SE
Date Designed	1999
Foundries	Linotype
Number of weights	2

ABCDEFGHIJKLMNOPQRSTUVWXYZ
abcdefghijklmnopqrstuvwxyz1234567890
A large fawn jumped quickly over white zinc boxes.

Tetria

Designer	Martin Jagodzinski
Nationality	DE
Date Designed	1999
Foundries	Linotype
Number of weights	8

ABCDEFGHIJKLMNOPQRSTUVWXYZ
abcdefghijklmnopqrstuvwxyz1234567890
My help squeezed back in again and joined the weavers after six.

Signa

Designer Ole Søndergaard
Nationality DK
Date Designed 2000
Foundries FontFont
Number of weights 75

ABCDEFGHIJKLMNOPQRSTUVWXYZ
abcdefghijklmnopqrstuvwxyz1234567890
Many big jackdaws quickly zipped over the fox pen.

Storm Sans

Designer Nina Lee Storm
Nationality KR
Date Designed 2000
Foundries Monotype
Number of weights 5

ABCDEFGHIJKLMNOPQRSTUVWXYZ
abcdefghijklmnopqrstuvwxyz1234567890
The juke box music puzzled a gentle visitor from a quaint valley town.

Advert

Designer Just van Rossum
Nationality NL
Date Designed 2002
Foundries FontFont
Number of weights 13

ABCDEFGHIJKLMNOPQRSTUVWXYZ
abcdefghijklmnopqrstuvwxyz1234567890
Big July earthquakes confound zany experimental vow.

Bau

Designer Christian Schwartz
Nationality US
Date Designed 2002
Foundries FontFont
Number of weights 18

ABCDEFGHIJKLMNOPQRSTUVWXYZ
abcdefghijklmnopqrstuvwxyz1234567890
Exquisite farm wench gives body jolt to prize stinker.

Hydra Extended

Designer Silvio Napoleone
Nationality IT
Date Designed 2002
Foundries FontFont
Number of weights 24

ABCDEFGHIJKLMNOPQRSTUVWXYZ
abcdefghijklmnopqrstuvwxyz1234567890
Six big devils from Japan quickly forgot how to waltz.

Tabula ITC

Designer Julian Janiszewski
Nationality FR
Date Designed 2002
Foundries ITC
Number of weights 8

ABCDEFGHIJKLMNOPQRSTUVWXYZ
abcdefghijklmnopqrstuvwxyz1234567890
Just work for improved basic techniques to maximize your typing skill.

Zwo

Designer Jorg Hemker
Nationality DE
Date Designed 2002
Foundries FontFont
Number of weights 190

ABCDEFGHIJKLMNOPQRSTUVWXYZ
abcdefghijklmnopqrstuvwxyz1234567890
The Baby Belling kept me warm.

Zemestro

Designer Panache Typography
Nationality UK
Date Designed 2002
Foundries Monotype
Number of weights 6

ABCDEFGHIJKLMNOPQRSTUVWXYZ
abcdefghijklmnopqrstuvwxyz1234567890
Shall take Jamshyd and Kaikobad away.

Turmino

Designer Ole Schaefer
Nationality DE
Date Designed 2002
Foundries FontFont
Number of weights 24

ABCDEFGHIJKLMNOPQRSTUVWXYZ
abcdefghijklmnopqrstuvwxyz1234567890
A mad boxer shot a quick, gloved jab to the jaw of his dizzy opponent.

Plus Sans

Designer Jürgen Hüber
Nationality DE
Date Designed 2003
Foundries FontFont
Number of weights 32

ABCDEFGHIJKLMNOPQRSTUVWXYZ
abcdefghijklmnopqrstuvwxyz1234567890
Verbatim reports were quickly given by Jim Fox to his amazed audience.

Kabel

Designer	Rudolf Koch
Nationality	DE
Date Designed	1925
Foundries	Klingspor Bitstream ITC A BE BQ
Number of weights	5

ABCDEFGHIJKLMNOPQRSTUVWXYZ
abcdefghijklmnopqrstuvwxyz1234567890
When we go back to Juarez, Mexico, do we fly over picturesque Arizona?

Futura

Designer	Paul Renner
Nationality	DE
Date Designed	1927
Foundries	Bauer Fundacion Tipografica Neufville Adobe
Number of weights	21

ABCDEFGHIJKLMNOPQRSTUVWXYZ
abcdefghijklmnopqrstuvwxyz1234567890
Verbatim reports were quickly given by Jim Fox to his amazed audience.

DIN Neuzeit

Designer	Wilhelm Pischner
Nationality	DE
Date Designed	1928
Foundries	Linotype
Number of weights	2

ABCDEFGHIJKLMNOPQRSTUVWXYZ
abcdefghijklmnopqrstuvwxyz1234567890
King Alexander was partly overcome just after quizzing Diogenes in his tub.

PL Futura MaxiBook

Designer	Paul Renner
Nationality	DE
Date Designed	1928
Foundries	Monotype
Recut/Digitised by	Vic Caruso, 1960
Number of weights	4

ABCDEFGHIJKLMNOPQRSTUVWXYZ
abcdefghijklmnopqrstuvwxyz1234567890
Futura with an engorged x-height.

Century Gothic

Designer	Monotype
Nationality	US
Date Designed	1930
Foundries	Monotype
Number of weights	4

ABCDEFGHIJKLMNOPQRSTUVWXYZ
abcdefghijklmnopqrstuvwxyz1234567890
Was there a quorum of able whizzkids gravely exciting the jaded fish at ATypI?

Koch Original

Designer	Rudolf Koch
Nationality	DE
Date Designed	1930
Foundries	Monotype
Number of weights	1

ABCDEFGHIJKLMNOPQRSTUVWXYZ

abcdefghijklmnopqrstuvwxyz1234567890

The July sun caused a fragment of black pine wax to ooze on the velvet quilt.

Metro #2

Designer	W A Dwiggins
Nationality	US
Date Designed	1930
Foundries	Mergenthaler Linotype
Number of weights	3

ABCDEFGHIJKLMNOPQRSTUVWXYZ

abcdefghijklmnopqrstuvwxyz1234567890

Two hardy boxing kangaroos jet from Sydney to Zanzibar on quicksilver pinions.

CG Gothic

Designer	W A Dwiggins
Nationality	US
Date Designed	1932
Foundries	CA Partners
Recut/Digitised by	Compugraphic, 1993
Number of weights	4

ABCDEFGHIJKLMNOPQRSTUVWXYZ

abcdefghijklmnopqrstuvwxyz1234567890

Ebenezer unexpectedly bagged two tranquil aardvarks with his jiffy vacuum cleaner.

Berlinsans

Designer	Lucian Bernhard
Nationality	AT
Date Designed	1933
Foundries	FontFont
Recut/Digitised by	David Berlow, Matthew Butterick
Number of weights	12

ABCDEFGHIJKLMNOPQRSTUVWXYZ

abcdefghijklmnopqrstuvwxyz1234567890

Redrawn from one single font weight by Matthew Butterick and David Berlow.

Twentieth Century MT

Designer	Sol Hess
Nationality	US
Date Designed	1936
Foundries	Lanston Monotype
Number of weights	18

ABCDEFGHIJKLMNOPQRSTUVWXYZ

abcdefghijklmnopqrstuvwxyz1234567890

Perhaps President Clinton's amazing sax skills will be judged quite favourably.

Spartan Classified

Designer Linotype Design Staff
Nationality US
Date Designed 1951
Foundries Linotype Adobe Monotype
Number of weights 5

ABCDEFGHIJKLMNOPQRSTUVWXYZ
abcdefghijklmnopqrstuvwxyz1234567890
Designed for legibility at very small point sizes in newspaper classified ads.

Eurostile

Designer Aldo Novarese
Nationality IT
Date Designed 1962
Foundries Nebiolo Linotype Adobe URW++
Number of weights 10

ABCDEFGHIJKLMNOPQRSTUVWXYZ
abcdefghijklmnopqrstuvwxyz1234567890
Fabled reader with jaded, roving eye seized by quickened impulse to expand budget.

Avant Garde Gothic

Designer Herb Lubalin, Tom Carnase
Nationality US
Date Designed 1970
Foundries ITC
Number of weights 14

ABCDEFGHIJKLMNOPQRSTUVWXYZ
abcdefghijklmnopqrstuvwxyz1234567890
For only $49, jolly housewives made "inexpensive" meals using quick-frozen vegetables.

Russell Square

Designer John Russell
Nationality UK
Date Designed 1971
Foundries Visual Graphics Corporation Adobe
Number of weights 2

ABCDEFGHIJKLMNOPQRSTUVWXYZ
abcdefghijklmnopqrstuvwxyz1234567890
Cheap London hotels for visiting Americans.

Serpentine

Designer Dick Jensen
Nationality US
Date Designed 1972
Foundries Elsner+Flake Linotype Adobe Monotype URW++
Number of weights 6

ABCDEFGHIJKLMNOPQRSTUVWXYZ
abcdefghijklmnopqrstuvwxyz1234567890
Jimmy and Zack, the police explained, were last seen diving into a field of buttered quahogs.

Dungeon RR

Designer	Steve Jackaman
Nationality	US
Date Designed	1974
Foundries	Red Rooster
Number of weights	4

ABCDEFGHIJKLMNOPQRSTUVWXYZ
abcdefghijklmnopqrstuvwxyz1234567890
Creative Minds, Warlies Park.

Washington

Designer	Russell Bean
Nationality	AU
Date Designed	1973
Foundries	Type Associates URW++
Number of weights	5

ABCDEFGHIJKLMNOPQRSTUVWXYZ
abcdefghijklmnopqrstuvwxyz1234567890
Exquisite farm wench gives body jolt to prize stinker.

Bauhaus

Designer	Edward Benguiat
Nationality	US
Date Designed	1975
Foundries	ITC Linotype Bitstream Adobe
Recut/Digitised by	Benguiat, Caruso 1975
Number of weights	5

ABCDEFGHIJKLMNOPQRSTUVWXYZ
abcdefghijklmnopqrstuvwxyz 1234567890
Herbert Bayer's experimental abandonment of capital letters occurred in 1925.

Chicago

Designer	Susan Kare
Nationality	US
Date Designed	1980
Foundries	Apple Bigelow, E Holmes
Number of weights	1

ABCDEFGHIJKLMNOPQRSTUVWXYZ
abcdefghijklmnopqrstuvwxyz1234567890
A mad boxer shot a quick, gloved jab to the jaw of his dizzy opponent.

Avenir

Designer	Adrian Frutiger
Nationality	CH
Date Designed	1988
Foundries	Linotype
Number of weights	12

ABCDEFGHIJKLMNOPQRSTUVWXYZ
abcdefghijklmnopqrstuvwxyz1234567890
William said that everything about his jacket was in quite good condition except for the zipper.

AT Brazilia Seven

Designer Photo-Lettering
Nationality US
Date Designed 1990
Foundries Monotype
Number of weights 2

ABCDEFGHIJKLMNOPQRSTUVWXYZ
abcdefghijklmnopqrstuvwxyz1234567890
Sexy qua lijf, doch bang voor het zwempak.

Insignia

Designer Neville Brody
Nationality UK
Date Designed 1986
Foundries Linotype Adobe Monotype
Number of weights 2

ABCDEFGHIJKLMNOPQRSTUVWXYZ
abcdefghijklmnopqrstuvwxyz1234567890
An inspired calligrapher can create pages of beauty using stick ink,
quill, brush, pick-axe, buzz saw, or even strawberry jam.

Ambient

Designer Neville Brody
Nationality UK
Date Designed 1986
Foundries Apple Computer
Number of weights 1

ABCDEFGHIJKLMNOPQRSTUVWXYZ
ABCDEFGHIJKLMNOPQRSTUVWXYZ1234567890
BACK IN JUNE WE DELIVERED OXYGEN EQUIPMENT OF THE SAME SIZE.

PL Brazilia Three

Designer Photo-Lettering
Nationality UK
Date Designed 1990
Foundries Monotype
Number of weights 2

ABCDEFGHIJKLMNOPQRSTUVWXYZ
abcdefghijklmnopqrstuvwxyz1234567890
Jelly-like above the high wire, six quaking pachyderms kept
the climax of the extravaganza in a dazzling state of flux.

Jeunesse Sans

Designer Johannes Birkenbach
Nationality DE
Date Designed 1993
Foundries Creative Alliance ABC Design
Monotype
Number of weights 3

ABCDEFGHIJKLMNOPQRSTUVWXYZ
abcdefghijklmnopqrstuvwxyz1234567890
Puzzled women bequeath jerks very exotic gifts.

Jocelyn

Designer	Johannes Birkenbach
Nationality	DE
Date Designed	1993
Foundries	Creative Alliance ABC Design
Number of weights	4

ABCDEFGHIJKLMNOPQRSTUVWXYZ

abcdefghijklmnopqrstuvwxyz1234567890

Zwei Boxkämpfer jagen Eva quer durch Sylt.

Bailey Sans

Designer	Kevin Bailey
Nationality	UK
Date Designed	1996
Foundries	CA Partners Linotype
Number of weights	4

ABCDEFGHIJKLMNOPQRSTUVWXYZ

abcdefghijklmnopqrstuvwxyz1234567890

Quick wafting zephyrs vex bold Jim.

Cocon

Designer	Evert Bloemsma
Nationality	NL
Date Designed	1998
Foundries	FontFont
Number of weights	30

ABCDEFGHIJKLMNOPQRSTUVWXYZ

abcdefghijklmnopqrstuvwxyz1234567890

Sphinx of black quartz judge my vow.

Naniara

Designer	Bo Berndal
Nationality	SE
Date Designed	1998
Foundries	Monotype
Number of weights	5

ABCDEFGHIJKLMNOPQRSTUVWXYZ

abcdefghijklmnopqrstuvwxyz1234567890

Playing jazz vibe chords quickly excites my wife.

TypeStar

Designer	Steffen Sauerteig
Nationality	DE
Date Designed	1998
Foundries	FontFont
Number of weights	8

ABCDEFGHIJKLMNOPQRSTUVWXYZ

abcdefghijklmnopqrstuvwxyz1234567890

Quick zephyrs blow, vexing daft Jim.

SuperGrotesk

Designer	Svend Smital
Nationality	DE
Date Designed	1999
Foundries	FontFont
Number of weights	21

ABCDEFGHIJKLMNOPQRSTUVWXYZ

abcdefghijklmnopqrstuvwxyz1234567890

How quickly daft jumping zebras vex.

Linotype Kaliber

Designer	Linotype
Nationality	DE
Date Designed	2000
Foundries	Linotype
Number of weights	4

ABCDEFGHIJKLMNOPQRSTUVWXYZ

abcdefghijklmnopqrstuvwxyz1234567890

Jackdaws love my big sphinx of quartz.

FF Max

Designer	Morten Olsen
Nationality	DK
Date Designed	2001
Foundries	FontFont
Number of weights	112

ABCDEFGHIJKLMNOPQRSTUVWXYZ

abcdefghijklmnopqrstuvwxyz1234567890

The sex life of the woodchuck is a provocative question for most vertebrate zoology majors.

Cineplex

Designer	Dario Muhafara
Nationality	AR
Date Designed	2002
Foundries	Linotype
Number of weights	5

ABCDEFGHIJKLMNOPQRSTUVWXYZ

abcdefghijklmnopqrstuvwxyz 1234567890

Breezily jangling €3,416,857,209 wise advertiser ambles to the bank, his exchequer amplified.

Ginger

Designer	Jürgen Hüber
Nationality	DE
Date Designed	2002
Foundries	FontFont
Number of weights	13

ABCDEFGHIJKLMNOPQRSTUVWXYZ

abcdefghijklmnopqrstuvwxyz1234567890

Ginger includes a wildly decorative swirling *flamboyant* weight.

Square 40

Designer	Carlos Segura
Nationality	CU
Date Designed	2002
Foundries	T-26
Number of weights	4

ABCDEFGHIJKLMNOPQRSTUVWXYZ
abcdefghijklmnopqrstuvwxyz1234567890
Mr. Jock, TV quiz Ph.D., bags few lynx.

Cachet

Designer	Dave Farey
Nationality	UK
Date Designed	2003
Foundries	Monotype
Number of weights	3

ABCDEFGHIJKLMNOPQRSTUVWXYZ
abcdefghijklmnopqrstuvwxyz 1234567890
No kidding, Lorenzo called off his trip to visit Mexico City just because they told him the conquistadores were extinct.

Johnston's Railway Type

Designer	Edward Johnston
Nationality	UK
Date Designed	1918
Foundries	London Transport
Number of weights	9

ABCDEFGHIJKLMNOPQRSTUVWXYZ
abcdefghijklmnopqrstuvwxyz 1234567890
How long does it take to get from SLOANE SQUARE to FINSBURY PARK?

Gill Sans

Designer	Eric Gill
Nationality	UK
Date Designed	1928
Foundries	Monotype Adobe
Number of weights	15

ABCDEFGHIJKLMNOPQRSTUVWXYZ
abcdefghijklmnopqrstuvwxyz1234567890
The only major typeface to have been designed in Wales.

Goudy Sans

Designer	Frederic W Goudy
Nationality	US
Date Designed	1929
Foundries	Bitstream Lanston Monotype Bitstream ITC
Number of weights	8

ABCDEFGHIJKLMNOPQRSTUVWXYZ
abcdefghijklmnopqrstuvwxyz1234567890
An inspired calligrapher can create pages of beauty using stick ink, quill, brush, pick-axe, buzz saw, or even strawberry jam.

Stellar

Designer R Hunter Middleton
Nationality US
Date Designed 1929
Foundries Ludlow Monotype
Number of weights 4

ABCDEFGHIJKLMNOPQRSTUVWXYZ

abcdefghijklmnopqrstuvwxyzl234567890

Forsaking monastic tradition, twelve jovial friars gave up their vocation for a questionable existence on the flying trapeze.

Lydian

Designer Warren Chappell
Nationality US
Date Designed 1938
Foundries Monotype ATF Bitstream
Number of weights 2

ABCDEFGHIJKLMNOPQRSTUVWXYZ

abcdefghijklmnopqrstuvwxyz1234567890

No kidding, Lorenzo called off his trip to visit Mexico City just because they told him the conquistadores were extinct.

Optima

Designer Hermann Zapf
Nationality DE
Date Designed 1958
Foundries Stempel Linotype
Number of weights 11

ABCDEFGHIJKLMNOPQRSTUVWXYZ

abcdefghijklmnopqrstuvwxyz1234567890

The most elegant sans serif ever designed. New drawing named Optima Nova.

Antique Olive

Designer Roger Excoffon
Nationality FR
Date Designed 1962
Foundries Olive Adobe URW++
Number of weights 9

ABCDEFGHIJKLMNOPQRSTUVWXYZ

abcdefghijklmnopqrstuvwxyz1234567890

Portez ce vieux whisky au juge blond qui fume.

Eras

Designer Albert Boton, Studio Hollenstein
Nationality FR
Date Designed 1969
Foundries Wagner Monotype ITC
Number of weights 6

ABCDEFGHIJKLMNOPQRSTUVWXYZ

abcdefghijklmnopqrstuvwxyz1234567890

HPR Publicity, London and Frankfurt.

Agfa Waddy 81

Designer	Aiko & Hideaki Wada
Nationality	JP
Date Designed	1999
Foundries	Monotype
Number of weights	3

ABCDEFGHIJKLMNOPQRSTUVWXYZ
abcdefghijklmnopqrstuvwxyz1234567890
Neither can I.

Agfa Waddy 82

Designer	Aiko & Hideaki Wada
Nationality	JP
Date Designed	1999
Foundries	Monotype
Number of weights	1

ABCDEFGHIJKLMNOPQRSTUVWXYZ
abcdefghijklmnopqrstuvwxyz1234567890
Astronaut Quincy B. Zack defies gravity with six jet fuel pumps.

Agfa Waddy 83

Designer	Aiko & Hideaki Wada
Nationality	JP
Date Designed	1999
Foundries	Monotype
Number of weights	1

ABCDEFGHIJKLMNOPQRSTUVWXYZ
abcdefghijklmnopqrstuvwxyz1234567890
My help squeezed back in again and joined the weavers after six.

Souvenir Gothic

Designer	George Brian
Nationality	US
Date Designed	1977
Foundries	FC URW
Number of weights	3

ABCDEFGHIJKLMNOPQRSTUVWXYZ
abcdefghijklmnopqrstuvwxyz1234567890

Jelly-like above the high wire, six quaking pachyderms kept the climax of the extravaganza in a dazzling state of flux.

Shannon

Designer	Kris Holmes, Janice Prescott
Nationality	US
Date Designed	1982
Foundries	Monotype
Number of weights	6

ABCDEFGHIJKLMNOPQRSTUVWXYZ
abcdefghijklmnopqrstuvwxyz1234567890
Shannon is the major river in Ireland. The small caps and experts fonts are called Shannon Premier.

Meta

Designer Erik Spiekermann
Nationality DE
Date Designed 1985
Foundries FontFont
Number of weights 108

ABCDEFGHIJKLMNOPQRSTUVWXYZ
abcdefghijklmnopqrstuvwxyz1234567890
William said that everything about his jacket was in quite good condition except for the zipper.

Mixage

Designer Aldo Novarese
Nationality IT
Date Designed 1985
Foundries ITC URW++
Number of weights 10

ABCDEFGHIJKLMNOPQRSTUVWXYZ
abcdefghijklmnopqrstuvwxyz1234567890
A quahog is an American clam (Venus mercenaria). Highly valued as food.

Agfa Rotis

Designer Otl Aicher
Nationality DE
Date Designed 1988
Foundries Monotype
Number of weights 6

ABCDEFGHIJKLMNOPQRSTUVWXYZ
abcdefghijklmnopqrstuvwxyz1234567890
The most influential font of the 1990s. Adored by corporations.

Claude Sans

Designer Alan Meeks
Nationality UK
Date Designed 1988
Foundries ITC Letraset
Number of weights 3

ABCDEFGHIJKLMNOPQRSTUVWXYZ
abcdefghijklmnopqrstuvwxyz1234567890
Claude Gill was a famous London bookseller. Eric Gill designed Gill Sans.

Panache

Designer Ed Benguiat
Nationality US
Date Designed 1988
Foundries ITC Linotype
Number of weights 8

ABCDEFGHIJKLMNOPQRSTUVWXYZ
abcdefghijklmnopqrstuvwxyz1234567890
Back in June we delivered oxygen equipment of the same size.

Bulldog

Designer	Adrian Williams
Nationality	UK
Date Designed	1990
Foundries	Monotype
Number of weights	6

ABCDEFGHIJKLMNOPQRSTUVWXYZ

abcdefghijklmnopqrstuvwxyz1234567890

Jimmy and Zack, the police explained, were last seen diving into a field of buttered quahogs.

Quay Sans

Designer	David Quay
Nationality	UK
Date Designed	1990
Foundries	ITC URW++ AGP Elsner+Flake Franklin
Number of weights	8

ABCDEFGHIJKLMNOPQRSTUVWXYZ

abcdefghijklmnopqrstuvwxyz1234567890

Breezily jangling €3,416,857,209, wise advertiser ambles to the bank, his exchequer amplified.

Arta

Designer	David Quay
Nationality	UK
Date Designed	1991
Foundries	Monotype
Number of weights	8

ABCDEFGHIJKLMNOPQRSTUVWXYZ

abcdefghijklmnopqrstuvwxyz1234567890

For only $49, jolly housewives made inexpensive meals using quick-frozen vegetables.

Imperial

Designer	Edwin W. Schaar
Nationality	US
Date Designed	1957
Foundries	Intertype Bitstream URW++
Number of weights	1

ABCDEFGHIJKLMNOPQRSTUVWXYZ

abcdefghijklmnopqrstuvwxyz1234567890

Viewing quizzical abstracts mixed up hefty jocks.

Imperial URW

Designer	Albert-Jan Pool
Nationality	NL
Date Designed	1991
Foundries	URW++
Number of weights	51

ABCDEFGHIJKLMNOPQRSTUVWXYZ

abcdefghijklmnopqrstuvwxyz1234567890

Jaded reader with fabled roving eye seized by quickened impulse to expand budget.

Charlotte Sans

Designer	Michael Gills
Nationality	UK
Date Designed	1992
Foundries	Linotype ITC
Number of weights	5

ABCDEFGHIJKLMNOPQRSTUVWXYZ

abcdefghijklmnopqrstuvwxyz1234567890

Ebenezer unexpectedly bagged two tranquil aardvarks with his jiffy vacuum cleaner.

Congress Sans

Designer	Adrian Williams
Nationality	UK
Date Designed	1992
Foundries	Monotype
Number of weights	5

ABCDEFGHIJKLMNOPQRSTUVWXYZ

abcdefghijklmnopqrstuvwxyz1234567890

Was there a quorum of able whizzkids gravely exciting the jaded fish at ATypI?

Legacy Sans

Designer	Ronald Arnholm
Nationality	US
Date Designed	1992
Foundries	ITC Elsner+Flake Monotype Adobe
Number of weights	16

ABCDEFGHIJKLMNOPQRSTUVWXYZ

abcdefghijklmnopqrstuvwxyz1234567890

Perhaps President Clinton's amazing sax skills will be judged quite favourably.

Balance

Designer	Evert Bloemsma
Nationality	NL
Date Designed	1993
Foundries	FontFont
Number of weights	32

ABCDEFGHIJKLMNOPQRSTUVWXYZ

abcdefghijklmnopqrstuvwxyz1234567890

The July sun caused a fragment of black pine wax to ooze on the velvet quilt.

Dialog

Designer	Franko Luin
Nationality	SL
Date Designed	1993
Foundries	Omnibus Linotype
Number of weights	19

ABCDEFGHIJKLMNOPQRSTUVWXYZ

abcdefghijklmnopqrstuvwxyz1234567890

About sixty codfish eggs will make a quarter pound of very fizzy jelly.

Scala Sans

Designer	Martin Majoor
Nationality	NL
Date Designed	1993
Foundries	FontFont
Number of weights	35

ABCDEFGHIJKLMNOPQRSTUVWXYZ

abcdefghijklmnopqrstuvwxyz1234567890

Murky haze enveloped a city as jarring quakes broke forty-six windows.

Ulissa

Designer	Johannes Birkenbach
Nationality	DE
Date Designed	1993
Foundries	Creative Alliance ABC Design
Number of weights	12

ABCDEFGHIJKLMNOPQRSTUVWXYZ

abcdefghijklmnopqrstuvwxyz1234567890

King Alexander was partly overcome just after quizzing Diogenes in his tub.

Wunderlich

Designer	Martin Wunderlich
Nationality	DE
Date Designed	1993
Foundries	FontFont
Number of weights	14

ABCDEFGHIJKLMNOPQRSTUVWXYZ

abcdefghijklmnopqrstuvwxyz1234567890

Questions of a zealous nature have become by degrees petty waxen jokes.

Bradlo

Designer	Andrej Krátky
Nationality	SK
Date Designed	1994
Foundries	FontFont
Number of weights	10

ABCDEFGHIJKLMNOPQRSTUVWXYZ

abcdefghijklmnopqrstuvwxyz1234567890

When we go back to Juarez, Mexico, do we fly over picturesque Arizona?

Dorothea

Designer	Philip Bouwsma
Nationality	US
Date Designed	1994
Foundries	Monotype
Number of weights	1

ABCDEFGHIJKLMNOPQRSTUVWXYZ

abcdefghijklmnopqrstuvwxyz1234567890

The sex life of the woodchuck is a provocative question for most vertebrate zoology majors.

Maiandra

Designer Dennis Pasternak
Nationality US
Date Designed 1994
Foundries Galapagos
Number of weights 6

ABCDEFGHIJKLMNOPQRSTUVWXYZ
abcdefghijklmnopqrstuvwxyz1234567890
Verbatim reports were quickly given by Jim Fox to his amazed audience.

Norma

Designer Franko Luin
Nationality SL
Date Designed 1994
Foundries Linotype
Number of weights 17

ABCDEFGHIJKLMNOPQRSTUVWXYZ
abcdefghijklmnopqrstuvwxyz1234567890
A mad boxer shot a quick, gloved jab to the jaw of his dizzy opponent.

Odense

Designer Franko Luin
Nationality SL
Date Designed 1994
Foundries Linotype Omnibus
Number of weights 17

ABCDEFGHIJKLMNOPQRSTUVWXYZ
abcdefghijklmnopqrstuvwxyz1234567890
Just work for improved basic techniques to maximize your typing skill.

TF Forever

Designer Joseph D Treacy
Nationality US
Date Designed 1986
Foundries Treacyfaces Monotype
Number of weights 16

ABCDEFGHIJKLMNOPQRSTUVWXYZ
abcdefghijklmnopqrstuvwxyz1234567890
Hark! Toxic jungle water vipers quietly drop on zebras for meals!

TF Forever Two

Designer Joseph D Treacy
Nationality US
Date Designed 1992
Foundries Treacyfaces
Number of weights 16

ABCDEFGHIJKLMNOPQRSTUVWXYZ
abcdefghijklmnopqrstuvwxyz1234567890
Will Major Douglas be expected to take this true-false quiz very soon?

Mahsuri Sans

Designer Monotype
Nationality UK
Date Designed 1995
Foundries Monotype
Number of weights 16

ABCDEFGHIJKLMNOPQRSTUVWXYZ
abcdefghijklmnopqrstuvwxyz1234567890
Six big juicy steaks sizzled in a pan as five workmen left the quarry.

Profile

Designer Martin Wenzel
Nationality DE
Date Designed 1995
Foundries FontFont
Number of weights 30

ABCDEFGHIJKLMNOPQRSTUVWXYZ
abcdefghijklmnopqrstuvwxyz1234567890
New farm hand (picking just six quinces) proves strong but lazy.

Aperto

Designer Paul Veres
Nationality US
Date Designed 1996
Foundries Calligraphics Linotype
Number of weights 6

ABCDEFGHIJKLMNOPQRSTUVWXYZ
abcdefghijklmnopqrstuvwxyz1234567890
Jaded zombies acted quaintly but kept driving their oxen forward.

Augustal Cursiva

Designer Jean-Renaud Cuaz
Nationality FR
Date Designed 1996
Foundries Monotype
Number of weights 6

ABCDEFGHIJKLMNOPQRSTUVWXYZ
abcdefghijklmnopqrstuvwxyz1234567890
Back in my quaint garden jaunty zinnias vie with flaunting phlox.

Bebop

Designer Thierry Puyfoulhoux
Nationality FR
Date Designed 1996
Foundries CA Exclusives
Number of weights 6

ABCDEFGHIJKLMNOPQRSTUVWXYZ
abcdefghijklmnopqrstuvwxyz1234567890
Alfredo just must bring very exciting news to the plaza quickly.

Dax

Designer	Hans Reichel
Nationality	DE
Date Designed	1996
Foundries	FontFont
Number of weights	108

ABCDEFGHIJKLMNOPQRSTUVWXYZ
abcdefghijklmnopqrstuvwxyz1234567890
My help squeezed back in again and joined the weavers after six.

Linotype Brewery

Designer	Gustav Andrejs Grinbergs
Nationality	LV
Date Designed	1996
Foundries	Linotype
Number of weights	6

ABCDEFGHIJKLMNOPQRSTUVWXYZ
abcdefghijklmnopqrstuvwxyz1234567890
New farm hand (picking just six quinces) proves strong but lazy.

Schmalhans

Designer	Hans Reichel
Nationality	DE
Date Designed	1996
Foundries	FontFont
Number of weights	10

ABCDEFGHIJKLMNOPQRSTUVWXYZ
abcdefghijklmnopqrstuvwxyz1234567890
I don't associate him with any active verbs.

Ergo

Designer	Gary Munch
Nationality	US
Date Designed	1997
Foundries	Linotype
Number of weights	9

ABCDEFGHIJKLMNOPQRSTUVWXYZ
abcdefghijklmnopqrstuvwxyz1234567890
Six big juicy steaks sizzled in a pan as five workmen left the quarry.

Finnegan

Designer	Jürgen Weltin
Nationality	DE
Date Designed	1997
Foundries	Linotype
Number of weights	22

ABCDEFGHIJKLMNOPQRSTUVWXYZ
abcdefghijklmnopqrstuvwxyz1234567890
Now is the time for all brown dogs to jump over the lazy lynx.

Pisa

Designer	Lutz Baar
Nationality	SE
Date Designed	1997
Foundries	Linotype
Number of weights	5

ABCDEFGHIJKLMNOPQRSTUVWXYZ
abcdefghijklmnopqrstuvwxyz1234567890
Jaunty Suez sailors vomit abaft while waxing parquet decks.

Transit

Designer	Lucas de Groot
Nationality	NL
Date Designed	1997
Foundries	FontFont
Number of weights	35

ABCDEFGHIJKLMNOPQRSTUVWXYZ
abcdefghijklmnopqrstuvwxyz1234567890
Alexanderplatz nach Charlottenburg.

Woodland

Designer	Akira Kobayashi
Nationality	JP
Date Designed	1997
Foundries	ITC
Number of weights	4

ABCDEFGHIJKLMNOPQRSTUVWXYZ
abcdefghijklmnopqrstuvwxyz1234567890
Astronaut Quincy B. Zack defies gravity with six jet fuel pumps.

Dyadis

Designer	Yvonne Diedrich
Nationality	AT
Date Designed	1998
Foundries	ITC
Number of weights	15

ABCDEFGHIJKLMNOPQRSTUVWXYZ
abcdefghijklmnopqrstuvwxyz1234567890
Lazy movers quit hard-packing of papier-maché jewellery boxes.

Octone

Designer	Eric de Berranger
Nationality	FR
Date Designed	1998
Foundries	ITC
Number of weights	10

ABCDEFGHIJKLMNOPQRSTUVWXYZ
abcdefghijklmnopqrstuvwxyz1234567890
Moi, je veux quinze clubs a golf et du whisky pur.

Adderville ITC

Designer	George Ryan
Nationality	US
Date Designed	1999
Foundries	ITC
Number of weights	3

ABCDEFGHIJKLMNOPQRSTUVWXYZ

abcdefghijklmnopqrstuvwxyz1234567890

All questions asked by five watch experts amazed the judge.

Fago Office Sans

Designer	Ole Schaefer
Nationality	DE
Date Designed	1999
Foundries	FontFont
Number of weights	256

ABCDEFGHIJKLMNOPQRSTUVWXYZ

abcdefghijklmnopqrstuvwxyz1234567890

The risqué gown marked a brazen exposure of very juicy flesh.

Karbid

Designer	Verena Gerlach
Nationality	DE
Date Designed	1999
Foundries	FontFont
Number of weights	16

ABCDEFGHIJKLMNOPQRSTUVWXYZ

abcdefghijklmnopqrstuvwxyz1234567890

We promptly judged antique ivory buckles for the next prize.

Linotype Projekt

Designer	Andreas Koch
Nationality	DE
Date Designed	1999
Foundries	Linotype
Number of weights	6

ABCDEFGHIJKLMNOPQRSTUVWXYZ

abcdefghijklmnopqrstuvwxyz1234567890

Grumpy wizards make toxic brew for the evil Queen and Jack.

Luna

Designer	Akira Kobayashi
Nationality	JP
Date Designed	1999
Foundries	ITC Linotype Monotype
Number of weights	2

ABCDEFGHIJKLMNOPQRSTUVWXYZ

abcdefghijklmnopqrstuvwxyz1234567890

The exodus of jazzy pigeons is craved by squeamish walkers.

Scene

Designer Sebastian Lester
Nationality UK
Date Designed 2000
Foundries Monotype
Number of weights 24

ABCDEFGHIJKLMNOPQRSTUVWXYZ
abcdefghijklmnopqrstuvwxyz1234567890
A quick movement of the enemy will jeopardize six gunboats.

Kievit

Designer Mike Abbink
Nationality UK
Date Designed 2001
Foundries FontFont
Number of weights 48

ABCDEFGHIJKLMNOPQRSTUVWXYZ
abcdefghijklmnopqrstuvwxyz1234567890
Freight to me sixty dozen quart jars and twelve black pans.

Mosquito

Designer Eric de Berranger
Nationality FR
Date Designed 2001
Foundries Monotype
Number of weights 12

ABCDEFGHIJKLMNOPQRSTUVWXYZ
abcdefghijklmnopqrstuvwxyz1234567890
*foto*LIBRA.com's corporate font.

Mosquito Formal

Designer Eric de Berranger
Nationality FR
Date Designed 2004
Foundries Monotype
Number of weights 6

ABCDEFGHIJKLMNOPQRSTUVWXYZ
abcdefghijklmnopqrstuvwxyz1234567890
*foto*LIBRA.com's corporate font.

Sari

Designer Hans Reichel
Nationality DE
Date Designed 2001
Foundries FontFont
Number of weights 26

ABCDEFGHIJKLMNOPQRSTUVWXYZ
abcdefghijklmnopqrstuvwxyz1234567890
Jay visited back home and gazed upon a brown fox and quail.

Linotype Aroma

Designer Gianfredo Lopetz
Nationality CH
Date Designed 2002
Foundries Linotype
Number of weights 11

ABCDEFGHIJKLMNOPQRSTUVWXYZ
abcdefghijklmnopqrstuvwxyz1234567890
Just keep examining every low bid quoted for zinc etchings.

Strada

Designer Albert Pinggera
Nationality IT
Date Designed 2002
Foundries FontFont
Number of weights 60

ABCDEFGHIJKLMNOPQRSTUVWXYZ
abcdefghijklmnopqrstuvwxyz1234567890
Fred specialized in the job of making very quaint wax toys.

Unit

Designer Erik Spiekermann, Christian Schwartz
Nationality DE
Date Designed 2004
Foundries FontFont
Number of weights 49

ABCDEFGHIJKLMNOPQRSTUVWXYZ
abcdefghijklmnopqrstuvwxyz1234567890
West quickly gave Bert handsome prizes for six juicy plums.

AT Advertisers Gothic-Light

Designer Robert Wiebking
Nationality US
Date Designed 1917
Foundries Monotype
Number of weights 1

ABCDEFGHIJKLMNOPQRSTUVWXYZ
abcdefghijklmnopqrstuvwxyz1234567890
World's largest x-height—hardly any descenders.

Parisian

Designer Morris Fuller Benton
Nationality US
Date Designed 1928
Foundries ATF Bitstream
Number of weights 1

ABCDEFGHIJKLMNOPQRSTUVWXYZ
abcdefghijklmnopqrstuvwxyz1234567890
Jim just quit and packed extra bags for Liz Owen.

Misc

Bernhard Fashion

Designer	Lucian Bernhard
Nationality	AT
Date Designed	1929
Foundries	ATF Bitstream URW++
Number of weights	1

ABCDEFGHIJKLMNOPQRSTUVWXYZ

abcdefghijklmnopqrstuvwxyz1234567890

Quick zephyrs blow, vexing daft Jim.

Peignot

Designer	A M Cassandre
Nationality	FR
Date Designed	1937
Foundries	Deberny & Peignot Adobe URW++
Number of weights	3

ABCDEFGHIJKLMNOPQRSTUVWXYZ

abcdefghijklmnopqrstuvwxyz1234567890

Moi, je veux quinze clubs a golf et du whisky pur.

Vellvé

Designer	Tomas Vellvé
Nationality	ES
Date Designed	1971
Foundries	Bauer CA Exclusives
Number of weights	5

ABCDEFGHIJKLMNOPQRSTUVWXYZ

abcdefghijklmnopqrstuvwxyz1234567890

Big July earthquakes confound zany experimental vow.

Liant

Designer	Ingrid Lich
Nationality	DE
Date Designed	1976
Foundries	FontFont
Number of weights	5

ABCDEFGHIJKLMNOPQRSTUVWXYZ

abcdefghijklmnopqrstuvwxyz1234567890

Brawny gods just flocked up to quiz and vex him.

Squire

Designer	Michael Neugebauer
Nationality	AT
Date Designed	1980
Foundries	Letraset URW++ Linotype ITC Monotype
Number of weights	2

ABCDEFGHIJKLMNOPQRSTUVWXYZ

abcdefghijklmnopqrstuvwxyz1234567890

Five wine experts jokingly quizzed sample chablis.

Flora

Designer	Gerard Unger
Nationality	NL
Date Designed	1984
Foundries	ITC
Number of weights	2

ABCDEFGHIJKLMNOPQRSTUVWXYZ
abcdefghijklmnopqrstuvwxyz1234567890
Sexy qua lijf, doch bang voor het zwempak.

Tannhäuser

Designer	Alan Meeks
Nationality	UK
Date Designed	1988
Foundries	Monotype
Number of weights	1

ABCDEFGHIJKLMNOPQRSTUVWXYZ
abcdefghijklmnopqrstuvwxyz1234567890
Tannhäuser, a mediæval German minstrel, is the eponymous hero of Wagner's opera.

Tekton

Designer	David Siegel, Jim Wasco, Francis Ching
Nationality	US
Date Designed	1989
Foundries	Adobe Linotype Monotype
Number of weights	1

ABCDEFGHIJKLMNOPQRSTUVWXYZ
abcdefghijklmnopqrstuvwxyz1234567890
Multiple masters.

Wade Sans

Designer	Paul Hickson
Nationality	UK
Date Designed	1990
Foundries	Letraset Monotype ITC
Number of weights	1

ABCDEFGHIJKLMNOPQRSTUVWXYZ
abcdefghijklmnopqrstuvwxyz1234567890
Six big devils from Japan quickly forgot how to waltz.

Sassoon San Slope

Designer	Rosemary Sassoon
Nationality	UK
Date Designed	1990
Foundries	Monotype
Number of weights	2

ABCDEFGHIJKLMNOPQRSTUVWXYZ
abcdefghijklmnopqrstuvwxyz1234567890
Five wine experts jokingly quizzed sample chablis.

Sassoon Primary

Designer	Rosemary Sassoon
Nationality	UK
Date Designed	1990
Foundries	Monotype Adobe Linotype
Number of weights	4

ABCDEFGHIJKLMNOPQRSTUVWXYZ

abcdefghijklmnopqrstuvwxyz1234567890

Designer's name and the font's intended use in first schooling

Sassoon Infant

Designer	Rosemary Sassoon
Nationality	UK
Date Designed	1995
Foundries	Monotype Adobe Linotype
Number of weights	4

ABCDEFGHIJKLMNOPQRSTUVWXYZ

abcdefghijklmnopqrstuvwxyz1234567890

Many big jackdaws quickly zipped over the fox pen.

Sassoon Sans

Designer	Rosemary Sassoon
Nationality	UK
Date Designed	1995
Foundries	Monotype Adobe Linotype
Number of weights	12

ABCDEFGHIJKLMNOPQRSTUVWXYZ

abcdefghijklmnopqrstuvwxyz1234567890

Primary, Infant & Regular.

TF Maltby Antique

Designer	Joseph D Treacy
Nationality	US
Date Designed	1990
Foundries	Treacyfaces Monotype
Number of weights	9

ABCDEFGHIJKLMNOPQRSTUVWXYZ

abcdefghijklmnopqrstuvwxyz1234567890

Viewing quizzical abstracts mixed up hefty jocks.

Skia

Designer	Matthew Carter, David Berlow
Nationality	UK
Date Designed	1992
Foundries	Apple
Number of weights	1

ABCDEFGHIJKLMNOPQRSTUVWXYZ

abcdefghijklmnopqrstuvwxyz1234567890

Built to showcase Apple's defunct QuickDraw GX technology, with variable weight and axes. GX fonts are now called AAT fonts.

Chasline

Designer Charles Wiltgen
Nationality US
Date Designed 1993
Foundries T-26
Number of weights 4

ABCDEFGHIJKLMNOPQRSTUVWXYZ
abcdefghijklmnopqrstuvwxyz1234567890
Jackdaws love my big sphinx of quartz.

Highlander

Designer Dave Farey
Nationality UK
Date Designed 1993
Foundries ITC Adobe
Number of weights 14

ABCDEFGHIJKLMNOPQRSTUVWXYZ
abcdefghijklmnopqrstuvwxyz1234567890
Based on the handwriting of American designer Oswald Cooper, circa 1928.

Instanter

Designer Frank Heine
Nationality DE
Date Designed 1994
Foundries FontFont
Number of weights 4

ABCDEFGHIJKLMNOPQRSTUVWXYZ
abcdefghijklmnopqrstuvwxyz1234567890
Dumpy kibitzer jingles as exchequer overflows.

Primary

Designer Martin Wenzel
Nationality DE
Date Designed 1995
Foundries FontFont
Number of weights 15

ABCDEFGHIJKLMNOPQRSTUVWXYZ
abcdefghijklmnopqrstuvwxyz1234567890
Now is the time for all brown dogs to jump over the lazy lynx.

Engine

Designer Alex Scholing
Nationality NL
Date Designed 1995
Foundries FontFont
Number of weights 19

ABCDEFGHIJKLMNOPQRSTUVWXYZ
abcdefghijklmnopqrstuvwxyz1234567890
Sympathizing would fix Quaker objectives.

Ellipse

Designer	Jean-Renaud Cuaz
Nationality	FR
Date Designed	1996
Foundries	Monotype ITC
Number of weights	4

ABCDEFGHIJKLMNOPQRSTUVWXYZ

abcdefghijklmnopqrstuvwxyz1234567890

Five big quacking zephyrs jolt my wax bed.

Stoclet

Designer	Phill Grimshaw
Nationality	UK
Date Designed	1998
Foundries	Linotype Monotype ITC Letraset
Number of weights	2

ABCDEFGHIJKLMNOPQRSTUVWXYZ

abcdefghijklmnopqrstuvwxyz1234567890

Palais Stoclet is a fantastic Sezession palace in eastern Brussels.

Julius Primary

Designer	Julius de Goede
Nationality	NL
Date Designed	1999
Foundries	Monotype
Number of weights	8

ABCDEFGHIJKLMNOPQRSTUVWXYZ

abcdefghijklmnopqrstuvwxyz1234567890

Women bequeath puzzled jerks very exotic gifts.

Linotype Atlantis

Designer	Lutz Baar
Nationality	SE
Date Designed	1999
Foundries	Weber Linotype
Number of weights	4

ABCDEFGHIJKLMNOPQRSTUVWXYZ

abcdefghijklmnopqrstuvwxyz1234567890

May Jo equal the fine record by solving six puzzles a week?

Atelier

Designer	Nick Curtis
Nationality	US
Date Designed	2001
Foundries	ITC
Number of weights	4

ABCDEFGHIJKLMNOPQRSTUVWXYZ

abcdefghijklmnopqrstuvwxyz1234567890

French for workshop.

Alega

Designer	Siegfried Rückel
Nationality	DE
Date Designed	2002
Foundries	FontFont
Number of weights	20

ABCDEFGHIJKLMNOPQRSTUVWXYZ

abcdefghijklmnopqrstuvwxyz1234567890

Asociación de lesbianas y gais.

Page Sans

Designer	Albert Boton
Nationality	FR
Date Designed	2003
Foundries	FontFont
Number of weights	28

ABCDEFGHIJKLMNOPQRSTUVWXYZ

abcdefghijklmnopqrstuvwxyz1234567890

Back in my quaint garden jaunty zinnias vie with flaunting phlox.

Neuseidler Antiqua

Designer	Richard Yeend
Nationality	UK
Date Designed	2003
Foundries	Linotype
Number of weights	6

ABCDEFGHIJKLMNOPQRSTUVWXYZ

abcdefghijklmnopqrstuvwxyz1234567890

The Neuseidler See is a large shallow lake near Vienna.

Jackie

Designer	Dario Muhafara
Nationality	AR
Date Designed	2003
Foundries	FontFont
Number of weights	16

ABCDEFGHIJKLMNOPQRSTUVWXYZ

abcdefghijklmnopqrstuvwxyz1234567890

Jazzy saxophones blew over Mick's turgid quiff.

Roice

Designer	Alex Scholing
Nationality	NL
Date Designed	2003
Foundries	FontFont
Number of weights	1

ABCDEFGHIJKLMNOPQRSTUVWXYZ

abcdefghijklmnopqrstuvwxyz1234567890

Back in June we delivered oxygen equipment of the same size.

Arabdream

Designer	Michael Parson
Nationality	CH
Date Designed	2003
Foundries	Linotype
Number of weights	1

Arabia Felix

Designer	Judith Sutcliffe
Nationality	US
Date Designed	1991
Foundries	Electric Typographer Monotype
Number of weights	1

ABCDEEGHIIKLMNOPQRSTUVWXYZ
abcdefghijklmnopqrstuvwxyz1234567890
Doctor and saint, and heard great argument

Bousni Carré & Ronde

Designer	Bachir Soussi Chiadmi
Nationality	FR
Date Designed	2003
Foundries	Linotype
Number of weights	1

ABCDEFGHIJKLMNOPQRSTUVWXYZ
abcdefghijklmnopqrstuvwxyz1234567890
About it and about: but evermore

Falafel

Designer	Per Baasch Jørgensen
Nationality	DK
Date Designed	1994-2001
Foundries	FontFont
Number of weights	1

ABCDEFGHIJKLMNOPQRSTUVWXYZ
abcdefghijklmnopqrstuvwxyz1234567890
Came out by the same Door as in I went.

Pide Nashi

Designer	Verena Gerlach
Nationality	DE
Date Designed	1996
Foundries	Linotype
Number of weights	1

ABCDEFGHIJKLMNOPQRSTUVWXYZ
abcdefghijklmnopqrstuvwxyz1234567890
With them the seed of Wisdom did I sow

Kanban

Designer	Ed Bugg
Nationality	UK
Date Designed	1992
Foundries	Linotype ITC
Number of weights	1

ABCDEFGHIJKLMNOPQRSTUVWXYZ

ABCDEFGHIJKLMNOPQRSTUVWXYZ1234567890

JIM JUST QUIT AND PACKED EXTRA BAGS FOR LIZ OWEN.

Ginko

Designer	Paul Pegoraro
Nationality	CA
Date Designed	1994
Foundries	Monotype
Number of weights	1

ABCDEFGHIJKLMNOPQRSTUVWXYZ

ABCDEFGHIJKLMNOPQRSTUVWXYZ1234567890

FREIGHT TO ME SIXTY DOZEN QUART JARS AND TWELVE BLACK PANS.

Aleksei

Designer	Lewis Tsalis
Nationality	AU
Date Designed	1996
Foundries	T-26
Number of weights	1

ABCDEFGHIJKLMNOPQRSTUVWXYZ

abcdefghijklmnopqrstuvwxyz1234567890

Let me see the follies of Pavlovsk.

Xerxes

Designer	Dan X Solo
Nationality	US
Date Designed	1974
Foundries	Monotype Mecanorma
Number of weights	1

ABCDEFGHIJKLMNOPQRSTUVWXYZ

ABCDEFGHIJKLMNOPQRSTUVWXYZ1234567890

AN INSPIRED CALLIGRAPHER CAN CREATE PAGES OF BEAUTY USING STICK INK, QUILL, BRUSH, PICK-AXE, BUZZ SAW, OR EVEN STRAWBERRY JAM.

Morocco

Designer	Michael Parson
Nationality	CH
Date Designed	2002
Foundries	Linotype
Number of weights	1

ABCDEFGHIJKLMNOPQRSTUVWXYZ

αδcδefghijklmnopqrstuvwxyz1234567890

More Greek than Moroccan, I'd have thought.

Bagel

Designer	Per Baasch Jørgensen
Nationality	DK
Date Designed	2001
Foundries	FontFont
Number of weights	1

ABCDEFGHIJKLMNOPQRSTUVWXYZ

abcdefghijklmnopqrstuvwxyz 1234567890

Verily the dark ex-Jew quit Zionism, preferring the cabala.

Simran ITC

Designer	Satwinder Sehmi
Nationality	KE
Date Designed	1997
Foundries	ITC Fontek Linotype Creative Alliance
Number of weights	1

abcdefghijklmnopqrstuvwxyz

abcdefghijklmnopqrstuvwxyz1234567890

Simran means meditation on god.

Linotype Sansara

Designer	Grégoire Poget
Nationality	FR
Date Designed	1999
Foundries	Linotype
Number of weights	1

ABCDEFGHIJKLMNOPQRSTUVWXYZ

abcdefghijklmnopqrstuvwxyz1234567890

sphinx of black quartz judge my vow.

Fusaka

Designer	Michael Want
Nationality	UK
Date Designed	1996
Foundries	Adobe Linotype
Number of weights	1

ABCDEFGHIJKLMNOPQRSTUVWXYZ

ABCDEFGHIJKLMNOPQRSTUVWXYZ1234567890

Jaded reader with fabled roving eye seized by quickened impulse to expand budget.

HaManga Irregular LL

Designer	Alessio Leonardi
Nationality	IT
Date Designed	1994
Foundries	Linotype
Number of weights	1

ABCDEFGHIJKLMNOPQRSTUVWXYZ

ABCDEFGHIJKLMNOPQRSTUVWXYZ

1234567890

The signs are all original Japanese

Manga Steel

Designer	Donald Beekman
Nationality	NL
Date Designed	2001
Foundries	FontFont
Number of weights	8

ABCDEFGHIJKLMNOPQRSTUVWXYZ
ABCDEFGHIJKLMNOPQRSTUVWXYZ1234567890
MANY-WIVED JACK LAUGHS AT PROBES OF SEX QUIZ.

Manga Stone

Designer	Donald Beekman
Nationality	NL
Date Designed	2001
Foundries	FontFont
Number of weights	8

ABCDEFGHIJKLMNOPQRSTUVWXYZ
ABCDEFGHIJKLMNOPQRSTUVWXYZ1234567890
MIX ZAPF WITH VELJOVIC AND GET QUIRKY BEZIERS.

MhaiThaipe

Designer	Marcus Remscheid
Nationality	DE
Date Designed	1996
Foundries	Linotype
Number of weights	1

ABCDEFGHIJKLMNOPQRSTUVWXYZ
abcdefghijklmnopqrstuvwxyz1234567890
The July sun caused a fragment of black pine wax
to ooze on the velvet quilt.

Noni Wan

Designer	Donald Beekman
Nationality	NL
Date Designed	2000
Foundries	FontFont
Number of weights	16

ABCDEFGHIJKLMNOPQRSTUVWXYZ
ABCDEFGHIJKLMNOPQRSTUVWXYZ1234567890
FIVE WINE EXPERTS JOKINGLY QUIZZED SAMPLE CHABLIS.

Clearface

Designer	Morris Fuller Benton
Nationality	US
Date Designed	1908
Foundries	Adobe Monotype URW++
Number of weights	5

ABCDEFGHIJKLMNOPQRSTUVWXYZ
abcdefghijklmnopqrstuvwxyz1234567890
Jimmy and Zack, the police explained, were last seen diving into a field of
buttered quahogs.

Suites

Clearface Gothic

Designer	Morris Fuller Benton
Nationality	US
Date Designed	1908
Foundries	Adobe Monotype URW++
Number of weights	5

ABCDEFGHIJKLMNOPQRSTUVWXYZ

abcdefghijklmnopqrstuvwxyz1234567890

Jimmy and Zack, the police explained, were last seen diving into a field of buttered quahogs.

Lucida Blackletter

Designer	Kris Holmes
Nationality	US
Date Designed	1985
Foundries	Adobe Elsner+Flake Monotype
Number of weights	1

ABCDEFGHIJKLMNOPQRSTUVWXYZ

abcdefghijklmnopqrstuvwxyz1234567890

Many big jackdaws quickly zipped over the fox pen.

Lucida Bright

Designer	Charles Bigelow, Kris Holmes
Nationality	US
Date Designed	1985
Foundries	Adobe Elsner+Flake
Number of weights	4

ABCDEFGHIJKLMNOPQRSTUVWXYZ

abcdefghijklmnopqrstuvwxyz1234567890

But come with old Khayyam, and leave the Lot.

Lucida Calligraphy

Designer	Kris Holmes
Nationality	US
Date Designed	1985
Foundries	Elsner+Flake
Number of weights	1

ABCDEFGHIJKLMNOPQRSTUVWXYZ

abcdefghijklmnopqrstuvwxyz1234567890

The exodus of jazzy pigeons is craved by squeamish walkers.

Lucida Fax

Designer	Charles Bigelow, Kris Holmes
Nationality	US
Date Designed	1985
Foundries	Adobe Elsner+Flake Monotype
Number of weights	5

ABCDEFGHIJKLMNOPQRSTUVWXYZ

abcdefghijklmnopqrstuvwxyz1234567890

Of Kaikobad and Kaikhosru forgot:

Lucida Sans

Designer Charles Bigelow, Kris Holmes
Nationality US
Date Designed 1985
Foundries Adobe Monotype Linotype Microsoft Elsner+Flake
Number of weights 6

ABCDEFGHIJKLMNOPQRSTUVWXYZ
abcdefghijklmnopqrstuvwxyz1234567890
Fred specialized in the job of making very quaint wax toys.

Lucida Typewriter

Designer Charles Bigelow, Kris Holmes
Nationality US
Date Designed 1985
Foundries Adobe Elsner+Flake Monotype
Number of weights 4

ABCDEFGHIJKLMNOPQRSTUVWXYZ
abcdefghijklmnopqrstuvwxyz1234567890
Two hardy boxing kangaroos jet from Sydney to Zanzibar on quicksilver pinions.

Hiroshige Sans

Designer Cynthia Hollandsworth
Nationality US
Date Designed 1986
Foundries Glyph Systems
Number of weights 4

ABCDEFGHIJKLMNOPQRSTUVWXYZ
abcdefghijklmnopqrstuvwxyz1234567890
Jaded zombies acted quaintly but kept driving their oxen forward.

Hiroshige Serif

Designer Cynthia Hollandsworth
Nationality US
Date Designed 1986
Foundries Glyph Systems
Number of weights 4

ABCDEFGHIJKLMNOPQRSTUVWXYZ
abcdefghijklmnopqrstuvwxyz1234567890
Jaded zombies acted quaintly but kept driving their oxen forward.

Stone Informal

Designer Sumner Stone
Nationality US
Date Designed 1987
Foundries Adobe ITC Elsner+Flake Linotype Monotype URW++
Number of weights 6

ABCDEFGHIJKLMNOPQRSTUVWXYZ
abcdefghijklmnopqrstuvwxyz1234567890
Note the single storey a and g, the addition of the serif on A and the removal of the serif on K.

Stone Sans

Designer	Sumner Stone
Nationality	US
Date Designed	1987
Foundries	Adobe ITC
Number of weights	6

ABCDEFGHIJKLMNOPQRSTUVWXYZ
abcdefghijklmnopqrstuvwxyz1234567890
Sphinx of black quartz judge my vow.

Stone Serif

Designer	Sumner Stone
Nationality	US
Date Designed	1987
Foundries	ITC Adobe Elsner+Flake Linotype Monotype URW++
Recut/Digitised by	John Renner
Number of weights	6

ABCDEFGHIJKLMNOPQRSTUVWXYZ
abcdefghijklmnopqrstuvwxyz1234567890
Jim just quit and packed extra bags for Liz Owen.

Rotis Sans Serif

Designer	Otl Aicher
Nationality	DE
Date Designed	1988
Foundries	Monotype
Number of weights	6

ABCDEFGHIJKLMNOPQRSTUVWXYZ
abcdefghijklmnopqrstuvwxyz1234567890
Probably the most popular font of the 1990s.

Rotis Semi Sans

Designer	Otl Aicher
Nationality	DE
Date Designed	1988
Foundries	Monotype Adobe Linotype
Number of weights	6

ABCDEFGHIJKLMNOPQRSTUVWXYZ
abcdefghijklmnopqrstuvwxyz1234567890
Headley Plachta Rolfe – HPR Publicity.

Rotis Semi Serif

Designer	Otl Aicher
Nationality	DE
Date Designed	1988
Foundries	Monotype Adobe Linotype
Number of weights	6

ABCDEFGHIJKLMNOPQRSTUVWXYZ
abcdefghijklmnopqrstuvwxyz1234567890
Named after the designer's home town Rotis über Leutkirch in Bavaria, Germany.

Rotis Serif

Designer	Otl Aicher
Nationality	DE
Date Designed	1988
Foundries	Monotype Adobe Linotype
Number of weights	3

ABCDEFGHIJKLMNOPQRSTUVWXYZ

abcdefghijklmnopqrstuvwxyz1234567890

Probably the most popular font of the 1990s.

Officina Sans

Designer	Erik Spiekermann, Ole Schäfer
Nationality	DE
Date Designed	1990
Foundries	ITC Adobe Linotype
Number of weights	10

ABCDEFGHIJKLMNOPQRSTUVWXYZ

abcdefghijklmnopqrstuvwxyz1234567890

My help squeezed back in again and joined the weavers after six.

Officina Serif

Designer	Erik Spiekermann, Ole Schäfer
Nationality	DE
Date Designed	1990
Foundries	ITC Adobe
Number of weights	10

ABCDEFGHIJKLMNOPQRSTUVWXYZ

abcdefghijklmnopqrstuvwxyz1234567890

A large fawn jumped quickly over white zinc boxes.

Charlotte

Designer	Michael Gills
Nationality	UK
Date Designed	1992
Foundries	Linotype ITC
Number of weights	5

ABCDEFGHIJKLMNOPQRSTUVWXYZ

abcdefghijklmnopqrstuvwxyz1234567890

While waxing parquet decks, jaunty Suez sailors vomit abaft.

Congress

Designer	Adrian Williams
Nationality	UK
Date Designed	1992
Foundries	Elsner+Flake URW++
Number of weights	2

ABCDEFGHIJKLMNOPQRSTUVWXYZ

abcdefghijklmnopqrstuvwxyz1234567890

Verbatim reports were quickly given by Jim Fox to his amazed audience.

Mariposa Sans

Designer	Philip Bouwsma
Nationality	US
Date Designed	1994
Foundries	Monotype
Number of weights	5

ABCDEFGHIJKLMNOPQRSTUVWXYZ
abcdefghijklmnopqrstuvwxyz1234567890
Mariposa is the Spanish for butterfly.

Mariposa Serif

Designer	Philip Bouwsma
Nationality	US
Date Designed	1994
Foundries	Monotype
Number of weights	5

ABCDEFGHIJKLMNOPQRSTUVWXYZ
abcdefghijklmnopqrstuvwxyz1234567890
Mariposa is the Spanish for butterfly.

Alinea Incise

Designer	Thierry Puyfoulhoux
Nationality	FR
Date Designed	1995
Foundries	Presence
Number of weights	6

ABCDEFGHIJKLMNOPQRSTUVWXYZ
abcdefghijklmnopqrstuvwxyz1234567890
Let Rustum lay about him as he will,

Alinea Roman

Designer	Thierry Puyfoulhoux
Nationality	FR
Date Designed	1995
Foundries	Monotype
Number of weights	6

ABCDEFGHIJKLMNOPQRSTUVWXYZ
abcdefghijklmnopqrstuvwxyz1234567890
Two hardy boxing kangaroos jet from Sydney to Zanzibar on quicksilver pinions.

Alinea Sans

Designer	Thierry Puyfoulhoux
Nationality	FR
Date Designed	1995
Foundries	Presence
Number of weights	6

ABCDEFGHIJKLMNOPQRSTUVWXYZ
abcdefghijklmnopqrstuvwxyz1234567890
Perhaps President Clinton's amazing sax skills will be judged quite favourably.

Bradlo

Designer Andrej Krátky
Nationality SK
Date Designed 1995
Foundries FontFont
Number of weights 2

ABCDEFGHIJKLMNOPQRSTUVWXYZ
abcdefghijklmnopqrstuvwxyz1234567890
A Canadian town founded by Slovak emigrants.

Bradlo Slab

Designer Andrej Krátky
Nationality SK
Date Designed 1995
Foundries FontFont
Number of weights 2

ABCDEFGHIJKLMNOPQRSTUVWXYZ
abcdefghijklmnopqrstuvwxyz1234567890
A Canadian town founded by Slovak emigrants.

Corvallis

Designer Philip Bouwsma
Nationality US
Date Designed 1995
Foundries Monotype
Number of weights 2

ABCDEFGHIJKLMNOPQRSTUVWXYZ
abcdefghijklmnopqrstuvwxyz1234567890
A city in Oregon, USA, the name made up from the Latin for 'heart of the valley'.

Corvallis Sans

Designer Philip Bouwsma
Nationality US
Date Designed 1995
Foundries Monotype
Number of weights 2

ABCDEFGHIJKLMNOPQRSTUVWXYZ
abcdefghijklmnopqrstuvwxyz1234567890
A city in Oregon, USA, the name made up from the Latin for 'heart of the valley'.

Humana Serif ITC

Designer Timothy Donaldson
Nationality UK
Date Designed 1995
Foundries ITC Monotype
Number of weights 5

ABCDEFGHIJKLMNOPQRSTUVWXYZ
abcdefghijklmnopqrstuvwxyz1234567890
When we go back to Juarez, Mexico, do we fly over picturesque Arizona?

Humana Sans ITC

Designer	Timothy Donaldson
Nationality	UK
Date Designed	1995
Foundries	ITC
Number of weights	5

ABCDEFGHIJKLMNOPQRSTUVWXYZ
abcdefghijklmnopqrstuvwxyz1234567890
Quick wafting zephyrs vex bold Jim.

Humana Script ITC

Designer	Timothy Donaldson
Nationality	UK
Date Designed	1995
Foundries	ITC Monotype
Number of weights	5

ABCDEFGHIJKLMNOPQRSTUVWXYZ
abcdefghijklmnopqrstuvwxyz1234567890
Questions of a zealous nature have become by degrees petty waxen jokes.

Eaglefeather Formal

Designer	David Siegel
Nationality	US
Date Designed	1996
Foundries	CA Partners
Number of weights	7

ABCDEFGHIJKLMNOPQR/TUVWXYZ
abcdefghijklmnopqrstuvwxyz1234567890
Xavier, a wildly informal court jester, kept calling Queen Elizabeth 'Betty.'

Eaglefeather Informal

Designer	David Siegel
Nationality	US
Date Designed	1996
Foundries	CA Partners
Number of weights	7

ABCDEFGHIJKLMNOPQR/TUVWXYZ
abcdefghijklmnopqrstuvwxyz1234567890
Sexy qua lijf, doch bang voor het zwempak.

Info Text

Designer	Erik Spiekermann, Ole Schäfer
Nationality	DE
Date Designed	1996
Foundries	FontFont
Number of weights	112

ABCDEFGHIJKLMNOPQRSTUVWXYZ
abcdefghijklmnopqrstuvwxyz1234567890
Mr. Jock, TV quiz Ph.D., bags few lynx.

Info

Designer	Erik Spiekermann, Ole Schäfer
Nationality	DE
Date Designed	1996
Foundries	FontFont
Number of weights	112

ABCDEFGHIJKLMNOPQRSTUVWXYZ

abcdefghijklmnopqrstuvwxyz1234567890

Playing jazz vibe chords quickly excites my wife.

Linex Sweet

Designer	Albert Boton
Nationality	FR
Date Designed	1996
Foundries	Monotype
Number of weights	4

ABCDEFGHIJKLMNOPQRSTUVWXYZ

abcdefghijklmnopqrstuvwxyz1234567890

Sixty zippers were quickly picked from the woven jute bag.

Linex

Designer	Albert Boton
Nationality	FR
Date Designed	1996
Foundries	Monotype
Number of weights	4

ABCDEFGHIJKLMNOPQRSTUVWXYZ

abcdefghijklmnopqrstuvwxyz1234567890

Mr. Jock, TV quiz Ph.D., bags few lynx.

Quadraat

Designer	Fred Smeijers
Nationality	NL
Date Designed	1997
Foundries	FontFont
Number of weights	30

ABCDEFGHIJKLMNOPQRSTUVWXYZ

abcdefghijklmnopqrstuvwxyz1234567890

Xavier, a wildly informal court jester, kept calling Queen Elizabeth 'Betty.'

Quadraat Sans

Designer	Fred Smeijers
Nationality	NL
Date Designed	1997
Foundries	FontFont
Number of weights	30

ABCDEFGHIJKLMNOPQRSTUVWXYZ

abcdefghijklmnopqrstuvwxyz1234567890

How razorback-jumping frogs can level six piqued gymnasts!

Planet Serif

Designer	Mat Planet
Nationality	US
Date Designed	1998
Foundries	Creative Alliance
Number of weights	2

ΛBCDEFGHIJKLMNOPQRSTUVⲰXYZ
ΛbcdefghijkLmnopqrstuvφxyƬ1234567890
PLaying jaƬƬ vibe chords quickly excites my φife.

Planet Sans Book

Designer	Mat Planet
Nationality	US
Date Designed	1998
Foundries	Monotype
Number of weights	4

ΛBCDEF GHIJKLMNOPQRSTUVⲰXYZ
ΛbcdefghijklmnopqrstuvwxyƬ1234567890
Ƨexy φuΛ Lijf, doch bΛ∩g voor het ƬwempΛk.

Planet Informal

Designer	Mat Planet
Nationality	US
Date Designed	1998
Foundries	Monotype
Number of weights	2

ΛBCDEF GHIJKLMNOPQRSTUVⲰXYZ
ΛbcdefghijklmnopqrstuvwxyƬ1234567890
Six crΛƬy kings vowed to ΛboLish my quite pitifʊL jousts.

Linotype Authentic Sans

Designer	Karin Huschka
Nationality	DE
Date Designed	1999
Foundries	Linotype
Number of weights	8

ABCDEFGHIJKLMNOPQRSTUVWXYZ
abcdefghijklmnopqrstuvwxyz1234567890
How vexing a fumble to drop a jolly zucchini in
the quicksand.

Linotype Authentic Serif

Designer	Karin Huschka
Nationality	DE
Date Designed	1999
Foundries	Linotype
Number of weights	8

ABCDEFGHIJKLMNOPQRSTUVWXYZ
abcdefghijklmnopqrstuvwxyz1234567890
Or Hatim Tai cry Supper — heed them not.

Linotype Authentic Small Serif

Designer	Karin Huschka
Nationality	DE
Date Designed	1999
Foundries	Linotype
Number of weights	8

ABCDEFGHIJKLMNOPQRSTUVWXYZ

abcdefghijklmnopqrstuvwxyz1234567890

With me along some Strip of Herbage strown

Prater Block

Designer	Steffen Sauerteig, Henning Wagenbreth
Nationality	DE
Date Designed	2000
Foundries	FontFont
Number of weights	8

ABCDEFGHIJKLMNOPQRSTUVWXYZ

abcdefghijklmnopqrstuvwxyz1234567890

Waltz, nymph, for quick jigs vex Bud.

Prater Sans

Designer	Steffen Sauerteig, Henning Wagenbreth
Nationality	DE
Date Designed	2000
Foundries	FontFont
Number of weights	8

ABCDEFGHIJKLMNOPQRSTUVWXYZ

abcdefghijklmnopqrstuvwxyz1234567890

How vexing a fumble to drop a jolly zucchini in the quicksand.

Prater Serif

Designer	Steffen Sauerteig, Henning Wagenbreth
Nationality	DE
Date Designed	2000
Foundries	FontFont
Number of weights	8

ABCDEFGHIJKLMNOPQRSTUVWXYZ

abcdefghijklmnopqrstuvwxyz1234567890

Xavier, a wildly informal court jester, kept calling Queen Elizabeth 'Betty.'

Seria

Designer	Martin Majoor
Nationality	NL
Date Designed	2000
Foundries	FontFont
Number of weights	20

ABCDEFGHIJKLMNOPQRSTUVWXYZ

abcdefghijklmnopqrstuvwxyz1234567890

How razorback-jumping frogs can level six piqued gymnasts!

Seria Sans

Designer	Martin Majoor
Nationality	NL
Date Designed	2000
Foundries	FontFont
Number of weights	20

ABCDEFGHIJKLMNOPQRSTUVWXYZ

abcdefghijklmnopqrstuvwxyz1234567890

How vexing a fumble to drop a jolly zucchini in the quicksand.

Zine Sans

Designer	Ole Schäfer
Nationality	DE
Date Designed	2001
Foundries	FontFont
Number of weights	27

ABCDEFGHIJKLMNOPQRSTUVWXYZ

abcdefghijklmnopqrstuvwxyz1234567890

Zwei Boxkämpfer jagen Eva quer durch Sylt.

Zine Serif

Designer	Ole Schäfer
Nationality	DE
Date Designed	2001
Foundries	FontFont
Number of weights	27

ABCDEFGHIJKLMNOPQRSTUVWXYZ

abcdefghijklmnopqrstuvwxyz1234567890

Zwei Boxkämpfer jagen Eva quer durch Sylt.

Zine Slab

Designer	Ole Schäfer
Nationality	DE
Date Designed	2001
Foundries	FontFont
Number of weights	27

ABCDEFGHIJKLMNOPQRSTUVWXYZ

abcdefghijklmnopqrstuvwxyz1234567890

May Jo equal the fine record by solving six puzzles a week?

Compatil Exquisit

Designer	Olaf Leu
Nationality	DE
Date Designed	2002
Foundries	Linotype
Number of weights	4

ABCDEFGHIJKLMNOPQRSTUVWXYZ

abcdefghijklmnopqrstuvwxyz1234567890

None of the Compatil family

Compatil Fact

Designer Olaf Leu
Nationality DE
Date Designed 2002
Foundries Linotype
Number of weights 4

ABCDEFGHIJKLMNOPQRSTUVWXYZ
abcdefghijklmnopqrstuvwxyz1234567890
has an italic font because

Compatil Letter

Designer Olaf Leu
Nationality DE
Date Designed 2002
Foundries Linotype
Number of weights 4

ABCDEFGHIJKLMNOPQRSTUVWXYZ
abcdefghijklmnopqrstuvwxyz1234567890
Professor Olaf Leu, the creator of the concept,

Compatil Text

Designer Olaf Leu
Nationality DE
Date Designed 2002
Foundries Linotype
Number of weights 4

ABCDEFGHIJKLMNOPQRSTUVWXYZ
abcdefghijklmnopqrstuvwxyz1234567890
doesn't consider italic to be serious enough.

Bulletin Typewriter

Designer ATF
Nationality US
Date Designed 1925
Foundries ATF
Number of weights 1

ABCDEFGHIJKLMNOPQRSTUVWXYZ
abcdefghijklmnopqrstuvwxyz1234567890
Zwei Boxkämpfer jagen Eva quer durch Sylt.

Prestige Elite

Designer Clayton Smith
Nationality US
Date Designed 1953
Foundries Linotype
Number of weights 4

ABCDEFGHIJKLMNOPQRSTUVWXYZ
abcdefghijklmnopqrstuvwxyz1234567890
Exquisite farm wench gives body jolt to prize
stinker.

Monospace

Courier

Designer	Howard Kettler
Nationality	US
Date Designed	1956
Foundries	Linotype Adobe URW++
Number of weights	4

ABCDEFGHIJKLMNOPQRSTUVWXYZ

abcdefghijklmnopqrstuvwxyz1234567890

That just divides the desert from the sown.

Letter Gothic

Designer	Roger Robertson
Nationality	US
Date Designed	1956
Foundries	Monotype Adobe Bitstream Linotype URW++ FontFont
Recut/Digitised by	Albert Pinggera
Number of weights	1

ABCDEFGHIJKLMNOPQRSTUVWXYZ

abcdefghijklmnopqrstuvwxyz1234567890

Playing jazz vibe chords quickly excites my wife.

Letter Gothic Slang

Designer	Susanna Dulkinys
Nationality	US
Date Designed	1999
Foundries	FontFont
Number of weights	1

Δẞ©ÐƩFGHIJKŁMNØÞQ®$TUVWXYZ

αþcdɛƒghijk∠ʍn✳þqrstuvw×yz12ʒ4567890◊

Thɛ risquɛ g✳wn ʍɑrkɛd ɑ þrazɛn ɛxþ✳surɛ ✳ƒ vɛry juicy ƒ∠ɛsh.

Olympia Light

Designer	Hell Design Studio
Nationality	DE
Date Designed	1960
Foundries	Linotype Elsner
Number of weights	1

ABCDEFGHIJKLMNOPQRSTUVWXYZ

abcdefghijklmnopqrstuvwxyz1234567890

Puzzled women bequeath jerks very exotic gifts.

Orator

Designer	Leonard H. D. Smit
Nationality	NL
Date Designed	1962
Foundries	Amsterdam
Recut/Digitised by	John Scheppler
Number of weights	2

ABCDEFGHIJKLMNOPQRSTUVWXYZ

ABCDEFGHIJKLMNOPQRSTUVWXYZ1234567890

LAZY MOVERS QUIT HARD-PACKING OF PAPIER-MACHÉ JEWELLERY BOXES.

Lucida Sans Typewriter

Designer	Charles Bigelow, Kris Holmes
Nationality	US
Date Designed	1985
Foundries	Adobe
Number of weights	4

ABCDEFGHIJKLMNOPQRSTUVWXYZ
abcdefghijklmnopqrstuvwxyz1234567890
Fred specialized in the job of making very quaint wax toys.

Monaco

Designer	Carol Kulik
Nationality	US
Date Designed	1985
Foundries	Apple
Number of weights	1

ABCDEFGHIJKLMNOPQRSTUVWXYZ
abcdefghijklmnopqrstuvwxyz1234567890
Just keep examining every low bid quoted for zinc etchings.

Trixie

Designer	Erik van Blokland
Nationality	NL
Date Designed	1991
Foundries	FontFont
Number of weights	1

ABCDEFGHIJKLMNOPQRSTUVWXYZ
abcdefghijklmnopqrstuvwxyz1234567890
Quick wafting zephyrs vex bold Jim.

Lucida Typewriter

Designer	Charles Bigelow, Kris Holmes
Nationality	US
Date Designed	1992
Foundries	Adobe Elsner+Flake Monotype
Number of weights	4

ABCDEFGHIJKLMNOPQRSTUVWXYZ
abcdefghijklmnopqrstuvwxyz1234567890
Two hardy boxing kangaroos jet from Sydney to Zanzibar on quicksilver pinions.

Andale Mono

Designer	Steve Matteson
Nationality	US
Date Designed	1993
Foundries	Microsoft
Number of weights	1

ABCDEFGHIJKLMNOPQRSTUVWXYZ
abcdefghijklmnopqrstuvwxyz1234567890
We promptly judged antique ivory buckles for the next prize.

Isonorm

Designer Robert Kirchner
Nationality DE
Date Designed 1993
Foundries FontFont
Number of weights 1

ABCDEFGHIJKLMNOPQRSTUVWXYZ

abcdefghijklmnopqrstuvwxyz1234567890

Lazy movers quit hard-packing of papier-maché jewellery boxes.

Chandler 42

Designer Steve Mehallo
Nationality US
Date Designed 1994
Foundries Monotype
Number of weights 8

ABCDEFGHIJKLMNOPQRSTUVWXYZ

abcdefghijklmnopqrstuvwxyz1234567890

Moi, je veux quinze clubs a golf et du whisky pur.

Dynamoe

Designer Just van Rossum
Nationality NL
Date Designed 1995
Foundries FontFont
Number of weights 1

ABCDEFGHIJKLMNOPQRSTUVWXYZ

ABCDEFGHIJKLMNOPQRSTUVWXYZ1234567890

ZWEEDSE EX-VIP, BEHOORLIJK GEK OP QUANTUMFYSICA.

Magda

Designer Cornel Windlin
Nationality CH
Date Designed 1995
Foundries FontFont
Number of weights 1

ABCDEFGHIJKLMNOPQRSTUVWXYZ

abcdefghijklmnopqrstuvwxyz1234567890

A large fawn jumped quickly over white zinc boxes.

Hardcase

Designer Dmitri Lavrow
Nationality DE
Date Designed 1996
Foundries FontFont
Number of weights 1

ABCDEFGHIJKLMNOPQRSTUVWXYZ

abcdefghijklmnopqrstuvwxyz1234567890

Waltz, nymph, for quick jigs vex Bud.

Briem Mono

Designer	Gunnlaugur S E Briem
Nationality	IS
Date Designed	1997
Foundries	Monotype
Number of weights	12

ABCDEFGHIJKLMNOPQRSTUVWXYZ
abcdefghijklmnopqrstuvwxyz1234567890
Big July earthquakes confound zany
experimental vow.

Quadraat Sans Monospaced

Designer	Fred Smeijers
Nationality	NL
Date Designed	1997
Foundries	FontFont
Number of weights	1

ABCDEFGHIJKLMNOPQRSTUVWXYZ
abcdefghijklmnopqrstuvwxyz1234567890
Sexy qua lijf, doch bang voor het zwempak.

Unotype

Designer	Bo Berndal
Nationality	SE
Date Designed	1997
Foundries	Monotype
Number of weights	1

ABCDEFGHIJKLMNOPQRSTUVWXYZ
abcdefghijklmnopqrstuvwxyz1234567890
Lazy movers quit hard-packing of papier-maché
jewellery boxes.

Elementa

Designer	Mindaugas Strockis
Nationality	LT
Date Designed	1998
Foundries	FontFont
Number of weights	1

ABCDEFGHIJKLMNOPQRSTUVWXYZ
abcdefghijklmnopqrstuvwxyz1234567890
Astronaut Quincy B. Zack defies gravity with six
jet fuel pumps.

Koko

Designer	Kai Zimmerman
Nationality	DE
Date Designed	1998
Foundries	FontFont
Number of weights	1

ABCDEFGHIJKLMNOPQRSTUVWXYZ
abcdefghijklmnopqrstuvwxyz1234567890
We have just quoted on nine dozen boxes of
gray lamp wicks.

Fago Monospaced

Designer	Ole Schaefer
Nationality	DE
Date Designed	1999
Foundries	FontFont
Number of weights	1

ABCDEFGHIJKLMNOPQRSTUVWXYZ
abcdefghijklmnopqrstuvwxyz1234567890
Jeb quickly drove a few extra miles on the glazed pavement.

Linotype Typo American

Designer	Mark Stanczyk
Nationality	US
Date Designed	1999
Foundries	Linotype
Number of weights	1

ABCDEFGHIJKLMNOPQRSTUVWXYZ
abcdefghijklmnopqrstuvwxyzI234567890
Mr. Jock, TV quiz Ph.D., bags few lynx.

Eureka Mono

Designer	Peter Bilak
Nationality	SK
Date Designed	2001
Foundries	FontFont
Number of weights	1

ABCDEFGHIJKLMNOPQRSTUVWXYZ
abcdefghijklmnopqrstuvwxyz1234567890
Verily the dark ex-Jew quit Zionism, preferring the cabala.

Tronic

Designer	Hyun Cho, Sung Min Choi
Nationality	CN
Date Designed	2003
Foundries	FontFont
Number of weights	1

ABCDEFGHIJKLMNOPQRSTUVWXYZ
abcdefghijklmnopqrstuvwxyz
1234567890
While waxing parquet decks, jaunty.

American Typewriter

Designer	Joel Kadan, Tony Stan
Nationality	US
Date Designed	1974
Foundries	ITC Bitstream
Number of weights	12

ABCDEFGHIJKLMNOPQRSTUVWXYZ
abcdefghijklmnopqrstuvwxyz1234567890
The next three fonts are NOT monospaced, although they are typewriter based.

Typewriter

Designer	URW++
Nationality	DE
Date Designed	1990
Foundries	URW++ P22
Number of weights	1

ABCDEFGHIJKLMNOPQRSTUVWXYZ

abcdefghijklmnopqrstuvwxyz1234567890

Not monospaced.

Static

Designer	Fontek
Nationality	US
Date Designed	1996
Foundries	Monotype ITC
Number of weights	1

ABCDEFGHIJKLMNOPQRSTUVWXYZ

ABCDEFGHIJKLMNOPQRSTUVWXYZ1234567890

DISPLAY TYPEWRITER STYLE.

Adagio

Designer	Albert J Kim
Nationality	US
Date Designed	1994
Foundries	Reference Type Foundry
Number of weights	2

ABCDEFGHIJKLMNOPQRSTUVWXYZ

abcdefghijklmnopqrstuvwxyz1234567890

A slow movement in music.

Handwriter

Designer	Alessio Leonardi
Nationality	IT
Date Designed	1997
Foundries	FontFont
Number of weights	3

ABCDEFGHIJKLMNOPQRSTUVWXYZ

abcdefghijklmnopqrstuvwxyz1234567890

Drawn by hand, but with fixed width, a sort of portable typewriter for the hand.

Bank Script

Designer	James West
Nationality	UK
Date Designed	1895
Foundries	URW++
Number of weights	1

ABCDEFGHIJKLMNOPQRSTUVWXYZ

abcdefghijklmnopqrstuvwxyz 1234567890

Back in my quaint garden jaunty zinnias vie with flaunting phlox.

Sackers English Script

Designer	Monotype
Nationality	UK
Date Designed	1900
Foundries	Monotype
Number of weights	2

ABCDEFGHIJKLMNOPQRSTUVWXYZ
abcdefghijklmnopqrstuvwxyz 1234567890
The quick brown fox jumps over the lazy dog.

Sackers Italian Script

Designer	Monotype
Nationality	UK
Date Designed	1900
Foundries	Monotype
Number of weights	2

ABCDEFGHIJKLMNOPQRSTUVWXYZ
abcdefghijklmnopqrstuvwxyz 1234567890
When we go back to Juarez, Mexico, do we fly over picturesque Arizona?

Kuenstler Script

Designer	Hans Bohn
Nationality	DE
Date Designed	1902
Foundries	Linotype Stempel URW++ Adobe Bitstream
Number of weights	3

ABCDEFGHIJKLMNOPQRSTUVWXYZ
abcdefghijklmnopqrstuvwxyz1234567890
German for Artist.

Commercial Script

Designer	Morris Fuller Benton
Nationality	US
Date Designed	1908
Foundries	Bitstream URW++
Number of weights	1

ABCDEFGHIJKLMNOPQRSTUVWXYZ
abcdefghijklmnopqrstuvwxyz1234567890
No kidding, Lorenzo called off his trip to visit Mexico City just because they told him the conquistadores were extinct.

Old Fashion Script

Designer	Monotype
Nationality	UK
Date Designed	1920
Foundries	Monotype
Number of weights	1

ABCDEFGHIJKLMNOPQRSTUVWXYZ
abcdefghijklmnopqrstuvwxyz 1234567890
King Alexander was partly overcome just after quizzing Diogenes in his tub.

Palace Script

Designer Monotype

Nationality UK

Date Designed 1923

Foundries Stephenson Blake Monotype Adobe

Number of weights 2

ABCDEFGHIJKLMNOPQRSTUVWXYZ

abcdefghijklmnopqrstuvwxyz1234567890

Questions of a zealous nature have become by degrees petty waxen jokes.

Original Script

Designer Monotype

Nationality UK

Date Designed 1930

Foundries Monotype

Number of weights 1

ABCDEFGHIJKLMNOPQRSTUVWXYZ

abcdefghijklmnopqrstuvwxyz1234567890

Murky haze enveloped a city as jarring quakes broke forty-six windows.

Florentine Script II

Designer R Hunter Middleton

Nationality US

Date Designed 1958

Foundries Monotype

Number of weights 1

ABCDEFGHI JKLMNOPQRSTUVWXYZ

abcdefghijklmnopqrstuvwxyz1234567890

The sex life of the woodchuck is a provocative question for most vertebrate zoology majors.

Flemish Script

Designer Monotype

Nationality BE

Date Designed 1960

Foundries Photon Bitstream Monotype

Number of weights 1

ABCDEFGHI JKLMNOPQRSTUVWXYZ

abcdefghijklmnopqrstuvwxyz1234567890

For only €49, jolly housewives made inexpensive meals using quick-frozen vegetables.

Englische Schreibschrift

Designer H Berthold

Nationality DE

Date Designed 1972

Foundries Berthold URW++

Number of weights 4

ABCDEFGHIJKLMNOPQRSTUVWXYZ

abcdefghijklmnopqrstuvwxyz1234567890

German for 'English Handwriting'

Shelley Script

Designer	Matthew Carter
Nationality	UK
Date Designed	1972
Foundries	Linotype Adobe Bitstream Monotype URW++
Number of weights	3

ABCDEFGHIJKLMNOPQRSTUVWXYZ

abcdefghijklmnopqrstuvwxyz1234567890

Percy Bysshe Shelley was an English romantic poet of the early C19.

Boulevard

Designer	Günther Herhard Lange
Nationality	DE
Date Designed	1955
Foundries	Berthold Adobe
Number of weights	1

ABCDEFGHIJKLMNOPQRSTU-VWXYZ

abcdefghijklmnopqrstuvwxyz1234567890

No kidding, Lorenzo called off his trip to visit Mexico City just because.

Helinda Rook

Designer	Monotype
Nationality	NL
Date Designed	1980
Foundries	Monotype
Number of weights	1

ABCDEFGHIJKLMNOPRSTUVWXYZ

abcdefghijklmnopqrstuvwxyz1234567890

Was there a quorum of able whizzkids gravely exciting the jaded fish at AType?

Young Baroque

Designer	Doyald Young
Nationality	UK
Date Designed	1984
Foundries	Letraset Monotype ITC
Number of weights	1

ABCDEFGHIJKLMNOPQRSTUVWXYZ

abcdefghijklmnopqrstuvwxyz1234567890

Six big juicy steaks sizzled in a pan as five workmen left the quarry.

AT Citadel Script

Designer	anon
Nationality	UK
Date Designed	1980
Foundries	CA Partners
Number of weights	1

ABCDEFGHIJKLMNOPQRSTUVWXYZ

abcdefghijklmnopqrstuvwxyz1234567890

Jelly-like above the high wire, six quaking pachyderms kept the climax of the extravaganza in a dazzling state of flux.

Edwardian Script

Designer	Ed Benguiat
Nationality	US
Date Designed	1994
Foundries	ITC Monotype
Number of weights	2

ABCDEFGHIJKLMNOPQRSTUVWXYZ

abcdefghijklmnopqrstuvwxyz 1234567890

Jimmy and Zack, the police explained, were last seen diving into a field of buttered quahogs.

Adine Kirnberg

Designer	David Rakowski
Nationality	US
Date Designed	1992
Foundries	Precision
Number of weights	1

ABCDEFGHIJKLMNOPQRSTUVWXYZ

abcdefghijklmnopqrstuvwxyz1234567890

Forsaking monastic tradition, twelve jovial friars gave up their vocation for a questionable existence on the flying trapeze.

Aristocrat

Designer	Donald Stevens
Nationality	UK
Date Designed	1978
Foundries	Linotype ITC
Number of weights	1

ABCDEFGHIJKLMNOPQRSTUVWXYZ

abcdefghijklmnopqrstuvwxyz1234567890

An inspired calligrapher can create pages of beauty using stick ink, quill, brush, pick-axe, buzz saw, or even strawberry jam.

Balmoral

Designer	Martin Wait
Nationality	UK
Date Designed	1978
Foundries	Martin Wait Type Linotype
Number of weights	1

ABCDEFGHIJKLMNOPQRSTUVWXYZ

abcdefghijklmnopqrstuvwxyz1234567890

A castle in Scotland owned by the Queen

Bordeaux Script

Designer	David Quay
Nationality	UK
Date Designed	1987-1990
Foundries	ITC
Number of weights	1

ABCDEFGHIJKLMNOPQRSTUVWXYZ

abcdefghijklmnopqrstuvwxyz1234567890

William Jex quickly caught five dozen Conservatives.

Gravura

Designer	Phill Grimshaw
Nationality	UK
Date Designed	1995
Foundries	Letraset Linotype ITC
Number of weights	1

ABCDEFGHIJKLMNOPQRSTUVWXYZ
abcdefghijklmnopqrstuvwxyz1234567890
Ebenezer unexpectedly bagged two tranquil aardvarks with his jiffy vacuum cleaner.

Agfa Waddy 124

Designer	Aiko & Hideaki Wada
Nationality	JP
Date Designed	1997
Foundries	Monotype
Number of weights	1

ABCDEFGHIJKLMNOPQRSTUVWXYZ
abcdefghijklmnopqrstuvwxyz1234567890
Will Major Douglas be expected to take this true-false quiz very soon?

Liberty

Designer	W T Sniffin
Nationality	US
Date Designed	1927
Foundries	ATF CA Partners
Number of weights	1

ABCDEFGHIJKLMNOPQRSTUVWXYZ
abcdefghijklmnopqrstuvwxyz1234567890
Two hardy boxing kangaroos jet from Sydney to Zanzibar on quicksilver pinions.

Nuptial Script

Designer	Edwin Shaar
Nationality	US
Date Designed	1952
Foundries	Bitstream Adobe
Number of weights	1

ABCDEFGHIJKLMNOPQRSTUVWXYZ
abcdefghijklmnopqrstuvwxyz1234567890
How vexing a fumble to drop a jolly zucchini in the quicksand.

Carl Beck

Designer	Bo Berndal
Nationality	SE
Date Designed	1992
Foundries	Monotype
Number of weights	1

ABCDEFGHIJKLMNOPQRSTUVWXYZ
abcdefghijklmnopqrstuvwxyz1234567890
William said that everything about his jacket was in quite good condition except for the zipper.

Dorchester Script

Designer	Monotype
Nationality	UK
Date Designed	1938
Foundries	Monotype
Number of weights	1

ABCDEFGHIJKLMNOPQRSTUVWXYZ

abcdefghijklmnopqrstuvwxyz1234567890

A market town in Dorset, England and a posh hotel in London.

Marnie

Designer	Gérard Mariscalchi
Nationality	CA
Date Designed	1992
Foundries	CA Exclusives
Number of weights	1

ABCDEFGHIJKLMNOPQRSTUVWXYZ

abcdefghijklmnopqrstuvwxyz1234567890

The July sun caused a fragment of black pine wax to ooze on the velvet quilt.

Savoye

Designer	Alan Meeks
Nationality	UK
Date Designed	1992
Foundries	Letraset ITC
Number of weights	1

ABCDEFGHIJKLMNOPQRSTUVWXYZ

abcdefghijklmnopqrstuvwxyz1234567890

A mad boxer shot a quick, gloved jab to the jaw of his dizzy opponent.

Toots

Designer	Gérard Mariscalchi
Nationality	CA
Date Designed	1997
Foundries	CA Exclusives
Number of weights	2

ABCDEFGHIJKLMNOPQRSTUVWXYZ

abcdefghijklmnopqrstuvwxyz1234567890

Based on the calligraphy of Villu Toots.

Hogarth Script

Designer	Harald Brödel
Nationality	DE
Date Designed	1910
Foundries	URW++
Number of weights	1

ABCDEFGHIJKLMNOPQRSTUVWXYZ

abcdefghijklmnopqrstuvwxyz1234567890

Hogarth was a renowned 18th century English artist and cartoonist.

Snell Roundhand

Designer	Matthew Carter
Nationality	UK
Date Designed	1966
Foundries	Linofilm Adobe Monotype Linotype
Number of weights	3

ABCDEFGHIJKLMNOPQRSTUVWXYZ
abcdefghijklmnopqrstuvwxyz1234567890
Named for the C18 English writing master.

Inscription

Designer	Alan Meeks
Nationality	UK
Date Designed	1983
Foundries	Letraset Monotype ITC
Number of weights	1

ABCDEFGHIJKLMNOPQRSTUVWXYZ
abcdefghijklmnopqrstuvwxyz1234567890
Perhaps President Clinton's amazing sax skills will be judged quite favourably.

Oberon

Designer	Phill Grimshaw
Nationality	UK
Date Designed	1986
Foundries	Monotype ITC
Number of weights	1

ABCDEFGHIJKLMNOPQRSTUVWXYZ
abcdefghijklmnopqrstuvwxyz1234567890
About sixty codfish eggs will make a quarter pound of very fizzy jelly.

Isabella

Designer	Herman Ihlenburg
Nationality	DE
Date Designed	1892
Foundries	AGP Adobe
Number of weights	1

ABCDEFGHIJKLMNOPQRSTUVWXYZ
abcdefghijklmnopqrstuvwxyz1234567890
Quick zephyrs blow, vexing daft Jim.

French Script

Designer	William Schraubstädter
Nationality	DE
Date Designed	1905
Foundries	CA Partners
Number of weights	1

ABCDEFGHIJKLMNOPQRSTUVWXYZ
abcdefghijklmnopqrstuvwxyz1234567890
Portez ce vieux whisky au juge blond qui fume.

Calligraphic

LinoScript

Designer Morris Fuller Benton
Nationality US
Date Designed 1905
Foundries Linotype Monotype Adobe
Number of weights 1

ABCDEFGHIJKLMNOPQRSTUVWXYZ

abcdefghijklmnopqrstuvwxyz1234567890

How razorback-jumping frogs can level six piqued gymnasts!

Riviera Script

Designer Morris Fuller Benton
Nationality US
Date Designed 1905
Foundries CA Partners
Number of weights 1

ABCDEFGHIJKLMNOPQRSTUVWXYZ

abcdefghijklmnopqrstuvwxyz1234567890

The vixen jumped quickly on her foe barking with zeal.

Phyllis

Designer H Wieynck
Nationality DE
Date Designed 1911
Foundries Bauer
Number of weights 3

ABCDEFGHIJKLMNOPQRSTUVWXYZ

abcdefghijklmnopqrstuvwxyz1234567890

Grumpy wizards make toxic brew for the evil Queen and Jack.

Civilité

Designer Louis Ferrand
Nationality FR
Date Designed 1922
Foundries ATF Monotype Granjon
Number of weights 1

ABCDEFGHIJKLMNOPQRSTUVWXYZ

abcdefghijklmnopqrstuvwxyz1234567890

King Alexander was partly overcome just after quizzing Diogenes in his tub.

Redonda

Designer Gerard Mariscalchi
Nationality CA
Date Designed 1998
Foundries ITC
Number of weights 2

ABCDEFGHIJKLMNOPQRSTUVWXYZ

abcdefghijklmnopqrstuvwxyz1234567890

The Kingdom of Redonda is a lump of rock off the coast of Antigua.

Park Avenue

Designer	Robert E Smith
Nationality	US
Date Designed	1933
Foundries	ATF Bitstream URW
Number of weights	1

ABCDEFGHIJKLMNOPQRSTUVWXYZ

abcdefghijklmnopqrstuvwxyz1234567890

Freight to me sixty dozen quart jars and twelve black pans.

Fling

Designer	Michael Gills
Nationality	UK
Date Designed	1991
Foundries	Letraset Monotype ITC
Number of weights	1

ABCDEFGHIJKLMNOPQRSTUVWXYZ

abcdefghijklmnopqrstuvwxyz1234567890

Jail zesty vixen who grabbed pay from quack.

Coronet

Designer	R Hunter Middleton
Nationality	US
Date Designed	1937
Foundries	Ludlow URW++
Recut/Digitised by	Steve Jackaman
Number of weights	2

ABCDEFGHIJKLMNOPQRSTUVWXYZ

abcdefghijklmnopqrstuvwxyz1234567890

The sex life of the woodchuck is a provocative question for most vertebrate zoology majors.

Gavotte

Designer	Rudo Spemann
Nationality	DE
Date Designed	1940
Foundries	Klingspor Linotype
Number of weights	1

ABCDEFGHIJKLMNOPQRSTUVWXYZ

abcdefghijklmnopqrstuvwxyz1234567890

Five big quacking zephyrs jolt my wax bed.

Mahogany Script

Designer	E J Klumpp
Nationality	US
Date Designed	1956
Foundries	Monotype
Number of weights	1

ABCDEFGHIJKLMNOPQRSTUVWXYZ

abcdefghijklmnopqrstuvwxyz1234567890

Mahogany is a very hard, reddish brown wood, beautifully veined, which polishes well.

Bible Script

Designer Richard Bradley
Nationality UK
Date Designed 1979
Foundries Letraset
Number of weights 2

ABCDEFGHIJKLMNOPQRSTUVWXYZ
abcdefghijklmnopqrstuvwxyz1234567890
Jews, Turks, Infidels and Heretics!

AT Basilica

Designer anon
Nationality UK
Date Designed 1980
Foundries Monotype
Number of weights 1

ABCDEFGHIJKLMNOPQRSTUVWXYZ
abcdefghijklmnopqrstuvwxyz1234567890
Quick zephyrs blow, vexing daft Jim.

Hadfield

Designer Martin Wait
Nationality UK
Date Designed 1980
Foundries Letraset Linotype ITC
Elsner+Flake URW
Number of weights 1

ABCDEFGHIJKLMNOPQRSTUVWXYZ
abcdefghijklmnopqrstuvwxyz1234567890
West quickly gave Bert handsome prizes for six juicy plums.

Cancellaresca Script

Designer Alan Meeks
Nationality UK
Date Designed 1982
Foundries Letraset Linotype ITC
Number of weights 1

ABCDEFGHIJKLMNOPQRSTUVWXYZ
abcdefghijklmnopqrstuvwxyz1234567890
Cancellaresca is the Italian for Chancery, where scribes with elegant handwriting copied manuscripts before the invention of moveable type

Isadora

Designer Kris Holmes
Nationality US
Date Designed 1985
Foundries ITC Linotype Adobe
Elsner+Flake Franklin Monotype URW++
Number of weights 2

ABCDEFGHIJKLMNOPQRSTUVWXYZ
abcdefghijklmnopqrstuvwxyz1234567890
How quickly daft jumping zebras vex.

Papyrus

Designer	Chris Costello
Nationality	US
Date Designed	1983
Foundries	Letraset Elsner+Flake ITC
Number of weights	2

ABCDEFGHIJKLMNOPQRSTUVWXYZ
abcdefghijklmnopqrstuvwxyz1234567890
Where name of Slave and Sultan scarce is known,

Pelican

Designer	Arthur Baker
Nationality	US
Date Designed	1989
Foundries	Adobe Linotype
Number of weights	1

ABCDEFGHIJKLMNOPQRSTUVWXYZ
abcdefghijklmnopqrstuvwxyz1234567890
A curious bird is the pelican; his mouth can hold more than his belican.

Carolina

Designer	Gottfried Pott
Nationality	DE
Date Designed	1991
Foundries	Linotype Adobe
Number of weights	1

ABCDEFGHIJKLMNOPQRSTUVWXYZ
abcdefghijklmnopqrstuvwxyz1234567890
Just keep examining every low bid quoted for zinc etchings.

Dobkin

Designer	David Rakowski
Nationality	US
Date Designed	1992
Foundries	Rakowski
Number of weights	1

ABCDEFGHIJKLMNOPQRSTUVWXYZ
abcdefghijklmnopqrstuvwxyz1234567890
The job of waxing linoleum frequently peeves chintzy kids.

Poetica

Designer	Robert Slimbach
Nationality	US
Date Designed	1992
Foundries	Adobe
Number of weights	21

ABCDEFGHIJKLMNOPQRSTUVWXYZ
abcdefghijklmnopqrstuvwxyz1234567890
The job of waxing linoleum frequently peeves chintzy kids.

Marguerita

Designer David Quay
Nationality UK
Date Designed 1993
Foundries Monotype Letraset ITC
Number of weights 1

ABCDEFGHIJKLMNOPQRSTUVWXYZ
abcdefghijklmnopqrstuvwxyz1234567890
Job quickly drove a few extra miles on the glazed pavement.

Greyhound Script

Designer Dave Farey
Nationality UK
Date Designed 1994
Foundries Monotype
Number of weights 1

ABCDEFGHIJKLMNOPQRSTUVWXYZ
abcdefghijklmnopqrstuvwxyz1234567890
Questions of a zealous nature have become by degrees petty waxen jokes.

Polenta

Designer Philip Bouwsma
Nationality US
Date Designed 1994
Foundries Monotype
Number of weights 2

ABCDEFGHIJKLMNOPQRSTUVWXYZ
abcdefghijklmnopqrstuvwxyz1234567890
Italian peasant filler food sold at £5 a portion in London restaurants.

Riva

Designer Martin Wait
Nationality UK
Date Designed 1994
Foundries ITC
Number of weights 1

ABCDEFGHIJKLMNOPQRSTUVWXYZ
abcdefghijklmnopqrstuvwxyz1234567890
Jail zesty vixen who grabbed pay from quack.

Calligraphica

Designer Arthur Baker
Nationality US
Date Designed 1995
Foundries Glyph Systems
Number of weights 6

ABCDEFGHIJKLMNOPQRSTUVWXYZ
abcdefghijklmnopqrstuvwxyz1234567890
Fred specialized in the job of making very quaint wax toys.

Donatello

Designer	Philip Bouwsma
Nationality	US
Date Designed	1995
Foundries	Monotype
Number of weights	1

ABCDEFGHIJKLMNOPQRSTUVWXYZ

ABCDEFGHIJKLMNOPQRSTUVWXYZ1234567890

GREAT C15 ITALIAN SCULPTOR.

Nyfors

Designer	Franko Luin
Nationality	SL
Date Designed	1995
Foundries	Linotype
Number of weights	1

ABCDEFGHIJKLMNOPQRSTUVWXYZ

abcdefghijklmnopqrstuvwxyz1234567890

Mr. Jock, TV quiz Ph.D., bags few lynx.

Scriptease

Designer	Phill Grimshaw
Nationality	UK
Date Designed	1995
Foundries	Monotype Letraset ITC
Number of weights	1

ABCDEFGHIJKLMNOPQRSTUVWXYZ

abcdefghijklmnopqrstuvwxyz1234567890

Five or six big jet planes zoomed quickly by the tower.

Gneisenauette

Designer	Gustav Andrejs Grinbergs
Nationality	LV
Date Designed	1996
Foundries	Linotype
Number of weights	8

ABCDEFGHIJKLMNOPQRSTUVWXYZ

abcdefghijklmnopqrstuvwxyz1234567890

Gneisenau and Scharnhorst were battleships named after collieries.

Evita

Designer	Gérard Mariscalchi
Nationality	CA
Date Designed	1997
Foundries	Monotype
Number of weights	1

ABCDEFGHIJKLMNOPQRSTUVWXYZ

abcdefghijklmnopqrstuvwxyz1234567890

Six big juicy steaks sizzled in a pan as five workmen left the quarry.

Brigida

Designer	Bo Berndal
Nationality	SE
Date Designed	1998
Foundries	Monotype
Number of weights	1

ABCDEFGHIJKLMNOPQRSTUVWXYZ
abcdefghijklmnopqrstuvwxyz1234567890
Forsaking monastic tradition, twelve jovial friars gave up their vocation for a questionable existence on the flying trapeze.

Freemouse

Designer	Slobodan Miladinov
Nationality	YU
Date Designed	1998
Foundries	ITC Monotype
Number of weights	1

ABCDEFGHIJKLMNOPQRSTUVWXYZ
abcdefghijklmnopqrstuvwxyz1234567890
The five boxing wizards jump quickly.

Ballerino

Designer	Viktor Solt-Bittner
Nationality	AT
Date Designed	1999
Foundries	ITC
Number of weights	1

ABCDEFGHIJKLMNOPQRSTUVWXYZ
abcdefghijklmnopqrstuvwxyz1234567890
New farm hand (picking just six quinces) proves strong but lazy.

Wolftrack

Designer	Philip Bouwsma
Nationality	US
Date Designed	1998
Foundries	Monotype
Number of weights	1

ABCDEFGHIJKLMNOPQRSTUVWXYZ
abcdefghijklmnopqrstuvwxyz1234567890
Now is the time for all brown dogs to jump over the lazy lynx.

Aspera

Designer	Olivera Stojadinovic
Nationality	YU
Date Designed	2000
Foundries	ITC
Number of weights	1

ABCDEFGHIJKLMNOPQRSTUVWXYZ
abcdefghijklmnopqrstuvwxyz1234567890
Quick wafting zephyrs vex bold Jim.

Rastko ITC

Designer	Olivera Stojadinovic
Nationality	YU
Date Designed	2000
Foundries	ITC
Number of weights	1

ABCDEFGHIJKLMNOPQRSTUVWXYZ
abcdefghijklmnopqrstuvwxyz1234567890
Saint Sava (1175 -1235) was born as a Serbian prince, Rastko Nemanjic.

Hedera ITC

Designer	Olivera Stojadinovic
Nationality	YU
Date Designed	2001
Foundries	ITC Monotype
Number of weights	1

ABCDEFGHIJKLMNOPQRSTUVWXYZ
abcdefghijklmnopqrstuvwxyz1234567890
Hedera helix is the Linnean term for English ivy.

Tartine Script

Designer	Xavier Dupré
Nationality	FR
Date Designed	2002
Foundries	FontFont
Number of weights	3

ABCDEFGHIJKLMNOPQRSTUVWXYZ
abcdefghijklmnopqrstuvwxyz1234567890
Martin J. Hixeypozer quickly began his first word.

Anasdair

Designer	Richard Yeend
Nationality	UK
Date Designed	2003
Foundries	Linotype
Number of weights	4

ABCDEFGHIJKLMNOPQRSTUVWXYZ
abcdefghijklmnopqrstuvwxyz1234567890
Alt characters almost transform it into a blackletter.

Carlin Script

Designer	Hans-Jürgen Ellenberger
Nationality	DE
Date Designed	2003
Foundries	Linotype
Number of weights	10

ABCDEFGHIJKLMNOPQRSTUVWXYZ
abcdefghijklmnopqrstuvwxyz1234567890
How quickly daft jumping zebras vex.

Monotype Script Bold

Designer	E Lautenbach
Nationality	DE
Date Designed	1926
Foundries	Monotype
Number of weights	1

ABCDEFGHIJKLMNOPQRSTUVWXYZ

abcdefghijklmnopqrstuvwxyz1234567890

Hark! Toxic jungle water vipers quietly drop on zebras for meals!

Monoline Script

Designer	Monotype
Nationality	UK
Date Designed	1935
Foundries	Monotype Linotype Adobe
Number of weights	1

ABCDEFGHIJKLMNOPQRSTUVWXYZ

abcdefghijklmnopqrstuvwxyz1234567890

Back in my quaint garden jaunty zinnias vie with flaunting phlox.

Glastonbury

Designer	Alan Meeks
Nationality	UK
Date Designed	1979
Foundries	Linotype ITC
Number of weights	1

ABCDEFGHIJKLMNOPQRSTUVWXYZ

abcdefghijklmnopqrstuvwxyz1234567890

Jelly-like above the high wire, six quaking pachyderms kept the climax of the extravaganza in a dazzling state of flux.

Rondo

Designer	Stefan Schlesinger, Dick Dooijes
Nationality	NL
Date Designed	1948
Foundries	Amsterdam
Number of weights	1

ABCDEFGHIJKLMNOPQRSTUVWXYZ

abcdefghijklmnopqrstuvwxyz1234567890

Verbatim reports were quickly given by Jim Fox to his amazed audience.

Ariadne

Designer	Gudrun Zapf von Hesse
Nationality	DE
Date Designed	1954
Foundries	Stempel Adobe
Number of weights	1

ABCDEFGHIJKLMNOPQRSTUVWXYZ

ABCDEFGHIJKLMNOPQRSTUVWXYZ

FIVE OR SIX BIG JET PLANES ZOOMED QUICKLY BY THE TOWER.

Quill Script

Designer	Tommy Thompson
Nationality	US
Date Designed	1952
Foundries	Monotype
Number of weights	1

ABCDEFGHIJKLMNOPQRSTUVWXYZ

abcdefghijklmnopqrstuvwxyz1234567890

We promptly judged antique ivory buckles for the next prize.

Le Griffe

Designer	André-Michel Lubac
Nationality	FR
Date Designed	1973
Foundries	Letraset Linotype Monotype Elsner+Flake ITC
Number of weights	2

ABCDEFGHIJKLMNOPQRSTUVWXYZ

abcdefghijklmnopqrstuvwxyz1234567890

Portez ce vieux whisky au juge blond qui fume.

Medici Script

Designer	Hermann Zapf
Nationality	DE
Date Designed	1974
Foundries	Adobe
Number of weights	1

ABCDEFGHIJKLMNOPQRSTUVWXYZ

abcdefghijklmnopqrstuvwxyz1234567890

We promptly judged antique ivory buckles for the next prize.

Zapf Chancery

Designer	Hermann Zapf
Nationality	DE
Date Designed	1979
Foundries	ITC Adobe Franklin Linotype Monotype URW++ Bitstream Elsner+Flake
Number of weights	7

ABCDEFGHIJKLMNOPQRSTUVWXYZ

abcdefghijklmnopqrstuvwxyz1234567890

Available on almost every computer.

Monotype Corsiva

Designer	Patricia Saunders
Nationality	UK
Date Designed	1991
Foundries	Monotype
Number of weights	2

ABCDEFGHIJKLMNOPQRSTUVWXYZ

abcdefghijklmnopqrstuvwxyz1234567890

Portez ce vieux whisky au juge blond qui fume.

Tiranti Solid

Designer Tony Forster
Nationality UK
Date Designed 1993
Foundries Letraset
Number of weights 1

ABCDEFGHIJKLMNOPQRSTUVWXYZ
abcdefghijklmnopqrstuvwxyz1234567890

Tiranti's is a long-established London art materials shop.

Quill

Designer Manfred Klein
Nationality DE
Date Designed 1994
Foundries FontFont
Number of weights 6

ABCDEFGHIJKLMNOPQRSTUVWXYZ
abcdefghijklmnopqrstuvwxyz1234567890

Hark! Toxic jungle water vipers quietly drop on zebras for meals!

Arioso

Designer Gottfried Pott
Nationality DE
Date Designed 1995
Foundries Linotype
Number of weights 1

ABCDEFGHIJKLMNOPQRSTUVWXYZ
abcdefghijklmnopqrstuvwxyz1234567890

A short melodious composition in the style of an aria, but less rigid in its construction.

Carmela

Designer Philip Bouwsma
Nationality US
Date Designed 1995
Foundries Monotype
Number of weights 1

ABCDEFGHIJKLMNOPQRSTUVWXYZ
abcdefghijklmnopqrstuvwxyz1234567890

A quick movement of the enemy will jeopardize six gunboats.

Mercator

Designer Arthur Baker
Nationality US
Date Designed 1995
Foundries Monotype Glyph
Number of weights 2

ABCDEFGHIJKLMNOPQRSTUVWXYZ
abcdefghijklmnopqrstuvwxyz1234567890

Gerardus Mercator from the Low Countries was the most famous of the mediaeval map makers.

Ludovico Smooth

Designer	Philip Bouwsma
Nationality	US
Date Designed	1995
Foundries	Ludlow
Number of weights	2

ABCDEFGHIJKLMNOPQRSTUVWXYZ

abcdefghijklmnopqrstuvwxyz1234567890

Ludovico Ariosto published Orlando Furioso in 1532.

Göteborg

Designer	Paul Shaw
Nationality	US
Date Designed	1997
Foundries	Monotype CA Exclusives
Number of weights	1

ABCDEFGHIJKLMNOPQRSTUVWXYZ

abcdefghijklmnopqrstuvwxyz1234567890

My help squeezed back in again and joined the weavers after six.

Augusta

Designer	Julius de Goede
Nationality	NL
Date Designed	1998
Foundries	CA Exclusives
Number of weights	6

ABCDEFGHIJKLMNOPQRSTUVWXYZ

abcdefghijklmnopqrstuvwxyz1234567890

Sphinx of black quartz judge my vow.

Vivaldi

Designer	Fritz Peters
Nationality	DE
Date Designed	1970
Foundries	URW++ ITC
Number of weights	1

ABCDEFGHIJKLMNOPQRSTUVWXYZ

abcdefghijklmnopqrstuvwxyz1234567890

Alfredo just must bring very exciting news to the plaza quickly.

Codex

Designer	Georg Trump
Nationality	DE
Date Designed	1954
Foundries	Weber Linotype
Number of weights	1

ABCDEFGHIJKLMNOPQRSTUVWXYZ

abcdefghijklmnopqrstuvwxyz1234567890

Two hardy boxing kangaroos jet from Sydney to Zanzibar on quicksilver pinions.

Ondine

Designer Adrian Frutiger
Nationality CH
Date Designed 1954
Foundries Deberny & Peignot Haas URW++
Number of weights 1

ABCDEFGHIJKLMNOPQRSTUVWXYZ
abcdefghijklmnopqrstuvwxyz1234567890
The job of waxing linoleum frequently peeves chintzy kids.

Amigo

Designer Arthur Baker
Nationality US
Date Designed 1987
Foundries Adobe Glyph Systems
Number of weights 1

ABCDEFGHIJKLMNOPQRSTUVWXYZ
abcdefghijklmnopqrstuvwxyz1234567890
Mr. Jock, TV quiz Ph.D., bags few lynx.

Humanist

Designer Jürgen Brinckmann
Nationality DE
Date Designed 1993
Foundries FontFont
Number of weights 1

ABCDEFGHIJKLMNOPQRSTUVWXYZ
abcdefghijklmnopqrstuvwxyz1234567890
Moi, je veux quinze clubs a golf et du whisky pur.

Gianpoggio

Designer Bo Berndal
Nationality SE
Date Designed 1995
Foundries Monotype
Number of weights 4

ABCDEFGHIJKLMNOPQRSTUVWXYZ
abcdefghijklmnopqrstuvwxyz1234567890
We have just quoted on nine dozen boxes of gray lamp wicks.

Amanda

Designer Tom Rickner
Nationality US
Date Designed 1996
Foundries Creative Alliance URW++
Number of weights 1

ABCDEFGHIJKLMNOPQRSTUVWXYZ
abcdefghijklmnopqrstuvwxyz1234567890
Five wine experts jokingly quizzed sample chablis.

CG Chaplin

Designer	Willard T Sniffin
Nationality	UK
Date Designed	1933
Foundries	CA Partners
Number of weights	1

ABCDEFGHIJKLMNOPQRSTUVWXYZ

abcdefghijklmnopqrstuvwxyz1234567890

King Alexander was partly overcome just after quizzing Diogenes in his tub.

Lake Informal

Designer	Rudolph Ruzicka
Nationality	CZ
Date Designed	1935
Foundries	Linotype
Number of weights	2

ABCDEFGHIJKLMNOPQRSTUVWXYZ

abcdefghijklmnopqrstuvwxyz1234567890

Fred specialized in the job of making very quaint wax toys.

Ruzicka Freehand

Designer	Rudolph Ruzicka
Nationality	CZ
Date Designed	1939
Foundries	Linotype
Number of weights	3

ABCDEFGHIJKLMNOPQRSTUVWXYZ

abcdefghijklmnopqrstuvwxyz1234567890

Five big quacking zephyrs jolt my wax bed.

Brio

Designer	Umberto Fenocchio
Nationality	IT
Date Designed	1970
Foundries	Fonderia Tipografica
	Cooperitiva Mecanorma Monotype
Number of weights	1

ABCDEFGHIJKLMNOPQRSTUVWXYZ

abcdefghijklmnopqrstuvwxyz1234567890

Italian for oomph, passion, pep, sparkle, spirit, sprightliness, verve, vibrancy, vigour, vim.

Vladimir Script

Designer	Valdimir Andrich
Nationality	US
Date Designed	1970
Foundries	URW++
Number of weights	1

ABCDEFGHIJKLMNOPQRSTUVWXYZ

abcdefghijklmnopqrstuvwxyz1234567890

William Jex quickly caught five dozen Conservatives.

Floridian Script

Designer	Agfa Monotype
Nationality	US
Date Designed	1972
Foundries	Monotype
Number of weights	1

ABCDEFGHIJKLMNOPQRSTUVWXYZ

abcdefghijklmnopqrstuvwxyz1234567890

Many-wived Jack laughs at probes of sex quiz.

Jasper AT

Designer	Les Usherwood
Nationality	CA
Date Designed	1980
Foundries	AGP
Number of weights	1

ABCDEFGHIJKLMNOPQRSTUVWXYZ

abcdefghijklmnopqrstuvwxyz1234567890

Dumpy kibitzer jingles as exchequer overflows.

Sallwey Script

Designer	Friedrich Karl Sallwey
Nationality	DE
Date Designed	1980
Foundries	Linotype
Number of weights	1

ABCDEFGHIJKLMNOPQRSTUVWXYZ

abcdefghijklmnopqrstuvwxyz1234567890

Quick wafting zephyrs vex bold Jim.

Freestyle Script

Designer	Martin Wait
Nationality	UK
Date Designed	1981
Foundries	Adobe ITC Letraset
Number of weights	2

ABCDEFGHIJKLMNOPQRSTUVWXYZ

abcdefghijklmnopqrstuvwxyz1234567890

Six big devils from Japan quickly forgot how to waltz.

Underscript

Designer	Jan van Dijk
Nationality	NL
Date Designed	1982
Foundries	Letraset Linotype ITC URW++
Recut/Digitised by	Peter O'Donnell, 1986
Number of weights	1

ABCDEFGHIJKLMNOPQRSTUVWXYZ

ABCDEFGHIJKLMNOPQRSTUVWXYZ1234567890

SYMPATHIZING WOULD FIX QUAKER OBJECTIVES.

Demian

Designer	Jan van Dijk
Nationality	NL
Date Designed	1984
Foundries	Linotype ITC
Number of weights	2

ABCDEFGHIJKLMNOPQRSTUVWXYZ

abcdefghijklmnopqrstuvwxyz1234567890

No verse can give pleasure for long, nor last, that is written by water-drinkers.

Rage

Designer	Ron Zwingelberg
Nationality	US
Date Designed	1984
Foundries	Letraset Elsner+Flake Linotype ITC
Number of weights	2

ABCDEFGHIJKLMNOPQRSTUVWXYZ

abcdefghijklmnopqrstuvwxyz1234567890

Viewing quizzical abstracts mixed up hefty jocks.

Sayer Script

Designer	Manfred Sayer
Nationality	DE
Date Designed	1984
Foundries	CA Partners
Number of weights	3

ABCDEFGHIJKLMNOPQRSTUVWXYZ

abcdefghijklmnopqrstuvwxyz1234567890

Many big jackdaws quickly zipped over the fox pen.

Limehouse Script

Designer	Alan Meeks
Nationality	UK
Date Designed	1986
Foundries	ITC Fontek Monotype Linotype Letraset
Number of weights	1

ABCDEFGHIJKLMNOPQRSTUVWXYZ

abcdefghijklmnopqrstuvwxyz1234567890

Martin J. Hixeypozer quickly began his first word.

Fine Hand

Designer	Richard Bradley
Nationality	UK
Date Designed	1987
Foundries	ITC Linotype
Number of weights	1

ABCDEFGHIJKLMNOPQRSTUVWXYZ

abcdefghijklmnopqrstuvwxyz1234567890

How quickly daft jumping zebras vex.

Laser

Designer Martin Wait
Nationality UK
Date Designed 1987
Foundries Martin Wait Type Letraset
Monotype Linotype ITC
Number of weights 1

ABCDEFGHIJKLMNOPQRSTUVWXYZ
abcdefghijklmnopqrstuvwxyz1234567890
Not as popular as Laser Chrome.

Laser Chrome

Designer Martin Wait
Nationality UK
Date Designed 1987
Foundries Martin Wait Type Letraset
Monotype Linotype ITC
Number of weights 1

ABCDEFGHIJKLMNOPQRSTUVWXYZ
abcdefghijklmnopqrstuvwxyz1234567890
Laser Chrome is a popular with car magazines.

Signature

Designer Greg Kolodziejzyk
Nationality CA
Date Designed 1987
Foundries IMA
Number of weights 2

ABCDEFGHIJKLMNOPQRSTUVWXYZ
abcdefghijklmnopqrstuvwxyz1234567890
Jim just quit and packed extra bags for Liz Owen.

Boscribe

Designer Bo Berndal
Nationality SE
Date Designed 1989
Foundries Monotype
Number of weights 1

ABCDEFGHIJKLMNOPQRSTUVWXYZ
abcdefghijklmnopqrstuvwxyz1234567890
Martin J. Hixeypozer quickly began his first word.

Florens

Designer Garrett Boge
Nationality US
Date Designed 1989
Foundries Monotype Adobe
Number of weights 1

ABCDEFGHIJKLMNOPQRSTUVWXYZ
abcdefghijklmnopqrstuvwxyz1234567890
Jazzy saxophones blew over Mick's turgid quiff.

Informal Roman

Designer	Martin Wait
Nationality	UK
Date Designed	1989
Foundries	Letraset Monotype ITC
Number of weights	1

ABCDEFGHIJKLMNOPQRSTUVWXYZ

abcdefghijklmnopqrstuvwxyz1234567890

Perhaps President Clinton's amazing sax skills will be judged quite favourably.

Rapier

Designer	Martin Wait
Nationality	UK
Date Designed	1989
Foundries	Letraset Martin Wait Type ITC
Number of weights	1

ABCDEFGHIJKLMNOPQRSTUVWXYZ

abcdefghijklmnopqrstuvwxyz1234567890

A straight sword with a fine point, used for a thrust in fencing.

Tiger Rag

Designer	John Viner
Nationality	UK
Date Designed	1989
Foundries	Letraset Monotype ITC
Number of weights	1

ABCDEFGHIJKLMNOPQRSTUVWXYZ

abcdefghijklmnopqrstuvwxyz1234567890

Jack amazed a few girls by dropping the antique onyx vase!

Ulysses

Designer	Timothy Donaldson
Nationality	UK
Date Designed	1991
Foundries	ITC
Number of weights	1

ABCDEFGHIJKLMNOPQRSTUVWXYZ

abcdefghijklmnopqrstuvwxyz1234567890

Anna Cheifetz edited this book.

Tomboy

Designer	Garrett Boge
Nationality	US
Date Designed	1989
Foundries	LPT MTD
Number of weights	3

ABCDEFGHIJKLMNOPQRSTUVWXYZ

abcdefghijklmnopqrstuvwxyz1234567890

Fred specialized in the job of making very quaint wax toys.

Indy Italic

Designer Charles Hughes

Nationality US

Date Designed 1990

Foundries Letraset Linotype ITC Monotype

Number of weights 1

ABCDEFGHIJKLMNOPQRSTUVWXYZ
abcdefghijklmnopqrstuvwxyz1234567890
Mix Zapf with Veljovic and get quirky Beziers.

Justlefthand

Designer Just van Russum

Nationality NL

Date Designed 1990

Foundries FontFont

Number of weights 2

ABCDEFGHIJKLMNOPQRSTUVWXYZ
abcdefghijklmnopqrstuvwxyz1234567890
May Jo equal the fine record by solving six puzzles a week?

Studio Script

Designer Pat Hickson

Nationality US

Date Designed 1990

Foundries ITC Linotype

Number of weights 3

ABCDEFGHIJKLMNOPQRSTUVWXYZ
abcdefghijklmnopqrstuvwxyz1234567890
Five wine experts jokingly quizzed sample chablis.

Wendy

Designer Garrett Boge

Nationality US

Date Designed 1990

Foundries Monotype Adobe

Number of weights 3

ABCDEFGHIJKLMNOPQRSTUVWXYZ
abcdefghijklmnopqrstuvwxyz1234567890
A name invented by J M Barrie from "Friendy-wendy".

Bickley Script

Designer Alan Meeks

Nationality UK

Date Designed 1986

Foundries Linotype ITC Letraset

Number of weights 1

ABCDEFGHIJKLMNOPQRSTUVWXYZ
abcdefghijklmnopqrstuvwxyz1234567890
Jail zesty vixen who grabbed pay from quack.

Giddyup

Designer	Laurie Szujewska
Nationality	US
Date Designed	1995
Foundries	Adobe
Number of weights	2

ABCDEFGHIJKLMNOPQRSTUVWXYZ

abcdefghijklmnopqrstuvwxyz1234567890

The sex life of the woodchuck is a provocative question for most vertebrate zoology majors.

Clover

Designer	Jill Bell
Nationality	US
Date Designed	1997
Foundries	ITC
Number of weights	1

ABCDEFGHIJKLMNOPQRSTUVWXYZ

abcdefghijklmnopqrstuvwxyz1234567890

Many-wived Jack laughs at probes of sex quiz.

Jiffy

Designer	Linotype
Nationality	DE
Date Designed	1995
Foundries	Linotype
Number of weights	1

ABCDEFGHIJKLMNOPQRSTUVWXYZ

abcdefghijklmnopqrstuvwxyz1234567890

Big July earthquakes confound zany experimental vow.

Agfa Nadianne

Designer	Aldo Novarese
Nationality	IT
Date Designed	1991
Foundries	Monotype
Number of weights	6

ABCDEFGHIJKLMNOPQRSTUVWXYZ

abcdefghijklmnopqrstuvwxyz1234567890

The quick brown fox jumps over the lazy dog.

Erikrighthand

Designer	Erik van Blokland
Nationality	NL
Date Designed	1991
Foundries	FontFont
Number of weights	2

ABCDEFGHIJKLMNOPQRSTUVWXYZ

abcdefghijklmnopqrstuvwxyz1234567890

Six crazy kings vowed to abolish my quite pitiful jousts.

Newberlin

Designer	Peter Verheul
Nationality	NL
Date Designed	1991
Foundries	FontFont
Number of weights	4

ABCDEFGHIJKLMNOPQRSTUVWXYZ

abcdefghijklmnopqrstuvwxyz1234567890

Zweedse ex-VIP, behoorlijk gek op quantumfysica.

Schulschrift

Designer	Just van Rossum
Nationality	NL
Date Designed	1991
Foundries	FontFont
Number of weights	12

ABCDEFGHIJKLMNOPQRSTUVWXYZ

abcdefghijklmnopqrstuvwxyz1234567890

Quick wafting zephyrs vex bold Jim.

Coptek

Designer	David Quay
Nationality	UK
Date Designed	1992
Foundries	Linotype ITC Letraset
Number of weights	1

ABCDEFGHIJKLMNOPQRSTUVWXYZ

abcdefghijklmnopqrstuvwxyz1234567890

About sixty codfish eggs will make a quarter pound of very fizzy jelly.

DuChirico

Designer	D van Meerbeeck
Nationality	NL
Date Designed	1992
Foundries	FontFont
Number of weights	1

ABCDEFGHIJKLMNOPQRSTUVWXYZ

abcdefghijklmnopqrstuvwxyz1234567890

Giorgio de Chirico (1888-1978)

DuDuchamp

Designer	D van Meerbeeck
Nationality	NL
Date Designed	1992
Foundries	FontFont
Number of weights	1

ABCDEFGHIJKLMNOPQRSTUVWXYZ

abcdefghijklmnopqrstuvwxyz1234567890

Marcel Duchamp (1887-1968)

DuGauguin

Designer	D van Meerbeeck
Nationality	NL
Date Designed	1992
Foundries	FontFont
Number of weights	1

ABCDEFGHIJKLMNOPQRSTUVWXYZ

abcdefghijklmnopqrstuvwxyz1234567890

Paul Gauguin (1848-1903)

DuMifu

Designer	D van Meerbeeck
Nationality	NL
Date Designed	1992
Foundries	FontFont
Number of weights	1

ABCDEFGHIJKLMNOPQRSTUVWXYZ

abcdefghijklmnopqrstuvwxyz1234567890

Mi Fu was a Chinese calligrapher (1051-1107)

DuMoore

Designer	D van Meerbeeck
Nationality	NL
Date Designed	1992
Foundries	FontFont
Number of weights	1

ABCDEFGHIJKLMNOPQRSTUVWXYZ

abcdefghijklmnopqrstuvwxyz1234567890

Henry Moore (1898-1986)

DuTurner

Designer	D van Meerbeeck
Nationality	NL
Date Designed	1992
Foundries	FontFont
Number of weights	1

ABCDEFGHIJKLMNOPQRSTUVWXYZ

abcdefghijklmnopqrstuvwxyz1234567890

J M W Turner (1775-1851)

Grimshaw Hand

Designer	Phill Grimshaw
Nationality	UK
Date Designed	1992
Foundries	Monotype Linotype ITC
Number of weights	1

ABCDEFGHIJKLMNOPQRSTUVWXYZ

abcdefghijklmnopqrstuvwxyz1234567890

The five boxing wizards jump quickly.

Fortuna

Designer	Franko Luin
Nationality	SL
Date Designed	1993
Foundries	Linotype
Number of weights	2

ABCDEFGHIJKLMNOPQRSTUVWXYZ

abcdefghijklmnopqrstuvwxyz1234567890

The vixen jumped quickly on her foe barking with zeal.

Inkspot

Designer	Howard Cuttle
Nationality	UK
Date Designed	1992
Foundries	Monotype
Number of weights	3

ABCDEFGHIJKLMNOPQRSTUVWXYZ

abcdefghijklmnopqrstuvwxyz1234567890

Was there a quorum of able whizzkids gravely exciting the jaded fish at ATypI?

Juliana

Designer	Philip Bouwsma
Nationality	US
Date Designed	1992
Foundries	Alphabets Inc
Number of weights	1

ABCDEFGHIJKLMNOPQRSTUVWXYZ

abcdefghijklmnopqrstuvwxyz1234567890

Zweedse ex-VIP, behoorlijk gek op quantumfysica.

Blueprint MT

Designer	Steve Matteson
Nationality	US
Date Designed	1993
Foundries	Monotype
Number of weights	4

ABCDEFGHIJKLMNOPQRSTUVWXYZ

abcdefghijklmnopqrstuvwxyz1234567890

How quickly daft jumping zebras vex.

Jacoby

Designer	Calvin Glenn
Nationality	US
Date Designed	1993
Foundries	Monotype NIMX
Number of weights	12

ABCDEFGHIJKLMNOPQRSTUVWXYZ

abcdefghijklmnopqrstuvwxyz1234567890

Mr. Jock, TV quiz Ph.D., bags few lynx.

Roundy

Designer	Friedrich Karl Sallwey
Nationality	DE
Date Designed	1993
Foundries	Linotype
Number of weights	2

ABCDEFGHIJKLMNOPQRSTUVWXYZ

abcdefghijklmnopqrstuvwxyz1234567890

Playing jazz vibe chords quickly excites my wife.

Wiesbaden Swing

Designer	Rosemarie Kloos-Rau
Nationality	DE
Date Designed	1993
Foundries	Linotype
Number of weights	2

ABCDEFGHIJKLMNOPQRSTUVWXYZ

abcdefghijklmnopqrstuvwxyz1234567890

Martin J. Hixeypozer quickly began his first word.

Daly Hand

Designer	Judith Sutcliffe
Nationality	US
Date Designed	1994
Foundries	The Electric Typographer
	Monotype
Number of weights	1

ABCDEFGHIJKLMNOPQRSTUVWXYZ

abcdefghijklmnopqrstuvwxyz1234567890

Now is the time for all brown dogs to jump over the lazy lynx.

Daly Text

Designer	Judith Sutcliffe
Nationality	US
Date Designed	1994
Foundries	The Electric Typographer
	Monotype
Number of weights	1

ABCDEFGHIJKLMNOPQRSTUVWXYZ

abcdefghijklmnopqrstuvwxyz1234567890

While waxing parquet decks, jaunty Suez sailors vomit abaft.

Balzano

Designer	John Benson
Nationality	US
Date Designed	1994
Foundries	Adobe
Number of weights	1

ABCDEFGHIJKLMNOPQRSTUVWXYZ

abcdefghijklmnopqrstuvwxyz1234567890

Big July earthquakes confound zany experimental vow.

Havergal

Designer Holly Goldsmith
Nationality US
Date Designed 1994
Foundries Monotype
Number of weights 4

ABCDEFGHIJKLMNOPQRSTUVWXYZ
abcdefghijklmnopqrstuvwxyz 1234567890
Astronaut Quincy B. Zack defies gravity with six jet fuel pumps.

Lebensjoy

Designer Bo Berndal
Nationality SE
Date Designed 1994
Foundries Monotype
Number of weights 3

ABCDEFGHIJKLMNOPQRSTUVWXYZ
abcdefghijklmnopqrstuvwxyz1234567890
Dumpy kibitzer jingles as exchequer overflows.

Lightnin

Designer Alan Meeks
Nationality UK
Date Designed 1994
Foundries Linotype Letraset Monotype ITC
Number of weights 1

ABCDEFGHIJKLMNOPQRSTUVWXYZ
abcdefghijklmnopqrstuvwxyz1234567890
Viewing quizzical abstracts mixed up hefty jocks.

Matthia

Designer Dieter Kurz
Nationality DE
Date Designed 1994
Foundries Linotype
Number of weights 1

ABCDEFGHIJKLMNOPQRSTUVWXYZ
abcdefghijklmnopqrstuvwxyz1234567890
Jaded zombies acted quaintly but kept driving their oxen forward.

Pristina

Designer Phill Grimshaw
Nationality UK
Date Designed 1994
Foundries ITC Fontek
Number of weights 1

ABCDEFGHIJKLMNOPQRSTUVWXYZ
abcdefghijklmnopqrstuvwxyz1234567890
Mike Shatzkin's Idea Logical Company.

ReadMyHand

Designer	Léon Hulst
Nationality	NL
Date Designed	1994
Foundries	Linotype
Number of weights	1

ABCDEFGHIJKLMNOPQRSTUVWXYZ
abcdefghijklmnopqrstuvwxyz1234567890
Zweedse ex-VIP, behoorlijk gek op quantumfysica.

Roughedge

Designer	Robert J. Howell
Nationality	US
Date Designed	1994
Foundries	CA Partners
Number of weights	1

ABCDEFGHIJKLMNOPQRSTUVWXYZ
abcdefghijklmnopqrstuvwxyz1234567890
The five boxing wizards jump quickly.

Saxony Script

Designer	Richard Yeend
Nationality	UK
Date Designed	1994
Foundries	CA Partners
Number of weights	1

ABCDEFGHIJKLMNOPQRSTUVWXYZ
abcdefghijklmnopqrstuvwxyz1234567890
William Jex quickly caught five dozen Conservatives.

School Script

Designer	Type Revivals
Nationality	US
Date Designed	1994
Foundries	Monotype
Number of weights	5

ABCDEFGHIJKLMNOPQRSTUVWXYZ
abcdefghijklmnopqrstuvwxyz1234567890
Big July earthquakes confound zany experimental vow.

School Oblique

Designer	SourceNet
Nationality	US
Date Designed	1994
Foundries	Monotype
Number of weights	5

ABCDEFGHIJKLMNOPQRSTUVWXYZ
abcdefghijklmnopqrstuvwxyz1234567890
Jackdaws love my big sphinx of quartz.

Stylus

Designer	Dennis Pasternak
Nationality	US
Date Designed	1994
Foundries	Galapagos ITC
Number of weights	2

ABCDEFGHIJKLMNOPQRSTUVWXYZ

abcdefghijklmnopqrstuvwxyz1234567890

A pointed instrument for writing, then the needle which produced sound from vinyl discs.

Belltrap

Designer	Bo Berndal
Nationality	SE
Date Designed	1995
Foundries	CA Exclusives
Number of weights	1

ABCDEFGHIJKLMNOPQRSTUVWXYZ

abcdefghijklmnopqrstuvwxyz1234567890

Mr. Jock, TV quiz Ph.D., bags few lynx.

Caliban

Designer	John Benson
Nationality	US
Date Designed	1995
Foundries	Adobe
Number of weights	1

ABCDEFGHIJKLMNOPQRSTUVWXYZ

abcdefghijklmnopqrstuvwxyz1234567890

Zwei Boxkämpfer jagen Eva quer durch Sylt.

Bradley Hand

Designer	Richard Bradley
Nationality	UK
Date Designed	1995
Foundries	ITC Linotype Letraset
Number of weights	2

ABCDEFGHIJKLMNOPQRSTUVWXYZ

abcdefghijklmnopqrstuvwxyz1234567890

Quick wafting zephyrs vex bold Jim.

Fineprint

Designer	Steve Matteson
Nationality	US
Date Designed	1995
Foundries	Monotype
Number of weights	8

ABCDEFGHIJKLMNOPQRSTUVWXYZ

abcdefghijklmnopqrstuvwxyz1234567890

Waltz, nymph, for quick jigs vex Bud.

Epaulet

Designer	Chris McGregor
Nationality	US
Date Designed	1995
Foundries	T-26
Number of weights	1

ABCDEFGHIJKLMNOPQRSTUVWXYZ

abcdefghijklmnopqrstuvwxyz1234567890

The five boxing wizards jump quickly.

Flight

Designer	Timothy Donaldson
Nationality	UK
Date Designed	1995
Foundries	Monotype ITC
Number of weights	1

ABCDEFGHIJKLMNOPQRSTUVWXYZ

abcdefghijklmnopqrstuvwxyz1234567890

Breezily jangling $3,416,857,209, wise advertiser ambles to the bank, his exchequer amplified.

Friday, Saturday, Sunday

Designer	Jan Jedding
Nationality	DE
Date Designed	1995
Foundries	FontFont
Number of weights	3

ABCDEFGHIJKLMNOPQRSTUVWXYZ

abcdefghijklmnopqrstuvwxyz1234567890

The job of waxing linoleum frequently peeves chintzy kids.

Graphite

Designer	David Siegel
Nationality	US
Date Designed	1995
Foundries	Font Bureau Adobe
Number of weights	40

ABCDEFGHIJKLMNOPQRSTUVWXYZ

abcdefghijklmnopqrstuvwxyz1234567890

Based on the handwriting of Anthony Celis La Rosa.

Hairspray

Designer	Christian Schwartz
Nationality	US
Date Designed	1995
Foundries	Monotype
Number of weights	1

ABCDEFGHIJKLMNOPQRSTUVWXYZ

abcdefghijklmnopqrstuvwxyz1234567890

Just keep examining every low bid quoted for zinc etchings.

Jesper

Designer	Franko Luin
Nationality	SE
Date Designed	1995
Foundries	Linotype
Number of weights	1

ABCDEFGHIJKLMNOPQRSTUVWXYZ

abcdefghijklmnopqrstuvwxyz1234567890

A large fawn jumped quickly over white zinc boxes.

John Handy

Designer	Timothy Donaldson
Nationality	UK
Date Designed	1995
Foundries	Letraset Monotype ITC
Number of weights	1

ABCDEFGHIJKLMNOPQRSTUVWXYZ

abcdefghijklmnopqrstuvwxyz1234567890

Puzzled women bequeath jerks very exotic gifts.

Jonatan

Designer	Franko Luin
Nationality	SL
Date Designed	1995
Foundries	Linotype
Number of weights	1

ABCDEFGHIJKLMNOPQRSTUVWXYZ

abcdefghijklmnopqrstuvwxyz1234567890

Exquisite farm wench gives body jolt to prize stinker.

Kasper

Designer	Franko Luin
Nationality	SL
Date Designed	1995
Foundries	Linotype
Number of weights	1

ABCDEFGHIJKLMNOPQRSTUVWXYZ

abcdefghijklmnopqrstuvwxyz1234567890

West quickly gave Bert handsome prizes for six juicy plums.

Pablo

Designer	Trevor Pettit
Nationality	UK
Date Designed	1995
Foundries	Letraset Linotype ITC Monotype
Number of weights	1

ABCDEFGHIJKLMNOPQRSTUVWXYZ

abcdefghijklmnopqrstuvwxyz1234567890

Based on the Spanish painter Pablo Picasso's signature.

Postcard

Designer	Perry Whittle
Nationality	US
Date Designed	1995
Foundries	Monotype
Number of weights	5

ABCDEFGHIJKLMNOPQRSTUVWXYZ

abcdefghijklmnopqrstuvwxyz1234567890

Five big quacking zephyrs jolt my wax bed.

Skippy Sharp

Designer	Steve McFadden, Chank Diesel
Nationality	US
Date Designed	1995
Foundries	Monotype
Number of weights	1

ABCDEFGHIJKLMNOPQRSTUVWXYZ

abcdefghijklmnopqrstuvwxyz1234567890

The job of waxing linoleum frequently peeves chintzy kids.

Skylark

Designer	Patty King
Nationality	US
Date Designed	1995
Foundries	Monotype ITC
Number of weights	1

ABCDEFGHIJKLMNOPQRSTUVWXYZ

abcdefghijklmnopqrstuvwxyz1234567890

We have just quoted on nine dozen boxes of gray lamp wicks.

Trackpad

Designer	Timothy Donaldson
Nationality	UK
Date Designed	1995
Foundries	ITC
Number of weights	1

ABCDEFGHIJKLMNOPQRSTUVWXYZ

abcdefghijklmnopqrstuvwxyz1234567890

Jeb quickly drove a few extra miles on the glazed pavement.

Viner Hand

Designer	John Viner
Nationality	US
Date Designed	1995
Foundries	ITC Monotype
Number of weights	1

ABCDEFGHIJKLMNOPQRSTUVWXYZ

abcdefghijklmnopqrstuvwxyz1234567890

Ebenezer unexpectedly bagged two tranquil aardvarks with his jiffy vacuum cleaner.

Wild Thing

Designer	Martin Wait
Nationality	UK
Date Designed	1995
Foundries	Martin Wait Type
Number of weights	1

ABCDEFGHIJKLMNOPQRSTUVWXYZ

abcdefghijklmnopqrstuvwxyz1234567890

Portez ce vieux whisky au juge blond qui fume.

FancyWriting

Designer	Timothy Donaldson
Nationality	UK
Date Designed	1996
Foundries	FontFont
Number of weights	3

ABCDEFGHIJKLMNOPQRSTUVWXYZ

abcdefghijklmnopqrstuvwxyz1234567890

How razorback-jumping frogs can level six piqued gymnasts!

Graphena

Designer	Giancarlo Barison
Nationality	IT
Date Designed	1996
Foundries	Linotype
Number of weights	1

ABCDEFGHIJKLMNOPQRSTUVWXYZ

abcdefghijklmnopqrstuvwxyz1234567890

Quick wafting zephyrs vex bold Jim.

Layout

Designer	Gerd Wippich
Nationality	DE
Date Designed	1996
Foundries	FontFont
Number of weights	4

ABCDEFGHIJKLMNOPQRSTUVWXYZ

abcdefghijklmnopqrstuvwxyz1234567890

Used for layouts. Oxomox replaces all characters with o, x, and m, and Tramline substitutes grayed out text.

Nowe Ateny

Designer	Dariusz Nowak-Nova
Nationality	PL
Date Designed	1996
Foundries	Linotype
Number of weights	1

ABCDEFGHIJKLMNOPQRSTUVWXYZ

abcdefghijklmnopqrstuvwxyz1234567890

The five boxing wizards jump quickly.

Market

Designer	H A Simon
Nationality	DE
Date Designed	1996
Foundries	FontFont
Number of weights	3

ABCDEFGHIJKLMNOPQRSTUVWXYZ
abcdefghijklmnopqrstuvwxyz1234567890
Astronaut Quincy B. Zack defies gravity with six jet fuel pumps.

Sketch

Designer	Dieter Kurz
Nationality	DE
Date Designed	1996
Foundries	Linotype
Number of weights	1

ABCDEFGHIJKLMNOPQRSTUVWXYZ
abcdefghijklmnopqrstuvwxyz1234567890
The vixen jumped quickly on her foe barking with zeal.

Synthetica

Designer	Philip Bouwsma, Cynthia Batty
Nationality	US
Date Designed	1996
Foundries	Monotype
Number of weights	2

ABCDEFGHIJKLMNOPQRSTUVWXYZ
abcdefghijklmnopqrstuvwxyz1234567890
We promptly judged antique ivory buckles for the next prize.

Arid

Designer	Rob Leuschke
Nationality	US
Date Designed	1997
Foundries	Linotype ITC
Number of weights	1

ABCDEFGHIJKLMNOPQRSTUVWXYZ
abcdefghijklmnopqrstuvwxyz1234567890
Crazy Fredericka bought many very exquisite opal jewels.

Bergell

Designer	Thomas Finke
Nationality	DE
Date Designed	1997
Foundries	Linotype ITC
Number of weights	1

ABCDEFGHIJKLMNOPQRSTUVWXYZ
abcdefghij-klmnopqrstuvwxyz1234567890
The quick brown fox jumps over the lazy dog.

Cyberkugel

Designer Timothy Donaldson
Nationality UK
Date Designed 1997
Foundries Bitstream ITC Letraset
Number of weights 1

ABCDEFGHIJKLMNOPQRSTUVWXYZ
abcdefghijklmnopqrstuvwxyz1234567890
For only $49, jolly housewives made inexpensive meals using quick-frozen vegetables.

Feltpen

Designer Lutz Baar
Nationality SE
Date Designed 1997
Foundries Linotype
Number of weights 2

ABCDEFGHIJKLMNOPQRSTUVWXYZ
abcdefghijklmnopqrstuvwxyz1234567890
A mad boxer shot a quick, gloved jab to the jaw of his dizzy opponent.

Inky Script

Designer Thomas Schnäbele
Nationality DE
Date Designed 1997
Foundries Linotype
Number of weights 1

ABCDEFGHIJKLMNOPQRSTUVWXYZ
abcdefghijklmnopqrstuvwxyz1234567890
We have just quoted on nine dozen boxes of gray lamp wicks.

Finer Liner

Designer Gary Munch
Nationality US
Date Designed 1997
Foundries Linotype
Number of weights 2

ABCDEFGHIJKLMNOPQRSTUVWXYZ
abcdefghijklmnopqrstuvwxyz1234567890
Sixty zippers were quickly picked from the woven jute bag.

Agogo

Designer Ed Bugg
Nationality UK
Date Designed 1997
Foundries Linotype
Number of weights 5

ABCDEFGHIJKLMNOPQRSTUVWXYZ
abcdefghijklmnopqrstuvwxyz1234567890
Five big quacking zephyrs jolt my wax bed.

Kulukundis

Designer	Daniel Pelavin
Nationality	US
Date Designed	1997
Foundries	Monotype ITC
Number of weights	1

ABCDEFGHIJKLMNOPQRSTUVWXYZ
abcdefghijklmnopqrstuvwxyz1234567890
Pack my box with five dozen liquor jugs.

Linotype Mild

Designer	Martina Schikorski
Nationality	DE
Date Designed	1997
Foundries	Linotype
Number of weights	1

ABCDEFGHIJKLMNOPQRSTUVWXYZ
abcdefghijklmnopqrstuvwxyz1234567890
Was there a quorum of able whizzkids gravely exciting the jaded fish at ATypI?

Peter's Miro

Designer	John Peter
Nationality	UK
Date Designed	1997
Foundries	ITC
Number of weights	2

ABCDEFGHIJKLMNOPQRSTUVWXYZ
abcdefghijklmnopqrstuvwxyz1234567890
Freight to me sixty dozen quart jars and twelve black pans.

Nora

Designer	James Montalbano
Nationality	US
Date Designed	1997
Foundries	Monotype
Number of weights	1

ABCDEFGHIJKLMNOPQRSTUVWXYZ
abcdefghijklmnopqrstuvwxyz1234567890
The risque gown marked a brazen exposure of very juicy flesh.

Rana

Designer	Hans-Jürgen Ellenberger
Nationality	DE
Date Designed	1997
Foundries	Linotype
Number of weights	6

ABCDEFGHIJKLMNOPQRSTUVWXYZ
abcdefghijklmnopqrstuvwxyz1234567890
How razorback-jumping frogs can level six piqued gymnasts!

Salamander

Designer	Michael Struller
Nationality	DE
Date Designed	1997
Foundries	Linotype
Number of weights	4

ABCDEFGHIJKLMNOPQRSTUVWXYZ
abcdefghijklmnopqrstuvwxyz1234567890
Lizard-like creatures which were thought to live in fire. They don't and can't.

Stranger

Designer	Jill Bell
Nationality	US
Date Designed	1997
Foundries	Linotype ITC Monotype
Number of weights	1

ABCDEFGHIJKLMNOPQRSTUVWXYZ
abcdefghijklmnopqrstuvwxyz1234567890
We promptly judged antique ivory buckles for the next prize.

Samuel

Designer	Phill Grimshaw
Nationality	UK
Date Designed	1998
Foundries	ITC
Number of weights	1

ABCDEFGHIJKLMNOPQRSTUVWXYZ
abcdefghijklmnopqrstuvwxyz1234567890
Playing jazz vibe chords quickly excites my wife.

Aspectintro LT

Designer	Hans-Jürgen Elllenberger
Nationality	DE
Date Designed	1999
Foundries	Linotype
Number of weights	1

ABCDEFGHIJKLMNOPQRSTUVWXYZ
abcdefghijklmnopqrstuvwxyz1234567890
Sphinx of black quartz judge my vow.

Longhand

Designer	Garrett Boge
Nationality	US
Date Designed	1998
Foundries	Monotype
Number of weights	2

ABCDEFGHIJKLMNOPQRSTUVWXYZ
abcdefghijklmnopqrstuvwxyz1234567890
Sympathizing would fix Quaker objectives.

Masterpiece

Designer	Peter Bilak
Nationality	SK
Date Designed	1996
Foundries	FontFont
Number of weights	4

ABCDEFGHIJKLMNOPQRSTUVWXYZ

abcdefghijklmnopqrstuvwxyz1234567890

New farm hand (picking just six quinces) proves strong but lazy.

Underscript

Designer	Claudia Rocha
Nationality	BR
Date Designed	1997
Foundries	ITC
Number of weights	1

ABCDEFGHIJKLMNOPQRSTUVWXYZ

ABCDEFGHIJKLMNOPQRSTUVWXYZ1234567890

ALL QUESTIONS ASKED BY FIVE WATCH EXPERTS
AMAZED THE JUDGE.

Bruno

Designer	Jill Bell
Nationality	US
Date Designed	1998
Foundries	CA Partners Monotype
Number of weights	1

ABCDEFGHIJKLMNOPQRSTUVWXYZ

abcdefghijklmnopqrstuvwxyz1234567890

How vexing a fumble to drop a jolly zucchini in the quicksand.

Dartangnon ITC

Designer	Nick Cooke
Nationality	UK
Date Designed	1998
Foundries	Monotype ITC
Number of weights	1

ABCDEFGHIJKLMNOPQRSTUVWXYZ

abcdefghijklmnopqrstuvwxyz1234567890

Breezily jangling £3,416,857,209 wise advertiser ambles to the bank, his exchequer amplified.

Highscript

Designer	Bayer Corporation
Nationality	US
Date Designed	1998
Foundries	CA Partners Monotype
Number of weights	6

ABCDEFGHIJKLMNOPQRSTUVWXYZ

abcdefghijklmnopqrstuvwxyz1234567890

Jackdaws love my big sphinx of quartz.

Maricava

Designer	Bo Berndal
Nationality	SE
Date Designed	1998
Foundries	Monotype
Number of weights	2

ABCDEFGHIJKLMNOPQRSTUVWXYZ

abcdefghijklmnopqrstuvwxyz1234567890

The vixen jumped quickly on her foe barking with zeal.

Regallia

Designer	Phill Grimshaw
Nationality	UK
Date Designed	1998
Foundries	ITC
Number of weights	1

ABCDEFGHIJKLMNOPQRSTUVWXYZ

abcdefghijklmnopqrstuvwxyz1234567890

Jay visited back home and gazed upon a brown fox and quail.

Johann Sparkling

Designer	Viktor Solt-Bittner
Nationality	AT
Date Designed	1997
Foundries	Monotype ITC
Number of weights	1

ABCDEFGHIJKLMNOPQRSTUVWXYZ

abcdefghijklmnopqrstuvwxyz1234567890

An inspired calligrapher can create pages of beauty using stick ink, quill, brush, pick-axe, buzz saw, or even strawberry jam.

Treefrog

Designer	Brian Willson
Nationality	US
Date Designed	1998
Foundries	Three Islands Press
Number of weights	1

ABCDEFGHIJKLMNOPQRSTUVWXYZ

abcdefghijklmnopqrstuvwxyz1234567890

Based on the display lettering style of Philip D. Cyr.

Texas Hero

Designer	Brian Willson
Nationality	US
Date Designed	1998
Foundries	Three Islands Press
Number of weights	1

ABCDEFGHIJKLMNOPQRSTUVWXYZ

abcdefghijklmnopqrstuvwxyz1234567890

Based on the handwriting of C19 Texan General Thomas J. Rusk.

Linotype Constitution

Designer	Frank Marciuliano
Nationality	US
Date Designed	2001
Foundries	Linotype
Number of weights	1

ABCDEFGHIJKLMNOPQRSTUVWXYZ

abcdefghijklmnopqrstuvwxyz1234567890

John Hancock's signature on the American constitution.

Voluta Script

Designer	Viktor Solt-Bittner
Nationality	AT
Date Designed	1998
Foundries	Adobe
Number of weights	3

ABCDEFGHIJKLMNOPQRSTUVWXYZ

abcdefghijklmnopqrstuvwxyz1234567890

Many-wived Jack laughs at probes of sex quiz.

Houston Pen

Designer	Brian Willson
Nationality	US
Date Designed	1998
Foundries	Type Quarry
Number of weights	2

ABCDEFGHIJKLMNOPQRSTUVWXYZ

abcdefghijklmnopqrstuvwxyz1234567890

About sixty codfish eggs will make a quarter pound of very fizzy jelly.

Solace

Designer	Adam Roe
Nationality	US
Date Designed	1995
Foundries	Monotype
Number of weights	1

ABCDEFGHIJKLMNOPQRSTUVWXYZ

abcdefghijklmnopqrstuvwxyz1234567890

Freight to me sixty dozen quart jars and twelve black pans.

Blackadder

Designer	Bob Anderton
Nationality	UK
Date Designed	1996
Foundries	ITC Linotype
Number of weights	1

ABCDEFGHIJKLMNOPQRSTUVWXYZ

abcdefghijklmnopqrstuvwxyz1234567890

Breezily jangling $3,416,857,209, wise advertiser ambles to the bank, his exchequer amplified.

Zapfino

Designer	Hermann Zapf
Nationality	DE
Date Designed	1998
Foundries	Linotype Apple
Number of weights	6

ABCDEFGHIJKLMNOPQRST...
abcdefghijklmnopqrstuvwxyz1234567890

Amadeo

Designer	Julius de Goede, Fiel van der Veen
Nationality	NL
Date Designed	1999
Foundries	Monotype
Number of weights	6

ABCDEFGHIJKLMNOPQRSTUVWXYZ
abcdefghijklmnopqrstuvwxyz1234567890
The exodus of jazzy pigeons is craved by squeamish walkers.

Coolman

Designer	Per Elstrom
Nationality	SE
Date Designed	1999
Foundries	ITC
Number of weights	1

ABCDEFGHIJKLMNOPQRSTUVWXYZ
abcdefghijklmnopqrstuvwxyz1234567890
Jim just quit and packed extra bags for Liz Owen.

Linotype Notec

Designer	Franciszek Otto
Nationality	PL
Date Designed	1999
Foundries	Linotype
Number of weights	1

ABCDEFGHIJKLMNOPQRSTUVWXYZ
abcdefghijklmnopqrstuvwxyz1234567890
Just keep examining every low-bid quoted for zinc etchings.

Schooner Script

Designer	Brian Willson
Nationality	US
Date Designed	1999
Foundries	Three Islands Press
Number of weights	5

ABCDEFGHIJKLMNOPQRSTUVWXYZ
abcdefghijklmnopqrstuvwxyz1234567890
Based on the 1825 handwriting of Samuel Clarke, a Princeton, Mass., pastor.

Styleboy

Designer	Chester Wajda
Nationality	US
Date Designed	1999
Foundries	ITC Monotype
Number of weights	1

ABCDEFGHIJKLMNOPQRSTUVWXYZ
abcdefghijklmnopqrstuvwxyz1234567890
Just keep examining every low bid quoted for zinc etchings.

Comedia Medium

Designer	Olivier Nineuil
Nationality	FR
Date Designed	2000
Foundries	Monotype
Number of weights	1

ABCDEFGHIJKLMNOPQRSTUVWXYZ
abcdefghijklmnopqrstuvwxyz1234567890
The juke box music puzzled a gentle visitor from a quaint valley town.

Weber Hand

Designer	Lisabeth Weber
Nationality	DE
Date Designed	1999
Foundries	ITC
Number of weights	1

ABCDEFGHIJKLMNOPQRSTUVWXYZ
abcdefghijklmnopqrstuvwxyz1234567890
Lazy movers quit hard-packing of papier-maché jewellery boxes.

Berranger Hand

Designer	Eric de Berranger
Nationality	FR
Date Designed	2001
Foundries	ITC
Number of weights	1

ABCDEFGHIJKLMNOPQRSTUVWXYZ
abcdefghijklmnopqrstuvwxyz1234567890
Portez ce vieux whisky au juge blond qui fume.

Django ITC

Designer	Wayne Thompson
Nationality	AU
Date Designed	2000
Foundries	ITC
Number of weights	1

ABCDEFGHIJKLMNOPQRSTUVWXYZ
abcdefghijklmnopqrstuvwxyz1234567890
The gypsy guitarist Django Reinhardt was illiterate.

Linotype Ego

Designer	Joern Lehnhoff
Nationality	DE
Date Designed	2000
Foundries	Linotype
Number of weights	1

ABCDEFGHIJKLMNOPQRSTUVWXYZ

abcdefghijklmnopqrstuvwxyz 1234567890

Quixotic Conservatives vet first key zero-growth jeremiad.

Linotype Elisa

Designer	Christopher Young
Nationality	NZ
Date Designed	2000
Foundries	Linotype
Number of weights	1

ABCDEFGHIJKL MNOPQRSTUV W X Y Z

abcdefghijklmnopqrstuvwxyz1234567890

My help squeezed back in again and joined the weavers after six.

Out of the Fridge

Designer	Jochen Schuss
Nationality	DE
Date Designed	2000
Foundries	ITC Monotype
Number of weights	1

ABCDEFGHIJKLMNOPQRSTUVWXYZ

abcdefghijklmnopqrstuvwxyz1234567890

Viewing quizzical abstracts mixed up hefty jocks.

Schuss Hand

Designer	Jochen Schuss
Nationality	DE
Date Designed	2000
Foundries	ITC
Number of weights	2

ABCDEFGHIJKLMNOPQRSTUVWXYZ

abcdefghijklmnopqrstuvwxyz1234567890

Back in June we delivered oxygen equipment of the same size.

Briem Script

Designer	Gunnlaugur S E Briem
Nationality	IS
Date Designed	2001
Foundries	Monotype
Number of weights	3

ABCDEFGHIJKLMNOPQRSTUVWXYZ

abcdefghijklmnopqrstuvwxyz1234567890

Six big devils from Japan quickly forgot how to waltz.

Ropsen Script

Designer	Jürgen Brinckmann
Nationality	DE
Date Designed	2001
Foundries	FontFont
Number of weights	1

ABCDEFGHIJKLMNOPQRSTUVWXYZ

abcdefghijklmnopqrstuvwxyz1234567890

The risque gown marked a brazen exposure of very juicy flesh.

Tuscany

Designer	Hans Bacher
Nationality	DE
Date Designed	2001
Foundries	Monotype
Number of weights	1

AbcDEFGhiJKLMNOPQRSTUVWXYZ

AbcDEFGhiJKLMNOPQRSTUVWXYZ1234567890

WhY NOT TOSCANA? OR EVEN TOSKANA?

Gaius

Designer	Julius de Goede
Nationality	NL
Date Designed	2002
Foundries	Linotype
Number of weights	12

ABCDEFGHIJKLMNOPQRSTUVWXYZ

abcdefghijklmnopqrstuvwxyz1234567890

Grumpy wizards make toxic brew for the evil Queen and Jack.

Pepe

Designer	Pepe Gimeno
Nationality	ES
Date Designed	2002
Foundries	FontFont
Number of weights	4

ABCDEFGHIJKLMNOPQRSTUVWXYZ

abcdefghijklmnopqrstuvwxyz1234567890

The risque gown marked a brazen exposure of very juicy flesh.

Arab Stroke

Designer	Mauro Carichini
Nationality	IT
Date Designed	2002
Foundries	Linotype
Number of weights	3

ABCDEFGHIJKLMNOPQRSTUVWXYZ

abcdefghijklmnopqrstuvwxyz1234567890

Sphinx of black quartz judge my vow.

Alexa

Designer	John Benson
Nationality	US
Date Designed	1995
Foundries	Adobe
Number of weights	1

ABCDEFGHIJKLMNOPQRSTUVWXYZ

abcdefghijklmnopqrstuvwxyz1234567890

A large fawn jumped quickly over white zinc boxes.

Andy

Designer	Steve Matteson
Nationality	US
Date Designed	1995
Foundries	Monotype
Number of weights	4

ABCDEFGHIJKLMNOPQRSTUVWXYZ

abcdefghijklmnopqrstuvwxyz1234567890

Quick wafting zephyrs vex bold Jim.

Flamme

Designer	Schelter & Giesecke
Nationality	DE
Date Designed	1933
Foundries	Linotype Monotype Letraset ITC
Recut/Digitised by	Alan Meeks 1993
Number of weights	1

ABCDEFGHIJKLMNOPQRSTUVWXYZ

abcdefghijklmnopqrstuvwxyz1234567890

Jackdaws love my big sphinx of quartz.

Blizzard

Designer	Julius Kim
Nationality	DE
Date Designed	1935
Foundries	Wagner URW++
Number of weights	1

ABCDEFGHIJKLMNOPQRSTUVWXYZ

abcdefghijklmnopqrstuvwxyz1234567890

As a typeface this was originally called Bison.

Gillies Gothic

Designer	William S Gillies
Nationality	US
Date Designed	1935
Foundries	Monotype URW++ Bauer ITC
Number of weights	4

ABCDEFGHIJKLMNOPQRSTUVWXYZ

abcdefghijklmnopqrstuvwxyz1234567890

Just keep examining every low bid quoted for zinc etchings.

Kaufmann

Designer M R Kaufmann
Nationality US
Date Designed 1936
Foundries ATF Bitstream Elsner+Flake URW
Number of weights 2

ABCDEFGHIJKLMNOP2RSTUVWXYZ
abcdefghijklmnopqrstuvwxyz1234567890
Five wine experts jokingly quizzed sample chablis.

Swing

Designer Max Kaufmann
Nationality US
Date Designed 1936
Foundries Monotype
Number of weights 2

ABCDEFGHIJKLMNOP2RSTUVWXYZ
abcdefghijklmnopqrstuvwxyz1234567890
Here with a Loaf of Bread beneath the Bough,

Malibu

Designer Alan Meeks
Nationality UK
Date Designed 1992
Foundries Monotype ITC Letraset
Number of weights 1

ABCDEFGHIJKLMNOPQRSTUVWXYZ
abcdefghijklmnopqrstuvwxyz1234567890
Verily the dark ex-Jew quit Zionism, preferring the cabala.

Harlow

Designer Colin Brignall
Nationality UK
Date Designed 1977
Foundries Letraset Linotype ITC
Number of weights 2

ABCDEFGHIJKLMNOPQRSTUVWXYZ
abcdefghijklmnopqrstuvwxyz1234567890
Jazzy saxophones blew over Mick's turgid quiff.

Santa Fé

Designer David Quay
Nationality UK
Date Designed 1983
Foundries Letraset Linotype ITC
Number of weights 1

ABCDEFGHIJKLMNOPQRSTUVWXYZ
abcdefghijklmnopqrstuvwxyz1234567890
Jail zesty vixen who grabbed pay from quack.

Reporter #2

Designer	Carlos Winkow
Nationality	ES
Date Designed	1938
Foundries	Wagner Linotype
Number of weights	1

ABCDEFGHJJKLMNOPQRSTUVWXYZ

abcdefghijklmnopqrstuvwxyz1234567890

Now is the time for all brown dogs to jump over the lazy lynx.

Brush Script

Designer	Robert E Smith
Nationality	US
Date Designed	1942
Foundries	Monotype Bitstream Adobe URW++
Number of weights	1

ABCDEFGHIJKLMNOPQRSTUVWXYZ

abcdefghijklmnopqrstuvwxyz1234567890

A Flask of Wine, a Book of Verse—and Thou.

Flash

Designer	Edwin W Shaar
Nationality	US
Date Designed	1939
Foundries	Monotype Letraset ITC Elsner+Flake URW++ Linotype
Number of weights	4

ABCDEFGHIJKLMNOPQRSTUVWXYZ

abcdefghijklmnopqrstuvwxyz1234567890

My grandfather picks up quartz and valuable onyx jewels.

Balloon

Designer	M R Kaufmann
Nationality	US
Date Designed	1939
Foundries	ATF URW++
Number of weights	2

ABCDEFGHIJKLMNOPQRSTUVWXYZ

ABCDEFGHIJKLMNOPQRSTUVWXYZ1234567890

A QUICK MOVEMENT OF THE ENEMY WILL JEOPARDIZE SIX GUNBOATS.

PL Davison Zip Bold

Designer	M Davison
Nationality	US
Date Designed	1950
Foundries	Monotype
Number of weights	1

ABCDEFGHIJKLMNOPQRSTUVWXYZ

ABCDEFGHIJKLMNOPQRSTUVWXYZ1234567890

PERHAPS PRESIDENT CLINTON'S AMAZING SAX SKILLS WILL BE JUDGED QUITE FAVOURABLY.

Dom Casual

Designer	Pete Dom
Nationality	US
Date Designed	1951
Foundries	ATF
Number of weights	2

ABCDEFGHIJKLMNOPQRSTUVWXYZ

abcdefghijklmnopqrstuvwxyz1234567890

Beside me singing in the Wilderness—

Marker Felt

Designer	Pat Snyder
Nationality	US
Date Designed	1955
Foundries	Erik.co.uk Linotype
Recut/Digitised by	Dieter Steffman
Number of weights	2

ABCDEFGHIJKLMNOPQRSTUVWXYZ

abcdefghijklmnopqrstuvwxyz1234567890

Felt markers were beloved of layout artists the world over.

PL Benguiat Frisky

Designer	Ed Benguiat
Nationality	US
Date Designed	1960
Foundries	Monotype
Number of weights	1

ABCDEFGHIJKLMNOPQRSTUVWXYZ

abcdefghijklmnopqrstuvwxyz1234567890

The July sun caused a fragment of black pine wax to ooze on the velvet quilt.

Churchward Brush

Designer	Joseph Churchward
Nationality	NZ
Date Designed	1970
Foundries	URW++
Number of weights	2

ABCDEFGHIJKLMNOPQRSTUVWXYZ

abcdefghijklmnopqrstuvwxyz1234567890

All questions asked by five watch experts amazed the judge.

Challenge

Designer	Martin Wait
Nationality	UK
Date Designed	1982
Foundries	Linotype Monotype ITC Letraset
Number of weights	2

ABCDEFGHIJKLMNOPQRSTUVWXYZ

abcdefghijklmnopqrstuvwxyz1234567890

Lazy movers quit hard-packing of papier-mache jewellery boxes.

One Stroke Script

Designer Paul Clarke
Nationality UK
Date Designed 1984
Foundries Letraset Linotype ITC
Number of weights 3

ABCDEFGHIJKLMNOPQRSTUVWXYZ

abcdefghijklmnopqrstuvwxyzl234567890

Hark! Toxic jungle water vipers quietly drop on zebras for meals!

Fluidum Bold

Designer Alessandro Butti
Nationality IT
Date Designed 1951
Foundries Nebiolo Monotype
Number of weights 1

ABCDEFGHIJKLMNOPQRSTUVWXYZ

abcdefghijklmnopqrstuvwxyz1234567890

The original Regular version is not available digitally.

Palette

Designer Martin Wilke
Nationality DE
Date Designed 1951
Foundries Berthold URW++
Number of weights 1

ABCDEFGHIJKLMNOPQRSTUVWXYZ

abcdefghijklmnopqrstuvwxyz1234567890

May Jo equal the fine record by solving six puzzles a week?

Salto

Designer Karlgeorg Hoefer
Nationality DE
Date Designed 1952
Foundries Klingspor Linotype
Number of weights 1

ABCDEFGHIJKLMNOPQRSTUVWXYZ

abcdefghijklmnopqrstuvwxyz1234567890

Murky haze enveloped a city as jarring quakes broke forty-six windows.

Saltino

Designer Karlgeorg Hoefer
Nationality DE
Date Designed 1953
Foundries Klingspor Monotype
Number of weights 1

ABCDEFGHIJKLMNOPQRSTUVWXYZ

abcdefghijklmnopqrstuvwxyz1234567890

About sixty codfish eggs will make a quarter pound of very fizzy jelly.

Mistral

Designer	Roger Excoffon
Nationality	FR
Date Designed	1953
Foundries	Olive Monotype URW++ ITC Adobe Linotype
Number of weights	3

ABCDEFGHIJKLMNOPQRSTUVWXYZ

abcdefghijklmnopqrstuvwxyz1234567890

The hot late summer wind that blows up from North Africa into the south of France, where Fonderie Olive was based.

Ashley Script

Designer	Ashley Havinden
Nationality	UK
Date Designed	1955
Foundries	Monotype Adobe
Number of weights	1

ABCDEFGHIJKLMNOPQRSTUVWXYZ

abcdefghijklmnopqrstuvwxyz1234567890

Sixty zippers were quickly picked from the woven jute bag.

Choc

Designer	Roger Excoffon
Nationality	FR
Date Designed	1955
Foundries	Olive ITC URW++
Number of weights	3

ABCDEFGHIJKLMNOPQRSTUVWXYZ

abcdefghijklmnopqrstuvwxyz1234567890

Moi, je veux quinze clubs a golf et du whisky pur.

Diskus

Designer	Martin Wilke
Nationality	DE
Date Designed	1955
Foundries	Stempel Adobe URW++
Number of weights	2

ABCDEFGHIJKLMNOPQRSTUVWXYZ

abcdefghijklmnopqrstuvwxyz1234567890

Jelly-like above the high wire, six quaking pachyderms kept the climax of the extravaganza in a dazzling state of flux.

Klang

Designer	Will Carter
Nationality	UK
Date Designed	1955
Foundries	Monotype Adobe
Number of weights	1

ABCDEFGHIJKLMNOPQRSTUVWXYZ

abcdefghijklmnopqrstuvwxyz1234567890

William Jex quickly caught five dozen Conservatives.

Time Script

Designer Georg Trump
Nationality DE
Date Designed 1956
Foundries URW++
Number of weights 3

ABCDEFGHIJKLMNOPQRSTUVWXYZ
abcdefghijklmnopqrstuvwxyz1234567890
We have just quoted on nine dozen boxes of gray lamp wicks.

Mercurius Script Bold

Designer Imre Reiner
Nationality HU
Date Designed 1957
Foundries Linotype Adobe
Number of weights 1

ABCDEFGHIJKLMNOPQRSTUVWXYZ
abcdefghijklmnopqrstuvwxyz1234567890
The risque gown marked a brazen exposure of very juicy flesh.

Slogan

Designer Aldo Novarese
Nationality IT
Date Designed 1957
Foundries Nebiolo
Number of weights 1

ABCDEFGHIJKLMNOPQRSTUVWXYZ
abcdefghijklmnopqrstuvwxyz1234567890
Was there a quorum of able whizzkids gravely exciting the jaded fish at ATypI?

Charme

Designer Helmut Matheis
Nationality DE
Date Designed 1958
Foundries Ludwig & Mayer Adobe Bauer
Number of weights 1

ABCDEFGHIJKLMNOPQRSTUVWXYZ
abcdefghijklmnopqrstuvwxyz1234567890
Questions of a zealous nature have become by degrees petty waxen jokes.

Slogan

Designer Helmut Matheis
Nationality DE
Date Designed 1959
Foundries Ludwig & Mayer Linotype URW++ Elsner+Flake
Number of weights 1

ABCDEFGHIJKLMNOPQRSTUVWXYZ
abcdefghijklmnopqrstuvwxyz1234567890
Astonishingly similar to Aldo Novarese's font of the same name, created two years earlier.

Pepita

Designer	Imre Reiner
Nationality	HU
Date Designed	1959
Foundries	Monotype
Number of weights	1

ABCDEFGHIJKLMNOPQRSTUVWXYZ

abcdefghijklmnopqrstuvwxyz1234567890

A quick movement of the enemy will jeopardize six gunboats.

Forte

Designer	Carl Reissberger
Nationality	DE
Date Designed	1962
Foundries	Monotype Adobe
Number of weights	1

ABCDEFGHIJKLMNOPQRSTUVWXYZ

abcdefghijklmnopqrstuvwxyz1234567890

Mr. Jock, TV quiz Ph.D., bags few lynx.

Biffo

Designer	David Marshall
Nationality	UK
Date Designed	1964
Foundries	Monotype Linotype Adobe
Number of weights	1

ABCDEFGHIJKLMNOPQRSTUVWXYZ

abcdefghijklmnopqrstuvwxyz1234567890

Sixty zippers were quickly picked from the woven jute bag.

Stentor

Designer	Heinz Schumann
Nationality	CZ
Date Designed	1964
Foundries	Typoart Elsner+Flake Linotype URW++
Number of weights	1

ABCDEFGHIJKLMNOPQRSTUVWXYZ

abcdefghijklmnopqrstuvwxyz1234567890

Ebenezer unexpectedly bagged two tranquil aardvarks with his jiffy vacuum cleaner.

New Berolina

Designer	Martin Wilke
Nationality	DE
Date Designed	1965
Foundries	Monotype
Number of weights	1

ABCDEFGHIJKLMNOPQRSTUVWXYZ

abcdefghijklmnopqrstuvwxyz1234567890

Just work for improved basic techniques to maximize your typing skill.

Cascade Script

Designer Matthew Carter
Nationality UK
Date Designed 1966
Foundries Linofilm Adobe Linotype
Number of weights 1

ABCDEFGHIJKLMNOPQRSTUVWXYZ
abcdefghijklmnopqrstuvwxyz 1234567890
A mad boxer shot a quick, gloved jab to the jaw of his dizzy opponent.

Present

Designer F K Sallwey
Nationality DE
Date Designed 1974
Foundries Linotype
Number of weights 5

ABCDEFGHIJKLMNOPQRSTUVWXYZ
abcdefghijklmnopqrstuvwxyz1234567890
Verily the dark ex-Jew quit Zionism, preferring the cabala.

Pendry Script

Designer Martin Wait
Nationality UK
Date Designed 1981
Foundries ITC
Number of weights 2

ABCDEFGHIJKLMNOPQRSTUVWXYZ
abcdefghijklmnopqrstuvwxyz1234567890
The sex life of the woodchuck is a provocative question for most vertebrate zoology majors.

Becka Script

Designer David Harris
Nationality UK
Date Designed 1985
Foundries Linotype ITC
Number of weights 1

ABCDEFGHIJKLMNOPQRSTUVWXYZ
abcdefghijklmnopqrstuvwxyz1234567890
Six big devils from Japan quickly forgot how to waltz.

Bronx

Designer David Quay
Nationality UK
Date Designed 1986
Foundries Linotype ITC
Number of weights 1

ABCDEFGHIJKLMNOPQRSTUVWXYZ
abcdefghijklmnopqrstuvwxyz1234567890
Crazy Fredericka bought many very exquisite opal jewels.

Spring

Designer	Garrett Boge
Nationality	US
Date Designed	1988
Foundries	LPT Monotype Adobe
Number of weights	2

ABCDEFGHIJKLMNOPQRSTUVWXYZ

abcdefghijklmnopqrstuvwxyz1234567890

Exquisite farm wench gives body jolt to prize stinker.

Visigoth

Designer	Arthur Baker
Nationality	US
Date Designed	1988
Foundries	Adobe Glyph Systems Monotype Linotype
Number of weights	1

ABCDEFGHIJKLMNOPQRSTUVWXYZ

abcdefghijklmnopqrstuvwxyz1234567890

New farm hand (picking just six quinces) proves strong but lazy.

Ru'ach

Designer	Timothy Donaldson
Nationality	UK
Date Designed	1990
Foundries	ITC
Number of weights	1

ABCDEFGHIJKLMNOPQRSTUVWXYZ

abcdefghijklmnopqrstuvwxyz1234567890

Mix Zapf with Veljovic and get quirky Beziers.

Quixley

Designer	Zoltan Nagy
Nationality	HU
Date Designed	1991
Foundries	Letraset Monotype ITC
Recut/Digitised by	Vince Whitlock
Number of weights	1

ABCDEFGHIJKLMNOPQRSTUVWXYZ

abcdefghijklmnopqrstuvwxyz1234567890

An inspired calligrapher can create pages of beauty using stick ink, quill, brush, pick-axe, buzz saw, or even strawberry jam.

Siena Black

Designer	Wagner & Schmidt
Nationality	DE
Date Designed	1991
Foundries	Monotype
Number of weights	1

ABCDEFGHIJKLMNOPQRSTUVWXYZ

abcdefghijklmnopqrstuvwxyz1234567890

Six crazy kings vowed to abolish my quite pitiful jousts.

DuMathieu

Designer D van Meerbeeck
Nationality NL
Date Designed 1992
Foundries FontFont
Number of weights 1

ABCDEFGHIJKLMNOPQRSTUVWXYZ

abcdefghijklmnopqrstuvwxyz1234567890

The risque gown marked a brazen exposure of very juicy flesh.

Koffee

Designer anon
Nationality US
Date Designed 1992
Foundries Apple URW++
Number of weights 1

ABCDEFGHIJKLMNOPQRSTUVWXYZ

abcdefghijklmnopqrstuvwxyz 1234567890

Six big juicy steaks sizzled in a pan as five workmen left the quarry.

Ruling Script Two

Designer Gottfried Pott
Nationality DE
Date Designed 1992
Foundries Linotype
Number of weights 1

ABCDEFGHIJKLMNOPQRSTUVWXYZ

abcdefghijklmnopqrstuvwxyz1234567890

Mr. Jock, TV quiz Ph.D., bags few lynx.

Bendigo

Designer Phill Grimshaw
Nationality UK
Date Designed 1993
Foundries FontFont Linotype ITC Letraset
Number of weights 1

ABCDEFGHIJKLMNOPQRSTUVWXYZ

abcdefghijklmnopqrstuvwxyz1234567890

A horse that built a mausoleum in Wales.

Pierre Bonnard Toulouse Lautrec

Designer Luiz Da Lomba
Nationality ES
Date Designed 1995
Foundries CA Partners
Number of weights 1

ABCDEFGHIJKLMNOPQRSTUVWXYZ

ABCDEFGHIJKLMNOPQRSTUVWXYZ1234567890

A QUICK MOVEMENT OF THE ENEMY WILL JEOPARDIZE SIX GUNBOATS.

Scotty

Designer	Scott Smith
Nationality	UK
Date Designed	1993
Foundries	T-26
Number of weights	1

ABCDEFGHIJKLMNOPQRSTUVWXYZ

abcdefghijklmnopqrstuvwxyz1234567890

Jail zesty vixen who grabbed pay from quack.

Sho

Designer	Karlgeorg Hoefer
Nationality	DE
Date Designed	1993
Foundries	Adobe
Number of weights	1

ABCDEFGHIJKLMNOPQRSTUVWXYZ

abcdefghijklmnopqrstuvwxyz1234567890

Brawny gods just flocked up to quiz and vex him.

Blacklight

Designer	URW++
Nationality	DE
Date Designed	1994
Foundries	URW++
Number of weights	1

ABCDEFGHIJKLMNOPQRSTUVWXYZ

abcdefghijklmnopqrstuvwxyz1234567890

Murky haze enveloped a city as jarring quakes broke forty-six windows.

Immi 505

Designer	Timothy Donaldson
Nationality	UK
Date Designed	1994
Foundries	Adobe
Number of weights	1

ABCDEFGHIJKLMNOPQRSTUVWXYZ

abcdefghijklmnopqrstuvwxyz1234567890

Mix Zapf with Veljovic and get quirky Beziers.

Smudger

Designer	Andrew Smith
Nationality	UK
Date Designed	1994
Foundries	Letraset Monotype ITC
Number of weights	1

ABCDEFGHIJKLMNOPQRSTUVWXYZ

abcdefghijklmnopqrstuvwxyz1234567890

A large fawn jumped quickly over white zinc boxes.

Blaze

Designer	Patty King
Nationality	US
Date Designed	1995
Foundries	Monotype ITC
Number of weights	1

ABCDEFGHIJKLMNOPQRSTUVWXYZ
abcdefghijklmnopqrstuvwxyz1234567890
Puzzled women bequeath jerks very exotic gifts.

Clair

Designer	Ingrid Lich
Nationality	DE
Date Designed	1995
Foundries	FontFont
Number of weights	8

ABCDEFGHIJKLMNOPQRSTUVWXYZ
abcdefghijklmnopqrstuvwxyz1234567890
Pack my box with five dozen liquor jugs.

Galahad

Designer	Alan Blackman
Nationality	US
Date Designed	1995
Foundries	Adobe
Number of weights	3

ABCDEFGHIJKLMNOPQRSTUVWXYZ
abcdefghijklmnopqrstuvwxyz1234567890
The quick brown fox jumps over the lazy dog.

Jawbox

Designer	Chank Diesel
Nationality	US
Date Designed	1995
Foundries	Chank
Number of weights	3

ABCDEFGHIJKLMNOPQRSTUVWXYZ
abcdefghijklmnopqrstuvwxyz1234567890
Jimmy and Zack, the police explained, were last seen diving into a field of buttered quahogs.

Kick

Designer	Patty King
Nationality	US
Date Designed	1995
Foundries	Monotype ITC
Number of weights	1

ABCDEFGHIJKLMNOPQRSTUVWXYZ
abcdefghijklmnopqrstuvwxyz1234567890
Sphinx of black quartz judge my vow.

Le Chat Noir Toulouse Lautrec

Designer	Luiz Da Lomba
Nationality	ES
Date Designed	1995
Foundries	CA Partners
Number of weights	1

ABCDEFGHIJKLMNOPQRSTUVWXYZ
abcdefghijklmnopqrstuvwxyz1234567890

Inspired by the lettering on a Toulouse-Lautrec poster for the Black Cat night club.

Scratch ITC

Designer	Andrew Smith
Nationality	UK
Date Designed	1995
Foundries	ITC Letraset
Number of weights	1

ABCDEFGHIJKLMNOPQRSTUVWXYZ
abcdefghijklmnopqrstuvwxyz1234567890

Mix Zapf with Veljovic and get quirky Beziers.

Twang

Designer	Timothy Donaldson
Nationality	UK
Date Designed	1995
Foundries	ITC
Number of weights	1

ABCDEFGHIJKLMNOPQRSTUVWXYZ
abcdefghijklmnopqrstuvwxyz1234567890

Jay visited back home and gazed upon a brown fox and quail.

Wisteria

Designer	Michael Stacey
Nationality	UK
Date Designed	1995
Foundries	ITC
Number of weights	1

ABCDEFGHIJKLMNOPQRSTUVWXYZ
abcdefghijklmnopqrstuvwxyz1234567890

Properly spelt Wistaria, after the plant's discoverer Caspar Wistar.

Zennor

Designer	Phill Grimshaw
Nationality	UK
Date Designed	1995
Foundries	Monotype ITC
Number of weights	1

ABCDEFGHIJKLMNOPQRSTUVWXYZ
abcdefghijklmnopqrstuvwxyz1234567890

A village in Cornwall, England.

Jaft

Designer Frank Marciuliano
Nationality US
Date Designed 1996
Foundries Monotype ITC Galapagos
Number of weights 1

ABCDEFGHIJKLMNOPQRSTUVWXYZ

abcdefghijklmnopqrstuvwxyz1234567890

Breezily jangling $3,416,857,209, wise advertiser ambles to the bank, his exchequer amplified.

Musica

Designer Galapagos
Nationality US
Date Designed 1996
Foundries ITC Monotype
Number of weights 3

ABCDEFGHIJKLMNOPQRSTUVWXYZ

abcdefghijklmnopqrstuvwxyz1234567890

Xavier, a wildly informal court jester, kept calling Queen Elizabeth 'Betty.'

Riptide

Designer Timothy Donaldson
Nationality UK
Date Designed 1996
Foundries ITC
Number of weights 1

ABCDEFGHIJKLMNOPQRSTUVWXYZ

abcdefghijklmnopqrstuvwxyz1234567890

Professor Luc Devroye's font site is a stunning piece of work.

Sale

Designer Tony Booth
Nationality UK
Date Designed 1996
Foundries FontFont
Number of weights 4

ABCDEFGHIJKLMNOPQRSTUVWXYZ

abcdefghijklmnopqrstuvwxyz1234567890

Xavier, a wildly informal court jester, kept calling Queen Elizabeth 'Betty.'

Arnova

Designer Genevieve Cerasoli
Nationality US
Date Designed 1997
Foundries Monotype ITC
Number of weights 1

ABCDEFGHIJKLMNOPQRSTUVWXYZ

abcdefghijklmnopqrstuvwxyz1234567890

My grandfather picks up quartz and valuable onyx jewels.

Banshee

Designer	Timothy Donaldson
Nationality	UK
Date Designed	1997
Foundries	Adobe
Number of weights	1

ABCDEFGHIJKLMNOPQRSTUVWXYZ
abcdefghijklmnopqrstuvwxyz1234567890
A shrieking female portent of impending death.

Linotype Seven

Designer	Christian Vornehm
Nationality	DE
Date Designed	1997
Foundries	Linotype
Number of weights	1

ABCDEFGHIJKLMNOPQRSTUVWXYZ
abcdefghijklmnopqrstuvwxyz1234567890
Zwei Boxkämpfer jagen Eva quer durch Sylt.

Linotype Inagur

Designer	Hans-Jürgen Ellenberger
Nationality	DE
Date Designed	1999
Foundries	Linotype
Number of weights	8

ABCDEFGHIJKLMNOPQRSTUVWXYZ
abcdefghijklmnopqrstuvwxyz1234567890
Jack amazed a few girls by dropping the antique onyx vase!

Whiskey

Designer	Jochen Schuss
Nationality	DE
Date Designed	1999
Foundries	ITC
Number of weights	1

ABCDEFGHIJKLMNOPQRSTUVWXYZ
abcdefghijklmnopqrstuvwxy31234567890
Scotch whisky doesn't have an e; every other whiskey does.

Cinderella ITC

Designer	Patricia Lillie
Nationality	US
Date Designed	2001
Foundries	Monotype
Number of weights	2

ABCDEFGHIJKLMNOPQRSTUVWXYZ
abcdefghijklmnopqrstuvwxyz1234567890
Quick wafting zephyrs vex bold Jim.

Jambono

Designer	Xavier Dupré
Nationality	FR
Date Designed	2002
Foundries	FontFont
Number of weights	5

ABCDEFGHIJKLMNOPQRSTUVWXYZ

abcdefghijklmnopqrstuvwxyz1234567890

We promptly judged antique ivory buckles for the next prize.

Teebrush Paint

Designer	Tomi Haaparaanta
Nationality	FI
Date Designed	2003
Foundries	Linotype
Number of weights	2

ABCDEFGHIJKLMNOPQRSTUVWXYZ

abcdefghijklmnopqrstuvwxyz1234567890

And Wilderness is Paradise now.

Champers

Designer	Alan Meeks
Nationality	UK
Date Designed	1988
Foundries	Letraset ITC
Number of weights	1

ABCDEFGHIJKLMNOPQRSTUVWXYZ

abcdefghijklmnopqrstuvwxyz1234567890

How vexing a fumble to drop a jolly zucchini in the quicksand.

Brody

Designer	Harold Brodersen
Nationality	US
Date Designed	1953
Foundries	ATF Linotype URW++
Number of weights	2

ABCDEFGHIJKLMNOPQRSTUVWXYZ

abcdefghijklmnopqrstuvwxyz1234567890

Alfredo just must bring very exciting news to the plaza quickly.

Brophy Script

Designer	Harold Brodersen
Nationality	US
Date Designed	1953
Foundries	Monotype
Number of weights	1

ABCDEFGHIJKLMNOPQRSTUVWXYZ

abcdefghijklmnopqrstuvwxyz1234567890

My grandfather picks up quartz and valuable onyx jewels.

Arab Brushstroke

Designer	URW++
Nationality	DE
Date Designed	1990
Foundries	URW++
Number of weights	1

ABCDEFGHIJKLMNOPQRSTUVWXYZ

abcdefghijklmnopqrstuvwxyz1234567890

Back in June we delivered oxygen equipment of the same size.

Dolores

Designer	Tobias Frere-Jones
Nationality	US
Date Designed	1991
Foundries	FontFont
Number of weights	5

ABCDEFGHIJKLMNOPQRSTUVWXYZ

abcdefghijklmnopqrstuvwxyz1234567890

Just keep examining every low bid quoted for zinc etchings.

Tweed

Designer	Jim Spiece
Nationality	US
Date Designed	1992
Foundries	Spiece Graphics
Number of weights	1

ABCDEFGHIJKLMNOPQRSTUVWXYZ

abcdefghijklmnopqrstuvwxyz1234567890

Murky haze enveloped a city as jarring quakes broke forty-six windows.

Bokka

Designer	John Critchley, Darren Raven
Nationality	UK
Date Designed	1993
Foundries	FontFont
Number of weights	7

ABCDEFGHIJKLMNOPQRSTUVWXYZ

abcdefghijklmnopqrstuvwxyz1234567890

Now is the time for all brown dogs to jump over the lazy lynx.

Child's Play

Designer	John Critchley
Nationality	UK
Date Designed	1993
Foundries	FontFont
Number of weights	7

ABCDEFGHIJKLMNOPQRSTUVWXYZ

abcdefghijklmnopqrstuvwxyz1234567890

Pack my box with five dozen liquor jugs.

Langer

Designer	Paul Lang
Nationality	UK
Date Designed	1993
Foundries	Monotype
Number of weights	8

ABCDEFGHIJKLMNOPQRSTUVWXYZ
abcdefghijklmnopqrstuvwxyz1234567890
The vixen jumped quickly on her foe barking with zeal.

Providence Sans

Designer	Guy Jeffrey Nelson
Nationality	US
Date Designed	1993
Foundries	FontFont
Number of weights	4

ABCDEFGHIJKLMNOPQRSTUVWXYZ
abcdefghijklmnopqrstuvwxyz1234567890
Jeb quickly drove a few extra miles on the glazed pavement.

Scotty Normal

Designer	Scott Smith
Nationality	US
Date Designed	1993
Foundries	CA Partners
Number of weights	1

ABCDEFGHIJKLMNOPQRSTUVWXYZ
abcdefghijklmnopqrstuvwxyz1234567890
Six big devils from Japan quickly forgot how to waltz.

Soupbone

Designer	Bruce Alcock
Nationality	CA
Date Designed	1993
Foundries	FontFont
Number of weights	6

ABCDEFGHIJKLMNOPQRSTUVWXYZ
abcdefghijklmnopqrstuvwxyz1234567890
Crazy Fredericka bought many very exquisite opal jewels.

Agrafie

Designer	Roland John Goulsbra
Nationality	DE
Date Designed	1994
Foundries	Linotype
Number of weights	1

ABCDEFGHIJKLMNOPQRSTUVWXYZ
abcdefghijklmnopqrstuvwxyz1234567890
A quick movement of the enemy will jeopardize six gunboats.

Alexie

Designer	Roland John Goulsbra
Nationality	DE
Date Designed	1994
Foundries	Linotype
Number of weights	1

ABCDEFGHIJKLMNOPQRSTUVWxYZ
abcdefghijklmnopqrstuvwxyz1234567890 IIIIIIIIIIIH   H
All questions asked by five watch experts amazed the judge.

Tag Team 1 Marker Skinny

Designer	Thomas Marecki
Nationality	DE
Date Designed	1994
Foundries	FontFont
Number of weights	2

ABCDEFGHIJKLMNOPQRSTUVWXYZ
abcdefghijklmnopqrstuvwxyz1234567890
Xavier, a wild's informal court jester, kept calling Queen Elizabeth "Betts." ??

Kristen Normal

Designer	George Ryan
Nationality	US
Date Designed	1995
Foundries	Galapagos ITC Linotype
Number of weights	2

ABCDEFGHIJKLMNOPQRSTUVWXYZ
abcdefghijklmnopqrstuvwxyz1234567890
May Jo equal the fine record by solving six puzzles a week?

Escript LL

Designer	Hans-Jürgen Ellenburger
Nationality	DE
Date Designed	1996
Foundries	Linotype
Number of weights	1

ABCDEFGHIJKLMNOPQRSTUVWXYZ
abcdefghijklmnopqrstuvwxyz1234567890
Back in my quaint garden jaunty zinnias vie with flaunting phlox.

Zemke Hand

Designer	Deborah Zemke
Nationality	US
Date Designed	1997
Foundries	Monotype ITC
Number of weights	1

ABCDEFGHIJKLMNOPQRSTUVWXYZ
abcdefghijklmnopqrstuvwxyz1234567890
Zweedse ex-VIP, behoorlijk gek op quantumfysica.

Coconino

Designer Slobodan Miladinov
Nationality YU
Date Designed 1998
Foundries ITC
Number of weights 1

ABCDEFGHIJKLMNOPQRSTUVWXYZ
abcdefghijklmnopqrstuvwxyz1234567890
Hark! Toxic jungle water vipers quietly drop on zebras for meals!

Tapioca

Designer Eric Stevens
Nationality US
Date Designed 1997
Foundries Monotype ITC
Number of weights 1

ABCDEFGHIJKLMNOPQRSTUVWXYZ
abcdefghijklmnopqrstuvwxyz1234567890
King Alexander was partly overcome just after quizzing Diogenes in his tub.

Kumquat

Designer Eric Stevens
Nationality US
Date Designed 1998
Foundries Monotype Linotype ITC
Number of weights 1

ABCDEFGHIJKLMNOPQRSTUVWXYZ
abcdefghijklmnopqrstuvwxyz1234567890
The quick brown fox jumps over the lazy dog.

Scrawlz

Designer Mark Harris
Nationality US
Date Designed 1998
Foundries Monotype
Number of weights 1

ABCDEFGHIJKLMNOPQRSTUVWXYZ
abcdefghijklmnopqrstuvwxyz1234567890
The vixen jumped quickly on her foe barking with zeal.

Linotype Colibri

Designer Hans-Jürgen Ellenburger
Nationality DE
Date Designed 1999
Foundries Linotype
Number of weights 2

ABCDEFGHIJKLMNOPQRSTUVWXYZ
abcdefghijklmnopqrstuvwxyz1234567890
Dumpy kibitzer jingles as exchequer overflows.

Tickle

Designer	Patricia Lillie
Nationality	US
Date Designed	2001
Foundries	Monotype
Number of weights	1

ABCDEFGHIJKLMNOPQRSTUVWXYZ
abcdefghijklmnopqrstuvwxyz1234567890
The job of waxing linoleum frequently peeves chintzy kids.

Chalkboard

Designer	anon
Nationality	US
Date Designed	2000
Foundries	Apple
Number of weights	1

ABCDEFGHIJKLMNOPQRSTUVWXYZ
abcdefghijklmnopqrstuvwxyz1234567890
Breezily jangling €3,416,857,209, wise advertiser ambles to the bank, his exchequer amplified.

Kid TYPE

Designer	DS Design
Nationality	US
Date Designed	2000
Foundries	Monotype
Number of weights	4

ABCDEFGHIJKLMNOPQRSTUVWXYZ
abcdefghijklmnopqrstuvwxyz1234567890
Crazy Fredericka bought many very exquisite opal jewels.

Kidprint

Designer	Monotype
Nationality	US
Date Designed	2000
Foundries	Monotype
Number of weights	2

ABCDEFGHIJKLMNOPQRSTUVWXYZ
abcdefghijklmnopqrstuvwxyz1234567890
How quickly daft jumping zebras vex.

Rattlescript

Designer	Marten Thavenius
Nationality	NO
Date Designed	2000
Foundries	FontFont
Number of weights	24

ABCDEFGHIJKLMNOPQRSTUVWXYZ
abcdefghijklmnopqrstuvwxyz1234567890
The vixen jumped quickly on her foe barking with zeal.

Eddie

Designer	Eddie Baret
Nationality	FR
Date Designed	2001
Foundries	FontFont CA
Number of weights	3

ABCDEFGHIJKLMNOPQRSTUVWXYZ

abcdefghijkl mnopqrstuvwxyz1234567890

Quick waflting zephyrs vex bold Jim.

New Gothic Light

Designer	Hans Bacher
Nationality	DE
Date Designed	2001
Foundries	Monotype
Number of weights	1

ABCDEFGHIJKLMNOPQRSTUVWXYZ

abcdefghijklmnopqrstuvwxyz1234567890

Was there a quorum of able whizzkids gravely exciting the jaded fish at FiTypI?

Chauncy

Designer	Chank Diesel
Nationality	US
Date Designed	2002
Foundries	Chank
Number of weights	2

ABCDEFGHIJKLMNOPQRSTUVWXYZ

abcdefghijklmnopqrstuvwxyz1234567890

Now is the time for all brown dogs to jump over the lazy lynx.

Double Dutch

Designer	Marianne van Ham
Nationality	NL
Date Designed	1992
Foundries	FontFont
Number of weights	1

ABCDEFGHIJKLMNOPQRSTUVWXYZ

abcdefghijklmnopqrstuvwxyz1234567890

Wim Meulenkamp: Bizarre Bouwwerkeu in Nederlands & Belgie.

Katfish

Designer	Michael Gills
Nationality	UK
Date Designed	1994
Foundries	Monotype ITC
Number of weights	1

ABCDEFGHIJKLMNOPQRSTUVWXYZ

abcdefghijklmnopqrstuvwxyz1234567890

Sexy qua lijf, doch bang voor het zwempak.

Kendo

Designer	Phill Grimshaw
Nationality	UK
Date Designed	1997
Foundries	Letraset Linotype ITC Monotype
Number of weights	2

ABCDEFGHIJKLMNOPQRSTUVWXYZ
abcdefghijklmnopqrstuvwxyz1234567890
Xavier, a wildly informal court jester, kept calling Queen
Elizabeth 'Betty.'

Tempus

Designer	Phill Grimshaw
Nationality	UK
Date Designed	1995
Foundries	ITC Linotype Letraset Monotype
Number of weights	4

ABCDEFGHIJKLMNOPQRSTUVWXYZ
abcdefghijklmnopqrstuvwxyz1234567890
Will Major Douglas be expected to take this true-false quiz very soon?

Tempus Sans

Designer	Phill Grimshaw
Nationality	UK
Date Designed	1995
Foundries	ITC Linotype Letraset Monotype
Number of weights	2

ABCDEFGHIJKLMNOPQRSTUVWXYZ
abcdefghijklmnopqrstuvwxyz1234567890
The juke box music puzzled a gentle visitor from a quaint valley town.

Tapeside

Designer	Stephan B Murphy
Nationality	UK
Date Designed	1996
Foundries	Linotype
Number of weights	2

ABCDEFGHIJKLMNOPQRSTUVWXYZ
abcdefghijklmnopqrstuvwxyz1234567890
Murky haze enveloped a city as jarring quakes broke forty-six windows.

TwoVooDoo

Designer	Mark Harris
Nationality	US
Date Designed	1998
Foundries	CA Exclusives
Number of weights	1

ABCDEFGHIJKLMNOPQRSTUVWXYZ
abcdefghijklmnopqrstuvwxyz1234567890
King Alexander was partly overcome just after quizzing Diogenes in his tub.

Linotype Rough

Designer Christophe Badani
Nationality FR
Date Designed 1998
Foundries Linotype
Number of weights 9

ABCDEFGHIJKLMNOPQRSTUVWXYZ
abcdefghijklmnopqrstuvwxyz1234567890
Hark! Toxic jungle water vipers quietly drop on zebras for meals!

Lintball

Designer Eric Stevens
Nationality US
Date Designed 1999
Foundries ITC
Number of weights 1

ABCDEFGHIJKLMNOPQRSTUVWXYZ
abcdefghijklmnopqrstuvwxyz1234567890
The quick brown fox jumps over the lazy dog.

Ludwig ITC

Designer Giuseppe Errico
Nationality IT
Date Designed 1999
Foundries ITC
Number of weights 1

ABCDEFGHIJKLMNOPQRSTUVWXYZ
abcdefghijklmnopqrstuvwxyz1234567890
Jail zesty vixen who grabbed pay from quack.

Comix

Designer Richard Yeend
Nationality UK
Date Designed 2000
Foundries Monotype
Number of weights 1

ABCDEFGHIJKLMNOPQRSTUVWXYZ
abcdefghijklmnopqrstuvwxyz1234567890
Just work for improved basic techniques to maximize your typing skill.

Elegie

Designer Albert Boton
Nationality FR
Date Designed 2002
Foundries FontFont
Number of weights 8

ABCDEFGHIJKLMNOPQRSTUVWXYZ
abcdefghijklmnopqrstuvwxyz1234567890
A quick movement of the enemy will jeopardize six gunboats.

Bodoni Unique

Designer	Giambattista Bodoni
Nationality	IT
Date Designed	1780
Foundries	Monotype
Number of weights	1

ABCDEFGHIJKLMNOPQRSTUVWXYZ

ABCDEFGHIJKLMNOPQRSTUVWXYZ1234567890

AWAKE! FOR MORNING IN THE BOWL OF NIGHT

Salut

Designer	H Maehler
Nationality	DE
Date Designed	1931
Foundries	Klingspor Monotype
Number of weights	1

ABCDEFGHIJKLMNOPQRSTUVWXYZ

abcdefghijklmnopqrstuvwxyz1234567890

King Alexander was partly overcome just after quizzing Diogenes in his tub.

Matura

Designer	Imre Reiner
Nationality	HU
Date Designed	1938
Foundries	Monotype Linotype FF Adobe
Number of weights	2

ABCDEFGHIJKLMNOPQRSTUVWXYZ

abcdefghijklmnopqrstuvwxyz1234567890

HAS FLUNG THE STONE THAT PUTS THE STARS TO FLIGHT:

CG Lisbon

Designer	Warren Chappell
Nationality	US
Date Designed	1938
Foundries	Miles
Number of weights	4

ABCDEFGHIJKLMNOPQRSTUVWXYZ

abcdefghijklmnopqrstuvwxyz1234567890

About sixty codfish eggs will make a quarter pound of very fizzy jelly.

Ritmo Bold

Designer	Aldo Novarese
Nationality	IT
Date Designed	1955
Foundries	CA Partners CG
Number of weights	1

ABCDEFGHIJKLMNOPQRSTUVWXYZ

abcdefghijklmnopqrstuvwxyz1234567890

Quick zephyrs blow, vexing daft Jim.

Estro

Designer	Aldo Novarese
Nationality	IT
Date Designed	1961
Foundries	Nebiolo T-26 URW++
Number of weights	1

ABCDEFGHIJKLMNOPQRSTUVWXYZ
abcdefghijklmnopqrstuvwxyz1234567890

Xavier, a wildly informal court jester, kept calling Queen
Elizabeth 'Betty.'

Cruz Swinger

Designer	Ray Cruz
Nationality	US
Date Designed	1970
Foundries	Monotype
Number of weights	1

ABCDEFGHIJKLMNOPQRSTUVWXYZ
abcdefghijklmnopqrstuvwxyz1234567890

Was there a quorum of able whizzkids gravely exciting the jaded fish at ATypI?

Sprint

Designer	Aldo Novarese
Nationality	IT
Date Designed	1974
Foundries	Linotype
Number of weights	1

ABCDEFGHIJKLMNOPQRSTUVWXYZ
abcdefghijklmnopqrstuvwxy21234567890

Quixotic Conservatives vet first key zero-growth jeremiad.

Stuyvesant

Designer	W A Dwiggins
Nationality	US
Date Designed	1955
Foundries	AGP Bitstream
Number of weights	1

ABCDEFGHIJKLMNOPQRSTUVWXYZ
abcdefghijklmnopqrstuvwxyz1234567890

Verbatim reports were quickly given by Jim Fox to his amazed audience.

Cabarga Cursiva

Designer	Leslie Cabarga, Demetrio R Cabarga
Nationality	US
Date Designed	1982
Foundries	Linotype ITC
Number of weights	1

ABCDEFGHIJKLMNOPQRSTUVWXYZ
abcdefghijklmnopqrstuvwxyz1234567890

William said that everything about his jacket was in quite good condition
except for the zipper.

Greyton Script

Designer	Gerhard Schwekendiek
Nationality	DE
Date Designed	1991
Foundries	Monotype ITC
Number of weights	1

ABCDEFGHIJKLMNOPQRSTUVWXYZ

abcdefghijklmnopqrstuvwxyz1234567890

Jaded reader with fabled roving eye seized by quickened impulse to expand budget.

Tropica Script

Designer	Vince Whitlock
Nationality	UK
Date Designed	1988
Foundries	ITC
Number of weights	1

ABCDEFGHIJKLMNOPQRSTUVWXYZ

abcdefghijklmnopqrstuvwxyz1234567890

Quick zephyrs blow, vexing daft Jim.

Retail Script

Designer	Vince Whitlock
Nationality	UK
Date Designed	1987
Foundries	ITC
Number of weights	1

ABCDEFGHIJKLMNOPQRSTUVWXYZ

abcdefghijklmnopqrstuvwxyz1234567890

Sphinx of black quartz judge my vow.

Varga

Designer	Alan Meeks
Nationality	UK
Date Designed	1991
Foundries	Monotype Letraset ITC
Number of weights	1

ABCDEFGHIJKLMNOPQRSTUVWXYZ

abcdefghijklmnopqrstuvwxyz1234567890

The exodus of jazzy pigeons is craved by squeamish walkers.

Squickt

Designer	Gert Wiescher
Nationality	DE
Date Designed	1991
Foundries	Monotype
Number of weights	1

ABCDEFGHIJKLMNOPQRSTUVWXYZ

abcdefghijklmnopqrstuvwxyz1234567890

Jeb quickly drove a few extra miles on the glazed pavement.

Spontan

Designer Manfred Klein
Nationality DE
Date Designed 1991
Foundries FontFont
Number of weights 4

ABCDEFGHIJKLMNOPQRSTUVWXYZ
ABCDEFGHIJKLMNOPQRSTUVWXYZ1234567890
MY GRANDFATHER PICKS UP QUARTZ AND VALUABLE
ONYX JEWELS.

Jacque

Designer Max Kisman
Nationality US
Date Designed 1991
Foundries FontFont
Number of weights 1

ABCDEFGHIJKLMNOPQRSTUVWXYZ
abcdefghijklmnopqrstuvwxyz1234567890
Five wine experts jokingly quizzed sample chablis.

Scarborough

Designer Akira Kobayashi
Nationality JP
Date Designed 1998
Foundries ITC Linotype
Number of weights 2

ABCDEFGHIJKLMNOPQRSTUVWXYZ
abcdefghijklmnopqrstuvwxyz1234567890
Quick wafting zephyrs vex bold Jim.

Neo Bold

Designer Carlos Segura
Nationality CU
Date Designed 1993
Foundries Monotype
Number of weights 1

AbCDEFGHIJKLMNOPQPSTUVIJXYZ
AbCDEFGHIJKLMNOPQPSTUVIJXYZ1234567890
AND LO! THE HUNTEP OF THE EAST HAS CAUGHT

Bogatyr

Designer David F Nalle
Nationality US
Date Designed 1993
Foundries Scriptorium
Number of weights 1

АБЦДЕФГИЮЖКЛМНОПРСТУВЭХЯЗ
ABCDEFGHIJKLMNOPQRSTUVWXY3
THE SULTANS TURRET IN A NOOSE OF LIGHT

Kosmik

Designer	Erik van Blokland
Nationality	NL
Date Designed	1993
Foundries	FontFont
Number of weights	1

ABCDEFGHIJKLMNOPQRSTUVWXYZ

abcdefghijklmnopqrstuvwxyz1234567890

Sexy qua lijf, doch bang voor het zwempak.

Merlin LT

Designer	Anne Boskamp
Nationality	DE
Date Designed	1994
Foundries	Linotype
Number of weights	1

ABCDEFGHIJKLMNOPQRSTUVWXYZ

ABCDEFGHIJKLMNOPQRSTUVWXYZ1234567890

SIX CRAZY KINGS VOWED TO ABOLISH MY PITIFUL JOUSTS.

Skidoos

Designer	anon
Nationality	DE
Date Designed	1994
Foundries	URW++
Number of weights	3

ABCDEFGHIJKLMNOPQRSTUVWXYZ

abcdefghijklmnopqrstuvwxyz1234567890

William Jex quickly caught five dozen Conservatives.

Kigali

Designer	Arthur Baker
Nationality	US
Date Designed	1994
Foundries	Adobe
Number of weights	1

ABCDEFGHIJKLMNOPQRSTUVWXYZ

abcdefghijklmnopqrstuvwxyz1234567890

Waltz, nymph, for quick jigs vex Bud.

Ashtray

Designer	Ashtray
Nationality	UK
Date Designed	1994
Foundries	Monotype
Number of weights	2

ABCDEFGHIJKLMNOPQRSTUVWXYZ

abcdefghijklmnopqrstuvwxyz1234567890

The job of waxing linoleum frequently peeves chintzy kids.

Klunder Script

Designer	Barbara Klunder
Nationality	CA
Date Designed	1994
Foundries	FontFont
Number of weights	1

ABCDEFGHIJKLMNOPQRSTUVWXYZ
abcdefghijkLmnopqrstuvwxyz1234567890
How vexing a fumble to drop a joLLy zucchini in the quicksand.

Palekin

Designer	Bo Berndal
Nationality	SE
Date Designed	1994
Foundries	Monotype
Number of weights	1

ABCDEFGHIJKLMNOPQRSTUVWXYZ
abcdefghijklmnopqrstuvwxyz1234567890
Two hardy boxing kangaroos jet from Sydney to Zanzibar on quicksilver pinions.

Elroy

Designer	Christian Schwartz
Nationality	US
Date Designed	1994
Foundries	Fonthaus Monotype
Number of weights	1

ABCDEFGHIJKLMNOPQRSTUVWXYZ
abcdefghijklmnopqrstuvwxyz1234567890
Casual serif.

Providence

Designer	Guy Jeffrey Nelson
Nationality	US
Date Designed	1994
Foundries	FontFont
Number of weights	1

ABCDEFGHIJKLMNOPQRSTUVWXYZ
abcdefghijklmnopqrstuvwxyz1234567890
Alfredo just must bring very exciting news to the plaza quickly.

Balder

Designer	Lutz Baar
Nationality	SE
Date Designed	1994
Foundries	Linotype
Number of weights	1

ABCDEFGHIJKLMNOPQRSTUVWXYZ
ABCDEFGHIJKLMNOPQRSTUVWXYZ1234567890
MY HELP SQUEEZED BACK IN AGAIN AND JOINED THE WEAVERS AFTER SIX.

Rekord

Designer	Martin Wenzel
Nationality	DE
Date Designed	1994
Foundries	FontFont
Number of weights	5

ABCDEFGHIJKLMNOPQRSTUVWXYZ

ABCDEFGHIJKLMNOPQRSTUVWXYZ1234567890

THE JOB OF WAXING LINOLEUM FREQUENTLY PEEVES CHINTZY KIDS.

Fontesque

Designer	Nick Shinn
Nationality	UK
Date Designed	1994
Foundries	FontFont
Number of weights	1

ABCDEFGHIJKLMNOPQRSTUVWXYZ

abcdefghijklmnopqrstuvwxyz1234567890

King Alexander was partly overcome just after quizzing Diogenes in his tub.

Schnitz

Designer	Osmo Niemi
Nationality	FI
Date Designed	1994
Foundries	Linotype
Number of weights	1

ABCDEFGHIJKLMNOPQRSTUVWXYZ

abcdefghijklmnopqrstuvwxyz1234567890

The five boxing wizards jump quickly.

Indus

Designer	P M Hashim
Nationality	IN
Date Designed	1994
Foundries	Linotype
Number of weights	1

ABCDEFGHIJKLMNOPQRSTUVWXYZ

abcdefghijklmnopqrstuvwxyz1234567890

Dumpy kibitzer jingles as exchequer overflows.

Sinah

Designer	Peter Huschka
Nationality	DE
Date Designed	1994
Foundries	Linotype
Number of weights	12

ABCDEFGHIJKLMNOPQRSTUVWXYZ

abcdefghijklmnopqrstuvwxyz1234567890

Big July earthquakes confound zany experimental vow.

Boink

Designer Robert Petrick
Nationality US
Date Designed 1994
Foundries Linotype ITC Letraset
Number of weights 1

ABCDEFGHIJKLMNOPQRSTUVWXYZ
ABCDEFGHIJKLMNOPQRSTUVWXYZ1234567890
DREAMING WHEN DAWN'S LEFT HAND WAS IN THE SKY.

Trombo

Designer Andreas Jung
Nationality DE
Date Designed 1995
Foundries FontFont
Number of weights 1

ABCDEFGHIJKLMNOPQRSTUVWXYZ
abcdefghijklmnopqrstuvwxyz1234567890
Sphinx of black quartz judge my vow.

Chiller

Designer Andrew Smith
Nationality UK
Date Designed 1995
Foundries Linotype ITC
Number of weights 1

ABCDEFGHIJKLMNOPQRSTUVWXYZ
abcdefghijklmnopqrstuvwxyz1234567890
My help squeezed back in again and joined the weavers after six.

Cold Mountain

Designer Arthur Baker
Nationality US
Date Designed 1995
Foundries Glyph Systems Monotype
Number of weights 6

ABCDEFGHIJKLMNOPQRSTUVWXYZ
abcdefghijklmnopqrstuvwxyz1234567890
Quick wafting zephyrs vex bold Jim.

Juice

Designer David Sagorski
Nationality US
Date Designed 1995
Foundries Monotype ITC
Number of weights 1

ABCDEFGHIJKLMNOPQRSTUVWXYZ
abcdefghijklmnopqrstuvwxyz1234567890
Moi, je veux quinze clubs a golf et du whisky pur.

Snap

Designer	David Sagorski
Nationality	US
Date Designed	1995
Foundries	Monotype ITC
Number of weights	1

ABCDEFGHIJKLMNOPQRSTUVWXYZ
abcdefghijklmnopqrstuvwxyz1234567890
Just keep examining every low bid quoted for zinc etchings

Howl

Designer	Jon H Clinch
Nationality	US
Date Designed	1995
Foundries	Monotype
Number of weights	1

ABCDEFGHIJKLMNOPQRSTUVWXYZ
abcdefghijklmnopqrstuvwxyz1234567890
Verbatim reports were quickly given by Jim Fox to his amazed audience.

Le Petit Trottin Toulouse Lautrec

Designer	Luiz Da Lomba
Nationality	ES
Date Designed	1995
Foundries	CA Partners
Number of weights	1

ABCDEFGHIJKLMNOPQRSTUVWXYZ
abcdefghijklmnopqrstuvwxyz1234567890
No kidding, Lorenzo called off his trip to visit Mexico City just because they told him the conquistadores were extinct.

Moulin Rouge Toulouse Lautrec

Designer	Luiz Da Lomba
Nationality	ES
Date Designed	1995
Foundries	CA Partners
Number of weights	1

ABCDEFGHIJKLMNOPQRSTUVWXYZ
ABCDEFGHIJKLMNOPQRSTUVWXYZ1234567890
FORSAKING MONASTIC TRADITION, TWELVE JOVIAL FRIARS GAVE UP THEIR VOCATION FOR A QUESTIONABLE EXISTENCE ON THE FLYING TRAPEZE.

True Grit

Designer	Michael Stacey
Nationality	UK
Date Designed	1995
Foundries	ITC
Number of weights	1

ABCDEFGHIJKLMNOPQRSTUVWXYZ
abcdefghijklmnopqrstuvwxyz1234567890
How quickly daft jumping zebras vex.

Penguin

Designer	Nick Cooke
Nationality	UK
Date Designed	1995
Foundries	FontFont
Number of weights	1

ABCDEFGHIJKLMNOPQRSTUVWXYZ

abcdefghijklmnopqrstuvwxyz1234567890

Jay visited back home and gazed upon a brown fox and quail.

Green

Designer	Timothy Donaldson
Nationality	UK
Date Designed	1995
Foundries	ITC Letraset Linotype
Number of weights	1

ABCDEFGHIJKLMNOPQRSTUVWXYZ

abcdefghijklmnopqrstuvwxyz1234567890

I HEARD A VOICE WITHIN THE TAVERN CRY,

Telegram

Designer	Timothy Donaldson
Nationality	UK
Date Designed	1995
Foundries	Linotype Letraset ITC
Number of weights	1

ABCDEFGHIJKLMNOPQRSTUVWXYZ

abcdefghijklmnopqrstuvwxyz1234567890

Jaded zombies acted quaintly but kept driving their oxen forward.

Chelsea FF

Designer	Frank Heine
Nationality	DE
Date Designed	1994
Foundries	FontFont
Number of weights	2

ABCDEFGHIJKLMNOPQRSTUVWXYZ

ABCDEFGHIJKLMNOPQRSTUVWXYZ1234567890

THE FIVE BOXING WIZARDS JUMP QUICKLY.

Etruscan

Designer	Timothy Donaldson
Nationality	UK
Date Designed	1995
Foundries	Monotype ITC
Number of weights	1

ABCDEFGHIJKLMNOPQRSTUVWXYZ

abcdefghijklmnopqrstuvwxyz1234567890

About sixty codfish eggs will make a quarter pound of very fizzy jelly

Cethubala

Designer	Patricia Carvalha
Nationality	PO
Date Designed	1996
Foundries	Linotype
Number of weights	1

ƷBCDꝶꝶꝶꝶJKLMNOPꝶRSTUVWXYZ

ƷBCDeꝶꝶꝶꝶJKLMNOPꝶRSTUVWXYZ1234567890

ꝶow quꝶckly Dꝶꝶꝶ Jumpꝶnꝶ zeBꝶꝶꝶ vex.

Neo Neo

Designer	Timothy Donaldson
Nationality	UK
Date Designed	1995
Foundries	ITC
Number of weights	1

ABCDEFGHIJKLMNOPQRSTUVWXYZ

abcdefghijklmnopqrstuvwxyz1234567890

Sphinx of black quartz judge my vow.

Wildstyle

Designer	Vincent Connare
Nationality	US
Date Designed	1995
Foundries	CA Partners
Number of weights	1

ABCDEFGHIJKLMNOPQRSTUVWXYZ

ABCDEFGHIJKLMNOPQRSTUVWXYZ1234567890

JIM JUST QUIT AND PACKED EXTRA BAGS FOR LIZ OWEN.

Temble

Designer	Andreu Balius
Nationality	ES
Date Designed	1996
Foundries	Monotype Linotype ITC
Number of weights	1

ABCDEFGHIJKLMNOPQRSTUVWXYZ

abcdefghijklmnopqrstuvwxyz1234567890

Hark! Toxic jungle water vipers quietly drop on zebras for meals!

Boundaround

Designer	Christina Sachse
Nationality	DE
Date Designed	1996
Foundries	Linotype
Number of weights	1

ABCDEFGHIJKLMNOPQRSTUVWXYZ

abcdefghijklmnopqrstuvwxyz1234567890

Jelly-like above the high wire, six quaking pachyderms kept the climax of the extravaganza in a dazzling state of flux.

Bodoni Brush

Designer	John Viner
Nationality	UK
Date Designed	1996
Foundries	ITC Linotype
Number of weights	1

ABCDEFGHIJKLMNOPQRSTUVWXYZ

abcdefghijklmnopqrstuvwxyz1234567890

The sex life of the woodchuck is a provocative question for most vertebrate zoology majors.

Braganza

Designer	Phill Grimshaw
Nationality	UK
Date Designed	1996
Foundries	Letraset ITC / Fontek Creative Alliance Linotype
Number of weights	4

ABCDEFGHIJKLMNOPQRSTUVWXYZ

abcdefghijklmnopqrstuvwxyz1234567890

Many big jackdaws quickly zipped over the fox pen.

Khaki

Designer	Stephen Miggas
Nationality	US
Date Designed	1996
Foundries	Aerotype Adobe
Number of weights	1

ABCDEFGHIJKLMNOPQRSTUVWXYZ

abcdefghijklmnopqrstuvwxyz1234567890

Quick wafting zephyrs vex bold Jim.

Cancione

Designer	Brenda Walton
Nationality	US
Date Designed	1997
Foundries	Linotype ITC Monotype
Number of weights	1

ABCDEFGHIJKLMNOPQRSTUVWXYZ

1234567890

THE LOWER CASE CONSISTS OF ELEGANT SORTS.

Down Town

Designer	Critzler
Nationality	DE
Date Designed	1997
Foundries	Linotype
Number of weights	1

ABCDEFGHIJKLMNOPQRSTUVWXYZ

abcdefghijklmnopqrstuvwxyz1234567890

Grumpy wizards make toxic brew for the evil Queen and Jack.

Linotype Sunburst

Designer	Ed Bugg
Nationality	UK
Date Designed	1997
Foundries	Linotype
Number of weights	1

ABCDEFGHIJKLMNOPQRSTUVWXYZ

abcdefghijklmnopqrstuvwxyz1234567890

Jaded reader with fabled roving eye seized by quickened impulse to expand budget.

Baylac

Designer	Gérard Mariscalchi
Nationality	CA
Date Designed	1997
Foundries	Monotype
Number of weights	1

ABCDEFGHIJKLMNOPQRSTUVWXYZ

abcdefghijklmnopqrstuvwxyz1234567890

The five boxing wizards jump quickly.

Inkling

Designer	Joel Decker
Nationality	DE
Date Designed	1997
Foundries	FontFont
Number of weights	2

ABCDEFGHIJKLMNOPQRSTUVWXYZ

abcdefghijklmnopqrstuvwxyz1234567890

Quick wafting zephyrs vex bold Jim.

Araby Rafique

Designer	Themina Rafique
Nationality	UK
Date Designed	1997
Foundries	Linotype
Number of weights	1

ABCDEFGHIJKLMNOPQRSTUVWXYZ

abcdefghijklmnopqrstuvwxyz1234567890

Lazy movers quit hard-packing of papier-mâché jewellery boxes.

Musclehead

Designer	Timothy Donaldson
Nationality	UK
Date Designed	1997
Foundries	Monotype ITC
Number of weights	1

ABCDEFGHIJKLMNOPQRSTUVWXYZ

abcdefghijklmnopqrstuvwxyz1234567890

All questions asked by five watch experts amazed the judge.

F2F Czykago Trans

Designer	Alexander Branczyk
Nationality	DE
Date Designed	1998
Foundries	LT Take Type 5
Number of weights	1

ABCDEFGHIJKLMNOPQRSTUVWXYZ
abcdefghijklmnopqrstuvwxyz
1234567890
The Polish spelling of Chicago.

ROM

Designer	Atelier de Rouen
Nationality	FR
Date Designed	1998
Foundries	CA Exclusives
Number of weights	4

ABCDEFGHIJKLMNOPQRSTUVWXYZ

abcdefghijklmnopqrstuvwxyz1234567890

Silly name for a font. You'll find 5,116 similar names when searching on your hard drive.

Deelirious

Designer	Dee Densmore D'Amico
Nationality	US
Date Designed	1998
Foundries	ITC
Number of weights	1

ABCDEFGHIJKLMNOPQRSTUVWXYZ
abcdefghijklmnopqrstuvwxyz1234567890
William said that everything about his jacket was in quite good condition except for
the zipper.

Postino

Designer	Timothy Donaldson
Nationality	UK
Date Designed	1998
Foundries	Adobe Linotype
Number of weights	2

ABCDEFGHIJKLMNOPQRSTUVWXYZ
abcdefghijklmnopqrstuvwxyz1234567890
Just keep examining every low bid quoted for
zinc etchings.

Cult

Designer	Timothy Donaldson
Nationality	UK
Date Designed	1998
Foundries	Linotype ITC Letraset
Number of weights	1

ABCDEFGHIJKLMNOPQRSTUVWXYZ
abcdefghijklmnopqrstuvwxyz1234567890
A large fawn jumped quickly over white zinc boxes.

Airstream

Designer	Timothy Donaldson
Nationality	UK
Date Designed	1998
Foundries	Linotype
Number of weights	1

ABCDEFGHIJKLMNOPQRSTUVWXYZ
abcdefghijklmnopqrstuvwxyz1234567890
Many-wived Jack laughs at probes of sex quiz.

Angry Hog

Designer	Timothy Donaldson
Nationality	UK
Date Designed	1998
Foundries	ITC Linotype
Number of weights	1

ABCDEFGHIJKLMNOPQRSTUVWXYZ
abcdefghijklmnopqrstuvwxyz1234567890
A large fawn jumped quickly over white zinc boxes.

Silvermoon

Designer	Akira Kobayashi
Nationality	JP
Date Designed	1999
Foundries	Monotype ITC
Number of weights	2

ABCDEFGHIJKLMNOPQRSTUVWXYZ
abcdefghijklmnopqrstuvwxyz1234567890
Sixty zippers were quickly picked from the woven jute bag.

Linotype Zurpreis

Designer	Bo Berndal
Nationality	SE
Date Designed	1999
Foundries	Linotype
Number of weights	2

ABCDEFGHIJKLMNOPQRSTUVWXYZ
abcdefghijklmnopqrstuvwxyz1234567890
Five or six big jet planes zoomed quickly by the tower.

Breeze

Designer	Donald Beekman
Nationality	NL
Date Designed	1999
Foundries	Linotype
Number of weights	2

ABCDEFGHIJKLMNOPQRSTUVWXYZ
abcdefghijklmnopqrstuvwxyz1234567890
William Jex quickly caught five dozen Conservatives.

Linotype Belle

Designer Isabelle Stutz
Nationality CH
Date Designed 1999
Foundries Linotype
Number of weights 2

ABCDEFGH IJKL MNOPQRSTUVWXYZ
ABCDEFGH IJKL MNOPQRSTUVWXYZ1234567890
JUST WORK FOR IMPROVED BASIC TECHNIQUES TO
MAXIMIZE YOUR TYPING SKILL.

Posterboy ITC

Designer Chester Wajda
Nationality US
Date Designed 2000
Foundries ITC
Number of weights 1

ABCDEFGHIJKLMNOPQRSTUVWXYZ
abcdefghijklmnopqrstuvwxyz1234567890
Six big devils from Japan quickly forgot how to waltz.

Eborg ITC

Designer George Ryan
Nationality US
Date Designed 2000
Foundries ITC
Number of weights 1

ABCDEFGHIJKLMNOPQRSTUVWXYZ
abcdefghijklmnopqrstuvwxyz1234567890
Waltz, nymph, for quick jigs vex Bud.

Dreamland

Designer Andreas Nylin
Nationality SE
Date Designed 2001
Foundries DustBustFonts
Number of weights 1

ABCDEFGHIJKLMNOPQRSTUVWXYZ
abcdefghijklmnopqrstuvwxyz1234567890
Just keep examining every low bid quoted for zinc etchings.

Haarlem

Designer Leslie Cabarga
Nationality US
Date Designed 2000
Foundries Flashfonts
Number of weights 2

ABCDEFGHIJKLMNOPQRSTUVWXYZ
abcdefghijklmnopqrstuvwxyz1234567890
We have just quoted on nine dozen boxes of gray lamp wicks.

Linotype Charon

Designer	Renate Weise
Nationality	DE
Date Designed	2000
Foundries	Linotype
Number of weights	5

ABCDEFGHIJKLMNOPQRSTUVWXYZ

abcdefghijklmnopqrstuvwxyz1234567890

Waltz, nymph, for quick jigs vex Bud.

Linotype Sicula

Designer	Roberto Mannella
Nationality	DE
Date Designed	2000
Foundries	Linotype
Number of weights	1

ABCDEFGHIJKLMNOPQRSTUVWXYZ

abcdefghijklmnopqrstuvwxyz1234567890

The Latin name for Sicily.

Prater Script

Designer	Steffen Sauerteig, Henning Wagenbreth
Nationality	DE
Date Designed	2000
Foundries	FontFont
Number of weights	1

ABCDEFGHIJKLMNOPQRSTUVWXYZ

abcdefghijklmnopqrstuvwxyz1234567890

How vexing a fumble to drop a jolly zucchini in the quicksand.

Boomerang Outline

Designer	Greg Bastin
Nationality	AU
Date Designed	2001
Foundries	JY&A Fonts
Recut/Digitised by	David Philpott, 2002
Number of weights	1

ABCDEFGHIJKLMNOPQRSTUVWXYZ

abcdefghijklmnopqrstuvwxyz1234567890

Five wine experts jokingly quizzed sample chablis.

Nelio

Designer	Sami Kortemaeki
Nationality	FI
Date Designed	2001
Foundries	FontFont
Number of weights	7

ABCDEFGHIJKLMNOPQRSTUVWXYZ

abcdefghijklmnopqrstuvwxyz1234567890

Quick, lazy vamp, just fix the drab gown.

Gillies Gothic Ex Bd Shaded

Designer William S Gillies
Nationality US
Date Designed 1935
Foundries Monotype
Number of weights 1

ABCDEFGHIJKLMNOPQRSTUVWXYZ

abcdefghijklmnopqrstuvwxyz1234567890

Jimmy and Zack, the police explained, were last seen diving into a field of buttered quahogs.

Highlight

Designer Tony Watson
Nationality UK
Date Designed 1978
Foundries Linotype ITC Letraset
Number of weights 1

ABCDEFGHIJKLMNOPQRSTUVWXYZ

abcdefghijklmnopqrstuvwxyz1234567890

Back in my quaint garden jaunty zinnias vie with flaunting phlox.

Vegas

Designer David Quay
Nationality UK
Date Designed 1984
Foundries Linotype ITC
Number of weights 1

ABCDEFGHIJKLMNOPQRSTUVWXYZ

abcdefghijklmnopqrstuvwxyz1234567890

The risque gown marked a brazen exposure of very juicy flesh.

Milano

Designer David Quay
Nationality UK
Date Designed 1985
Foundries Letraset ITC
Number of weights 1

ABCDEFGHIJKLMNOPQRSTUVWXYZ

abcdefghijklmnopqrstuvwxyz1234567890

Perhaps President Clinton's amazing sax skills will be judged quite favourably

Laura

Designer Tony Watson
Nationality UK
Date Designed 1990
Foundries Letraset Linotype Monotype ITC
Number of weights 1

ABCDEFGHIJKLMNOPQRSTUVWXYZ

abcdefghijklmnopqrstuvwxyz1234567890

My grandfather picks up quartz and valuable onyx jewels.

Artiste

Designer	Martin Wait
Nationality	UK
Date Designed	1991
Foundries	Linotype Letraset ITC
Number of weights	1

ABCDEFGHIJKLMNOPQRSTUVWXYZ
ABCDEFGHIJKLMNOPQRSTUVWXYZ1234567890
AWAKE, MY LITTLE ONES, AND FILL THE CUP.

Klee

Designer	Timothy Donaldson
Nationality	UK
Date Designed	1992
Foundries	Monotype ITC Letraset
Number of weights	1

ABCDEFGHIJKLMNOPQRSTUVWXYZ
abcdefghijklmnopqrstuvwxyz1234567890
Jackdaws love my big sphinx of quartz.

Bermuda

Designer	Garrett Boge, Paul Shaw
Nationality	US
Date Designed	1996
Foundries	Monotype Adobe LetterPerfect
Number of weights	4

ABCDEFGHIJKLMNOPQRSTUVWXYZ
ABCDEFGHIJKLMNOPQRSTUVWXYZ1234567890
ANOTHER FONT CALLED BERMUDA BY WAYNE DWIGGINS.

Banner

Designer	Martin Wait
Nationality	UK
Date Designed	1996
Foundries	Letraset Linotype ITC
Number of weights	1

ABCDEFGHIJKLMNOPQRSTUVWXYZ
abcdefghijklmnopqrstuvwxyz1234567890
Many big jackdaws quickly zipped over the fox pen.

Zaragoza

Designer	Phill Grimshaw
Nationality	UK
Date Designed	1996
Foundries	Linotype Letraset ITC
Number of weights	1

ABCDEFGHIJKLMNOPQRSTUVWXYZ
abcdefghijklmnopqrstuvwxyz1234567890
Moi, je veux quinze clubs a golf et du whisky pur.

Linotype Mineru

Designer Ronny Edelstein
Nationality DE
Date Designed 1996
Foundries Linotype
Number of weights 1

ABCDEFGHIJKLMNOPQRSTUVWXYZ
abcdefghijklmnopqrstuvwxyz1234567890
Jaded reader with fabled roving eye seized by quickened
impulse to expand budget.

Access

Designer A Accent
Nationality FR
Date Designed 1980
Foundries Mecanorma
Number of weights 1

ABCDEFGHIJKLMNOPQRSTUVWXYZ
ABCDEFGHIJKLMNOPQRSTUVWXYZ1234567890
BEFORE LIFE'S LIQUOR IN ITS CUP BE DRY.

Comic Strip

Designer Gérard Mariscalchi
Nationality FR
Date Designed 1985
Foundries Monotype
Number of weights 6

ABCDEFGHIJKLMNOPQRSTUVWXYZ
ABCDEFGHIJKLMNOPQRSTUVWXYZ1234567890
AND, AS THE COCK CREW, THOSE WHO STOOD
BEFORE

Olaus Bandus

Designer Bo Berndal
Nationality SE
Date Designed 1992
Foundries Monotype
Number of weights 1

ABCDEFGHIJKLMNOPQRSTUVWXYZ
ABCDEFGHIJKLMNOPQRSTUVWXYZ1234567890
ALFREDO JUST MUST BRING VERY EXCITING NEWS TO THE PLAZA QUICKLY.

Olaus Magnus

Designer Bo Berndal
Nationality SE
Date Designed 1992
Foundries Monotype
Number of weights 1

ABCDEFGHIJKLMNOPQRSTUVWXYZ
ABCDEFGHIJKLMNOPQRSTUVWXYZ1234567890
BACK IN MY QUAINT GARDEN JAUNTY ZINNIAS VIE WITH PHLOX.

Herculanum

Designer	Adrian Frutiger
Nationality	CH
Date Designed	1990
Foundries	Adobe
Number of weights	1

ABCDEFGHIJKLMNOPQRSTUVWXYZ

ABCDEFGHIJKLMNOPQRSTUVWXYZ1234567890

HERCULANEUM WAS DESTROYED ALONG WITH POMPEII.
WHAT IS HERCULANUM?

Pompeijana

Designer	Adrian Frutiger
Nationality	CH
Date Designed	1993
Foundries	Linotype
Number of weights	2

ABCDEFGHIJKLMNOPQRSTUVWXYZ

ABCDEFGHIJKLMNOPQRSTUVWXYZ1234567890

POMPEII WAS DESTROYED IN THE ERUPTION OF MT. VESUVIUS IN AD79.

Rusticana

Designer	Adrian Frutiger
Nationality	CH
Date Designed	1992
Foundries	Linotype
Number of weights	2

ABCDEFGHIJKLMNOPQRSTUVWXYZ

ABCDEFGHIJKLMNOPQRSTUVWXYZ1234567890

SYMPATHIZING WOULD FIX QUAKER OBJECTIVES.

Revolver

Designer	Rian Hughes
Nationality	UK
Date Designed	1990
Foundries	FontFont
Number of weights	2

ABCDEFGHIJKLMNOPQRSTUVWXYZ

ABCDEFGHIJKLMNOPQRSTUVWXYZ1234567890

NEW FARM HAND (PICKING JUST SIX QUINCES) PROVES STRONG BUT LAZY.

Squash

Designer	Jan van Dijk
Nationality	NL
Date Designed	1991
Foundries	Mecanorma CA Partners
Number of weights	2

ABCDEFGHIJKLMNOPQRSTUVWXYZ

ABCDEFGHIJKLMNOPQRSTUVWXYZ1234567890

THE TAVERN SHOUTED—"OPEN THEN THE DOOR.

Pneuma

Designer	Timothy Donaldson
Nationality	UK
Date Designed	1991
Foundries	ITC
Number of weights	1

ABCDEFGHIJKLMNOPQRSTUVWXYZ

ABCDEFGHIJKLMNOPQRSTUVWXYZ1234567890

YOU KNOW HOW LITTLE WHILE WE HAVE TO STAY,

Hazel

Designer	Phill Grimshaw
Nationality	UK
Date Designed	1992
Foundries	Monotype ITC
Number of weights	1

ABCDEFGHIJKLMNOPQRSTUVWXYZ

ABCDEFGHIJKLMNOPQRSTUVWXYZ1234567890

AND, ONCE DEPARTED, MAY RETURN NO MORE."

Kiilani

Designer	Judith Sutcliffe
Nationality	US
Date Designed	1993
Foundries	Monotype
Number of weights	1

ABCDEFGHIJKLMNOPQRSTUVWXYZ

ABCDEFGHIJKLMNOPQRSTUVWXYZ1234567890

QUICK WAFTING ZEPHYRS VEX BOLD JIM.

Cartoon Script

Designer	Linotype Library
Nationality	DE
Date Designed	1993
Foundries	Linotype
Number of weights	1

ABCDEFGHIJKLMNOPQRSTUVWXYZ

ABCDEFGHIJKLMNOPQRSTUVWXYZ1234567890

XAVIER, A WILDLY INFORMAL COURT JESTER, KEPT CALLING
QUEEN ELIZABETH 'BETTY.'

Roquette

Designer	Martin Wait
Nationality	UK
Date Designed	1993
Foundries	Martin Wait Type
Number of weights	1

ABCDEFGHIJKLMNOPQRSTUVWXYZ

ABCDEFGHIJKLMNOPQRSTUVWXYZ1234567890

NOW THE NEW YEAR REVIVING OLD DESIRES,

Hand Drawn

Designer	Michael Gills
Nationality	UK
Date Designed	1993
Foundries	Letraset ITC
Number of weights	1

ABCDEFGHIJKLMNOPQRSTUVWXYZ

ABCDEFGHIJKLMNOPQRSTUVWXYZ1234567890

THE THOUGHTFUL SOUL TO SOLITUDE RETIRES.

Bluntz

Designer	David Sagorski
Nationality	US
Date Designed	1994
Foundries	Linotype ITC
Number of weights	1

ABCDEFGHIJKLMNOPQRSTUVWXYZ

ABCDEFGHIJKLMNOPQRSTUVWXYZ1234567890

WHERE THE WHITE HAND OF MOSES ON THE BOUGH

Tag

Designer	David Sagorski
Nationality	US
Date Designed	1994
Foundries	Linotype ITC
Number of weights	1

ABCDEFGHIJKLMNOPQRSTUVWXYZ

ABCDEFGHIJKLMNOPQRSTUVWXYZ1234567890

PUTS OUT, AND JESUS FROM THE GROUND SUSPIRES.

Mateo

Designer	Hans-Jürgen Ellenburger
Nationality	DE
Date Designed	1994
Foundries	Linotype
Number of weights	1

ABCDEFGHIJKLMNOPQRSTUVWXYZ

abcdefghijklmnopqrstuvwxyz1234567890

Alfredo just must bring very exciting news to the plaza quickly.

CrashBangWallop

Designer	Rian Hughes
Nationality	UK
Date Designed	1994
Foundries	FontFont
Number of weights	1

ABCDEFGHIJKLMNOPQRSTUVWXYZ

abcdefghijklmnopqrstuvwxyz

1234567890

Many big jackdaws quickly zipped over.

Virgile

Designer	Franck Jalleau
Nationality	FR
Date Designed	1995
Foundries	Monotype
Number of weights	2

ABCDEFGHIJKLMNOPQRSTUVWXYZ

ABCDEFGHIJKLMNOPQRSTUVWXYZ1234567890

IRAM INDEED IS GONE WITH ALL ITS ROSE,

Matisse

Designer	Gregory Grey
Nationality	FR
Date Designed	1995
Foundries	ITC Linotype Monotype
Number of weights	1

ABCDEFGHIJKLMNOPQRSTUVWXYZ

ABCDEFGHIJKLMNOPQRSTUVWXYZ1234567890

CRAZY FREDERICKA BOUGHT MANY VERY EXQUISITE OPAL JEWELS.

Little Louis

Designer	Panache Typography
Nationality	UK
Date Designed	1995
Foundries	Monotype
Number of weights	3

ABCDEFGHIJKLMNOPQRSTUVWXYZ

ABCDEFGHIJKLMNOPQRSTUVWXYZ1234567890

WE HAVE JUST QUOTED ON NINE DOZEN BOXES OF GRAY LAMP WICKS.

Spirit

Designer	Patty King
Nationality	US
Date Designed	1995
Foundries	Linotype ITC Monotype
Number of weights	1

ABCDEFGHIJKLMNOPQRSTUVWXYZ

ABCDEFGHIJKLMNOPQRSTUVWXYZ1234567890

VERILY THE DARK EX-JEW QUIT ZIONISM, PREFERRING THE CABALA.

Wolfdance

Designer	Philip Bouwsma
Nationality	US
Date Designed	1995
Foundries	CA Partners
Number of weights	1

ABCDEFGHIJKLMNOPQRSTUVWXYZ

ABCDEFGHIJKLMNOPQRSTUVWXYZ1234567890

QUICK WAFTING ZEPHYRS VEX BOLD JIM.

Mission

Designer	Stephen Miggas
Nationality	US
Date Designed	1995
Foundries	Aerotype Monotype
Number of weights	1

ABCDEFGHIJKLMNOPQRSTUVWXYZ

ABCDEFGHIJKLMNOPQRSTUVWXYZ1234567890

WILLIAM SAID THAT EVERYTHING ABOUT HIS JACKET WAS IN QUITE GOOD CONDITION EXCEPT FOR THE ZIPPER.

Mod

Designer	Tim Ryan
Nationality	IE
Date Designed	1995
Foundries	Type Revivals Monotype
Number of weights	1

ABCDEFGHIJKLMNOPQRSTUVWXYZ?

ABCDEFGHIJKLMNOPQRSTUVWXYZ1234567890?

JACK AMAZED A FEW GIRLS BY DROPPING THE ANTIQUE ONYX VASE!

Quake

Designer	Fryda Berd
Nationality	US
Date Designed	1989
Foundries	Adobe
Number of weights	1

ABCDEFGHIJKLMNOPQRSTUVWXYZ

abcdefghijklmnopqrstuvwxyz1234567890

Forsaking monastic tradition, twelve jovial friars gave up their vocation for a questionable existence on the flying trapeze.

Merlin FF

Designer	Nick Shinn
Nationality	UK
Date Designed	1997
Foundries	FontFont
Number of weights	5

ABCDEFGHIJKLMNOPQRSTUVWXYZ

abcdefghijklmnopqrstuvwxyz1234567890

The Welsh wizard – enduring and wonderful.

Drycut

Designer	Serge Pichii
Nationality	CA
Date Designed	1997
Foundries	ITC
Number of weights	1

ABCDEFGHIJKLMNOPQRSTUVWXYZ

ABCDEFGHIJKLMNOPQRSTUVWXYZ1234567890

WE PROMPTLY JUDGED ANTIQUE IVORY BUCKLES FOR THE NEXT PRIZE.

Martini At Joes

Designer Steve Mehallo
Nationality US
Date Designed 1997
Foundries Monotype
Number of weights 1

ABCDEFGHIJKLMNOPQRST
UVWXYZ1234567890
FIVE OR SIX BIG JET PLANES
ZOOMED QUICKLY BY THE TOWER.

Surfboard

Designer Teri Kahan
Nationality US
Date Designed 1997
Foundries Monotype ITC
Number of weights 1

ABCDEFGHIJKLMNOPQRSTUVWXYZ
ABCDEFGHIJKLMNOPQRSTUVWXYZ1234567890
HOW VEXING A FUMBLE TO DROP A JOLLY ZUCCHINI IN
THE QUICKSAND.

Gema

Designer Claudia Rocha
Nationality BR
Date Designed 1998
Foundries Monotype ITC
Number of weights 1

ABCDEFGHIJKLMNOPQRSTUVWXYZ
ABCDEFGHIJKLMNOPQRSTUVWXYZ1234567890
SIXTY ZIPPERS WERE QUICKLY PICKED FROM THE WOVEN
JUTE BAG.

Flood

Designer Joachim Müller-Lancé
Nationality DE
Date Designed 2000
Foundries Adobe
Number of weights 1

ABCDEFGHIJKLMNOPQRSTUVWXYZ
ABCDEFGHIJKLMNOPQRSTUVWXYZ1234567890
MURKY HAZE ENVELOPED A CITY AS JARRING QUAKES BROKE
FORTY-SIX WINDOWS.

Architec

Designer Hans Bacher
Nationality DE
Date Designed 2001
Foundries Monotype
Number of weights 1

ABCDEFGHIJKLMNOPQRSTUVWXYZ
ABCDEFGHIJKLMNOPQRSTUVWXYZ1234567890
ALFREDO JUST MUST BRING VERY EXCITING NEWS TO THE PLAZA QUICKLY.

Twist

Designer Christian Schwartz
Nationality US
Date Designed 2004
Foundries Monotype
Number of weights 4

ABCDEFGHIJKLMNOPQRSTUVWXYZ

ABCDEFGHIJKLMNOPQRSTUVWXYZ1234567890

A QUICK MOVEMENT OF THE ENEMY WILL JEOPARDIZE SIX GUNBOATS.

Typeface 4

Designer Neville Brody
Nationality UK
Date Designed 1992
Foundries FontFont
Number of weights 2

ABCDEFGHIJKLMNOPQRSTUVWXYZ

abcdefghijklmnopqrstuvwxyz1234567890

The five boxing wizards jump quickly.

Digitek

Designer David Quay
Nationality UK
Date Designed 1990
Foundries Letraset Linotype ITC
Number of weights 1

ABCDEFGHIJKLMNOPQRSTUVWXYZ

abcdefghijklmnopqrstuvwxyz1234567890

New farm hand (picking just six quinces) proves strong but lazy.

Dome

Designer Neville Brody
Nationality UK
Date Designed 1993
Foundries FontFont
Number of weights 1

ABCDEFGHIJKLMNOPQRSTUVWXYZ

abcdefghijklmnopqrstuvwxyz1234567890

Freight to me sixty dozen quart jars and twelve black pans.

Revolution

Designer Douglas Carter
Nationality UK
Date Designed 1993
Foundries T-26 Monotype
Number of weights 1

ABCDEFGHIJKLMNOPQRSTUVWXYZ

ABCDEFGHIJKLMNOPQRSTUVWXYZ1234567890

SYMPATHIZING WOULD FIX QUAKER OBJECTIVES.

Roswell

Designer	Jim Parkinson
Nationality	US
Date Designed	1998
Foundries	ITC
Number of weights	6

ABCDEFGHIJKLMNOPQRSTUVWXYZ
abcdefghijklmnopqrstuvwxyz1234567890
Six big juicy steaks sizzled in a pan as five workmen left the quarry.

Arcadia

Designer	Neville Brody
Nationality	UK
Date Designed	1990
Foundries	Linotype
Number of weights	1

ABCDEFGHIJKLMNOPQRSTUVWXYZ
abcdefghijklmnopqrstuvwxyz1234567890
Jail zesty vixen who grabbed pay from quack.

Agfa Waddy 27

Designer	Aiko & Hideaki Wada
Nationality	JP
Date Designed	1999
Foundries	Monotype
Number of weights	1

ABCDEFGHIJKLMNOPQRSTUVWXYZ
abcdefgbijklmnopqrstuvwxyz1234567890
New farm hand (picking just six quinces) proves strong but lazy.

Silhouette

Designer	Morris Fuller Benton
Nationality	US
Date Designed	1937
Foundries	Monotype
Recut/Digitised by	Garrett Boge, 1990
Number of weights	1

ABCDEFGHIJKLMNOPQRSTUVWXYZ
abcdefghijklmnopqrstuvwxyz1234567890
Viewing quizzical abstracts mixed up hefty jocks.

Agfa Waddy 28

Designer	Aiko & Hideaki Wada
Nationality	JP
Date Designed	1999
Foundries	Monotype
Number of weights	1

ABCDEFGHIJKLMNOPQRSTUVWXYZ
abcdefgbijklmnopqrstuvwxyz1234567890
New farm hand (picking just six quinces) proves strong but lazy.

Malstock

Designer Frantisek Storm
Nationality CZ
Date Designed 1996
Foundries ITC Linotype
Number of weights 1

ABCDEFGHIJKLMNOPQRSTUVWXYZ

abcdefghijklmnopqrstuvwxyz1234567890

Exquisite farm wench gives body jolt to prize stinker.

Agfa Waddy 125

Designer Aiko & Hideaki Wada
Nationality JP
Date Designed 1999
Foundries Monotype
Number of weights 1

ABCDEFGHIJKLMNOPQRSTUVWXYZ

abcdefghijklmnopqrstuvwxyz1234567890

New farm hand (picking just six quinces) proves strong but lazy.

Mekanik

Designer David Quay
Nationality UK
Date Designed 1998
Foundries Linotype ITC
Number of weights 2

ABCDEFGHIJKLMNOPQRSTUVWXYZ

abcdefghijklmnopqrstuvwxyz1234567890

Quick wafting zephyrs vex bold Jim.

Binner Gothic

Designer John F Cumming
Nationality UK
Date Designed 1898
Foundries Monotype
Number of weights 1

ABCDEFGHIJKLMNOPQRSTUVWXYZ

abcdefghijklmnopqrstuvwxyz1234567890

Mix Zapf with Veljovic and get quirky Beziers.

Linotype Lichtwerk

Designer Bernd Pfannkuchen
Nationality DE
Date Designed 1999
Foundries Linotype
Number of weights 1

ABCDEFGHIJKLMNOPQRSTUVWXYZ

abcdefghijklmnopqrstuvwxyz1234567890

A quick movement of the enemy will jeopardize six gunboats.

TF Hotelmoderne

Designer Joseph D Treacy

Nationality US

Date Designed 1985

Foundries Monotype

Number of weights 11

ABCDEFGHIJKLMNOPQRSTUVWXYZ

abcdefghijklmnopqrstuvwxyz1234567890

The juke box music puzzled a gentle visitor from a quaint valley town.

Obsessed

Designer Jamie Nazaroff

Nationality CA

Date Designed 1996

Foundries Monotype zang

Number of weights 1

ABCDEFGHIJKLMNOPQRSTUVWXYZ

abcdefghijklmnopqrstuvwxyz1234567890

Sympathizing would fix Quaker objectives.

Industria

Designer Neville Brody

Nationality UK

Date Designed 1990

Foundries Linotype Adobe

Number of weights 4

ABCDEFGHIJKLMNOPQRSTUVWXYZ

abcdefghijklmnopqrstuvwxyz1234567890

May Jo equal the fine record by solving six puzzles a week?

Tyson

Designer Neville Brody

Nationality UK

Date Designed 1990

Foundries FontFont

Number of weights 1

ABCDEFGHIJKLMNOPQRSTUVWXYZ

abcdefghijklmnopqrstuvwxyz1234567890

A heavyweight boxer and popular dog's name.

TF Raincheck

Designer Joseph D Treacy

Nationality US

Date Designed 1992

Foundries Treacyfaces Monotype

Number of weights 8

ABCDEFGHIJKLMNOPQRSTUVWXYZ

abcdefghijklmnopqrstuvwxyz1234567890

How quickly daft jumping zebras vex.

Linotype Reducta

Designer	Herbert O Modelhart
Nationality	AT
Date Designed	1996
Foundries	Linotype
Number of weights	1

ABCDEFGHIJKLMNOPQRSTUVWXYZ

abcdefghijklmnopqrstuvwxyz1234567890

Lazy movers quit hard-packing of papier-maché jewellery boxes.

Freytag

Designer	Arne Freytag
Nationality	DE
Date Designed	1998
Foundries	Linotype
Number of weights	1

ABCDEFGHIJKLMNOPQRSTUVWXYZ

abcdefghijklmnopqrstuvwxyz1234567890

Crazy Fredericka bought many very exquisite opal jewels.

Phenix American

Designer	Morris Fuller Benton
Nationality	US
Date Designed	1935
Foundries	Monotype
Number of weights	1

ABCDEFGHIJKLMNOPQRSTUVWXYZ

abcdefghijklmnopqrstuvwxyz1234567890

Jimmy and Zack, the police explained, were last seen diving into a field of buttered quahogs.

TF Akimbo

Designer	Joseph D Treacy
Nationality	US
Date Designed	1990
Foundries	Treacyfaces Monotype
Number of weights	7

ABCDEFGHIJKLMNOPQRSTUVWXYZ

abcdefghijklmnopqrstuvwxyz1234567890

Mix Zapf with Veljovic and get quirky Beziers.

Compacta

Designer	Fred Lambert
Nationality	UK
Date Designed	1963
Foundries	Letraset Linotype ITC
Number of weights	1

ABCDEFGHIJKLMNOPQRSTUVWXYZ

abcdefghijklmnopqrstuvwxyz1234567890

Ebenezer unexpectedly bagged two tranquil aardvarks with his jiffy vacuum cleaner.

Hadrian

Designer	anon
Nationality	UK
Date Designed	1965
Foundries	Monotype
Number of weights	1

ABCDEFGHIJKLMNOPQRSTUVWXYZ

abcdefghijklmnopqrstuvwxyz1234567890

Quick wafting zephyrs vex bold Jim.

Motter Festival

Designer	Othmar Motter
Nationality	DE
Date Designed	2000
Foundries	FontFont
Number of weights	6

ABCDEFGHIJKLMNOPQRSTUVWXYZ

abcdefghijklmnopqrstuvwxyz1234567890

Brawny gods just flocked up to quiz and vex him.

Integral

Designer	Jim Marcus
Nationality	US
Date Designed	1996
Foundries	Monotype
Number of weights	1

ABCDEFGHIJKLMNOPQRSTUVWXYZ

abcdefghijklmnopqrstuvwxyz 1234567890

Ebenezer unexpectedly bagged two tranquil aardvarks with his jiffy vacuum cleaner.

Lennox

Designer	Alexander Rühl
Nationality	DE
Date Designed	1996
Foundries	Monotype ITC Linotype
Number of weights	1

ABCDEFGHIJKLMNOPQRSTUVWXYZ

abcdefghijklmnopqrstuvwxyz1234567890

Jazzy saxophones blew over Mick's turgid quiff.

Modernique

Designer	Morris Fuller Benton
Nationality	US
Date Designed	1928
Foundries	ATF
Number of weights	1

ABCDEFGHIJKLMNOPQRSTUVWXYZ

abcdefghijklmnopqrstuvwxyz1234567890

Six big devils from Japan quickly forgot how to waltz.

Dolmen

Designer	Max Salzmann
Nationality	DE
Date Designed	1922
Foundries	Schelter & Giesecke
Number of weights	1

ABCDEFGHIJKLMNOPQRSTUVWXYZ

abcdefghijklmnopqrstuvwxyz1234567890

A cromlech; a prehistoric Celtic burial chamber with two uprights and a capstone.

Koloss

Designer	J Erbar
Nationality	DE
Date Designed	1923
Foundries	Ludwig & Mayer Linotype FC Castle
Number of weights	1

ABCDEFGHIJKLMNOPQRSTUVWXYZ

abcdefghijklmnopqrstuvwxyz1234567890

Martin J. Hixeypozer quickly began his first word.

Einhorn

Designer	Letraset
Nationality	UK
Date Designed	1980
Foundries	Letraset Linotype
Number of weights	1

ABCDEFGHIJKLMNOPQRSTUVWXYZ

abcdefghijklmnopqrstuvwxyz1234567890

Zweedse ex-VIP, behoorlijk gek op quantumfysica.

Black Boton

Designer	Albert Boton
Nationality	FR
Date Designed	1970
Foundries	Monotype
Number of weights	1

ABCDEFGHIJKLMNOPQRSTUVWXYZ

ABCDEFGHIJKLMNOPQRSTUVWXYZ1234567890

HOW SWEET IS MORTAL SOVRANTY!—THINK SOME:

Schildersblad Capitals

Designer	Philip Bouwsma
Nationality	US
Date Designed	1997
Foundries	Monotype
Number of weights	1

ABCDEFGHIJKLMNOPQRSTUVWXYZ

ABCDEFGHIJKLMNOPQRSTUVWXYZ1234567890

JADED READER WITH FABLED ROVING EYE SEIZED BY QUICKENED IMPULSE TO EXPAND BUDGET.

Alex

Designer	J-J Tachdjian, I comme image
Nationality	FR
Date Designed	1995
Foundries	Radiateur Fontes, Union Type Supply
Number of weights	2

ABCDEFGHIJKLMNOPQRSTUVWXYZ
ABCDEFGHIJKLMNOPQRSTUVWXYZ1234567890
ASTRONAUT QUINCY B. ZACK DEFIES GRAVITY WITH SIX JET FUEL PUMPS.

Mister Chuckles

Designer	Nick Curtis
Nationality	US
Date Designed	2001
Foundries	ITC
Number of weights	1

ABCDEFGHIJKLMNOPQRSTUVWXYZ
ABCDEFGHIJKLMNOPQRSTUVWXYZ1234567890
JAZZY SAXOPHONES BLEW OVER MICK'S TURGID QUIFF.

Broadway

Designer	Morris Fuller Benton
Nationality	US
Date Designed	1929
Foundries	ATF URW++
Number of weights	2

ABCDEFGHIJKLMNOPQRSTUVWXYZ
abcdefghijklmnopqrstuvwxyz1234567890
New farm hand (picking just six quinces) proves strong but lazy.

Kobalt

Designer	Leslie Cabarga
Nationality	US
Date Designed	1994
Foundries	Monotype
Number of weights	1

ABCDEFGHIJKLMNOPQRSTUVWXYZ
abcdefghijklmnopqrstuvwxyz1234567890
Pack my box with five dozen liquor jugs.

TC Broadway

Designer	Morris Fuller Benton
Nationality	US
Date Designed	1929
Foundries	TC
Number of weights	2

ABCDEFGHIJKLMNOPQRSTUVWXYZ
ABCDEFGHIJKLMNOPQRSTUVWXYZ1234567890
TWO DIFFERENT FONTS NAMED BROADWAY.

Broadway Poster

Designer	Morris Fuller Benton
Nationality	US
Date Designed	1928
Foundries	Monotype
Number of weights	1

ABCDEFGHIJKLMNOPQRSTUVWXYZ
abcdefghijklmnopqrstuvwxyz1234567890
Martin J. Hixeypozer quickly began his first word.

Linotype Scott Mars

Designer	Hellmut Bomm
Nationality	DE
Date Designed	2000
Foundries	Linotype
Number of weights	1

ABCDEFGHIJKLMNOPQRSTUVWXYZ
abcdefghijklmnopqrstuvwxyz1234567890
five big quacking zephyrs jolt my wax bed.

Linotype Scott Venus

Designer	Hellmut Bomm
Nationality	DE
Date Designed	2000
Foundries	Linotype
Number of weights	1

ABCDEFGHIJKLMNOPQRSTUVWXYZ
abcdefghijklmnopqrstuvwxyz1234567890
the quick brown fox jumps over the lazy dog.

Deli Deluxe

Designer	Jim Spiece
Nationality	US
Date Designed	1999
Foundries	ITC
Number of weights	1

ABCDEFGHIJKLMNOPQRSTUVWXYZ
ABCDEFGHIJKLMNOPQRSTUVWXYZ1234567890
CRAZY FREDERICKA BOUGHT MANY VERY EXQUISITE
OPAL JEWELS.

Zeppelin

Designer	Frantisek Storm
Nationality	CZ
Date Designed	1991
Foundries	Storm
Number of weights	1

ABCDEFGHIJKLMNOPQRSTUVWXYZ
abcdefghijklmnopqrstuvwxyz1234567890
Zweedse ex-VIP, behoorlijk gek op quantumfysica.

Mustang Sally

Designer	Nick Curtis
Nationality	US
Date Designed	2001
Foundries	Monotype
Number of weights	1

ABCDEFGHIJKLMNOPQRSTUVWXYZ
abcdefghijklmnopqrstuvwxyz1234567890
The vixen jumped quickly on her foe barking with zeal.

Pump

Designer	Letraset
Nationality	UK
Date Designed	1970
Foundries	Letraset
Number of weights	1

ABCDEFGHIJKLMNOPQRSTUVWXYZ
abcdefghijklmnopqrstuvwxyz1234567890
Jaded zombies acted quaintly but kept driving their oxen forward.

Blippo

Designer	Foto Star
Nationality	US
Date Designed	1973
Foundries	Bitstream Linotype URW++
Number of weights	1

ABCDEFGHIJKLMNOPQRSTUVWXYZ
abcdefghijklmnopqrstuvwxyz1234567890
Compare this and Pump with Bauhaus for text.

Capone Light

Designer	Tony Geddes
Nationality	UK
Date Designed	1994
Foundries	Monotype
Number of weights	1

ABCDEFGHIJKLMNOPQRSTUVWXYZ
abcdefghijklmnopqrstuvwxyz1234567890
West quickly gave Bert handsome prizes for six juicy plums.

Hardwood

Designer	Willard T Sniffin
Nationality	UK
Date Designed	1932
Foundries	Monotype Adobe
Recut/Digitised by	Garrett Boge, 1992
Number of weights	1

ABCDEFGHIJKLMNOPQRSTUVWXYZ
abcdefghijklmnopqrstuvwxyz1234567890
How vexing a fumble to drop a jolly zucchini in the quicksand.

BeoSans

Designer	Erik van Blokland, Just van Rossum
Nationality	NL
Date Designed	1991
Foundries	FontFont
Number of weights	1

ABCDEFGHIJKLMNOPQRSTUVWXYZ

abcdefghijklmnopqrstuvwxyz1234567890

BeoSans is a so called RandomFont. This means that every time you print a character, it will look slightly different.

McCollough

Designer	Gustav F Schroeder
Nationality	DE
Date Designed	1994
Foundries	Monotype
Number of weights	1

ABCDEFGHIJKLMNOPQRSTUVWXYZ

abcdefghijklmnopqrstuvwxyz1234567890

The exodus of jazzy pigeons is craved by squeamish walkers.

Ritmo

Designer	Aldo Novarese
Nationality	IT
Date Designed	1955
Foundries	Nebiolo
Number of weights	1

ABCDEFGHIJKLMNOPQRSTUVWXYZ

abcdefghijklmnopqrstuvwxyz1234567890

Strongly influenced by BANCO but with a lower case.

Autotrace

Designer	Neville Brody
Nationality	UK
Date Designed	1994
Foundries	FontFont
Number of weights	1

ABCDEFGHIJKLMNOPQRSTUVWXYZ

abcdefghijklmnopqrstuvwxyz1234567890

Shows its character best in large point sizes.

Flexure

Designer	Stephen Farrell
Nationality	US
Date Designed	1993
Foundries	T-26
Number of weights	1

ABCDEFGHIJKLMNOPQRSTUVWXYZ

abcdefghijklmnopqrstuvwxyz1234567890

Quick wafting zephyrs vex bold Jim.

Cartonnage

Designer	Yanek Iontef
Nationality	IL
Date Designed	2003
Foundries	FontFont
Number of weights	1

ABCDEFGHIJKLMNOPQRSTUVWXYZ

abcdefghijklmnopqrstuvwxyz1234567890

Freight to me sixty dozen quart jars and twelve black pans.

Linotype Bariton

Designer	Alexei Chekoulaev
Nationality	RU
Date Designed	1997
Foundries	Linotype
Number of weights	1

ABCDEFGHIJKLMNOPQRSTUVWXYZ

abcdefghijklmnopqrstuvwxyz1234567890

Hark! Toxic jungle water vipers quietly drop on zebras for meals!

TF Adepta

Designer	Joseph D Treacy
Nationality	US
Date Designed	1992
Foundries	Treacyfaces Monotype
Number of weights	1

ABCDEFGHIJKLMNOPQRSTUVWXYZ

abcdefghijklmnopqrstuvwxyz1234567890

Jackdaws love my big sphinx of quartz.

Balance

Designer	Noah Rothschild
Nationality	US
Date Designed	1999
Foundries	Victory Type
Number of weights	32

ABCDEFGHIJKLMNOPQRSTUVWXYZ

abcdefghijklmnopqrstuvwxyz1234567890

Jay visited back home and gazed upon a brown fox and quail.

Block

Designer	H Hoffman
Nationality	DE
Date Designed	1908
Foundries	Berthold URW++
Number of weights	1

ABCDEFGHIJKLMNOPQRSTUVWXYZ

abcdefghijklmnopqrstuvwxyz1234567890

Digitised as HERMES by Matthew Butterick, 1995.

Britannic

Designer	Stephenson Blake
Nationality	UK
Date Designed	1895
Foundries	Stephenson Blake Linotype URW++
Number of weights	1

ABCDEFGHIJKLMNOPQRSTUVWXYZ
abcdefghijklmnopqrstuvwxyz1234567890
Others—"How blest the Paradise to come!"

Hobo

Designer	Morris Fuller Benton
Nationality	US
Date Designed	1910
Foundries	ATF Bitstream
Number of weights	10

ABCDEFGHIJKLMNOPQRSTUVWXYZ
abcdefghijklmnopqrstuvwxyz1234567890
One of Benton's least attractive fonts, used by people with no interest in design or typography. Perplexingly popular for nearly a century.

Kino

Designer	M Dovey
Nationality	UK
Date Designed	1930
Foundries	Monotype Adobe
Number of weights	1

ABCDEFGHIJKLMNOPQRSTUVWXYZ
abcdefghijklmnopqrstuvwxyz1234567890
Ah, take the Cash in hand and waive the Rest;

Cosmic

Designer	Chank Diesel
Nationality	US
Date Designed	1996
Foundries	Chank
Number of weights	1

ABCDEFGHIJKLMNOPQRSTUVWXYZ
abcdefghijklmnopqrstuvwxyz1234567890
King Alexander was partly overcome just after quizzing Diogenes in his tub.

Anzeigen Grotesk

Designer	Haas
Nationality	DE
Date Designed	1896
Foundries	Elsner+Flake Linotype URW++
Number of weights	2

ABCDEFGHIJKLMNOPQRSTUVWXYZ
abcdefghijklmnopqrstuvwxyz1234567890
Pack my box with five dozen liquor jugs.

Gill Kayo Condensed

Designer	Eric Gill
Nationality	UK
Date Designed	1930
Foundries	ITC
Number of weights	1

ABCDEFGHIJKLMNOPQRSTUVWXYZ

abcdefghijklmnopqrstuvwxyz1234567890

Jimmy and Zack, the police explained, were last seen diving into a field of buttered quahogs.

Helvetica Inserat

Designer	Max Miedinger
Nationality	CH
Date Designed	1957
Foundries	Monotype
Number of weights	1

ABCDEFGHIJKLMNOPQRSTUVWXYZ

abcdefghijklmnopqrstuvwxyz1234567890

Moi, je veux quinze clubs a golf et du whisky pur.

Haettenschweiler

Designer	Robert Norton
Nationality	UK
Date Designed	1994
Foundries	Apple
Number of weights	1

ABCDEFGHIJKLMNOPQRSTUVWXYZ

abcdefghijklmnopqrstuvwxyz1234567890

Oh, the brave Music of a distant Drum!

Myriad Headline

Designer	Robert Slimbach, Carol Twombly
Nationality	US
Date Designed	1992
Foundries	Adobe
Number of weights	1

ABCDEFGHIJKLMNOPQRSTUVWXYZ

abcdefghijklmnopqrstuvwxyz1234567890

Multiple Master font.

Briem Akademi

Designer	Gunnlaugur S E Briem
Nationality	IS
Date Designed	2001
Foundries	Monotype Adobe
Number of weights	27

ABCDEFGHIJKLMNOPQRSTUVWXYZ

abcdefghijklmnopqrstuvwxyz1234567890

Compressed weight is unbelievably ▮; Multiple Master.

Outback

Designer	Bob Alonso
Nationality	US
Date Designed	1996
Foundries	Monotype ITC
Number of weights	1

ABCDEFGHIJKLMNOPQRSTUVWXYZ

abcdefghijklmnopqrstuvwxyz1234567890

Murky haze enveloped a city as jarring quakes broke forty-six windows.

Ad Hoc

Designer	Franko Luin
Nationality	SL
Date Designed	1994
Foundries	Linotype
Number of weights	1

ABCDEFGHIJKLMNOPQRSTUVWXYZ

abcdefghijklmnopqrstuvwxyz1234567890

Jay visited back home and gazed upon a brown fox and quail.

Liverpool

Designer	anon
Nationality	UK
Date Designed	1994
Foundries	ITC
Number of weights	1

ABCDEFGHIJKLMNOPQRSTUVWXYZ

abcdefghijklmnopqrstuvwxyz1234567890

Grumpy wizards make toxic brew for the evil Queen and Jack.

Impact

Designer	Geoffrey Lee
Nationality	UK
Date Designed	1964
Foundries	Stephenson Blake Letraset Linotype Monotype The Font Company Adobe
Number of weights	1

ABCDEFGHIJKLMNOPQRSTUVWXYZ

abcdefghijklmnopqrstuvwxyz1234567890

Chosen as a core font for Microsoft Windows. Impact Wide designed in 2002.

Tempo

Designer	Robert Hunter Middleton
Nationality	US
Date Designed	1930
Foundries	Ludlow Linotype
Number of weights	2

ABCDEFGHIJKLMNOPQRSTUVWXYZ

abcdefghijklmnopqrstuvwxyz1234567890

Middleton was born in Scotland and emigrated to the USA when he was ten.

Zipper

Designer	Philip Kelly
Nationality	UK
Date Designed	1970
Foundries	Letraset Linotype
Number of weights	1

ABCDEFGHIJKLMNOPQRSTUUWXYZ

abcdefghijklmnopqrstuuwxyz1234567890

Sexy qua lijf, doch bang voor het zwempak.

Flyer

Designer	Linotype
Nationality	DE
Date Designed	1955
Foundries	Linotype Adobe Elsner+Flake Monotype Letraset
Number of weights	2

ABCDEFGHIJKLMNOPQRSTUVWXYZ

abcdefghijklmnopqrstuvwxyz1234567890

Elsner's Bold is effectively Flyer Extended.

Placard

Designer	anon
Nationality	UK
Date Designed	1958
Foundries	Monotype
Number of weights	1

ABCDEFGHIJKLMNOPQRSTUVWXYZ

abcdefghijklmnopqrstuvwxyz1234567890

An obsolescent word for poster.

Aura

Designer	E-lan Ronen
Nationality	US
Date Designed	1928
Foundries	T-26 Monotype
Number of weights	4

ABCDEFGHIJKLMNOPQRSTUVWXYZ

abcdefghijklmnopqrstuvwxyz1234567890

Playing jazz vibe chords quickly excites my wife.

Impacta

Designer	Marc Lubbers
Nationality	NL
Date Designed	1994
Foundries	Linotype
Number of weights	1

ABCDEFGHIJKLMNOPQRSTUVWXYZ

abcdefghijklmnopqrstuvwxyz1234567890

Zweedse ex-VIP, behoorlijk gek op quantumfysica.

Ewie

Designer	URW++
Nationality	DE
Date Designed	1993
Foundries	URW++
Number of weights	2

ABCDEFGHIJKLMNOPQRSTUVWXYZ

abcdefghijklmnopqrstuvwxyz1234567890

Will Major Douglas be expected to take this true-false quiz very soon?

TF Roux

Designer	Joseph D Treacy
Nationality	US
Date Designed	1973
Foundries	Treacyfaces
Number of weights	1

ABCDEFGHIJKLMNOPQRSTUVWXYZ

abcdefghijklmnopqrstuvwxyz 1234567890

Many-wived Jack laughs at probes of sex quiz.

Bigband

Designer	Karlgeorg Hoefer
Nationality	DE
Date Designed	1994
Foundries	Linotype
Number of weights	1

ABCDEFGHIJKLMNOPQRSTUVWXYZ

abcdefghijklmnopqrstuvwxyz1234567890

When we go back to Juarez, Mexico, do we fly over picturesque Arizona?

Derek

Designer	Monotype
Nationality	UK
Date Designed	1994
Foundries	Monotype
Number of weights	1

ABCDEFGHIJKLMNOPQRSTUVWXYZ

abcdefghijklmnopqrstuvwxyz 1234567890

Derek Cross rekindled my interest in type.

Renee Display

Designer	Renée Ramsey-Passmore
Nationality	US
Date Designed	1997
Foundries	Linotype
Number of weights	1

ABCDEFGHIJKLMNOPQRSTUVWXYZ

abcdefghijklmnopqrstuvwxyz 1234567890

While waxing parquet decks, jaunty Suez.

Agfa Waddy 93

Designer Aiko & Hideaki Wada
Nationality JP
Date Designed 1999
Foundries Monotype
Number of weights 1

ABCDEFGHIJKLMNOPQRSTUVWXYZ

abcdefghijklmnopqrstuvwxyz1234567890

New farm hand (picking just six quinces) proves strong but lazy.

Cirrus

Designer Maryanne Mastandrea
Nationality US
Date Designed 1993
Foundries T-26
Number of weights 1

ABCDEFGHIJKLMNOPQRSTUVWXYZ

abcdefghijklmnopqrstuvwxyz1234567890

Back in my quaint garden jaunty zinnias vie with flaunting phlox.

Commonworld

Designer Stephen Farrell
Nationality US
Date Designed 1995
Foundries T-26
Number of weights 1

ABCDEFGHIJKLMNOPQRSTUVWXYZ

ABCDEFGHIJKLMNOPQRSTUVWXYZ1234567890

A MAD BOXER SHOT A QUICK, GLOVED JAB TO THE JAW OF HIS DIZZY OPPONENT.

Equinox

Designer Vince Whitlock
Nationality UK
Date Designed 1988
Foundries Monotype Letraset ITC
Number of weights 1

ABCDEFGHIJKLMNOPQRSTUVWXYZ

abcdefghijklmnopqrstuvwxyz1234567890

When we go back to Juarez, Mexico, do we fly over picturesque Arizona?

Dog

Designer Paul Sych
Nationality CA
Date Designed 1991
Foundries FontFont
Number of weights 1

ABCDEFGHIJKLMNOPQRSTUVWXYZ

abcdefghijklmnopqrstuvwxyz1234567890

Will Major Douglas be expected to take this true-false quiz very soon?

Pop

Designer	Neville Brody
Nationality	UK
Date Designed	1993
Foundries	FontFont
Number of weights	2

ABCDEFGHIJKLMNOPQRSTUVWXYZ

abcdefghijklmnopqrstuvwxyz1234567890

Lazy movers quit hard-packing of papier-maché jewellery boxes.

Beckett

Designer	Gustav Jaeger
Nationality	DE
Date Designed	1994
Foundries	Linotype
Number of weights	1

ABCDEFGHIJKLMNOPQRSTUVWXYZ

abcdefghijklmnopqrstuvwxyz1234567890

Who will rid me of this turbulent priest?

F2F Frontpage Four

Designer	Alexander Branczyk
Nationality	DE
Date Designed	1994
Foundries	Linotype
Number of weights	1

ABCDEFGHIJKLMNOPQRSTUVWXYZ

abcdefghijklmnopqrstuvwxyz1234567890

Jack amazed a few girls by dropping the antique onyx vase!

Black Tulip

Designer	Dudley Rees
Nationality	UK
Date Designed	1997
Foundries	Linotype ITC
Number of weights	1

ABCDEFGHIJKLMNOPQRSTUVWXYZ

abcdefghijklmnopqrstuvwxyz1234567890

Mix Zapf with Veljovic and get quirky Beziers.

Gothic

Designer	Neville Brody
Nationality	UK
Date Designed	2002
Foundries	FontFont
Number of weights	6

ABCDEFGHIJKLMNOPQRSTUVWXYZ

abcdefghijklmnopqrstuvwxyz

1234567890

Pack my box with five dozen liquor jugs.

Lineale

Designer	Gérard Mariscalchi
Nationality	CA
Date Designed	1997
Foundries	Monotype
Number of weights	1

ABCDEFGHIJKLMNOPQRSTUVWXYZ
abcdefghijklmnopqrstuvwxyz1234567890

Breezily jangling $3,416,857,209,wise advertiser ambles to the bank, his exchequer amplified.

Anlinear

Designer	Michael Parson
Nationality	CH
Date Designed	2003
Foundries	Linotype
Number of weights	1

ABCDEFGHIJKLMNOPQRSTUVWXYZ
abcdefghijklmnopqrstuvwxyz1234567890

Look to the Rose that blows about us? - "Lo

Ned

Designer	Michael Parson
Nationality	CH
Date Designed	2003
Foundries	Linotype
Number of weights	1

ABCDEFGHIJKLMNOPQRSTUVWXYZ
abcdefghijklmnopqrstuvwxyz1234567890

Laughing," she says, "into the World I blow."

Bandolero Bandolera

Designer	Ray Cruz
Nationality	US
Date Designed	1998
Foundries	CA Exclusives
Number of weights	1

ABCDEFGHIJKLMNOPQRSTUVWXYZ
abcdefghijklmnopqrstuvwxyz1234567890

Sphinx of black quartz judge my vow.

Headline MT

Designer	Monotype
Nationality	UK
Date Designed	1895
Foundries	Monotype
Number of weights	1

ABCDEFGHIJKLMNOPQRSTUVWXYZ
abcdefghijklmnopqrstuvwxyz1234567890

Jackdaws love my big sphinx of quartz.

Gothic 13

Designer anon
Nationality UK
Date Designed 1900
Foundries Monotype Linotype Bitstream Adobe
Number of weights 1

ABCDEFGHIJKLMNOPQRSTUVWXYZ

abcdefghijklmnopqrstuvwxyz1234567890

Grumpy wizards make toxic brew for the evil Queen and Jack.

Golota

Designer Bo Berndal
Nationality SE
Date Designed 1998
Foundries Monotype
Number of weights 1

ABCDEFGHIJKLMNOPQRSTUVWXYZ

abcdefghijklmnopqrstuvwxyz1234567890

All questions asked by five watch experts amazed the judge.

Gothic Extra Light Extended

Designer Monotype
Nationality UK
Date Designed 1994
Foundries Creative Alliance
Number of weights 1

ABCDEFGHIJKLMNOPQRSTUVWXYZ

abcdefghijklmnopqrstuvwxyz1234567890

No kidding, Lorenzo called off his trip to visit Mexico City just because they told him the conquistadores were extinct.

TF Dierama

Designer Joseph D Treacy
Nationality US
Date Designed 1994
Foundries Monotype
Number of weights 2

ABCDEFGHIJKLMNOPQRSTUVWXYZ

abcdefghijklmnopqrstuvwxyz1234567890

Moi, je veux quinze clubs a golf et du whisky pur.

Eumundi Sans

Designer Russell Bean
Nationality AU
Date Designed 1994
Foundries Monotype
Number of weights 1

ABCDEFGHIJKLMNOPQRSTUVWXYZ

abcdefghijklmnopqrstuvwxyz1234567890

The quick brown fox jumps over the lazy dog.

Fontoon

Designer Steve Zafarana
Nationality US
Date Designed 1995
Foundries Galapagos ITC
Number of weights 1

ABCDEFGHIJKLMNOPQRSTUVWXYZ
abcdefghijklmnopqrstuvwxyz1234567890
A large fawn jumped quickly over white zinc boxes.

Generica

Designer Jim Parkinson
Nationality US
Date Designed 1995
Foundries Monotype
Number of weights 1

ABCDEFGHIJKLMNOPQRSTUVWXYZ
abcdefghijklmnopqrstuvwxyz1234567890
The job of waxing linoleum frequently peeves chintzy kids.

Glowworm

Designer Bogdan Zochowski
Nationality PL
Date Designed 1971
Foundries Mecanorma Monotype
Number of weights 2

ABCDEFGHIJKLMNOPQRSTUVWXYZ
abcdefghijklmnopqrstuvwxyz1234567890
A quick movement of the enemy will jeopardize six gunboats.

Kit

Designer Albert Boton
Nationality FR
Date Designed 1998
Foundries Monotype
Number of weights 6

ABCDEFGHIJKLMNOPQRSTUVWXYZ
abcdefghijklmnopqrstuvwxyz1234567890
The five boxing wizards jump quickly.

Klepto

Designer Phill Grimshaw
Nationality UK
Date Designed 1996
Foundries Monotype ITC
Number of weights 1

ABCDEFGHIJKLMNOPQRSTUVWXYZ
abcdefghijklmnopqrstuvwxyz1234567890
Mr. Jock, TV quiz Ph.D., bags few lynx.

Noovo

Designer Phill Grimshaw
Nationality UK
Date Designed 1997
Foundries Linotype LAT Monotype
Number of weights 2

ABCDEFGHIJKLMNOPQRSTUVWXYZ

abcdefghijklmnopqrstuvwxyz1234567890

We promptly judged antique ivory buckles for the next prize.

Banjoman

Designer Paul Veres
Nationality HU
Date Designed 1996
Foundries Calligraphics
Number of weights 9

ABCDEFGHIJKLMNOPQRSTUVWXYZ

abcdefghijklmnopqrstuvwxyz1234567890

How quickly daft jumping zebras vex.

Swingbill

Designer Bo Berndal
Nationality SE
Date Designed 1995
Foundries Monotype
Number of weights 1

ABCDEFGHIJKLMNOPQRSTUVWXYZ

abcdefghijklmnopqrstuvwxyz1234567890

Astronaut Quincy B. Zack defies gravity with six jet fuel pumps.

Trotzkopf

Designer Bo Berndal
Nationality SE
Date Designed 1997
Foundries Monotype
Number of weights 2

ABCDEFGHIJKLMNOPQRSTUVWXYZ

abcdefghijklmnopqrstuvwxyz1234567890

Questions of a zealous nature have become by degrees petty waxen jokes.

Verkehr

Designer Mott Jordan
Nationality US
Date Designed 1996
Foundries Monotype ITC
Number of weights 2

ABCDEFGHIJKLMNOPQRSTUVWXYZ

abcdefghijklmnopqrstuvwxyz1234567890

Was there a quorum of able whizzkids gravely exciting the jaded fish at ATypI?

Gothic FF

Designer Neville Brody
Nationality UK
Date Designed 1992
Foundries FontFont
Number of weights 6

ABCDEFGHIJKLMNOPQRSTUVWXYZ
abcdefghijklmnopqrstuvwxyz
1234567890
Sphinx of black quartz judge my vow.

PL Britannia Bold

Designer Stephenson Blake
Nationality UK
Date Designed 1900
Foundries Wagner & Schmidt
Number of weights 1

ABCDEFGHIJKLMNOPQRSTUVWXYZ
abcdefghijklmnopqrstuvwxyz1234567890
Two hardy boxing kangaroos jet from Sydney to Zanzibar on quicksilver pinions.

PL Radiant Bold Extra Condensed

Designer R Hunter Middleton
Nationality US
Date Designed 1938
Foundries Photo-Lettering
Number of weights 1

ABCDEFGHIJKLMNOPQRSTUVWXYZ
abcdefghijklmnopqrstuvwxyz1234567890
The sex life of the woodchuck is a provocative question for most vertebrate zoology majors.

Pritchard

Designer Martin Wait
Nationality UK
Date Designed 1990
Foundries ITC
Number of weights 1

ABCDEFGHIJKLMNOPQRSTUVWXYZ
ABCDEFGHIJKLMNOPQRSTUVWXYZ1234567890
WILLIAM SAID THAT EVERYTHING ABOUT HIS JACKET WAS IN QUITE GOOD CONDITION EXCEPT FOR THE ZIPPER.

Regatta Condensed

Designer Alan Meeks
Nationality UK
Date Designed 1987
Foundries ITC
Number of weights 1

ABCDEFGHIJKLMNOPQRSTUVWXYZ
abcdefghijklmnopqrstuvwxyz1234567890
Xavier, a wildly informal court jester, kept calling Queen Elizabeth 'Betty.'

F2F Czykago Light

Designer	Alexander Branczyk
Nationality	DE
Date Designed	1998
Foundries	LT Take Type 5
Number of weights	1

ABCDEFGHIJKLMNOPQRSTUVWXYZ
abcdefghijklmnopqrstuvwxyz1234567890
A very European take on the Mac system font Chicago.

Globe Gothic

Designer	Joseph W Phinney
Nationality	US
Date Designed	1897
Foundries	Lanston Monotype URW++ Mecanorma
Number of weights	3

ABCDEFGHIJKLMNOPQRSTUVWXYZ
abcdefghijklmnopqrstuvwxyz1234567890
Kenny Grant designed this book.

Grafilone

Designer	Bo Berndal
Nationality	SE
Date Designed	1996
Foundries	Linotype
Number of weights	3

ABCDEFGHIJKLMNOPQRSTUVWXYZ
abcdefghijklmnopqrstuvwxyz1234567890
Sexy qua lijf, doch bang voor het zwempak.

Jigger

Designer	Steffen Sauerteig
Nationality	DE
Date Designed	2000
Foundries	FontFont
Number of weights	12

ABCDEFGHIJKLMNOPQRSTUVWXYZ
abcdefghijklmnopqrstuvwxyz1234567890
The font comes in layers to make colours, a 3D font.

Kipp

Designer	Claudia Kipp
Nationality	DE
Date Designed	1993
Foundries	FontFont
Number of weights	1

ABCDEFGHIJKLMNOPQRSTUVWXYZ
abcdefghijklmnopqrstuvwxyz1234567890
Six crazy kings vowed to abolish my quite pitiful jousts.

Linotype Marcu San

Designer Marcus McCallion
Nationality UK
Date Designed 1996
Foundries Linotype
Number of weights 1

ABCDEFGHIJKLMNOPQRSTUVUXYZ
abcdefghijklmnopqrstuvwxyz1234567890
Sphinx of black quartz judge ny vow.

Minimum

Designer Pierre di Sciullo
Nationality IT
Date Designed 1993-1995
Foundries FontFont
Number of weights 1

ABCDEFGHIJKLMNOPQRSTUVWXYZ

abcdefghijklmnopqrstuvwxyz1234567890

The sex life of the woodchuck is a provocative question for most vertebrate
zoology majors.

Plak

Designer Paul Renner
Nationality DE
Date Designed 1928
Foundries Heidelberger Linotype
Number of weights 3

ABCDEFGHIJKLMNOPQRSTUVWXYZ
abcdefghijklmnopqrstuvwxyz1234567890
Quixotic Conservatives vet first key zero-growth jeremiad.

Linotype Rezident

Designer Paul van der Laan
Nationality NL
Date Designed 1999
Foundries Linotype
Number of weights 4

ABCDEFGHIJKLMNOPQRSTUVWXYZ
abcdefghijklmnopqrstuvwxyz1234567890
Sexy qua lijf, doch bang voor het zwempak.

Rosetta

Designer Max Kisman
Nationality US
Date Designed 1991
Foundries FontFont
Number of weights 1

ABCDEFGHIJKLMNOPQRSTUVWXYZ
abcdefghijklmnopqrstuvwxyz1234567890
Hark! Toxic jungle water vipers quietly drop on zebras for meals!

Rundfunk Grotesk

Designer	Esselte Letraset
Nationality	DE
Date Designed	1987
Foundries	Letraset
Number of weights	1

ABCDEFGHIJKLMNOPQRSTUVWXYZ
abcdefghijklmnopqrstuvwxyz1234567890
A mad boxer shot a quick, gloved jab to the jaw of his dizzy
opponent.

Tokyo

Designer	Neville Brody
Nationality	UK
Date Designed	1993
Foundries	FontFont
Number of weights	4

ABCDEFGHIJKLMNOPQRSTUVWXYZ
ABCDEFGHIJKLMNOPQRSTUVWXYZ1234567890
WILLIAM SAID THAT EVERYTHING ABOUT HIS JACKET WAS IN QUITE GOOD CONDITION EXCEPT
FOR THE ZIPPER.

TradeMarker

Designer	Critzler
Nationality	DE
Date Designed	1999
Foundries	FontFont
Number of weights	16

ABCDEFGHIJKLMNOPQRSTUVWXYZ
abcdefghijklmnopqrstuvwxyz1234567890
Moi, je veux quinze clubs a golf et du whisky pur.

Typeface 6 & 7

Designer	Vaughan Sedore
Nationality	US
Date Designed	1991
Foundries	FontFont
Number of weights	3

ABCDEFGHIJKLMNOPQRSTUVWXYZ
ABCDEFGHIJKLMNOPQRSTUVWXYZ1234567890
JACKDAWS LOVE MY BIG SPHINX OF QUARTZ.

World

Designer	Neville Brody
Nationality	UK
Date Designed	1993
Foundries	FontFont
Number of weights	3

ABCDEFGHIJKLMNOPQRSTUVWXYZ
abcdefghijklmnopqrstuvwxyz1234567890
Big July earthquakes confound zany experimental vow.

Balega

Designer	Jürgen Weltin
Nationality	DE
Date Designed	2003
Foundries	Linotype
Number of weights	1

ABCDEFGHIJKLMNOPQRSTUVWXYZ
abcdefghijklmnopqrstuvwxyz1234567890
At once the silken Tassel of my Purse.

Binner Poster

Designer	John F Cumming
Nationality	UK
Date Designed	1898
Foundries	Monotype
Number of weights	1

ABCDEFGHIJKLMNOPQRSTUVWXYZ
abcdefghijklmnopqrstuvwxyz1234567890
Sexy qua lijf, doch bang voor het zwempak.

Govan

Designer	Ole Schaefer, Erik Spiekermann
Nationality	DE
Date Designed	2001
Foundries	FontFont
Number of weights	1

ABCDEFGHIJKLMNOPQRSTUVWXYZ
abcdefghijklmnopqrstuvwxyz1234567890
Jackdaws love my big sphinx of quartz.

Moderne

Designer	Jim Parkinson
Nationality	US
Date Designed	1996
Foundries	FontFont
Number of weights	4

ABCDEFGHIJKLMNOPQRSTUVWXYZ
ABCDEFGHIJKLMNOPQRSTUVWXYZ1234567890
THE EXODUS OF JAZZY PIGEONS IS CRAVED BY
SQUEAMISH WALKERS.

Linotype Puritas

Designer	Linotype
Nationality	DE
Date Designed	2002
Foundries	Linotype
Number of weights	7

ABCDEFGHIJKLMNOPQRSTUVWXYZ
abcdefghijklmnopqrstuvwxyz1234567890
Top heavy.

CG Gothic No 1

Designer	W A Dwiggins
Nationality	US
Date Designed	1936
Foundries	CA Partners
Number of weights	1

ABCDEFGHIJKLMNOPQRSTUVWXYZ

abcdefghijklmnopqrstuvwxyz1234567890

Just work for improved basic techniques to maximize your typing skill.

CG Gothic No 3

Designer	W A Dwiggins
Nationality	US
Date Designed	1936
Foundries	CA Partners
Number of weights	1

ABCDEFGHIJKLMNOPQRSTUVWXYZ

abcdefghijklmnopqrstuvwxyz1234567890

A mad boxer shot a quick, gloved jab to the jaw of his dizzy opponent.

CG Gothic No 4

Designer	W A Dwiggins
Nationality	US
Date Designed	1936
Foundries	CA Partners
Number of weights	1

ABCDEFGHIJKLMNOPQRSTUVWXYZ

abcdefghijklmnopqrstuvwxyz1234567890

Verbatim reports were quickly given by Jim Fox to his amazed audience.

Aircraft

Designer	Albert Boton
Nationality	FR
Date Designed	2002
Foundries	FontFont
Number of weights	1

ABCDEFGHIJKLMNOPQRSTUVWXYZ

abcdefghijklmnopqrstuvwxyz1234567890

No kidding, Lorenzo called off his trip to visit Mexico City just because they told him the conquistadores were extinct.

Studio

Designer	Albert Boton
Nationality	FR
Date Designed	2002
Foundries	FontFont
Number of weights	1

ABCDEFGHIJKLMNOPQRSTUVWXYZ

abcdefghijklmnopqrstuvwxyz1234567890

Forsaking monastic tradition, twelve jovial friars gave up their vocation for a questionable existence on the flying trapeze.

District

Designer	Albert Boton
Nationality	FR
Date Designed	2002
Foundries	FontFont
Number of weights	1

ABCDEFGHIJKLMNOPQRSTUVWXYZ

abcdefghijklmnopqrstuvwxyz1234567890

An inspired calligrapher can create pages of beauty using stick ink, quill, brush, pick-axe, buzz saw, or even strawberry jam.

Odyssée

Designer	Roselyne Besnard, Michel Besnard
Nationality	FR
Date Designed	1996
Foundries	ITC Monotype
Number of weights	7

ABCDEFGHIJKLMNOPQRSTUVWXYZ

abcdefghijklmnopqrstuvwxyz1234567890

Portez ce vieux whisky au juge blond qui fume.

Tugboat Annie

Designer	Nick Curtis
Nationality	US
Date Designed	2001
Foundries	Monotype
Number of weights	1

ABCDEFGHIJKLMNOPQRSTUVWXYZ

abcdefghijklmnopqrstuvwxyz1234567890

Forsaking monastic tradition, twelve jovial friars gave up their vocation for a questionable existence on the flying trapeze.

Premier Lightline

Designer	Letraset
Nationality	UK
Date Designed	1969
Foundries	Letraset
Number of weights	1

ABCDEFGHIJKLMNOPQRSTUVWXYZ

abcdefghijklmnopqrstuvwxyz1234567890

While waxing parquet decks, jaunty Suez sailors vomit abaft.

Modern Poster

Designer	Alf R Becker
Nationality	US
Date Designed	1932
Foundries	The Fontry
Recut/Digitised by	Michael Gene Adkins, 1998
Number of weights	1

ABCDEFGHIJKLMNOPQRSTUVWXYZ

abcdefghijklmnopqrstuvwxyz1234567890

The July sun caused a fragment of black pine wax to ooze on the velvet quilt.

Orbon

Designer	James Montalbano
Nationality	US
Date Designed	1995
Foundries	Linotype ITC Monotype
Recut/Digitised by	ITC
Number of weights	4

ABCDEFGHIJKLMNOPQRSTUUWXYZ

abcdefghijklmnopqrstuvwxyz1234567890

The juke box music puzzled a gentle visitor from a quaint valley town.

Metronome Gothic

Designer	Anistatia Miller
Nationality	US
Date Designed	1989
Foundries	Chartpak Monotype
Number of weights	1

ABCDEFGHIJKLMNOPQRSTUVWXYZ

abcdefghijklmnopqrstuvwxyz1234567890

Originally named Miller, after the designer.

Migrate

Designer	George Ryan
Nationality	US
Date Designed	1994
Foundries	Galapagos
Number of weights	1

ABCDEFGHIJKLMNOPQRSTUVWXYZ

abcdefghijklmnopqrstuvwxyz1234567890

Formalised version of Oz Handicraft.

Octane

Designer	Norbert Reiners
Nationality	DE
Date Designed	1997
Foundries	Linotype
Number of weights	2

ABCDEFGHIJKLMNOPQRSTUVWXYZ

abcdefghijklmnopqrstuvwxyz1234567890

Jail zesty vixen who grabbed pay from quack.

Motter Sparta

Designer	Otmar Motter
Nationality	DE
Date Designed	1976
Foundries	Linotype ITC
Number of weights	1

ABCDEFGHIJKLMNOPQRSTUVWXYZ

abcdefghijklmnopqrstuvwxyz1234567890

Jeb quickly drove a few extra miles on the glazed pavement.

Dalcora HE

Designer Erwin Koch
Nationality DE
Date Designed 1989
Foundries Linotype
Number of weights 1

ABCDEFGHIJKLMNOPQRSTUVWXYZ

abcdefghijklmnopqrstuvwxyz1234567890

Five or six big jet planes zoomed quickly by the tower.

Fehrle Display

Designer Erich Fehrle
Nationality DE
Date Designed 1976
Foundries Linotype
Number of weights 1

ABCDEFGHIJKLMNOPQRSTUVWXYZ

abcdefghijklmnopqrstuvwxyz1234567890

Just work for improved basic techniques to maximize your typing skill.

Grapefruit

Designer Györi Attila
Nationality HU
Date Designed 1997
Foundries ITC
Number of weights 1

ABCDEFGHIJKLMNOPQRSTUVWXYZ

abcdefghijklmnopqrstuvwxyz1234567890

Xavier, a wildly informal court jester, kept calling Queen Elizabeth 'Betty.'

TF Simper

Designer Joseph D Treacy
Nationality US
Date Designed 1992
Foundries Treacyfaces Monotype
Number of weights 4

ABCDEFGHIJKLMNOPQRSTUVWXYZ

abcdefghijklmnopqrstuvwxyz1234567890

Simper Serif has imperceptibly enlarged blobs for serifs.

Hexatype

Designer Michael Parson
Nationality CH
Date Designed 2003
Foundries Linotype
Number of weights 1

ABCDEFGHIJKLMNOPQRSTUVWXYZ

abcdefghijklmnopqrstuvwxyz1234567890

Tear, and its Treasure on the Garden throw.

Piercing LT

Designer	Michael Parson
Nationality	CH
Date Designed	2003
Foundries	Linotype
Number of weights	3

ABCDEFGHIJKLMDOPQRSTUUXYZ

abcdefghijklmnopqrstuvwxyz1234567890

the Moddy Dope men set their Beards upon.

Leopard

Designer	Christof Gassner
Nationality	DE
Date Designed	1976
Foundries	Mecanorma CA Partners
Number of weights	1

ABCDEFGHIJKLMNOPQRSTUVWXYZ

ABCDEFGHIJKLMNOPQRSTUVWXYZ1234567890

BRAWNY GODS JUST FLOCKED UP TO QUIZ AND VEX HIM.

Techno Outline

Designer	Vaughan Sedore
Nationality	US
Date Designed	1995
Foundries	Monotype
Number of weights	1

ABCDEFGHIJKLMNOPQRSTUVWXYZ

abcdefghijklmnopqrstuvwxyz1234567890

Was there a quorum of able whizzkids gravely
exciting the jaded fish at ATypI?

Odessa

Designer	Peter O'Donnell
Nationality	UK
Date Designed	1988
Foundries	Letraset ITC
Number of weights	1

ABCDEFGHIJKLMNOPQRSTUVWXYZ

abcdefghijklmnopqrstuvwxyz1234567890

Astronaut Quincy B. Zack defies gravity with six jet fuel pumps.

Bandolero

Designer	Ray Cruz
Nationality	US
Date Designed	1998
Foundries	Monotype
Number of weights	1

ABCDEFGHIJKLMNOPQRSTUVWXYZ

abcdefghijklmnopqrstuvwxyz1234567890

Alfredo just must bring very exciting news to the plaza quickly.

FontSoup

Designer Andreu Balius, Joan Carles Casasin

Nationality ES

Date Designed 1997

Foundries FontFont

Number of weights 12

ABCDEFGHIJKLMNOPQRSTUVWXYZ

abcdefghijklmnopqrstuvwxyz1234567890

The July sun caused a fragment of black pine wax to ooze on the velvet quilt.

Science Regular

Designer Val Fullard

Nationality CA

Date Designed 1995

Foundries CA Exclusives

Number of weights 1

ABCDEFGHIJKLMNOPQRSTUVWXYZ

abcdefghijklmnopqrstuvwxyz1234567890

Exquisite farm wench gives body jolt to prize stinker.

Albawing

Designer Linotype Library

Nationality DE

Date Designed 1994

Foundries Linotype

Number of weights 1

ABCDEFGHIJKLMNOPQRSTUVWXYZ

abcdefghijklmnopqrstuvwxyz1234567890

The July sun caused a fragment of black pine wax to ooze on the velvet quilt.

Delilah

Designer Patricia Lillie

Nationality US

Date Designed 1993

Foundries erik.co.uk

Number of weights 1

ABCDEFGHIJKLMNOPQRSTUVWXYZ

abcdefghijklmnopqrstuvwxyz1234567890

Samson's nemesis.

Iris

Designer Letraset

Nationality UK

Date Designed 1994

Foundries Letraset ITC

Number of weights 1

ABCDEFGHIJKLMNOPQRSTUVWXYZ

ABCDEFGHIJKLMNOPQRSTUVWXYZ1234567890

QUICK WAFTING ZEPHYRS VEX BOLD JIM.

Agfa Waddy 213

Designer Aiko & Hideaki Wada
Nationality JP
Date Designed 1999
Foundries Monotype
Number of weights 1

ABCDEFGHIJKLMNOPQRSTUVWXYZ

ABCDEFGHIJKLMNOPQRSTUVWXYZ1234567890

NEW FARM HAND (PICKING JUST SIX QUINCES) PROVES STRONG BUT LAZY.

Neon Extra Condensed

Designer G de Milano
Nationality IT
Date Designed 1935
Foundries Paratype
Number of weights 1

ABCDEFGHIJKLMNOPQRSTUVWXYZ

ABCDEFGHIJKLMNOPQRSTUVWXYZ1234567890

WILL MAJOR DOUGLAS BE EXPECTED TO TAKE THIS TRUE-FALSE QUIZ VERY SOON?

Quasaria

Designer Armin Retzko
Nationality DE
Date Designed 1994
Foundries Linotype
Number of weights 4

ABCDEFGHIJKLMNOPQRSTUVWXYZ

ABCDEFGHIJKLMNOPQRSTUVWXYZ1234567890

WE PROMPTLY JUDGED ANTIQUE IVORY BUCKLES FOR THE NEXT PRIZE.

Diner

Designer David Rakowski
Nationality US
Date Designed 1992
Foundries Font Diner
Number of weights 1

ABCDEFGHIJKLMNOPQRSTUVWXYZ

ABCDEFGHIJKLMNOPQRSTUVWXYZ1234567890

EVOKING A UNIQUELY AMERICAN CUISINE.

Compress

Designer Achaz Reuss
Nationality DE
Date Designed 1993
Foundries URW++
Number of weights 1

ABCDEFGHIJKLMNOPQRSTUVWXYZ

ABCDEFGHIJKLMNOPQRSTUVWXYZ1234567890

JELLY-LIKE ABOVE THE HIGH WIRE, SIX QUAKING PACHYDERMS KEPT THE CLIMAX OF THE EXTRAVAGANZA IN A DAZZLING STATE OF FLUX.

Agfa Waddy 182

Designer Aiko & Hideaki Wada
Nationality JP
Date Designed 1999
Foundries Monotype
Number of weights 1

ABCDEFGHIJKLMNOPQRSTUVWXYZ
ABCDEFGHIJKLMNOPQRSTUVWXYZ1234567890
AN HUNDRED YEARS SHOULD GO TO PRAISE

Agfa Waddy 188

Designer Aiko & Hideaki Wada
Nationality JP
Date Designed 1999
Foundries Monotype
Number of weights 1

ABCDEFGHIJKLMNOPQRSTUVWXYZ
ABCDEFGHIJKLMNOPQRSTUVWXYZ1234567890
THINE EYES AND ON THY FOREHEAD GAZE;

Agfa Waddy 186

Designer Aiko & Hideaki Wada
Nationality JP
Date Designed 1999
Foundries Monotype
Number of weights 1

ABCDEFGHIJKLMNOPQRSTUVWXYZ
ABCDEFGHIJKLMNOPQRSTUVWXYZ1234567890
TWO HUNDRED TO ADORE EACH BREAST,

Agfa Waddy 187

Designer Aiko & Hideaki Wada
Nationality JP
Date Designed 1999
Foundries Monotype
Number of weights 1

ABCDEFGHIJKLMNOPQRSTUVWXYZ
ABCDEFGHIJKLMNOPQRSTUVWXYZ1234567890
BUT CUT THE CRAP — JUST GET UNDRESSED.

Serengetti

Designer Bob Alonso
Nationality US
Date Designed 1996
Foundries Monotype ITC
Number of weights 1

ABCDEFGHIJKLMNOPQRSTUVWXYZ
ABCDEFGHIJKLMNOPQRSTUVWXYZ1234567890
MY GRANDFATHER PICKS UP QUARTZ AND VALUABLE ONYX JEWELS.

Anna

Designer	Daniel Pelavin
Nationality	US
Date Designed	1990
Foundries	ITC
Number of weights	1

ABCDEFGHIJKLMNOPQRSTUVWXYZ

ABCDEFGHIJKLMNOPQRSTUVWXYZ1234567890

THE FIVE BOXING WIZARDS JUMP QUICKLY.

Aldous Vertical

Designer	Walter Huxley
Nationality	UK
Date Designed	1935
Foundries	Monotype
Number of weights	1

ABCDEFGHIJKLMNOPQRSTUVWXYZ

ABCDEFGHIJKLMNOPQRSTUVWXYZ1234567890

PUZZLED WOMEN BEQUEATH JERKS VERY EXOTIC GIFTS.

Plaza

Designer	Letraset
Nationality	UK
Date Designed	1975
Foundries	Letraset
Number of weights	1

ABCDEFGHIJKLMNOPQRSTUVWXYZ

ABCDEFGHIJKLMNOPQRSTUVWXYZ1234567890

THE RISQUE GOWN MARKED A BRAZEN EXPOSURE OF VERY JUICY FLESH.

Organda

Designer	Mecanorma
Nationality	FR
Date Designed	1975
Foundries	Mecanorma
Number of weights	2

ABCDEFGHIJKLMNOPQRSTUVWXYZ

ABCDEFGHIJKLMNOPQRSTUVWXYZ1234567890

A MAD BOXER SHOT A QUICK, GLOVED JAB TO THE JAW OF HIS DIZZY OPPONENT.

DeStijl

Designer	Garrett Boge
Nationality	US
Date Designed	1992
Foundries	P22
Number of weights	2

ABCDEFGHIJKLMNOPQRSTUVWXYZ

ABCDEFGHIJKLMNOPQRSTUVWXYZ1234567890

Quixotic Conservatives vet first key zero-growth jeremiad.

Avenida

Designer John Chippindale

Nationality UK

Date Designed 1994

Foundries Letraset Linotype ITC Monotype

Number of weights 1

ABCDEFGHIJKLMNOPQRSTUVWXYZ

ABCDEFGHIJKLMNOPQRSTUVWXYZ1234567890O

JIM JUST QUIT AND PACKED EXTRA BAGS FOR LIZ OWEN.

Caribbean

Designer Jill Bell

Nationality US

Date Designed 1996

Foundries Linotype ITC Monotype

Number of weights 1

ABCDEFGHIJKLMNOPQRSTUVWXYZ

ABCDEFGHIJKLMNOPQRSTUVWXYZ1234567890

JAY VISITED BACK HOME AND GAZED UPON A BROWN FOX AND QUAIL.

Nordica

Designer Lutz Baar

Nationality SE

Date Designed 1996

Foundries Linotype

Number of weights 2

ABCDEFGHIJKLMNOPQRSTUVWXYZ

ABCDEFGHIJKLMNOPQRSTUVWXYZ1234567890

HOW QUICKLY DAFT JUMPING ZEBRAS VEX.

Golden Gate Gothic

Designer Jim Parkinson

Nationality US

Date Designed 1996

Foundries FontFont

Number of weights 1

ABCDEFGHIJKLMNOPQRSTUVWXYZ

ABCDEFGHIJKLMNOPQRSTUVWXYZ1234567890

AN INSPIRED CALLIGRAPHER CAN CREATE PAGES OF BEAUTY USING STICK INK, QUILL, BRUSH, PICK-AXE, BUZZ SAW, OR EVEN STRAWBERRY JAM.

ZiP

Designer Lennart Hansson

Nationality SE

Date Designed 1998

Foundries Creative Alliance Monotype

Number of weights 1

ABCDEFGHIJKLMNOPQRSTUVWXYZ

ABCDEFGHIJKLMNOPQRSTUVWXYZ1234567890

SEXY QUA LIJF, DOCH BANG VOOR HET ZWEMPAK.

Busorama

Designer	Herb Lubalin, Tom Carnase
Nationality	US
Date Designed	1970
Foundries	ITC Bitstream
Number of weights	3

ABCDEFGHIJKLMNOPQRSTUVWXYZ
ABCDEFGHIJKLMNOPQRSTUVWXYZ1234567890
FIVE BIG QUACKING ZEPHYRS JOLT MY WAX BED.

Neuland

Designer	Rudolf Koch
Nationality	DE
Date Designed	1923
Foundries	Klingspor Alphabets Inc
Number of weights	1

ABCDEFGHIJKLMNOPQRSTUVWXYZ
ABCDEFGHIJKLMNOPQRSTUVWXYZ1234567890
FIVE OR SIX BIG JET PLANES ZOOMED QUICKLY BY THE TOWER.

Diablo

Designer	Jim Parkinson
Nationality	US
Date Designed	2002
Foundries	Monotype
Number of weights	1

ABCDEFGHIJKLMNOPQRSTUVWXYZ
ABCDEFGHIJKLMNOPQRSTUVWXYZ1234567890
PORTEZ CE VIEUX WHISKY AU JUGE BLOND QUI FUME.

Phosphor

Designer	Jakob Erbar
Nationality	DE
Date Designed	1930
Foundries	Linotype Monotype
Number of weights	1

ABCDEFGHIJKLMNOPQRSTUVWXYZ
ABCDEFGHIJKLMNOPQRSTUVWXYZ1234567890
QUICK WAFTING ZEPHYRS VEX BOLD JIM.

Follies

Designer	Alan Meeks
Nationality	UK
Date Designed	1991
Foundries	Creative Alliance Linotype
Number of weights	1

ABCDEFGHIJKLMNOPQRSTUVWXYZ
ABCDEFGHIJKLMNOPQRSTUVWXYZ1234567890
FOLLY THE CAT. 1988–2005. R.I.P.

Bertram

Designer	Martin Wait
Nationality	UK
Date Designed	1991
Foundries	Martin Wait Type Linotype ITC Letraset
Number of weights	1

ABCDEFGHIJKLMNOPQRSTUVWXYZ
ABCDEFGHIJKLMNOPQRSTUVWXYZ1234567890
THE RISQUE GOWN MARKED A BRAZEN EXPOSURE OF VERY JUICY FLESH.

Boul Mich

Designer	Dan X Solo
Nationality	US
Date Designed	1974
Foundries	Dover
Number of weights	1

ABCDEFGHIJKLMNOPQRSTUVWXYZ
ABCDEFGHIJKLMNOPQRSTUVWXYZ1234567890
SHORT FOR BOULEVARD ST MICHEL, PARIS'S ANSWER TO BROADWAY.

Grock

Designer	Dan X Solo
Nationality	US
Date Designed	1935
Foundries	Dover
Recut/Digitised by	Dan X Solo
Number of weights	1

ABCDEFGHIJKLMNOPQRSTUVWXYZ
ABCDEFGHIJKLMNOPQRSTUVWXYZ1234567890
PUZZLED WOMEN BEQUEATH JERKS VERY EXOTIC GIFTS.

Kolo

Designer	Paul Shaw
Nationality	US
Date Designed	1994
Foundries	Monotype Adobe LetterPerfect
Number of weights	4

ABCDEFGHIJKLMNOPQRSTUVWXYZ
ABCDEFGHIJKLMNOPQRSTUVWXYZ1234567890
FIVE BIG QUACKING ZEPHYRS JOLT MY WAX BED.

Killer

Designer	André Nossek
Nationality	DE
Date Designed	1996
Foundries	Linotype
Number of weights	1

ABCDEFGHIJKLMNOPQRSTUVWXYZ
ABCDEFGHIJKLMNOPQRSTUVWXYZ1234567890
MY GRANDFATHER PICKS UP QUARTZ.

Beekman

Designer	Donald Beekman
Nationality	NL
Date Designed	1999
Foundries	FontFont
Number of weights	1

ABCDEFGHIJKL
NOPQRSTUVWXYZ
1234567890
ZWEEDSE EX-VIP, BEHOORLIJK.

Achtung Baby

Designer	John Roshell
Nationality	US
Date Designed	1999
Foundries	ITC
Number of weights	1

ABCDEFGHIJKLMNOPQRSTUVWXYZ
ABCDEFGHIJKLMNOPQRSTUVWXYZ1234567890
QUICK ZEPHYRS BLOW, VEXING DAFT JIM.

Copal

Designer	David Lemon
Nationality	US
Date Designed	1995
Foundries	Adobe
Number of weights	3

ABCDEFGHIJKLMNOPQRSTUVWXYZ
ABCDEFGHIJKLMNOPQRSTUVWXYZ1234567890
ZWEEDSE EX-VIP, BEHOORLIJK GEK OP QUANTUMFYSICA.

Extra

Designer	Paul H Neville
Nationality	US
Date Designed	1995
Foundries	FontFont
Number of weights	2

ABCDEFGHIJKLMNOPQRSTUVWXYZ
ABCDEFGHIJKLMNOPQRSTUVWXYZ1234567890
WORLD'S BOLDEST FONT?

Van Der Hoef Capitals

Designer	Philip Bouwsma
Nationality	US
Date Designed	1999
Foundries	Monotype
Number of weights	1

ABCDEFGHIJKLMNOPQRSTUVWXYZ
ABCDEFGHIJKLMNOPQRSTUVWXYZ1234567890
PORTEZ CE VIEUX WHISKY AU JUGE BLOND QUI FUME.

Chromium One

Designer David Harris
Nationality UK
Date Designed 1983
Foundries ITC
Number of weights 1

ABCDEFGHIJKLMNOPQRSTUVWXYZ
ABCDEFGHIJKLMNOPQRSTUVWXYZ1234567890
NEW FARM HAND (PICKING JUST SIX QUINCES) PROVES STRONG BUT LAZY.

Buzzer Three

Designer Paul Crome, Tony Lyons
Nationality DE
Date Designed 1995
Foundries Linotype ITC Letraset
Number of weights 1

ABCDEFGHIJKLMNOPQRSTUVWXYZ
ABCDEFGHIJKLMNOPQRSTUVWXYZ1234567890
WEST QUICKLY GAVE BERT HANDSOME PRIZES FOR SIX JUICY PLUMS.

Bobo

Designer S E Norton, Tim Ryan
Nationality US
Date Designed 1995
Foundries Monotype
Number of weights 1

ABCDEFGHIJKLMNOPQRSTUVWXYZ
ABCDEFGHIJKLMNOPQRSTUVWXYZ1234567890
KIND WORDS BUTTER NO PARSNIPS.

Ramiz

Designer Greg Samata
Nationality US
Date Designed 1993
Foundries CA Partners
Number of weights 1

ABCDEFGHIJKLM
NOPQRSTUVWXYZ
1234567890
ZWEEDSE EX-VIP.

Kryptic

Designer Garrett Boge
Nationality US
Date Designed 1992
Foundries Monotype
Number of weights 1

ABCDEFGHIJKLMNOPQRSTUVWXYZ
ABCDEFGHIJKLMNOPQRSTUVWXYZ
1234567890
BIG JULY EARTHQUAKES CONFOUND.

Stenberg

Designer	Tagir Safeyev
Nationality	RU
Date Designed	1997
Foundries	ITC Linotype Monotype
Number of weights	1

ABCDEFGHIJKLMNOPQRSTUVWXYZ

ABCDEFGHIJKLMNOPQRSTUVWXYZ1234567890

MAY JO EQUAL THE FINE RECORD BY SOLVING SIX PUZZLES A WEEK?

Linotype Spacera

Designer	Louis Lemoine
Nationality	US
Date Designed	2002
Foundries	Linotype
Number of weights	1

ABCDEFGHIJKLMNOPQRSTUVWXYZ

ABCDEFGHIJKLMNOPQRSTUVWXYZ

1234567890

QUICK WAFTING ZEPHYRS VEX BOLD JIM.

Monolith

Designer	Anthony Mayers
Nationality	UK
Date Designed	1994
Foundries	Monotype
Number of weights	1

abcdefghijklm
nopqrstuvwxyz
1234567890

FRed SPeCIaLIZed eaRLY.

Flatiron

Designer	Photo Lettering Collection
Nationality	UK
Date Designed	1997
Foundries	ITC Monotype
Number of weights	1

ABCDEFGHIJKLMN
OPQRSTUVWXYZ
1234567890

THIS IS THE WIDEST FONT.

Vienna Extended

Designer	Anthony de Meester
Nationality	NL
Date Designed	1989
Foundries	Linotype ITC
Number of weights	1

ABCDEFGHIJKLMN
OPQRSTUVWXYZ
1234567890

NOW IS THE TIME FOR DOGS.

Monolith Square

Designer	Jun Tomita
Nationality	JP
Date Designed	1998
Foundries	Monotype
Number of weights	4

abcdefGHIJKLMNOPQRSTUVWXYZ

abcdefGHIJKLMNOPQRSTUVWXYZ1234567890

an inspired calligrapher can create pages of
beauty using stick ink, quill, brush.

Beata

Designer	Garrett Boge
Nationality	US
Date Designed	1997
Foundries	Monotype
Number of weights	1

ABCDEFGHIJKLMNOPQRSTUVWXYZ

ABCDEFGHIJKLMNOPQRSTUVWXYZ1234567890

JACKDAWS LOVE MY BIG SPHINX OF QUARTZ.

Lithos

Designer	Carol Twombly
Nationality	US
Date Designed	1989
Foundries	Adobe Linotype Monotype
Number of weights	2

ABCDEFGHIJKLMNOPQRSTUVWXYZ

ABCDEFGHIJKLMNOPQRSTUVWXYZ1234567890

JACK AMAZED A FEW GIRLS BY DROPPING THE ANTIQUE
ONYX VASE!

Linotype Syntax Lapidar

Designer	Hans-Eduard Meier
Nationality	DE
Date Designed	1969
Foundries	Linotype
Number of weights	1

ABCDEFGHIJKLMNOPQRSTUVWXYZ

ABCDEFGHIJKLMNOPQRSTUVWXYZ1234567890

VERILY THE DARK EX-JEW QUIT ZIONISM, PREFERRING
THE CABALA.

Camellia

Designer	Tony Wenman
Nationality	UK
Date Designed	1972
Foundries	Letraset Linotype
Number of weights	1

abcdefghijklmnopqrstuvwxyz

abcdefghijklmnopqrstuvwxyz1234567890

the juke box music puzzled a gentle visitor from a quaint
valley town.

Gabardine

Designer	Richard Dawson
Nationality	UK
Date Designed	1994
Foundries	Monotype
Number of weights	1

ABCDEFGHIJKLMNOPQRSTUVWXYZ

ABCDEFGHIJKLMNOPQRSTUVWXYZ1234567890

CRAZY FREDERICKA BOUGHT MANY VERY EXQUISITE OPAL JEWELS.

Minimal

Designer	Doug Olena
Nationality	US
Date Designed	1995
Foundries	Monotype
Number of weights	1

ABCDEFGHIJKLMNOPQRSTUVWXYZ

ABCDEFGHIJKLMNOPQRSTUVWXYZ1234567890

FOR ONLY $49, JOLLY HOUSEWIVES MADE INEXPENSIVE MEALS USING QUICK-FROZEN VEGETABLES.

Modified Gothic

Designer	Heidelberger
Nationality	DE
Date Designed	1994
Foundries	Linotype
Number of weights	1

ABCDEFGHIJKLMNOPQRSTUVWXYZ

ABCDEFGHIJKLMNOPQRSTUVWXYZ1234567890

FORSAKING MONASTIC TRADITION, TWELVE JOVIAL FRIARS GAVE UP THEIR VOCATION FOR A QUESTIONABLE EXISTENCE ON THE FLYING TRAPEZE.

Circle

Designer	Michael Neugebauer
Nationality	AT
Date Designed	1970
Foundries	URW++
Number of weights	1

abcdefghijklmnopqrstuvwxyz

abcdefghijklmnopqrstuvwxyz1234567890

Five big quacking zephyrs jolt my wax bed.

Double Back

Designer	Robert Schenk
Nationality	US
Date Designed	2000
Foundries	Ingrimayne
Number of weights	1

ABCDEFGHIJKLMNOPQRSTUVWXYZ

ABCDEFGHIJKLMNOPQRSTUVWXYZ1234567890

ZWEI BOXKÄMPFER JAGEN EVA QUER DURCH SYLT.

Ghiberti

Designer	Garrett Boge, Paul Shaw
Nationality	US
Date Designed	1997
Foundries	Monotype
Number of weights	1

ABCDEFGHIJKLMNOPQRSTUVWXYZ

ABCDEFGHIJKLMNOPQRSTUVWXYZ1234567890

JACK AMAZED A FEW GIRLS BY DROPPING THE ANTIQUE ONYX VASE!

Harvey

Designer	Dale R Kramer
Nationality	US
Date Designed	1989
Foundries	Monotype Linotype ITC
Number of weights	1

ABCDEFGHIJKLMNOPQRSTUVWXYZ

ABCDEFGHIJKLMNOPQRSTUVWXYZ1234567890

WHILE WAXING PARQUET DECKS, JAUNTY SUEZ SAILORS VOMIT ABAFT.

Vino Bianco

Designer	Jochen Schuss
Nationality	DE
Date Designed	1998
Foundries	Monotype ITC
Number of weights	1

ABCDEFGHIJKLMNOPQRSTUVWXYZ

ABCDEFGHIjKLMNOPQRSTUVWXYZ

1234567890

JADED READER WITH FABLED ROVING EYE.

Refracta

Designer	Martin Wait
Nationality	UK
Date Designed	1988
Foundries	ITC
Number of weights	1

ABCDEFGHIJKLMNOPQRSTUVWXYZ

ABCDEFGHIJKLMNOPQRSTUVWXYZ1234567890

SEXY QUA LIJF, DOCH BANG VOOR HET ZWEMPAK.

Vere Dignum

Designer	Phil Baines
Nationality	UK
Date Designed	2003
Foundries	Linotype
Number of weights	1

ABCDEFGHIJKLMNOPQRSTUVWXYZ

ABCDEFGHIJKLMNOPQRSTUVWXYZ1234567890

TURNS ASHES—OR IT PROSPERS; AND ANON,

Elefont

Designer Bob McGrath
Nationality UK
Date Designed 1978
Foundries URW++
Number of weights 1

ABCDEFGHIJKLMNOPQRSTUVWXYZ
ABCDEFGHIJKLMNOPQRSTUVWXYZ1234567890
NEW FARM HAND (PICKING JUST SIX QUINCES) PROVES STRONG BUT LAZY.

Outlander

Designer Rian Hughes
Nationality UK
Date Designed 1995
Foundries FontFont
Number of weights 1

ABCDEFGHIJKLMNOPQRSTUVWXYZ
ABCDEFGHIJKLMNOPQRSTUVWXYZ
1234567890
PLAYING JAZZ VIBE CHORDS QUICKLY.

Matinee Gothic

Designer Jim Parkinson
Nationality US
Date Designed 1996
Foundries FontFont
Number of weights 1

ABCDEFGHIJKLMNOPQRSTUVWXYZ
ABCDEFGHIJKLMNOPQRSTUVWXYZ1234567890
BACK IN MY QUAINT GARDEN JAUNTY ZINNIAS VIE WITH
FLAUNTING PHLOX.

Motel Gothic

Designer Jim Parkinson
Nationality US
Date Designed 1996
Foundries FontFont
Number of weights 1

ABCDEFGHIJKLMNOPQRSTUVWXYZ
ABCDEFGHIJKLMNOPQRSTUVWXYZ1234567890
ZWEEDSE EX-VIP, BEHOORLIJK GEK OP QUANTUMFYSICA.

Cuppajoe ITC

Designer Nick Curtis
Nationality US
Date Designed 2001
Foundries ITC
Number of weights 1

ABCDEFGHIJKLMNOPQRSTUVWXYZ
ABCDEFGHIJKLMNOPQRSTUVWXYZ1234567890
QUICK ZEPHYRS BLOW, VEXING DAFT JIM.

Premier

Designer	Letraset
Nationality	UK
Date Designed	1969
Foundries	Letraset
Number of weights	1

ABCDEFGHIJKLMNOPQRSTUVWXYZ

abcdefghijklmnopqrstuvwxyz1234567890

While waxing parquet decks, jaunty Suez sailors vomit abaft.

Empire

Designer	Morris Fuller Benton
Nationality	US
Date Designed	1938
Foundries	ATF Bitstream
Number of weights	1

ABCDEFGHIJKLMNOPQRSTUVWXYZ

ABCDEFGHIJKLMNOPQRSTUVWXYZ1234567890

SEXY QUA LIJF, DOCH BANG VOOR HET ZWEMPAK.

Slide

Designer	Jim Marcus
Nationality	US
Date Designed	1996
Foundries	Monotype
Number of weights	1

ABCDEFGHIJKLMNOPQRSTUVWXYZ

ABCDEFGHIJKLMNOPQRSTUVWXYZ1234567890

WEST QUICKLY GAVE BERT HANDSOME PRIZES FOR SIX
JUICY PLUMS.

Mata

Designer	Greg Samata
Nationality	US
Date Designed	1993
Foundries	T-26
Number of weights	4

ABCDEFGHIJKLMN
OPQRSTUVWXYZ
1234567890
GRUMPY WIZARDS MAKE TEA.

Stop

Designer	Aldo Novarese
Nationality	IT
Date Designed	1970
Foundries	Nebiolo Linotype Elsner+Flake URW++
Number of weights	1

ABCDEFGHIJKLMNOPQRSTUVWXYZ

ABCDEFGHIJKLMNOPQRSTUVWXYZ1234567890

MY GRANDFATHER PICKS UP QUARTZ AND VALUABLE ONYX JEWELS.

Dex Gothic

Designer	Lennart Hansson
Nationality	SE
Date Designed	1991
Foundries	Elsner+Flake Linotype URW++
Number of weights	2

ABCDEFGHIJKLMNOPQRSTUVWXYZ

ABCDEFGHIJKLMNOPQRSTUVWXYZ1234567890

HOW RAZORBACK-JUMPING FROGS CAN LEVEL SIX PIQUED GYMNASTS!

Agfa Waddy 211

Designer	Aiko & Hideaki Wada
Nationality	JP
Date Designed	1999
Foundries	Monotype
Number of weights	1

ABCDEFGHIJKLMNOPQRSTUVWXYZ

ABCDEFGHIJKLMNOPQRSTUVWXYZ1234567890

CAN YOU MAKE SENSE OF THE AGFA WADDY SERIES?

Ter Gast

Designer	Philip Bouwsma
Nationality	US
Date Designed	1995
Foundries	Monotype
Number of weights	2

ABCDEFGHIJKLMNOPQRSTUVWXYZ

ABCDEFGHIJKLMNOPQRSTUVWXYZ1234567890

JUST WORK FOR IMPROVED BASIC TECHNIQUES TO MAXIMIZE YOUR TYPING SKILL.

Taut

Designer	John Jones
Nationality	UK
Date Designed	1994
Foundries	Linotype
Number of weights	1

ABCDEFGHIJKLMNOPQRSTUVWXYZ

ABCDEFGHIJKLMNOPQRSTUVWXYZ1234567890

ON THE OTHER HAND, TAUT T-26 IS A HANDWRITING FONT BY EMMA ELDRIDGE.

Commerce Gothic

Designer	anon
Nationality	US
Date Designed	1939
Foundries	Monotype Ludlow
Recut/Digitised by	Jim Parkinson, 1998
Number of weights	1

ABCDEFGHIJKLMNOPQRSTUVWXYZ

ABCDEFGHIJKLMNOPQRSTUVWXYZ1234567890

WAS THERE A QUORUM OF ABLE WHIZZKIDS GRAVELY EXCITING THE JADED FISH AT ATYPI?

Festival Titling

Designer Philip Boydell
Nationality UK
Date Designed 1951
Foundries Creative Alliance
Number of weights 1

ABCDEFGHIJKLMNOPQRSTUVWXYZ
ABCDEFGHIJKLMNOPQRSTUVWXYZ1234567890
PLAYING JAZZ VIBE CHORDS QUICKLY EXCITES MY WIFE.

French Flash

Designer Enric Crous-Vidal
Nationality FR
Date Designed 1953
Foundries Française Neufville Digital
Bauer
Number of weights 1

ABCDEFGHIJKLMNOPQRSTUVWXYZ
ABCDEFGHIJKLMNOPQRSTUVWXYZ1234567890
ORIGINALLY CALLED PARIS FLASH, A SHADED VERSION OF THE
SAME DESIGNER'S PARIS.

Bonita

Designer Jim Parkinson
Nationality US
Date Designed 1998
Foundries Monotype
Number of weights 1

ABCDEFGHIJKLMNOPQRSTUVWXYZ
ABCDEFGHIJKLMNOPQRSTUVWXYZ1234567890
JIM JUST QUIT AND PACKED EXTRA BAGS FOR LIZ OWEN.

Confidential

Designer Just van Rossum
Nationality NL
Date Designed 1995
Foundries FontFont
Number of weights 1

ABCDEFGHIJKLMNOPQRSTUVWXYZ
ABCDEFGHIJKLMNOPQRSTUVWXYZ1234567890
JAZZY SAXOPHONES BLEW OVER MICK'S TURGID QUIFF.

Umbra

Designer R Hunter Middleton
Nationality US
Date Designed 1932
Foundries FC
Number of weights 1

ABCDEFGHIJKLMNOPQRSTUVWXYZ
ABCDEFGHIJKLMNOPQRSTUVWXYZ1234567890
PERHAPS PRESIDENT CLINTON'S AMAZING SAX SKILLS WILL BE
JUDGED QUITE FAVOURABLY.

Othello

Designer	Rudolf Koch
Nationality	DE
Date Designed	1923
Foundries	Klingspor Monotype ATF
Number of weights	3

ABCDEFGHIJKLMNOPQRSTUVWXYZ

ABCDEFGHIJKLMNOPQRSTUVWXYZ1234567890

WE HAVE JUST QUOTED ON NINE DOZEN BOXES OF GRAY LAMP WICKS.

Frankfurter

Designer	Nick Belshaw, Alan Meeks
Nationality	UK
Date Designed	1970
Foundries	Letraset Linotype ITC
Number of weights	4

ABCDEFGHIJKLMNOPQRSTUVWXYZ

ABCDEFGHIJKLMNOPQRSTUVWXYZ1234567890

PACK MY BOX WITH FIVE DOZEN LIQUOR JUGS.

Enviro

Designer	F Scott Garland
Nationality	US
Date Designed	1982
Foundries	URW++ Monotype
Number of weights	1

ABCDEFGHIJKLMNOPQRSTUVWXYZ

ABCDEFGHIJKLMNOPQRSTUVWXYZ1234567890

"THERE IS A LOWERCASE VERSION OF THIS, BUT I CAN'T FIND IT."

Banco

Designer	Roger Excoffon
Nationality	FR
Date Designed	1951
Foundries	Olive Adobe Linotype Monotype ITC
Number of weights	1

ABCDEFGHIJKLMNOPQRSTUVWXYZ

ABCDEFGHIJKLMNOPQRSTUVWXYZ1234567890

LIGHT DESIGNED BY PHIL GRIMSHAW.

Machine

Designer	Tom Carnase, Ronnie Onder
Nationality	US
Date Designed	1970
Foundries	ITC Bitstream
Number of weights	1

ABCDEFGHIJKLMNOPQRSTUVWXYZ

ABCDEFGHIJKLMNOPQRSTUVWXYZ1234567890

PUZZLED WOMEN BEQUEATH JERKS VERY EXOTIC GIFTS.

Superstar

Designer Colin Brignall
Nationality UK
Date Designed 1970
Foundries Letraset FTF ITC
Number of weights 1

ABCDEFGHIJKLMNOPQRSTUVWXYZ
ABCDEFGHIJKLMNOPQRSTUVWXYZ1234567890
SIX CRAZY KINGS VOWED TO ABOLISH MY QUITE PITIFUL JOUSTS.

Railroad Gothic

Designer Kingsley
Nationality UK
Date Designed 1906
Foundries Kingsley / ATF Linotype Red Rooster
Recut/Digitised by Steve Jackaman
Number of weights 1

ABCDEFGHIJKLMNOPQRSTUVWXYZ
ABCDEFGHIJKLMNOPQRSTUVWXYZ1234567890
BACK IN JUNE WE DELIVERED OXYGEN EQUIPMENT OF THE SAME SIZE.

Industrial Gothic

Designer Jim Parkinson
Nationality US
Date Designed 1997
Foundries Monotype
Number of weights 1

ABCDEFGHIJKLMNOPQRSTUVWXYZ
ABCDEFGHIJKLMNOPQRSTUVWXYZ1234567890
TWO HARDY BOXING KANGAROOS JET FROM SYDNEY TO ZANZIBAR ON QUICKSILVER PINIONS.

Logoform

Designer Bo Berndal
Nationality SE
Date Designed 1994
Foundries Monotype
Number of weights 2

ABCDEFGHIJKLMNOPQRSTUVWXYZ
ABCDEFGHIJKLMNOPQRSTUVWXYZ1234567890
WILLIAM JEX QUICKLY CAUGHT FIVE DOZEN CONSERVATIVES.

Franosch

Designer Max Franosch
Nationality UK
Date Designed 2002
Foundries Linotype
Number of weights 3

ABCDEFGHIJKLMNOPQRSTUVWXYZ
ABCDEFGHIJKLMNOPQRSTUVWXYZ1234567890
HOW QUICKLY DAFT JUMPING ZEBRAS VEX.

Andesite

Designer	James L Harris
Nationality	US
Date Designed	1991
Foundries	Harris
Number of weights	1

ABCDEFGHIJKLMNOPQRSTUVWXYZ
ABCDEFGHIJKLMNOPQRSTUVWXYZ1234567890
A VOLCANIC ROCK FOUND IN THE ANDES.

Trajan

Designer	Carol Twombly
Nationality	US
Date Designed	1989
Foundries	Adobe Linotype Monotype
Number of weights	1

ABCDEFGHIJKLMNOPQRSTUVWXYZ
ABCDEFGHIJKLMNOPQRSTUVWXYZ1234567890
DIGITISED IN 1989, BUT ORIGINALLY DESIGNED IN AD113.
PROBABLY THE DEFINITIVE ROMAN LETTER FORM.

Charlemagne

Designer	Carol Twombly
Nationality	US
Date Designed	1989
Foundries	Adobe
Number of weights	1

ABCDEFGHIJKLMNOPQRSTUVWXYZ
ABCDEFGHIJKLMNOPQRSTUVWXYZ1234567890
A QUICK MOVEMENT OF THE ENEMY WILL JEOPARDIZE
SIX GUNBOATS.

Serlio

Designer	Linotype
Nationality	DE
Date Designed	1994
Foundries	Linotype Adobe Monotype
Number of weights	1

ABCDEFGHIJKLMNOPQRSTUVWXYZ
ABCDEFGHIJKLMNOPQRSTUVWXYZ1234567890
THE SERLIAN WINDOW IS ALSO KNOWN AS THE VENETIAN WINDOW.

Felix

Designer	Felice Feliciano
Nationality	IT
Date Designed	1463
Foundries	Monotype
Number of weights	1

ABCDEFGHIJKLMNOPQRSTUVWXYZ
ABCDEFGHIJKLMNOPQRSTUVWXYZ1234567890
FIVE OR SIX BIG JET PLANES ZOOMED QUICKLY BY THE TOWER.

Bembo Titling

Designer Francesco Griffo
Nationality IT
Date Designed 1495
Foundries Aldus Manutius Adobe Monotype
Number of weights 24

ABCDEFGHIJKLMNOPQRSTUVWXYZ
ABCDEFGHIJKLMNOPQRSTUVWXYZ1234567890
HOW QUICKLY DAFT JUMPING ZEBRAS VEX.

Plantin Titling

Designer Robert Granjon
Nationality BE
Date Designed 1700
Foundries Plantin Monotype
Recut/Digitised by F H Pierpont, 1913
Number of weights 20

ABCDEFGHIJKLMNOPQRSTUVWXYZ
ABCDEFGHIJKLMNOPQRSTUVWXYZ1234567890
WE PROMPTLY JUDGED ANTIQUE IVORY BUCKLES FOR
THE NEXT PRIZE.

Caslon Titling

Designer William Caslon
Nationality UK
Date Designed 1725
Foundries Monotype
Number of weights 1

ABCDEFGHIJKLMNOPQRSTUVWXYZ
ABCDEFGHIJKLMNOPQRSTUVWXYZ1234567890
VERBATIM REPORTS WERE QUICKLY GIVEN BY JIM FOX
TO HIS AMAZED AUDIENCE.

Classic Roman

Designer Monotype
Nationality UK
Date Designed 1900
Foundries Monotype
Number of weights 1

ABCDEFGHIJKLMNOPQRSTUVWXYZ
ABCDEFGHIJKLMNOPQRSTUVWXYZ1234567890
LIKE SNOW UPON THE DESERT'S DUSTY FACE.

Perpetua Titling

Designer Eric Gill
Nationality UK
Date Designed 1928
Foundries Monotype
Number of weights 12

ABCDEFGHIJKLMNOPQRSTUVWXYZ
ABCDEFGHIJKLMNOPQRSTUVWXYZ1234567890
BIG JULY EARTHQUAKES CONFOUND ZANY EXPERIMENTAL VOW.

Aeneas

Designer	John Hudson
Nationality	UK
Date Designed	1996
Foundries	Tiro Typeworks
Number of weights	1

ABCDEFGHIJKLMNOPQRSTUVWXYZ

ABCDEFGHIJKLMNOPQRSTUVWXYZ1234567890

PACK MY BOX WITH FIVE DOZEN LIQUOR JUGS.

Cresci

Designer	Garrett Boge
Nationality	US
Date Designed	1996
Foundries	Monotype
Number of weights	1

ABCDEFGHIJKLMNOPQRSTUVWXYZ

ABCDEFGHIJKLMNOPQRSTUVWXYZ1234567890

TWO HARDY BOXING KANGAROOS JET FROM SYDNEY TO
ZANZIBAR ON QUICKSILVER PINIONS.

Galba

Designer	Claude Mediavilla
Nationality	FR
Date Designed	2003
Foundries	Monotype
Number of weights	1

ABCDEFGHIJKLMNOPQRSTUVWXYZ

ABCDEFGHIJKLMNOPQRSTUVWXYZ1234567890

AN ENDEARINGLY CRUEL ROMAN EMPEROR.

Pietra

Designer	Garrett Boge, Paul Shaw
Nationality	US
Date Designed	1996
Foundries	LetterPerfect
Number of weights	1

ABCDEFGHIJKLMNOPQRSTUVWXYZ

ABCDEFGHIJKLMNOPQRSTUVWXYZ1234567890

SPHINX OF BLACK QUARTZ JUDGE MY VOW.

Pontif

Designer	Garrett Boge
Nationality	US
Date Designed	1996
Foundries	LetterPerfect
Number of weights	1

ABCDEFGHIJKLMNOPQRSTUVWXYZ

ABCDEFGHIJKLMNOPQRSTUVWXYZ1234567890

WEST QUICKLY GAVE BERT HANDSOME PRIZES FOR SIX JUICY PLUMS.

Handle Old Style

Designer	Monotype
Nationality	UK
Date Designed	1994
Foundries	Monotype
Number of weights	1

ABCDEFGHIJKLMNOPQRSTUVWXYZ

ABCDEFGHIJKLMNOPQRSTUVWXYZ1234567890

VERILY THE DARK EX-JEW QUIT ZIONISM, PREFERRING THE CABALA.

Renasci

Designer	Lennart Hansson
Nationality	SE
Date Designed	1997
Foundries	Monotype
Number of weights	1

ABCDEFGHIJKLMNOPQRSTUVWXYZ

ADÆALAPARMDŒHEIJKLAMENNŒMPQRHTUETTTWYTY
1234567890

THE FIVE BOXING WIZARDS JUMP QUICKLY.

Palazzo

Designer	Johannes Birkenbach
Nationality	DE
Date Designed	1997
Foundries	Monotype
Number of weights	2

ABCDEFGHIJKLMNOPQRSTUVWXYZ

ABCDEFGHIJKLMNOPQRSTUVWXYZ1234567890

THE JULY SUN CAUSED A FRAGMENT OF BLACK PINE WAX TO OOZE
ON THE VELVET QUILT.

Invasion

Designer	Hellmut G Bomm
Nationality	DE
Date Designed	2002
Foundries	Linotype
Number of weights	1

ABCDEFGHIJKLMNOPQRSTUVWXYZ

ABCDEFGHIJKLMNOPQVRSTUVWXYZ1234567890

1066 AND THE BATTLE OF HASTINGS, CAPTURED IN THE BAYEUX
TAPESTRY BY TEAMS OF DEDICATED WAR EMBROIDERERS.

Eccentric

Designer	Gustav F Schroeder
Nationality	DE
Date Designed	1881
Foundries	Adobe
Number of weights	1

ABCDEFGHIJKLMNOPQRSTUVWXYZ

ABCDEFGHIJKLMNOPQRSTUVWXYZ1234567890

ALFREDO JUST MUST BRING VERY EXCITING NEWS TO THE PLAZA QUICKLY.

Davida

Designer Louis Minott
Nationality US
Date Designed 1965
Foundries Bitstream Elsner+Flake
Linotype
Number of weights 1

ABCDEFGHIJKLMNOPQRSTUVWXYZ
ABCDEFGHIJKLMNOPQRSTUVWXYZ1234567890
PLEASE DON'T USE THIS FONT ANY MORE. THANK YOU.

Desdemona

Designer anon
Nationality UK
Date Designed 1910
Foundries Font Bureau
Number of weights 1

ABCDEFGHIJKLMNOPQRSTUVWXYZ
ABCDEFGHIJKLMNOPQRSTUVWXYZ1234567890
NO RELATIONSHIP TO OTHELLO.

Epokha

Designer Colin Brignall
Nationality UK
Date Designed 1992
Foundries Monotype ITC Letraset
Number of weights 1

ABCDEFGHIJKLMNOPQRSTUVWXYZ
ABCDEFGHIJKLMNOPQRSTUVWXYZ1234567890
VERBATIM REPORTS WERE QUICKLY GIVEN BY JIM FOX TO
HIS AMAZED AUDIENCE.

Pullman

Designer Johannes Erler, Factor Design
Nationality US
Date Designed 1997
Foundries FontFont
Number of weights 1

abcdefghijklmnopqrstuvwxyz
ABCDEFGHIJKLMNOPQRSTUVWXYZ1234567890
BACK IN MY QUAINT GARDEN JAUNTY ZINNIAS VIE WITH
FLAUNTING PHLOX.

Agfa Waddy 144

Designer Aiko & Hideaki Wada
Nationality JP
Date Designed 1999
Foundries Monotype
Number of weights 1

ABCDEFGHIJKLMNOPQRSTUVWXYZ
ABCDEFGHIJKLMNOPQRSTUVWXYZ1234567890
NEW FARM HAND (PICKING JUST SIX QUINCES) PROVES STRONG
BUT LAZY.

Columna

Designer	Max Caflisch
Nationality	CH
Date Designed	1955
Foundries	Bauer Linotype Elsner+Flake
URW++	
Number of weights	1

ABCDEFGHIJKLMNOPQRSTUVWXYZ

ABCDEFGHIJKLMNOPQRSTUVWXYZ1234567890

PERHAPS PRESIDENT CLINTON'S AMAZING SAX SKILLS WILL BE JUDGED QUITE FAVOURABLY.

Pitchfork

Designer	Aerotype
Nationality	US
Date Designed	1995
Foundries	CA Partners
Number of weights	1

ABCDEFGHIJKLMNOPQRSTUVWXYZ

ABCDEFGHIJKLMNOPQRSTUVWXYZ1234567890

FORSAKING MONASTIC TRADITION, TWELVE JOVIAL FRIARS GAVE UP THEIR VOCATION.

MN Art World

Designer	J Dresscher
Nationality	FR
Date Designed	1994
Foundries	Mecanorma
Number of weights	1

ABCDEFGHIJKLMNOPQRSTUVWXYZ

ABCDEFGHIJKLMNOPQRSTUVWXYZ1234567890

NOW IS THE TIME FOR ALL BROWN DOGS TO JUMP OVER THE LAZY LYNX.

Magnifico Daytime

Designer	Akira Kobayashi
Nationality	JP
Date Designed	1999
Foundries	ITC
Number of weights	1

ABCDEFGHIJKLMNOPQRSTUVWXYZ 1234567890

IF YOU CAN'T STAND THE THOUGHT OF PROFIL.

Durendal

Designer	David F Nalle
Nationality	US
Date Designed	1993
Foundries	DFN
Number of weights	1

ABCDEFGHIJKLMNOPQRSTUVWX

abcdefghijklmnopqrstuvwxyz

Yet another mythical valley.

Algerian

Designer Phillip Kelly
Nationality UK
Date Designed 1998
Foundries Stephenson Blake Letraset
Linotype URW++
Number of weights 1

ABCDEFGHIJKLMNOPQRSTUVWXYZ
ABCDEFGHIJKLMNOPQRSTUVWXYZ1234567890
OVERUSED IN BRITISH SHOP FRONTS.

Saphir

Designer Hermann Zapf
Nationality DE
Date Designed 1953
Foundries Stempel Linotype
Number of weights 1

ABCDEFGHIJKLMNOPQRSTUVWXYZ
ABCDEFGHIJKLMNOPQRSTUVWXYZ
1234567890
WORKS WELL WITH HIS MELIOR.

Tattoo

Designer Tony Klassen
Nationality US
Date Designed 1993
Foundries T-26
Number of weights 1

ABCDEFGHIJKLMNOPQRSTUVWXYZ
ABCDEFGHIJKLMNOPQRSTUVWXYZ1234567890
BETTER IN LARGER SIZES

Ambrose

Designer Rudolf Koch
Nationality DE
Date Designed 1914
Foundries Monotype ITC
Number of weights 1

ABCDEFGHIJKLMNOPQRSTUVWXYZ
ABCDEFGHIJKLMNOPQRSTUVWXYZ1234567890
COMPARE THE H IN MAXIMILIAN.

Gill Floriated Caps MT

Designer Eric Gill
Nationality UK
Date Designed 1930
Foundries Monotype
Number of weights 1

ABCDEFGHIJKLMNOPQRSTUVWXYZ
ABCDEFGHIJKLMNOPQRSTUVWXYZ
ONE SHOULD NEVER BEGIN A PARAGRAPH WITH A NUMBER

Goudy Ornate MT

Designer	Monotype Design Studio
Nationality	US
Date Designed	1930
Foundries	Monotype
Number of weights	1

ABCDEFGHIJKLMNOPQRSTUVWXYZ
ABCDEFGHIJKLMNOPQRSTUVWXYZ1234567890
JAY VISITED BACK HOME AND GAZED UPON A BROWN
FOX AND QUAIL.

Bambus Initials

Designer	FontFont
Nationality	DE
Date Designed	1994
Foundries	FontFont
Number of weights	1

ABCDEFGHIJKLMNOPQRSTUVWXYZ
ABCDEFGHIJKLMNOPQRSTUVWXYZ
OSTENSIBLY BASED ON BODONI

Scala Jewels

Designer	Martin Majoor
Nationality	NL
Date Designed	1990-1998
Foundries	FontFont
Number of weights	63

ABCDEFGHIJKLMNOPQRSTUVWXYZ
ABCDEFGHIJKLMNOPQRSTUVWXYZ1234567890
A HUGE FAMILY OF SERIF AND SANS IN 63 WEIGHTS AND STYLES.

Orlando ITC

Designer	Freda Sack
Nationality	UK
Date Designed	1986
Foundries	ITC Letraset
Number of weights	1

ABCDEFGHIJKLMNOPQRSTUVWXYZ
ABCDEFGHIJKLMNOPQRSTUVWXYZ1234567890
A QUICK MOVEMENT OF THE ENEMY WILL JEOPARDIZE SIX GUNBOATS.

Delphian Open Titling

Designer	R Hunter Middleton
Nationality	US
Date Designed	1928
Foundries	Ludlow Monotype
Number of weights	1

ABCDEFGHIJKLMNOPQRSTUVWXYZ
ABCDEFGHIJKLMNOPQRSTUVWXYZ1234567890
JIMMY AND ZACK, THE POLICE EXPLAINED, WERE LAST SEEN DIVING
INTO A FIELD OF BUTTERED QUAHOGS.

Augustea Open

Designer	Alessandro Butti, Aldo Novarese
Nationality	IT
Date Designed	1951
Foundries	Nebiolo ITC
Number of weights	1

ABCDEFGHIJKLMNOPQRSTUVWXYZ
ABCDEFGHIJKLMNOPQRSTUVWXYZ1234567890
GREAT LION OF GOD.

Castellar

Designer	John Peters
Nationality	UK
Date Designed	1957
Foundries	Monotype Linotype Monotype Adobe
Number of weights	1

ABCDEFGHIJKLMNOPQRSTUVWXYZ
ABCDEFGHIJKLMNOPQRSTUVWXYZ1234567890
VERBATIM REPORTS WERE QUICKLY GIVEN BY JIM FOX TO
HIS AMAZED AUDIENCE.

Clascon

Designer	Rachel Godfrey
Nationality	UK
Date Designed	1997
Foundries	Linotype
Number of weights	1

ABCDEFGHIJKLMNOPQRSTUVWXYZ
ABCDEFGHIJKLMNOPQRSTUVWXYZ
1234567890
THE QUICK BROWN FOX JUMPS OVER.

Venezia

Designer	Robert Kolben
Nationality	DE
Date Designed	1997
Foundries	Linotype
Number of weights	1

ABCDEFGHIJKLMNOPQRSTUVWXYZ
ABCDEFGHIJKLMNOPQRSTUVWXYZ
QUICK WAFTING ZEPHYRS VEX BOLD JIM

Smaragd

Designer	Gudrun Zapf von Hesse
Nationality	DE
Date Designed	1953
Foundries	Stempel Linotype
Number of weights	1

ABCDEFGHIJKLMNOPQRSTUVWXYZ
ABCDEFGHIJKLMNOPQRSTUVWXYZ
1234567890
THE GERMAN FOR EMERALD.

Agfa Waddy 143

Designer Aiko & Hideaki Wada
Nationality JP
Date Designed 1999
Foundries Monotype
Number of weights 1

ABCDEFGHIJKLMNOPQRSTUVWXYZ
ABCDEFGHIJKLMNOPQRSTUVWXYZ1234567890
NEW FARM HAND (PICKING JUST SIX QUINCES) PROVES
STRONG BUT LAZY.

Lotus

Designer Monotype
Nationality UK
Date Designed 1994
Foundries Monotype
Number of weights 1

ABCDEFGHIJKLMNOPQRSTUVWXYZ
ABCDEFGHIJKLMNOPQRSTUVWXYZ
WEST QUICKLY GAVE BERT HANDSOME PRIZES FOR SIX
JUICY PLUMS

Madame

Designer Gillé
Nationality FR
Date Designed 1820
Foundries Linotype
Number of weights 1

ABCDEFGHIJKLMNOPQRSTUVWXYZ
1234567890
LETTERS COMPOSED OF MANY PARTS :
A B C D

Kath Condensed

Designer Paul H Neville
Nationality UK
Date Designed 1992
Foundries FontFont
Number of weights 1

ABCDEFGHIJKLMNOPQRSTUVWXYZ
ABCDEFGHIJKLMNOPQRSTUVWXYZ1234567890
FIVE OR SIX BIG JET PLANES ZOOMED QUICKLY BY THE TOWER.

Revolution Normal

Designer Dave Farey
Nationality UK
Date Designed 1994
Foundries Panache Typography
Number of weights 1

ABCDEFGHIJKLMNOPQRSTUVWXYZ
ABCDEFGHIJKLMNOPQRSTUVWXYZ123456789O
FIVE BIG QUACKING ZEPHYRS JOLT MY WAX BED.

Category

Designer	Adam Roe
Nationality	US
Date Designed	1993
Foundries	Monotype
Number of weights	2

ABCDEFGHIJKLMNOPQRSTUVWXYZ

ABCDEFGHIJKLMNOPQRSTUVWXYZ1234567890

WE PROMPTLY JUDGED ANTIQUE IVORY BUCKLES FOR THE NEXT PRIZE.

Dextor

Designer	L Meuffels
Nationality	BE
Date Designed	1994
Foundries	Mecanorma Elsner+Flake Linotype URW++
Number of weights	8

ABCDEFGHIJKLMNOPQRSTUVWXYZ

ABCDEFGHIJKLMNOPQRSTUVWXYZ1234567890

MY HELP SQUEEZED BACK IN AGAIN AND JOINED THE WEAVERS AFTER SIX.

Clyde

Designer	Dan X Solo
Nationality	US
Date Designed	1974
Foundries	Dover
Number of weights	1

ABCDEFGHIJKLMNOPQRSTUVWXYZ

ABCDEFGHIJKLMNOPQRSTUVWXYZ1234567890

BONNIE AND, RATHER THAN THE RIVER.

Yearbook

Designer	Monotype
Nationality	UK
Date Designed	1994
Foundries	Monotype
Number of weights	3

ABCDEFGHIJKLMNOPQRSTUVWXYZ

ABCDEFGHIJKLMNOPQRSTUVWXYZ1234567890

VERBATIM REPORTS WERE QUICKLY GIVEN BY JIM FOX TO HIS AMAZED AUDIENCE.

Princetown

Designer	Letraset
Nationality	UK
Date Designed	1981
Foundries	Letraset
Number of weights	1

ABCDEFGHIJKLMNOPQRSTUVWXYZ

ABCDEFGHIJKLMNOPQRSTUVWXYZ1234567890

WITH A LETTER ON FRONT I GOT FOR FOOTBALL AND TRACK.

Victoria Titling

Designer	Monotype
Nationality	UK
Date Designed	1924
Foundries	Monotype
Number of weights	1

ABCDEFGHIJKLMNOPQRSTUVWXYZ
ABCDEFGHIJKLMNOPQRSTUVWXYZ1234567890
HOW VEXING A FUMBLE TO DROP A JOLLY ZUCCHINI IN THE QUICKSAND.

Skjald

Designer	John F Cumming
Nationality	US
Date Designed	1884
Foundries	Monotype
Number of weights	1

ABCDEFGHIJKLMNOPQRSTUVWXYZ
abcdefghijklmnopqrstuvwxyz1234567890
Jack amazed a few girls by dropping the antique onyx vase!

Raphael

Designer	William F Jackson
Nationality	US
Date Designed	1885
Foundries	Adobe Monotype
Number of weights	1

ABCDEFGHIJKLMNOPQRSTUVWXYZ
abcdefghijklmnopqrstuvwxyz1234567890
Zwei Boxkämpfer jagen Eva quer durch Sylt.

Arnold Böcklin

Designer	Otto Weisert
Nationality	AT
Date Designed	1904
Foundries	Adobe URW++
Number of weights	1

ABCDEFGHIJKLMNOPQRSTUVWXYZ
abcdefghijklmnopqrstuvwxyz1234567890
Many-wived Jack laughs at probes of sex quiz.

Victorian

Designer	Letraset
Nationality	UK
Date Designed	1976
Foundries	Letraset Linotype ITC
Number of weights	1

ABCDEFGHIJKLMNOPQRSTUVWXYZ
abcdefghijklmnopqrstuvwxyz1234567890
PLEASE DON'T USE THIS ALL IN CAPS. Actually, please don't use this.

Bernhard Bold Condensed

Designer	Lucian Bernhard
Nationality	AT
Date Designed	1912
Foundries	Linotype
Number of weights	1

ABCDEFGHIJKLMNOPQRSTUVWXYZ

abcdefghijklmnopqrstuvwxyz1234567890

Crazy Fredericka bought many very exquisite opal jewels.

Bernhard Antique

Designer	Lucian Bernhard
Nationality	AT
Date Designed	1937
Foundries	Elsner+Flake URW++
Number of weights	1

ABCDEFGHIJKLMNOPQRSTUVWXYZ

abcdefghijklmnopqrstuvwxyz1234567890

Five or six big jet planes zoomed quickly by the tower.

Springfield

Designer	Bob McGrath
Nationality	UK
Date Designed	1979
Foundries	Linotype URW++
Number of weights	1

ABCDEFGHIJKLMNOPQRSTUVWXYZ

abcdefghijklmnopqrstuvwxyz1234567890

Six big devils from Japan quickly forgot how to waltz.

Goudy Heavyface

Designer	Frederic W Goudy
Nationality	US
Date Designed	1925
Foundries	Bitstream
Number of weights	1

ABCDEFGHIJKLMNOPQRSTUVWXYZ

abcdefghijklmnopqrstuvwxyz1234567890

Forsaking monastic tradition, twelve jovial friars gave up their vocation for a questionable existence.

Mithras

Designer	Bob Anderton
Nationality	UK
Date Designed	1995
Foundries	Linotype ITC Monotype
Number of weights	1

ABCDEFGHIJKLMNOPQRSTUVWXYZ

abcdefghijklmnopqrstuvwxyz1234567890

The job of waxing linoleum frequently peeves chintzy kids.

Attic Antique

Designer Brian Willson
Nationality US
Date Designed 1999
Foundries Three Islands Press
Number of weights 2

ABCDEFGHIJKLMNOPQRSTUVWXYZ
abcdefghijklmnopqrstuvwxyz1234567890
Jaded zombies acted quaintly but kept driving their
oxen forward.

Crillee

Designer Peter Connell, Dick Jones, Vince
Whitlock
Nationality UK
Date Designed 1980
Foundries Bitstream Elsner+Flake ITC
Number of weights 1

ABCDEFGHIJKLMNOPQRSTUVWXYZ
abcdefghijklmnopqrstuvwxyz1234567890
Perhaps President Clinton's amazing sax skills will be judged
quite favourably.

Technique

Designer Adam Roe
Nationality US
Date Designed 1993
Foundries T-26 Monotype
Number of weights 2

ABCDEFGHIJKLMNOPQRSTUVWXYZ
abcdefghijklmnopqrstuvwxyz1234567890
Back in my quaint garden jaunty zinnias vie with flaunting phlox.

Quirinus

Designer Alessandro Butti
Nationality IT
Date Designed 1939
Foundries Nebiolo Monotype
Number of weights 1

ABCDEFGHIJKLMNOPQRSTUVWXYZ
abcdefghijklmnopqrstuvwxyz1234567890
Compare this with Corvinus, by Imre Reiner, 1929.

Mister Frisky

Designer Chank Diesel
Nationality US
Date Designed 1995
Foundries T-26
Number of weights 1

ABCDEFGHIJKLMNOPQRSTUVWXYZ
abcdefghijklmnopqrstuvwxyz1234567890
Sixty zippers were quickly picked from the woven jute bag.

PL Latin

Designer	Photo-Lettering
Nationality	UK
Date Designed	1994
Foundries	CA Partners
Number of weights	2

ABCDEFGHIJKLMNOPQRSTUVWXYZ
abcdefghijklmnopqrstuvwxyzl234567890
For only $49, jolly housewives made inexpensive meals using quick-frozen vegetables.

Priska Serif

Designer	Alessio Leonardi
Nationality	IT
Date Designed	1993
Foundries	FontFont
Number of weights	1

ABCDEFGHIJKLMNOPQRSTUVWXYZ
abcdefghijklmnopqrstuvwxyz1234567890
Priska is the name of Leonardi's business partner.

Buccaneer

Designer	David F Nalle
Nationality	US
Date Designed	1995
Foundries	Monotype
Number of weights	1

ABCDEFGHIJKLMNOPQRSTUVWXYZ
abcdefghijklmnopqrstuvwxyz1234567890
How razorback-jumping frogs can level six piqued gymnasts!

Aikiko

Designer	Jasper Manchipp
Nationality	UK
Date Designed	1995
Foundries	Monotype
Number of weights	1

ABCDEFGHIJKLMNOPQRSTUVWXYZ
abcdefghijklmnopqrstuvwxyz1234567890
The quick brown fox jumps over the lazy dog.

Alexander

Designer	Adam Roe
Nationality	US
Date Designed	1993
Foundries	Monotype
Number of weights	6

ABCDEFGHIJKLMNOPQRSTUVWXYZ
abcdefghijklmnopqrstuvwxyz1234567890
Brawny gods just flocked up to quiz and vex him.

Bonehead

Designer	Chank Diesel
Nationality	US
Date Designed	1995
Foundries	Monotype
Number of weights	1

ABCDEFGHIJKLMNOPQRSTUVWXYZ
abcdefghijklmnopqrstuvwxyz1234567890
Playing jazz vibe chords quickly excites my wife.

Academy Engraved

Designer	Vince Whitlock
Nationality	UK
Date Designed	1989
Foundries	Monotype ITC
Number of weights	1

ABCDEFGHIJKLMNOPQRSTUVWXYZ
abcdefghijklmnopqrstuvwxyz1234567890
Quick zephyrs blow, vexing daft Jim.

Flamenco

Designer	Tony Geddes
Nationality	UK
Date Designed	1972
Foundries	Letraset Creative Alliance Linotype ITC URW++
Number of weights	1

ABCDEFGHIJKLMNOPQRSTUVWXYZ
abcdefghijklmnopqrstuvwxyz1234567890
The Inline version is far more widely used than the regular font.

Thorowgood

Designer	Stephenson Blake
Nationality	UK
Date Designed	1836
Foundries	Elsner+Flake URW++
Number of weights	1

ABCDEFGHIJKLMNOPQRSTUVWXYZ
abcdefghijklmnopqrstuvwxyz1234567890
Sixty zippers were quickly picked from the woven jute bag.

Falstaff

Designer	Heinz König
Nationality	DE
Date Designed	1906
Foundries	Monotype Adobe
Number of weights	1

ABCDEFGHIJKLMNOPQRSTUVWXYZ
abcdefghijklmnopqrstuvwxyz1234567890
Quick zephyrs blow, vexing daft Jim.

Poster Bodoni

Designer	Giambattista Bodoni
Nationality	IT
Date Designed	1929
Foundries	Mergenthaler Linotype
Number of weights	1

ABCDEFGHIJKLMNOPQRSTUVWXYZ
abcdefghijklmnopqrstuvwxyz1234567890
A distraction's only a distraction if you pay attention to it.

Ozwald

Designer	Dave Farey
Nationality	UK
Date Designed	1928
Foundries	ITC Adobe Creative Alliance
Number of weights	1

ABCDEFGHIJKLMN
OPQRSTUVWXYZ
abcdefghijklmnopqrstuvwxyz
1234567890

Spumoni

Designer	Garrett Boge
Nationality	US
Date Designed	1989
Foundries	LPT Monotype Adobe
Number of weights	1

ABCDEFGHIJKLMNOPQRSTUVWXYZ
abcdefghijklmnopqrstuvwxyz1234567890
The vixen jumped quickly on her foe barking with zeal.

Angle

Designer	Leslie Cabarga
Nationality	US
Date Designed	2000
Foundries	Flashfonts
Number of weights	1

ABCDEFGHIJKLMNOPQRSTUVWXYZ
abcdefghijklmnopqrstuvwxyz1234567890
Many big jackdaws quickly zipped over the fox pen.

Zapata

Designer	Erik van Blokland
Nationality	DE
Date Designed	1997
Foundries	FontFont
Number of weights	1

ABCDEFGHIJKLMN
OPQRSTUVWXYZ
abcdefghijklmn
opqrstuvwxyz1234567890

Motter Corpus

Designer	Othmar Motter
Nationality	DE
Date Designed	1994
Foundries	ITC Monotype Adobe
Number of weights	1

ABCDEFGHIJKLMNOPQRSTUVWXYZ
abcdefghijklmnopqrstuvwxyz1234567890
Zwei Boxkämpfer jagen Eva quer durch Sylt.

Chwast Buffalo

Designer	Seymour Chwast
Nationality	US
Date Designed	1981
Foundries	Linotype
Number of weights	1

ABCDEFGHIJKLMNOPQRSTUVWXYZ
abcdefghijklmnopqrstuvwxyz1234567890
Sympathizing would fix Quaker objectives.

Hadriano

Designer	Frederic W Goudy
Nationality	US
Date Designed	1918
Foundries	Goudy
Number of weights	1

ABCDEFGHIJKLMNOPQRSTUVWXYZ
abcdefghijklmnopqrstuvwxyz1234567890
Fred specialized in the job of making very quaint wax toys.

Romic

Designer	Letraset
Nationality	UK
Date Designed	1979
Foundries	Letraset
Number of weights	1

ABCDEFGHIJKLMNOPQRSTUVWXYZ
abcdefghijklmnopqrstuvwxyz1234567890
A mad boxer shot a quick, gloved jab to the jaw of his dizzy opponent.

Holland Title

Designer	Hollis Holland
Nationality	UK
Date Designed	1974
Foundries	Monotype
Number of weights	1

ABCDEFGHIJKLMNOPQRSTUVWXYZ
abcdefghijklmnopqrstuvwxyz1234567890
Sexy qua lijf, doch bang voor het zwempak.

Vortex

Designer	Max Kisman
Nationality	US
Date Designed	1990
Foundries	FontFont
Number of weights	1

ABCDEFGHIJKLMNOPQRSTUVWXYZ

abcdefghijklmnopqrstuvwxyz1234567890

Dumpy kibitzer jingles as exchequer overflows.

Werkstatt

Designer	Colin Brignall, Satwinder Sehmi
Nationality	UK
Date Designed	1999
Foundries	ITC Monotype
Number of weights	2

ABCDEFGHIJKLMNOPQRSTUVWXYZ

abcdefghijklmnopqrstuvwxyz1234567890

No kidding, Lorenzo called off his trip to visit Mexico City just because they told him the conquistadores were extinct.

Windsor

Designer	Stephenson Blake
Nationality	UK
Date Designed	1905
Foundries	Stephenson Blake
Recut/Digitised by	Edwin W Shaar
Number of weights	1

ABCDEFGHIJKLMNOPQRSTUVWXYZ

abcdefghijklmnopqrstuvwxyz1234567890

Queen Victoria had died two years earlier. Windsor Castle was her main residence. Probably named in patriotic fervour.

Disturbance

Designer	Jeremy Tankard
Nationality	UK
Date Designed	1993
Foundries	FontFont
Number of weights	1

abcdefghijklmnopqrstuvwxyz

abcdefghijklmnopqrstuvwxyz1234567890

west quickly gave bert handsome prizes for six juicy plums.

Jeepers ITC

Designer	Nick Curtis
Nationality	US
Date Designed	2001
Foundries	ITC
Number of weights	1

ABCDEFGHIJKLMNOPQRSTUVWXYZ

abcdefghijklmnopqrstuvwxyz1234567890

Pack my box with five dozen liquor jugs.

Photoplay ITC

Designer	Nick Curtis
Nationality	US
Date Designed	2002
Foundries	ITC
Number of weights	1

ABCDEFGHIJKLMNOPQRSTUVWXYZ

abcdefghijklmnopqrstuvwxyz1234567890

Big July earthquakes confound zany experimental vow.

Scram Gravy ITC

Designer	Nick Curtis
Nationality	US
Date Designed	2001
Foundries	ITC Monotype
Number of weights	1

ABCDEFGHIJKLMNOPQRSTUVWXYZ

abcdefghijklmnopqrstuvwxyz

1234567890

Six crazy kings vowed to abolish war.

Modern Roman

Designer	Alf R Becker
Nationality	US
Date Designed	1933
Foundries	The Fontry
Recut/Digitised by	Michael Gene Adkins, 1997
Number of weights	1

ABCDEFGHIJKLMNOPQRSTUVWXYZ

abcdefghijklmnopqrstuvwxyz1234567890

Two hardy boxing kangaroos jet from Sydney to Zanzibar on quicksilver pinions.

Agfa Waddy 95

Designer	Aiko & Hideaki Wada
Nationality	JP
Date Designed	1999
Foundries	Monotype
Number of weights	1

ABCDEFGHIJKLMNOPQRSTUVWXYZ

abcdefghijklmnopqrstuvwxyz1234567890

New farm hand (picking just six quinces) proves strong but lazy.

Chesterfield

Designer	Alan Meeks
Nationality	UK
Date Designed	1977
Foundries	Letraset Linotype
Number of weights	1

ABCDEFGHIJKLMNOPQRSTUVWXYZ

abcdefghijklmnopqrstuvwxyz1234567890

About sixty codfish eggs will make a quarter pound of very fizzy jelly.

Modernistic

Designer	W A Parker
Nationality	US
Date Designed	1927
Foundries	ATF Monotype
Number of weights	1

ABCDEFGHIJKLMNOPQRSTUVWXYZ
ABCDEFGHIJKLMNOPQRSTUVWXYZ1234567890
BREEZILY JANGLING $3,416,857,209, WISE ADVERTISER
AMBLES TO THE BANK, HIS EXCHEQUER AMPLIFIED.

Vermont

Designer	Freda Sack
Nationality	UK
Date Designed	1987
Foundries	Monotype ITC
Number of weights	1

ABCDEFGHIJKLMNOPQRSTUVWXYZ
abcdefghijklmnopqrstuvwxyz1234567890
Back in June we delivered oxygen equipment of the same size.

Eastwood

Designer	Martin Archer
Nationality	UK
Date Designed	1997
Foundries	Linotype ITC
Number of weights	1

ABCDEFGHIJKLMNOPQRSTUVWXYZ
abcdefghijklmnopqrstuvwxyz1234567890
New farm hand (picking just six quinces) proves strong but lazy.

Eckmann

Designer	Otto Eckmann
Nationality	DE
Date Designed	1900
Foundries	Klingspor Linotype URW++
Number of weights	1

ABCDEFGHIJKLMNOPQRSTUVWXYZ
abcdefghijklmnopqrstuvwxyz1234567890
Lighting a little hour or two — is gone.

Kompakt

Designer	Hermann Zapf
Nationality	DE
Date Designed	1954
Foundries	Stempel Adobe
Number of weights	1

ABCDEFGHIJKLMNOPQRSTUVWXYZ
abcdefghijklmnopqrstuvwxyz1234567890
Many big jackdaws quickly zipped over the fox pen.

Rialto

Designer	Letraset
Nationality	UK
Date Designed	1980
Foundries	Letraset
Number of weights	1

ABCDEFGHIJKLMNOPQRSTUVWXYZ

abcdefghijklmnopqrstuvwxyz1234567890

Will Major Douglas be expected to take this true-false quiz very soon?

Bordeaux

Designer	David Quay
Nationality	UK
Date Designed	1987
Foundries	Linotype
Number of weights	1

ABCDEFGHIJKLMNOPQRSTUVWXYZ

abcdefghijklmnopqrstuvwxyz1234567890

Five wine experts jokingly quizzed sample chablis.

Cantina

Designer	Ray Cruz
Nationality	US
Date Designed	1994
Foundries	Monotype
Number of weights	1

ABCDEFGHIJKLMNOPQRSTUVWXYZ

abcdefghijklmnopqrstuvwxyz1234567890

Verily the dark ex-Jew quit Zionism, preferring the cabala.

Central Station

Designer	Leslie Cabarga
Nationality	US
Date Designed	1999
Foundries	Flashfonts
Number of weights	1

ABCDEFGHIJKLMNOPQ RSTUVWXYZ

abcdefghijklmnopqrstuvwxyz1234567890

Back in June we delivered oxygen equipment of the same size.

Fashion Compressed

Designer	Alan Meeks
Nationality	UK
Date Designed	1986
Foundries	Monotype
Number of weights	1

ABCDEFGHIJKLMNOPQRSTUVWXYZ

abcdefghijklmnopqrstuvwxyz1234567890

Quick wafting zephyrs vex bold Jim.

Fashion Engraved

Designer	Alan Meeks
Nationality	UK
Date Designed	1991
Foundries	Letraset
Number of weights	1

ABCDEFGHIJKLMNOPQRSTUVWXYZ

abcdefghijklmnopqrstuvwxyz1234567890

Brawny gods just flocked up to quiz and vex him.

Robotik

Designer	David Quay
Nationality	UK
Date Designed	1989
Foundries	ITC
Number of weights	1

ABCDEFGHIJKLMNOPQRSTUVWXYZ

abcdefghijklmnopqrstuvwxyz1234567890

How quickly daft jumping zebras vex.

Teknik

Designer	David Quay
Nationality	UK
Date Designed	1989
Foundries	Letraset Linotype ITC
Number of weights	1

ABCDEFGHIJKLMNOPQRSTUVWXYZ

abcdefghijklmnopqrstuvwxyz1234567890

How razorback-jumping frogs can level six piqued gymnasts!

Heliotype

Designer	Lee Martin McAuley
Nationality	UK
Date Designed	1991
Foundries	Letraset ITC
Number of weights	1

ABCDEFGHIJKLMNOPQRSTUVWXYZ

abcdefghijklmnopqrstuvwxyz1234567890

New farm hand (picking just six quinces) proves strong but lazy.

Impakt

Designer	Leonard Currie
Nationality	UK
Date Designed	1995
Foundries	Letraset Linotype Monotype ITC
Number of weights	1

ABCDEFGHIJKLMNOPQRSTUVWXYZ

abcdefghijklmnopqrstuvwxyz1234567890

King Alexander was partly overcome just after quizzing Diogenes in his tub.

Hornpype

Designer Mott Jordan
Nationality US
Date Designed 1997
Foundries Linotype ITC Monotype
Number of weights 1

ABCDEFGHIJKLMNOPQRSTUVWXYZ
abcdefghijklmnopqrstuvwxyz1234567890
Six big juicy steaks sizzled in a pan as five workmen left the quarry.

Malaise

Designer Adam Roe
Nationality US
Date Designed 1995
Foundries Monotype
Number of weights 2

ABCDEFGHIJKLMNOPQRSTUVWXYZ
abcdefghijklmnopqrstuvwxyz1234567890
Big July earthquakes confound zany experimental vow.

Morticia

Designer Christian Schwartz
Nationality US
Date Designed 1995
Foundries Monotype
Number of weights 1

ABCDEFGHIJKLMNOPQRSTUVWXYZ
abcdefghijklmnopqrstuvwxyz1234567890
A quick movement of the enemy will jeopardize six gunboats.

Peplum

Designer Jean-Renaud Cuaz
Nationality FR
Date Designed 1997
Foundries Monotype
Number of weights 1

ABCDEFGHIJKLMNOPQRSTUVWXYZ
abcdefghijklmnopqrstuvwxyz1234567890
Breezily jangling $3,416,857,209, wise advertiser ambles to the bank, his exchequer amplified.

Quantum

Designer Trevor Scobie
Nationality UK
Date Designed 1996
Foundries Monotype
Number of weights 1

ABCDEFGHIJKLMNOPQRSTUVWXYZ
abcdefghijklmnopqrstuvwxyz1234567890
Quick zephyrs blow, vexing daft Jim.

Runic

Designer	Monotype
Nationality	UK
Date Designed	1991
Foundries	Monotype Adobe
Number of weights	1

ABCDEFGHIJKLMNOPQRSTUVWXYZ

abcdefghijklmnopqrstuvwxyz1234567890

Jazzy saxophones blew over Mick's turgid quiff.

Strayhorn

Designer	Michael Harvey
Nationality	UK
Date Designed	1998
Foundries	Monotype Adobe
Number of weights	1

ABCDEFGHIJKLMNOPQRSTUVWXYZ

abcdefghijklmnopqrstuvwxyz1234567890

A lineale version of Ellington, named after another jazz great, Billy Strayhorn.

Arsis

Designer	Gerry Powell
Nationality	UK
Date Designed	1939
Foundries	Tetterode Lettergieterij Amsterdam Linotype Adobe URW++
Number of weights	1

ABCDEFGHIJKLMNOPQRSTUVWXYZ

abcdefghijklmnopqrstuvwxyz1234567890

Dumpy kibitzer jingles as exchequer overflows.

Edwardian

Designer	Colin Brignall
Nationality	UK
Date Designed	1983
Foundries	Letraset ITC Linotype Monotype
Number of weights	1

ABCDEFGHIJKLMNOPQRSTUVWXYZ

abcdefghijklmnopqrstuvwxyz1234567890

Hark! Toxic jungle water vipers quietly drop on zebras for meals!

PL Tower Condensed

Designer	Morris Fuller Benton
Nationality	US
Date Designed	1934
Foundries	Photo-Lettering
Number of weights	1

ABCDEFGHIJKLMNOPQRSTUVWXYZ

abcdefghijklmnopqrstuvwxyz1234567890

Breezily jangling €3,416,857,209, wise advertiser ambles to the bank, his exchequer amplified.

TC Jasper

Designer	Les Usherwood
Nationality	CA
Date Designed	1997
Foundries	TC Typesettra
Number of weights	1

ABCDEFGHIJKLMNOPQRSTUVWXYZ

abcdefghijklmnopqrstuvwxyz1234567890

Quick wafting zephyrs vex bold Jim.

TF Simper Serif

Designer	Joseph D Treacy
Nationality	US
Date Designed	1991
Foundries	Treacyfaces
Number of weights	1

ABCDEFGHIJKLMNOPQRSTUVWXYZ

abcdefghijklmnopqrstuvwxyz1234567890

A large fawn jumped quickly over white zinc boxes.

Dharma

Designer	Gerd Sebastian Jakob, Ewald Meissner
Nationality	DE
Date Designed	1997
Foundries	Linotype
Number of weights	1

ABCDEFGHIJKLMNOPQRSTUVWXYZ

abcdefghijklmnopqrstuvwxyz1234567890

Sixty zippers were quickly picked from the woven jute bag.

Forbes

Designer	Linotype
Nationality	DE
Date Designed	1994
Foundries	Linotype
Number of weights	1

ABCDEFGHIJKLMNOPQRSTUVWXYZ

abcdefghijklmnopqrstuvwxyz1234567890

Two hardy boxing kangaroos jet from Sydney to Zanzibar on quicksilver pinions.

Kingsbury Condensed SG

Designer	Jim Spiece
Nationality	US
Date Designed	1992
Foundries	Spiece Graphics
Number of weights	1

ABCDEFGHIJKLMNOPQRSTUVWXYZ

abcdefghijklmnopqrstuvwxyz1234567890

Quixotic Conservatives vet first key zero-growth jeremiad.

Prague

Designer Michael Gills
Nationality UK
Date Designed 1991
Foundries ITC
Number of weights 1

ABCDEFGHIJKLMNOPQRSTUVWXYZ
ABCDEFGHIJKLMNOPQRSTUVWXYZ1234567890
FREIGHT TO ME SIXTY DOZEN QUART JARS AND TWELVE
BLACK PANS.

Retro Bold

Designer Colin Brignall, Andrew Smith
Nationality UK
Date Designed 1992
Foundries ITC
Number of weights 2

ABCDEFGHIJKLMNOPQRSTUVWXYZ
ABCDEFGHIJKLMNOPQRSTUVWXYZ1234567890
MY HELP SQUEEZED BACK IN AGAIN AND JOINED THE WEAVERS
AFTER SIX.

Roemisch

Designer Linotype-Hell
Nationality DE
Date Designed 1993
Foundries Linotype
Number of weights 1

ABCDEFGHIJKLMNOPQRSTUVWXYZ
abcdefghijklmnopqrstuvwxyz1234567890
Alfredo just must bring very exciting news to the plaza quickly.

Romantica Condensed

Designer Ray Cruz
Nationality US
Date Designed 1998
Foundries Monotype
Number of weights 1

ABCDEFGHIJKLMNOPQRSTUVWXYZ
abcdefghijklmnopqrstuvwxyz1234567890
Back in my quaint garden jaunty zinnias vie with flaunting phlox.

Rundfunk Antiqua

Designer Esselte Letraset
Nationality DE
Date Designed 1987
Foundries Letraset
Number of weights 1

ABCDEFGHIJKLMNOPQRSTUVWXYZ
abcdefghijklmnopqrstuvwxyz1234567890
Just work for improved basic techniques to maximize your
typing skill.

Tekno

Designer	Calvin Glenn
Nationality	US
Date Designed	1993
Foundries	Monotype
Number of weights	1

ABCDEFGHIJKLMNOPQRSTUVWXYZ

abcdefghijklmnopqrstuvwxyz1234567890

Ebenezer unexpectedly bagged two tranquil aardvarks with his jiffy vacuum cleaner.

Theatre Antoine Toulouse Lautrec

Designer	Luiz Da Lomba
Nationality	ES
Date Designed	1995
Foundries	CA Partners
Number of weights	1

ABCDEFGHIJKLMNOPQRSTUVWXYZ

abcdefghijklmnopqrstuvwxyz1234567890

An inspired calligrapher can create pages of beauty using stick ink, quill, brush, pick-axe, buzz saw, or even strawberry jam.

Woodstock

Designer	Linotype
Nationality	DE
Date Designed	1993
Foundries	Linotype
Number of weights	1

ABCDEFGHIJKLMNOPQRSTUVWXYZ

abcdefghijklmnopqrstuvwxyz1234567890

Many big jackdaws quickly zipped over the fox pen.

Devinne

Designer	Nicholas J Werner
Nationality	US
Date Designed	1893
Foundries	URW++
Number of weights	2

ABCDEFGHIJKLMNOPQRSTUVWXYZ

abcdefghijklmnopqrstuvwxyz1234567890

My help squeezed back in again and joined the weavers after six.

Bertie

Designer	Alan Meeks
Nationality	UK
Date Designed	1985
Foundries	Linotype Letraset ITC
Number of weights	1

ABCDEFGHIJKLMNOPQRSTUVWXYZ

abcdefghijklmnopqrstuvwxyz1234567890

Many-wived Jack laughs at probes of sex quiz.

Aitos

Designer	Kevin Simpson
Nationality	UK
Date Designed	2000
Foundries	Cybertype
Number of weights	1

ABCDEFGHIJKLMNOPQRSTUVWXYZ
abcdefghijklmnopqrstuvwxyz1234567890
Hark! Toxic jungle water vipers quietly drop on zebras
for meals!

Bonsai

Designer	Brian Willson
Nationality	US
Date Designed	1999
Foundries	Three Islands Press
Number of weights	2

ABCDEFGHIJKLMNOPQRSTUVWXYZ
abcdefghijklmnopqrstuvwxyz1234567890
Just work for improved basic techniques to maximize your
typing skill.

Castine

Designer	Brian Willson
Nationality	US
Date Designed	1999
Foundries	Three Islands Press
Number of weights	2

ABCDEFGHIJKLMNOPQRSTUVWXYZ
abcdefghijklmnopqrstuvwxyz1234567890
A mad boxer shot a quick, gloved jab to the jaw of
his dizzy opponent.

Batak ITC

Designer	Charles Nix
Nationality	US
Date Designed	2002
Foundries	Monotype
Number of weights	1

ABCDEFGHIJKLMNOPQRSTUVWXYZ
abcdefghijklmnopqrstuvwxyz1234567890
Zwei Boxkämpfer jagen Eva quer durch Sylt.

Mudville ITC

Designer	Christopher Wolff
Nationality	UK
Date Designed	1999
Foundries	ITC
Number of weights	1

ABCDEFGHIJKLMNOPQRSTUVWXYZ
abcdefghijklmnopqrstuvwxyz1234567890
Viewing quizzical abstracts mixed up hefty jocks.

Onyx

Designer Gerry Powell
Nationality UK
Date Designed 1937
Foundries Monotype ATF Bitstream Adobe
Number of weights 1

ABCDEFGHIJKLMNOPQRSTUVWXYZ

abcdefghijklmnopqrstuvwxyz1234567890

And those who husbanded the Golden Grain,

Latin Condensed

Designer Monotype
Nationality UK
Date Designed 1890
Foundries Monotype
Number of weights 1

ABCDEFGHIJKLMNOPQRSTUVWXYZ

abcdefghijklmnopqrstuvwxyz1234567890

Five or six big jet planes zoomed quickly by the tower.

Latino Elongated

Designer David Quay
Nationality UK
Date Designed 1988
Foundries Letraset Linotype Monotype ITC
Number of weights 1

ABCDEFGHIJKLMNOPQRSTUVWXYZ

abcdefghijklmnopqrstuvwxyz1234567890

Crazy Fredericka bought many very exquisite opal jewels.

Agfa Waddy 96

Designer Aiko & Hideaki Wada
Nationality JP
Date Designed 1999
Foundries Monotype
Number of weights 1

ABCDEFGHIJKLMNOPQRSTUVWXYZ

abcdefghijklmnopqrstuvwxyz1234567890

New farm hand (picking just six quinces) proves strong but lazy.

Spotlight

Designer Tony Geddes
Nationality UK
Date Designed 1989
Foundries Letraset Monotype ITC
Number of weights 1

ABCDEFGHIJKLMNOPQRSTUVWXYZ

abcdefghijklmnopqrstuvwxyz1234567890

Big July earthquakes confound zany experimental vow.

Inflex MT

Designer	Monotype
Nationality	UK
Date Designed	1994
Foundries	Monotype Linotype Adobe
Number of weights	1

ABCDEFGHIJKLMNOPQRSTUVWXYZ
abcdefghijklmnopqrstuvwxyz1234567890
And those who flung it to the Winds like rain,

Cooper Black

Designer	Oswald B. Cooper
Nationality	US
Date Designed	1921
Foundries	Barnhardt Bros. & Spindler Bitstream Adobe E+F URW++
Number of weights	1

ABCDEFGHIJKLMNOPQRSTUVWXYZ
abcdefghijklmnopqrstuvwxyz1234567890
Most often seen in *italic*.

Agfa Waddy 97

Designer	Aiko & Hideaki Wada
Nationality	JP
Date Designed	1999
Foundries	Monotype
Number of weights	1

ABCDEFGHIJKLMNOPQRSTUVWXYZ
abcdefghijklmnopqrstuvwxyz1234567890
Quick wafting zephyrs vex bold Jim.

Goudy Handtooled

Designer	Frederic W Goudy
Nationality	US
Date Designed	1932
Foundries	Bitstream Linotype Elsner+Flake URW++
Number of weights	1

ABCDEFGHIJKLMNOPQRSTUVWXYZ
abcdefghijklmnopqrstuvwxyz1234567890
The exodus of jazzy pigeons is craved by squeamish walkers.

Ignatius

Designer	Freda Sack
Nationality	UK
Date Designed	1987
Foundries	Linotype ITC
Number of weights	1

ABCDEFGHIJKLMNOPQRSTUVWXYZ
abcdefghijklmnopqrstuvwxyz1234567890
About sixty codfish eggs will make a quarter pound of very fizzy jelly.

Artisan Roman

Designer	Monotype
Nationality	UK
Date Designed	1994
Foundries	Monotype
Number of weights	1

ABCDEFGHIJKLMNOPQRSTUVWXYZ

abcdefghijklmnopqrstuvwxyz1234567890

Puzzled women bequeath jerks very exotic gifts.

Century Handtooled

Designer	Edward Benguiat
Nationality	US
Date Designed	1993
Foundries	ITC Linotype Monotype
Number of weights	4

ABCDEFGHIJKLMNOPQRSTUVWXYZ
abcdefghijklmnopqrstuvwxyz1234567890
Sphinx of black quartz judge my vow.

Cheltenham Handtooled

Designer	Morris Fuller Benton, Bertram Goodhue
Nationality	US
Date Designed	1900
Foundries	ITC Monotype Linotype
Number of weights	4

ABCDEFGHIJKLMNOPQRSTUVWXYZ
abcdefghijklmnopqrstuvwxyz1234567890
Jackdaws love my big sphinx of quartz.

Cloister

Designer	R Hunter Middletonn
Nationality	US
Date Designed	1920
Foundries	Adobe Bitstream
Number of weights	1

ABCDEFGHIJKLMNOPQRSTUVWXYZ

abcdefghijklmnopqrstuvwxyz1234567890

The covered walkway bordering a quadrangle in a monastery.

Monotype Old Style MT

Designer	Alexander Phemister
Nationality	UK
Date Designed	1860
Foundries	Monotype
Number of weights	1

ABCDEFGHIJKLMNOPQRSTUVWXYZ
abcdefghijklmnopqrstuvwxyz1234567890
Sphinx of black quartz judge my vow.

Colonna

Designer	Monotype
Nationality	UK
Date Designed	1936
Foundries	Monotype
Number of weights	1

ABCDEFGHIJKLMNOPQRSTUVWXYZ

abcdefghijklmnopqrstuvwxyz1234567890

William said that everything about his jacket was in quite good condition except for the zipper.

Woodley Park

Designer	Nick Curtis
Nationality	US
Date Designed	2001
Foundries	Monotype
Number of weights	1

ABCDEFGHIJKLMNOPQRSTUVWXYZ

abcdefghijklmnopqrstuvwxyz1234567890

Moi, je veux quinze clubs a golf et du whisky pur.

Gallia

Designer	Wadsworth A Parker
Nationality	US
Date Designed	1928
Foundries	Monotype Creative Alliance
Number of weights	1

ABCDEFGHIJKLMNOPQRSTUVWXYZ

ABCDEFGHIJKLMNOPQRSTUVWXYZ1234567890

SYMPATHIZING WOULD FIX QUAKER OBJECTIVES.

Forest Shaded

Designer	Martin Wait
Nationality	UK
Date Designed	1978
Foundries	Creative Alliance ITC
Number of weights	1

ABCDEFGHIJKLMNOPQRSTUVWXYZ

abcdefghijklmnopqrstuvwxyz1234567890

Big July earthquakes confound zany experimental vow.

Burlington

Designer	Alan Meeks
Nationality	UK
Date Designed	1985
Foundries	Linotype ITC Letraset
Number of weights	1

ABCDEFGHIJKLMNOPQRSTUVWXYZ

abcdefghijklmnopqrstuvwxyz1234567890

We have just quoted on nine dozen boxes of gray lamp wicks.

Teethreedee

Designer Tomi Haaparaanta
Nationality FI
Date Designed 2001
Foundries Monotype
Number of weights 1

ABCDEFGHIJKLMNOPQRSTUVWXYZ
abcdefghijklmnopqrstuvwxyz1234567890
Jelly-like above the high wire, six quaking pachyderms kept the climax of the extravaganza in a dazzling state of flux.

Old Style Bold Outline

Designer Alexander Phemister
Nationality UK
Date Designed 1860
Foundries Miller & Richard Adobe Monotype Linotype
Number of weights 1

ABCDEFGHIJKLMNOPQRSTUVWXYZ
abcdefghijklmnopqrstuvwxyz1234567890
Six crazy kings vowed to abolish my quite pitiful jousts.

Blue Island

Designer Jeremy Tankard
Nationality UK
Date Designed 1999
Foundries Adobe
Number of weights 1

ABCDEFGHIJKLMNOPQRSTUVWXYZ
abcdefghijklmnopqrstuvwxyz1234567890
Perhaps President Clinton's amazing sax skills will be judged quite favourably.

Pueblo

Designer Jim Parkinson
Nationality US
Date Designed 1998
Foundries Monotype
Number of weights 1

ABCDEFGHIJKLMNOPQRSTUVWXYZ
abcdefghijklmnopqrstuvwxyz1234567890
Sphinx of black quartz judge my vow.

PL Behemoth

Designer Dave West
Nationality UK
Date Designed 1960
Foundries Photo-Lettering Monotype
Number of weights 1

ABCDEFGHIJKLMNOPQRSTUVWXYZ
abcdefghijklmnopqrstuvwxyz1234567890
King Alexander was partly overcome just after quizzing Diogenes in his tub.

Pharaon Ultra Bold

Designer	Albert Boton
Nationality	FR
Date Designed	1998
Foundries	CA Exclusives
Number of weights	1

ABCDEFGHIJKLMNOPQRSTUVWXYZ
abcdefghijklmnopqrstuvwxyz1234567890
The vixen jumped quickly on her foe barking with zeal.

PL Barnum Block

Designer	Dave West
Nationality	UK
Date Designed	1960
Foundries	Monotype
Number of weights	1

ABCDEFGHIJKLMNOPQRSTUVWXYZ
abcdefghijklmnopqrstuvwxyz1234567890
The sex life of the woodchuck is a provocative question for most vertebrate zoology majors.

Scratch FF

Designer	Max Kisman
Nationality	US
Date Designed	1991
Foundries	FontFont
Number of weights	1

ABCDEFGHIJKLMNOPQRSTUVWXYZ
abcdefghijklmnopqrstuvwxyz1234567890
Moi, je veux quinze clubs a golf et du whisky pur.

Czykago Semiserif

Designer	Alexander Branczyk
Nationality	DE
Date Designed	1996
Foundries	Linotype
Number of weights	1

ABCDEFGHIJKLMNOPQRSTUVWXYZ
abcdefghijklmnopqrstuvwxyz1234567890
Like Chicago with serifs.

Stratford Bold

Designer	Vincent Pacella
Nationality	US
Date Designed	1982
Foundries	Monotype
Number of weights	1

ABCDEFGHIJKLMNOPQRSTUVWXYZ
abcdefghijklmnopqrstuvwxyz1234567890
There are two different fonts named Stratford Bold.

Aachen

Designer	Letraset
Nationality	UK
Date Designed	1977
Foundries	Letraset
Number of weights	2

ABCDEFGHIJKLMNOPQRSTUVWXYZ

abcdefghijklmnopqrstuvwxyzl234567890

A German town on the Dutch / Belgian border, a stronghold of Charlemagne and known in French and English as Aix-la-Chapelle.

Egiziano

Designer	Aldo Novarese
Nationality	IT
Date Designed	1955
Foundries	Nebiolo Monotype URW++
Recut/Digitised by	Dennis Ortiz-Lopez
Number of weights	4

ABCDEFGHIJKLMNOPQRSTUVWXYZ

abcdefghijklmnopqrstuvwxyz1234567890

An inspired calligrapher can create pages of beauty using stick ink, quill, brush, pick-axe or buzz saw.

Egyptienne

Designer	Adrian Frutiger
Nationality	CH
Date Designed	1956
Foundries	Lettergieterij Amsterdan URW++
Number of weights	1

ABCDEFGHIJKLMNOPQRSTUVWXYZ

abcdefghijklmnopqrstuvwxyz1234567890

While waxing parquet decks, jaunty Suez sailors vomit abaft.

Linotype Method

Designer	Thomas Schnäbele
Nationality	DE
Date Designed	1996
Foundries	Linotype
Number of weights	1

ABCDEFGHIJKLMNOPQRSTUVWXYZ

abcdefghijklmnopqrstuvwxyz1234567890

Murky haze enveloped a city as jarring quakes broke forty-six windows.

Eumundi Serif

Designer	Russell Bean
Nationality	AU
Date Designed	1994
Foundries	Type Associates
Number of weights	1

ABCDEFGHIJKLMNOPQRSTUVWXYZ

abcdefghijklmnopqrstuvwxyz1234567890

Back in my quaint garden jaunty zinnias vie with flaunting phlox.

Bailey Quad

Designer	Kevin Bailey
Nationality	UK
Date Designed	1996
Foundries	Monotype ITC
Number of weights	5

ABCDEFGHIJKLMNOPQRSTUVWXYZ

abcdefghijklmnopqrstuvwxyz1234567890

Quick wafting zephyrs vex bold Jim.

Waterloo

Designer	Alan Meeks
Nationality	UK
Date Designed	1992
Foundries	Letraset Monotype ITC
Number of weights	1

ABCDEFGHIJKLMNOPQRSTUVWXYZ

abcdefghijklmnopqrstuvwxyz1234567890

Jelly-like above the high wire, six quaking pachyderms kept the climax of the extravaganza in a dazzling state of flux.

Quadrus

Designer	Peter Fahrni
Nationality	CH
Date Designed	1990
Foundries	Letraset Monotype ITC
Number of weights	1

ABCDEFGHIJKLMNOPQRSTUVWXYZ

ABCDEFGHIJKLMNOPQRSTUVWXYZ1234567890

JELLY-LIKE ABOVE THE HIGH WIRE, SIX QUAKING PACHYDERMS KEPT THE CLIMAX OF THE EXTRAVAGANZA IN A DAZZLING STATE OF FLUX.

Linotype Really

Designer	Gary Munch
Nationality	US
Date Designed	1999
Foundries	Linotype
Number of weights	1

ABCDEFGHIJKLMNOPQRSTUVWXYZ

abcdefghijklmnopqrstuvwxyz1234567890

Sixty zippers were quickly picked from the woven jute bag.

Peregrine

Designer	Rodrigo Xavier Cavazos
Nationality	US
Date Designed	1996
Foundries	CA Partners Monotype
Number of weights	1

ABCDEFGHIJKLMNOPQRSTUVWXYZ

abcdefghijklmnopqrstuvwxyz1234567890

While waxing parquet decks, jaunty Suez sailors vomit abaft.

Futura Black

Designer	Paul Renner
Nationality	DE
Date Designed	1929
Foundries	Creative Alliance Bitstream
Number of weights	1

ABCDEFGHIJKLMNOPQRSTUVWXYZ

abcdefghijklmnopqrstuvwxyz1234567890

Jaded reader with fabled roving eye seized by quickened impulse to expand budget.

Braggadocio

Designer	W A Woolley
Nationality	UK
Date Designed	1930
Foundries	Monotype
Number of weights	1

ABCDEFGHIJKLMNOPQRSTUVWXYZ

abcdefghijklmnopqrstuvwxyz1234567890

A braggart and a boaster.

Stencil

Designer	R Hunter Middleton
Nationality	US
Date Designed	1938
Foundries	Ludlow Adobe Bitstream Linotype Monotype URW++
Number of weights	1

ABCDEFGHIJKLMNOPQRSTUVWXYZ

abcdefghijklmnopqrstuvwxyz1234567890

The definitive Stencil font.

Tea Chest

Designer	Robert Harling
Nationality	UK
Date Designed	1939
Foundries	Stephenson Blake Linotype Elsner+Flake
Number of weights	1

ABCDEFGHIJKLMNOPQRSTUVWXYZ

ABCDEFGHIJKLMNOPQRSTUVWXYZ1234567890

FOR ONLY $49, JOLLY HOUSEWIVES MADE INEXPENSIVE MEALS USING QUICK-FROZEN VEGETABLES.

Clarendon Stencil

Designer	R Besley
Nationality	UK
Date Designed	1970
Foundries	URW++
Number of weights	4

ABCDEFGHIJKLMNOPQRSTUVWXYZ

abcdefghijklmnopqrstuvwxyz1234567890

Pack my box with five dozen liquor jugs.

Caslon Stencil

Designer	William Caslon
Nationality	UK
Date Designed	1970
Foundries	Letraset URW++
Number of weights	1

ABCDEFGHIJKLMNOPQRSTUVWXYZ

abcdefghijklmnopqrstuvwxyz1234567890

Breezily jangling $3,416,857,209,wise advertiser ambles to the bank, his exchequer amplified.

Cooper Stencil

Designer	Oz Cooper
Nationality	US
Date Designed	1928
Foundries	URW++
Number of weights	1

ABCDEFGHIJKLMNOPQRSTUVWXYZ

abcdefghijklmnopqrstuvwxyz1234567890

My help squeezed back in again and joined the weavers after six.

Rubber Stamp

Designer	Alan R Birch
Nationality	UK
Date Designed	1983
Foundries	Letraset
Number of weights	1

ABCDEFGHIJKLMNOPQRSTUVWXYZ

ABCDEFGHIJKLMNOPQRSTUVWXYZ1234567890

JACKDAWS LOVE MY BIG SPHINX OF QUARTZ.

Sayer Interview

Designer	Manfred Sayer
Nationality	DE
Date Designed	1984
Foundries	Mecanorma
Number of weights	1

ABCDEFGHIJKLMNOPQRSTUVWXYZ

abcdefghijklmnopqrstuvwxyz1234567890

Martin J. Hixeypozer quickly began his first word.

Cargo

Designer	URW++
Nationality	DE
Date Designed	1990
Foundries	URW++
Number of weights	1

ABCDEFGHIJKLMNOPQRSTUVWXYZ

abcdefghijklmnopqrstuvwxyz1234567890

Two different stencil fonts called CARGO.

Jerrywi

Designer	Bo Berndal
Nationality	SE
Date Designed	1994
Foundries	Monotype
Number of weights	1

ABCDEFGHIJKLMNOPQRSTUVWXYZ
ABCDEFGHIJKLMNOPQRSTUVWXYZ1234567890
NO KIDDING, LORENZO CALLED OFF HIS TRIP TO VISIT
MEXICO CITY JUST BECAUSE.

Nyx

Designer	Rick Cusick
Nationality	US
Date Designed	1995
Foundries	Adobe
Number of weights	1

ABCDEFGHIJKLMNOPQRSTUVWXYZ
ABCDEFGHIJKLMNOPQRSTUVWXYZ1234567890
WHILE WAXING PARQUET DECKS, JAUNTY SUEZ SAILORS VOMIT ABAFT.

Flightcase

Designer	Just van Rossum
Nationality	NL
Date Designed	1995
Foundries	FontFont
Number of weights	1

ABCDEFGHIJKLMNOPQRSTUVWXYZ
ABCDEFGHIJKLMNOPQRSTUVWXYZ1234567890
ABOUT SIXTY CODFISH EGGS WILL MAKE A QUARTER POUND OF
VERY FIZZY JELLY.

Karton

Designer	Just van Rossum
Nationality	NL
Date Designed	1995
Foundries	FontFont
Number of weights	1

ABCDEFGHIJKLMNOPQRSTUVWXYZ
ABCDEFGHIJKLMNOPQRSTUVWXYZ1234567890
THE VIXEN JUMPED QUICKLY ON HER FOE.

Link

Designer	Gérard Mariscalchi
Nationality	CA
Date Designed	1995
Foundries	Monotype
Number of weights	4

ABCDEFGHIJKLMNOPQRSTUVWXYZ
abcdefghijklmnopqrstuvwxyz1234567890
Jim just quit and packed extra bags for Liz Owen.

Linotype Sjablony

Designer	Mark Van Wageningen
Nationality	NL
Date Designed	1996
Foundries	Linotype
Number of weights	1

ABCDEFGHIJKLMNOPQRSTUVWXYZ
ABCDEFGHIJKLMNOPQRSTUVWXYZ
1234567890
SIX BIG DEVILS FROM JAPAN.

Linotype Mindline

Designer	Critzler
Nationality	DE
Date Designed	1996
Foundries	Linotype
Number of weights	1

ABCDEFGHIJKLMNOPQRSTUVWXYZ
ABCDEFGHIJKLMNOPQRSTUVWXYZ1234567890
BRAVE JACKDAWS LOVE MY BIG SPHINX OF QUARTZ

Offline

Designer	Roelof Mulder
Nationality	DE
Date Designed	1996
Foundries	FontFont
Number of weights	1

ABCDEFGHIJKLMNOPQRSTUVWXYZ
abcdefghijklmnopqrstuvwxyz1234567890
Many-wived Jack laughs at probes of sex quiz.

Campaign

Designer	Alan Meeks
Nationality	UK
Date Designed	1997
Foundries	Linotype
Number of weights	1

ABCDEFGHIJKLMNOPQRSTUVWXYZ
ABCDEFGHIJKLMNOPQRSTUVWXYZ1234567890
MAY JO EQUAL THE FINE RECORD BY SOLVING SIX PUZZLES A WEEK?

Portago

Designer	Luis Siquot
Nationality	AR
Date Designed	1997
Foundries	ITC
Number of weights	1

ABCDEFGHIJKLMNOPQRSTUVWXYZ
ABCDEFGHIJKLMNOPQRSTUVWXYZ1234567890
FRED SPECIALIZED IN THE JOB OF MAKING VERY QUAINT WAX TOYS.

Isilda

Designer	Frank Marciuliano
Nationality	CA
Date Designed	1997
Foundries	Linotype
Number of weights	1

ABCDEFGHIJKLMNOPQRSTUVWXYZ

abcdefghijklmnopqrstuvwxyz1234567890

Astronaut Quincy B. Zack defies gravity with six jet fuel pumps.

Linotype Authentic Stencil

Designer	Karin Huschka
Nationality	DE
Date Designed	1999
Foundries	Linotype
Number of weights	1

ABCDEFGHIJKLMNOPQRSTUVWXYZ

abcdefghijklmnopqrstuvwxyz1234567890

And this delightful Herb has tender green stalks.

Chernobyl

Designer	Stefan Müller
Nationality	DE
Date Designed	1999
Foundries	FontFont
Number of weights	1

ABCDEFGHIJKLMNOPQRSTUVWXYZ

abcdefghijklmnopqrstuvwxyz1234567890

Jimmy and Zack, the police explained, were last seen diving into a field of buttered quahogs.

Container

Designer	Stefan Müller
Nationality	DE
Date Designed	1999
Foundries	FontFont
Number of weights	1

ABCDEFGHIJKLMNOPQRSTUVWXYZ

abcdefghijklmnopqrstuvwxyz1234567890

William said that everything about his jacket was in quite good condition except for the zipper.

Snafu

Designer	Jonathan Hitchen
Nationality	UK
Date Designed	2002
Foundries	FontFont
Number of weights	1

ABCDEFGHIJKLMNOPQRSTUVWXYZ

ABCDEFGHIJKLMNOPQRSTUVWXYZ1234567890

WWII ACRONYM FOR SITUATION NORMAL — ALL FUCKED UP.

Other

Swaak Centennial

Designer Mecanorma
Nationality FR
Date Designed 1994
Foundries Mecanorma Monotype
Number of weights 1

ABCDEFGHIJKLMNOPQRSTUVWXYZ

ABCDEFGHIJKLMNOPQRSTUVWXYZ1234567890

NOW IS THE TIME FOR ALL BROWN DOGS TO JUMP OVER THE LAZY LYNX.

Maigret

Designer Dave Farey
Nationality UK
Date Designed 2000
Foundries Monotype
Number of weights 1

ABCDEFGHIJKLMNOPQRSTUVWXYZ

ABCDEFGHIJKLMNOPQRSTUVWXYZ1234567890

A LARGE FAWN JUMPED QUICKLY OVER WHITE ZINC BOXES.

Ortem

Designer J H Crook
Nationality UK
Date Designed 1994
Foundries Mecanorma
Number of weights 1

ABCDEFGHIJKLMNOPQRSTUVWXYZ

ABCDEFGHIJKLMNOPQRSTUVWXYZ1234567890

WHEN WE GO BACK TO JUAREZ, MEXICO, DO WE FLY OVER PICTURESQUE ARIZONA?

Poster Gothic

Designer Agfa Monotype
Nationality UK
Date Designed 1900
Foundries Monotype
Number of weights 1

ABCDEFGHIJKLMNOPQRSTUVWXYZ

abcdefghijklmnopqrstuvwxyz1234567890

Zwei Boxkämpfer jagen Eva quer durch Sylt.

Willow Plain

Designer Tony Forster
Nationality UK
Date Designed 1990
Foundries ITC Linotype
Number of weights 1

ABCDEFGHIJKLMNOPQRSTUVWXYZ

ABCDEFGHIJKLMNOPQRSTUVWXYZ1234567890

THE WILLOW TEA ROOMS IN GLASGOW WERE DESIGNED BY CHARLES RENNIE MACKINTOSH, WHO MAY HAVE SUFFERED FROM ASPERGER'S SYNDROME.

Rennie Mackintosh

Designer	Phill Grimshaw
Nationality	UK
Date Designed	1996
Foundries	ITC
Number of weights	1

ABCDEFGHIJKLMNOPQRSTUVWXYZ

ABCDEFGHIJKLMNOPQRSTUVWXYZ1234567890

JACKDAWS LOVE MY BIG SPHINX OF QUARTZ.

Vintage

Designer	Hollly Goldsmith
Nationality	US
Date Designed	1996
Foundries	Linotype ITC Monotype
Number of weights	1

ABCDEFGHIJKLMNOPQRSTUVWXYZ

ABCDEFGHIJKLMNOPQRSTUVWXYZ1234567890

For only $49, jolly housewives made inexpensive meals using quick-frozen vegetables.

Virgin Roman

Designer	Dave Farey
Nationality	UK
Date Designed	1994
Foundries	Monotype
Number of weights	1

ABCDEFGHIJKLMNOPQRSTUVWXYZ

abcdefghijklmnopqrstuvwxyz1234567890

Jimmy and Zack, the police explained, were last seen diving into a field of buttered quahogs.

Boomerang

Designer	Tim Ryan
Nationality	IE
Date Designed	1995
Foundries	Monotype
Number of weights	1

ABCDEFGHIJKLMNOPQRSTUVWXYZ

abcdefghijklmnopqrstuvwxyz1234567890

Jack amazed a few girls by dropping the antique onyx vase!

Decco Modern

Designer	Andy Hullinger
Nationality	US
Date Designed	1994
Foundries	T-26 Monotype
Number of weights	2

ABCDEFGHIJKLMNOPQRSTUVWXYZ

abcdefghijklmnopqrstuvwxyz1234567890

Now is the time for all brown dogs to jump over the lazy lynx.

Milton Demibold

Designer Mecanorma
Nationality FR
Date Designed 1994
Foundries Mecanorma Monotype
Number of weights 1

ABCDEFGHIJKLMNOPQRSTUVWXYZ
abcdefghijklmnopqrstuvwxyz1234567890
While waxing parquet decks, jaunty Suez sailors vomit abaft.

Rosewood

Designer Kim Buker Chansler, Carl
Crossgrove, Carol Twombly
Nationality US
Date Designed 1994
Foundries Adobe
Number of weights 1

ABCDEFGHIJKLMNOPQRSTUVWXYZ
ABCDEFGHIJKLMNOPQRSTUVWXYZ1234567890
WALTZ, NYMPH, FOR QUICK JIGS VEX BUD.

Virile

Designer John F Cumming
Nationality US
Date Designed 1890
Foundries Monotype
Number of weights 1

ABCDEFGHIJKLMNOPQRSTUVWXYZ
abcdefghijklmnopqrstuvwxyz1234567890
Astronaut Quincy B. Zack defies gravity with six jet fuel pumps.

Typados

Designer Roselyne Besnard, Michel
Besnard
Nationality FR
Date Designed 1997
Foundries ITC
Number of weights 1

ABCDEFGHIJKLMNOPQRSTUVWXYZ
abcdefghijklmnopqrstuvwxyz1234567890
Based on M Besnard's imaginary friend Ado.

Artistik

Designer anon
Nationality FR
Date Designed 1903
Foundries Monotype
Number of weights 1

ABCDEFGHIJKLMNOPQRSTUVWXYZ
abcdefghijklmnopqrstuvwxyz1234567890
Brawny gods just flocked up to quiz and vex him.

Metropolitain

Designer	anon
Nationality	FR
Date Designed	1903
Foundries	Elsner+Flake Linotype URW++
Number of weights	5

ABCDEFGHIJKLMNOPQRSTUVWXYZ

ABCDEFGHIJKLMNOPQRSTUVWXYZ1234567890

KING ALEXANDER WAS PARTLY OVERCOME JUST AFTER QUIZZING DIOGENES IN HIS TUB.

Stealth

Designer	Malcolm Garrett
Nationality	UK
Date Designed	1991
Foundries	FontFont
Number of weights	1

ABCDEFGHIJKLMNOPQRSTUVWXYZ

1234567890

THE JOB OF WAXING LINOLEUM FREQUENTLY PEEVES CHINTZY KIDS.

Automatic

Designer	Donald Beekman
Nationality	NL
Date Designed	1999
Foundries	FontFont
Number of weights	1

ABCDEFGHIJKLMNOPQRSTUVWXYZ

abcdefghijklmnopqrstuvwxyz1234567890

Was there a quorum of able whizzkids gravely exciting the jaded fish at ATypI?

Jackson

Designer	B Jacquet
Nationality	FR
Date Designed	1971
Foundries	Creative Alliance Mecanorma
Number of weights	1

ABCDEFGHIJKLMNOPQRSTUVWXYZ

1234567890

THE SEX LIFE OF THE WOODCHUCK IS A PROVOCATIVE QUESTION FOR MOST VERTEBRATES.

Werkman

Designer	Lewis Tsalis
Nationality	AU
Date Designed	1996
Foundries	T-26
Number of weights	1

ABCDEFGHIJKLMNOPQRSTUVWXYZ

abcdefghijklmnopqrstuvwxyz1234567890

Six big juicy steaks sizzled in a pan as five workmen left the quarry.

Flava

Designer	Donald Beekman
Nationality	NL
Date Designed	2003
Foundries	FontFont
Number of weights	8

ABCDEFGHIJKLMNOPQRSTUVWXYZ
abcdefghijklmnopqrstuvwxyz1234567890
sexy qua lijf, doch bang voor het zwempak.

Atmosphere

Designer	Taouffik Semmad
Nationality	DZ
Date Designed	1997
Foundries	ITC
Number of weights	1

ABCDEFGHIJKLMNOPQRSTUVWXYZ
ABCDEFGHIJKLMNOPQRSTUVWXYZ1234567890
JUST KEEP EXAMINING EVERY LOW BID QUOTED FOR ZINC ETCHINGS.

Skid Row

Designer	Akira Kobayashi
Nationality	JP
Date Designed	1990
Foundries	Letraset Linotype Monotype ITC
Number of weights	1

ABCDEFGHIJKLMNOPQRSTUVWXYZ
ABCDEFGHIJKLMNOPQRSTUVWXYZ1234567890
FIVE WINE EXPERTS JOKINGLY QUIZZED SAMPLE CHABLIS.

Imperfect

Designer	Michael Strassburger
Nationality	DE
Date Designed	1994
Foundries	T-26
Number of weights	1

ABCDEFGHIJKLMNOPQRSTUVWXYZ
abcdefghijklmnopqrstuvwxyz1234567890
The July sun caused a fragment of black pine wax to ooze on the velvet quilt.

Bibracte

Designer	Michel Redon, Denis Patouillard Demriane
Nationality	FR
Date Designed	1997
Foundries	Monotype
Number of weights	1

ABCDEFGHIJKLMNOPQRSTUVWXYZ
ABCDEFGHIJKLMNOPQRSTUVWXYZ1234567890
A GALLIC HILL FORT IN BURGUNDY.

Metropolis

Designer	W Schwerdtner
Nationality	DE
Date Designed	1932
Foundries	Stempel Monotype Castle
Number of weights	1

ABCDEFGHIJKLMNOPQRSTUVWXYZ
abcdefghijklmnopqrstuvwxyz1234567890
Viewing quizzical abstracts mixed up hefty jocks.

Beverly Hills

Designer	Monotype
Nationality	US
Date Designed	1930
Foundries	Monotype
Number of weights	1

ABCDEFGHIJKLMNOPQRSTUVWXYZ
ABCDEFGHIJKLMNOPQRSTUVWXYZ1234567890
SIX CRAZY KINGS VOWED TO ABOLISH MY QUITE PITIFUL JOUSTS.

Mona Lisa

Designer	Albert Augspurg
Nationality	DE
Date Designed	1930
Foundries	Ludwig & Mayer ITC Adobe
Number of weights	1

ABCDEFGHIJKLMNOPQRSTUVWXYZ
abcdefghijklmnopqrstuvwxyz1234567890
Brawny gods just flocked up to quiz and vex him.

Joanna Solotype

Designer	Monotype
Nationality	UK
Date Designed	1994
Foundries	Monotype
Number of weights	1

ABCDEFGHIJKLMNOPQRSTUVWXYZ
abcdefghijklmnopqrstuvwxyz1234567890
A large fawn jumped quickly over white zinc boxes.

Manhattan

Designer	Tom Carnase
Nationality	US
Date Designed	1970
Foundries	ITC
Number of weights	1

ABCDEFGHIJKLMNOPQRSTUVWXYZ
abcdefghijklmnopqrstuvwxyz1234567890
A quick movement of the enemy will jeopardize six gunboats.

BlackWhite

Designer	Ferdinay Duman
Nationality	DE
Date Designed	1989
Foundries	Linotype
Number of weights	1

ABCDEFGHIJKLMNOPQRSTUVWXYZ
ABCDEFGHIJKLMNOPQRSTUVWXYZ
1234567890
KING ALEXANDER WAS PARTLY OVERCOME .

Art Deco Display

Designer	anon
Nationality	US
Date Designed	1929
Foundries	P22
Number of weights	1

ABCDEFGHIJKLMNOPQRSTUVWXYZ
ABCDEFGHIJKLMNOPQRSTUVWXYZ1234567890
FOR ONLY $49, JOLLY HOUSEWIVES MADE INEXPENSIVE MEALS USING
QUICK-FROZEN VEGETABLES.

Agfa Waddy 92

Designer	Aiko & Hideaki Wada
Nationality	JP
Date Designed	1999
Foundries	Monotype
Number of weights	1

ABCDEFGHIJKLMNOPQRSTUVWXYZ
abcdefghijklmnopqrstuvwxyz1234567890
New farm hand (picking just six quinces) proves strong but lazy.

Jazz

Designer	Alan Meeks
Nationality	UK
Date Designed	1992
Foundries	Letraset Linotype ITC
Number of weights	1

ABCDEFGHIJKLMNOPQRSTUVWXYZ
abcdefghijklmnopqrstuvwxyz1234567890
William said that everything about his jacket was in quite
good condition except for the zipper.

Ojaio

Designer	Leslie Cabarga
Nationality	US
Date Designed	1994
Foundries	Monotype
Number of weights	1

ABCDEFGHIJKLMNOPQRSTUVWXYZ
abcdefghijklmnopqrstuvwxyz1234567890
New farm hand (picking just six quinces) proves strong but lazy.

Sinaloa

Designer	Rosemarie Tissi
Nationality	CH
Date Designed	1974
Foundries	Letraset AGP URW++
Number of weights	1

ABCDEFGHIJKLMNOPQRSTUVWXYZ
abcdefghijklmnopqrstuvwxyz1234567890
Became very popular for perspex shop fronts in Great Britain.

Matra

Designer	A M Cassandre
Nationality	FR
Date Designed	1930
Foundries	Monotype
Number of weights	1

ABCDEFGHIJKLMNOPQRSTUVWXYZ
ABCDEFGHIJKLMNOPQRSTUVWXYZ1234567890
USE THIS IF YOU CAN'T GET CASSANDRE'S BIFUR.

Dinitials

Designer	Helga Jörgensen
Nationality	DK
Date Designed	1995
Foundries	Monotype ITC
Number of weights	1

ABCDEFGHIJKLMNOPQRSTUVWXYZ
ABCDEFGHIJKLMNOPQRSTUVWXYZ1234567890
ZWEEDSE EXVIP BEHOORLIJK GEK OP QUANTUMFYSICA

Hibiscus

Designer	Judith Sutcliffe
Nationality	US
Date Designed	1993
Foundries	Monotype
Number of weights	1

ABCDEFGHIJKLMNOP
QRSTUVWXYZ
ZWEI BOXKÄMPFER JAGEN EVA QUER
DURCH SYLT

A Lazy Day

Designer	Simone Schöpp
Nationality	DE
Date Designed	1995
Foundries	FontFont
Number of weights	1

ABCDEFGHIJKLMNOPQRSTUVWXYZ
ABCDEFGHIJKLMNOPQRSTUVWXYZ
VERILY THE DARK EX JEW QUIT ZIONISM
PREFERRING THE CABALA

Daylilies

Designer	Judith Sutcliffe
Nationality	US
Date Designed	1995
Foundries	Electric Typographer Monotype
Number of weights	1

ABCDEFGHIJKLMNOPQRSTUVWXYZ

ABCDEFGHIJKLMNOPQRSTUVWXYZ

GOUDY OLD STYLE CAPITALS DECORATED
WITH LILIES

Abacus

Designer	Panache Typography
Nationality	UK
Date Designed	1995
Foundries	ITC
Number of weights	1

ABCDEFGHIJKLMNOPQRSTUVWXYZ

ABCDEFGHIJKLMNOPQRSTUVWXYZ1234567890

A COUNTING AND CALCULATING DEVICE

Acorn

Designer	Richard Yeend
Nationality	UK
Date Designed	1997
Foundries	Monotype
Number of weights	1

ABCDEFGHIJKLMNOPQRSTUVWXYZ

abcdefghijklmnopqrstuvwxyz1234567890

How quickly daft jumping zebras vex.

Aftershock

Designer	Bob Alonso
Nationality	US
Date Designed	1996
Foundries	Linotype ITC
Number of weights	1

ABCDEFGHIJKLMNOPQRSTUVWXYZ

abcdefghijklmnopqrstuvwxyz1234567890

Sympathizing would fix Quaker objectives.

Alta California

Designer	Steve Mehallo
Nationality	US
Date Designed	1984
Foundries	Monotype
Number of weights	1

ABCDEFGHIJKLMNOPQRSTUVWXYZ

abcdefghijklmnopqrstuvwxyz1234567890

Jim just quit and packed extra bags for Liz Owen.

Amoeba

Designer	Peter Warren
Nationality	UK
Date Designed	1995
Foundries	FontFont
Number of weights	1

ABCDEFGHIJKLMNOPQRSTUVWXYZ
abcdefghijklmnopqrstuvwxyz1234567890
William Jex quickly caught five dozen Conservatives.

Amplifier

Designer	Frank Heine
Nationality	DE
Date Designed	1994
Foundries	T-26
Number of weights	1

ABCDEFGHIJKLMNOPQRSTUVWXYZ
abcdefghijklmnopqrstuvwxyz1234567890
Martin J. Hixeypozer quickly began his first word.

Dynamo

Designer	K Sommer
Nationality	DE
Date Designed	1930
Foundries	Ludwig & Mayer
Number of weights	1

ABCDEFGHIJKLMNOPQRSTUVWXYZ
abcdefghijklmnopqrstuvwxyz1234567890
No kidding. Lorenzo called off his trip to visit Mexico City just because they told him the conquistadores were extinct.

Blind Date

Designer	Adam Roe
Nationality	US
Date Designed	1992
Foundries	T-26
Number of weights	2

ABCDEFGHIJKLMNOPQRSTUVWXYZ
ABCDEFGHIJKLMNOPQRSTUVWXYZ1234567890
Jazzy saxophones blew over Mick's turgid quiff.

Broad Street

Designer	Richard Yeend
Nationality	UK
Date Designed	1994
Foundries	Monotype
Number of weights	1

ABCDEFGHIJKLMNOPQRSTUVWXYZ
abcdefghijklmnopqrstuvwxyz1234567890
Five or six big jet planes zoomed quickly by the tower.

Bubba Love

Designer	Todd Brei
Nationality	US
Date Designed	1994
Foundries	ITC
Number of weights	1

ABCDEFGHIJKLMNOPQRSTUVWXYZ

abcdefghi jklmnopqrstuvwxyz1234567890

Six crazy kings vowed to abolish my quite pitiful jousts.

Droplet

Designer	Hat Nguyen
Nationality	VT
Date Designed	1995
Foundries	T-26 Monotype
Number of weights	1

ABCDEFGHIJKLMNOPQRSTUVWXYZ

abcdefghijklmnopqrstuvwxyz1234567890

Sexy qua lijf, doch bang voor het zwempak.

Farmhaus

Designer	Timothy Donaldson
Nationality	UK
Date Designed	1995
Foundries	Monotype ~ITC
Number of weights	1

ABCDEFGHIJKLMNOPQRSTUVWXYZ

abcdefghijklmnopqrstuvwxyz1234567890

Jazzy saxophones blew over Mick's turgid quiff.

Freddo

Designer	James Montalbano
Nationality	US
Date Designed	1996
Foundries	Creative Alliance Linotype ITC
Number of weights	1

ABCDEFGHIJKLMNOPQRSTUVWXYZ

abcdefghijklmnopqrstuvwxyz

1234567890

Exquisite farm wench gives body jolt.

Sackers Solid Antique Roman

Designer	Monotype
Nationality	UK
Date Designed	1920
Foundries	Monotype
Number of weights	1

ABCDEFGHIJKLMNOPQRSTUVWXYZ

abcdefghijklmnopqrstuvwxyz1234567890

Viewing quizzical abstracts mixed up hefty jocks.

Baluster

Designer	Marcus Burlile
Nationality	US
Date Designed	1993
Foundries	Garagefonts
Number of weights	1

ABCDEFGHIJHLMNOPQRSTUUWKP2

ABCDEFGHIJHLMNOPQRSTUUWKP21234567890

WILLIAM JEK QUICHLP CAUGHT FIUE DOZEN CONSERUATIUES.

Cloister Open Face

Designer	R Hunter Middleton
Nationality	US
Date Designed	1920
Foundries	Adobe
Number of weights	1

ABCDEFGHIJKLMNOPQRSTUVWXYZ

abcdefghijklmnopqrstuvwxyz1234567890

Back in June we delivered oxygen equipment of the same size.

Devit

Designer	Lewis Tsalis
Nationality	AU
Date Designed	1996
Foundries	T-26
Number of weights	1

ABCDEFGHIJKLMNOPQRSTUVWXYZ

ABCDEFGHIJKLMNOPQRSTUVWXYZ1234567890

INSPIRED BY A CORGI BATMOBILE

Freakshow

Designer	Todd Brei
Nationality	US
Date Designed	1994
Foundries	Creative Alliance
Number of weights	2

ABCDEFGHIJKLMNOPQRSTUVWXYZ

abcdefghijklmnopqrstuvwxyz1234567890

Ebenezer unexpectedly bagged two tranquil aardvarks with his jiffy vacuum cleaner.

Gadzooks

Designer	Monotype
Nationality	UK
Date Designed	1994
Foundries	Creative Alliance
Number of weights	1

ABCDEFGHIJKLMNOPQRS
abcdefghijklmnopq
rstuvwxyz1234567890
Gadzooks! ejaculated Prince.

MN Fumo DropShadow

Designer	L Fumarolo
Nationality	FR
Date Designed	1994
Foundries	MN Creative Alliance
Number of weights	1

ABCDEFGHIJKLMNOPQRSTUVWXYZ
abcdefghijklmnopqrstuvwxyz1234567890
New farm hand (picking just six quinces) proves strong
but lazy.

TC Europa Bold

Designer	Les Usherwood
Nationality	CA
Date Designed	1997
Foundries	TC Typesettra Monotype
Number of weights	1

ABCDEFGHIJKLMNOPQRSTUVWXYZ
abcdefghijklmnopqrstuvwxyz1234567890
Not the same as Europa Grotesque.

Font

Designer	Dave Farey
Nationality	UK
Date Designed	1994
Foundries	Creative Alliance Panache
Number of weights	2

ABCDEFGHIJKLMNOPQRSTUVWXYZ
ABCDEFGHIJKLMNOPQRSTUVWXYZ
1234567890
ZWEI BOXKAMPFER JAGEN EVA QUER DURCH SYLT.

Macbeth

Designer	Linotype
Nationality	UK
Date Designed	1994
Foundries	Linotype
Number of weights	1

ABCDEFGHIJKLMNOPQRSTUVWXYZ
abcdefghijklmnopqrstuvwxyz1234567890
We promptly judged antique ivory buckles for the next prize.

Linotype Mailbox

Designer	Andreas Karl
Nationality	DE
Date Designed	1997
Foundries	Linotype
Number of weights	1

@abcdefghijklmnopqrstuvwxyz
@abcdefghijklmnopqrstuvwxyz1234567890
Quick waiting zephyr vex bald jim.

TF Avian

Designer Joseph D Treacy
Nationality US
Date Designed 1990
Foundries Monotype
Number of weights 1

ABCDEFGHIJKLMNO
PQRSTUVWXYZ
abcdefghijklmnopqrstuvwxyz
1234567890

Sweeney MT

Designer Kathryn Darnell
Nationality IE
Date Designed 2002
Foundries Monotype
Number of weights 1

ABCDEFGHIJKLMNOPQRSTUVWXYZ
ABCDEFGHIJKLMNOPQRSTUVWXYZ1234567890
THE RISQUE GOWN MARKED A BRAZEN EXPOSURE OF VERY
JUICY FLESH.

Zeitgeist

Designer Michael Johnson
Nationality UK
Date Designed 1990
Foundries MCL Monotype
Number of weights 1

ABCDEFGHIJKLMNOPQRSTUVWXYZ
abcdefgghijckchm n ofspqrstt u vwxy zy ①②③④⑤⑥⑦⑧⑨⓪
Questtiofnst ofét a zye a chofust nature shave bectofme by deggreest spetty
waXen jofckest

Claude

Designer Psychoglyph
Nationality US
Date Designed 1991
Foundries Psychoglyph
Number of weights 1

ABCDEFGHIJKLMNOPQRSTUVWXYZ
A PRETTY FEEBLE ATTEMPT AT A DOT MATRIX FONT

Talking Drum

Designer Timothy Donaldson
Nationality UK
Date Designed 2004
Foundries ITC
Number of weights 1

ABCDEFGHIJKLMNOPQRSTUVWXYZ
abcdefghijklmnopqrstuvwxyz1234567890
About sixty codfish eggs will make a quarter pound of
very fizzy jelly.

Hip

Designer	Paul Sych
Nationality	CA
Date Designed	1991
Foundries	FontFont
Number of weights	1

ABCDEFGHIJKLMNOPQRSTUVWXYZ

abcdefghijklmnopqrstuvwxyz1234567890

The juke box music puzzled a gentle visitor from a quaint valley town.

Imperial

Designer	Donald Beekman
Nationality	NL
Date Designed	2001
Foundries	FontFont
Number of weights	1

ABCDEFGHIJKLMNOPQRSTUVWXYZ

ABCDEFGHIJKLMNOPQRSTUVWXYZ1234567890

NEW FARM HAND (PICKING JUST SIX OUNCES) PROVES STRONG BUT LAZY.

Totem

Designer	Donald Beekman
Nationality	NL
Date Designed	1999
Foundries	FontFont
Number of weights	1

ABCDEFGHIJKLMNOPQRSTUVWXYZ

ABCDEFGHIJKLMNOPQRSTUVWXYZ1234567890

EBENEZER UNEXPECTEDLY BAGGED TWO TRANQUIL AARDVARKS WITH HIS JIFFY VACUUM CLEANER.

Revue

Designer	Letraset
Nationality	UK
Date Designed	1969
Foundries	Letraset
Number of weights	1

ABCDEFGHIJKLMNOPQRSTUVWXYZ

abcdefghijklmnopqrstuvwxyz1234567890

Six big juicy steaks sizzled in a pan as five workmen left the quarry.

Blocker

Designer	Hannes Famira
Nationality	DE
Date Designed	1998
Foundries	FontFont
Number of weights	1

ABCDEFGHIJKLMNOPQRSTUVWXYZ

abcdefghijklmnopqrstuvwxyz1234567890

While waxing parquet decks, jaunty Suez sailors vomit abaft.

Juanita

Designer Luis Siquot
Nationality AR
Date Designed 1996
Foundries ITC Linotype Monotype
Number of weights 1

ABCDEFGHIJKLMNOPQRSTUVWXYZ
ABCDEFGHIJKLMNOPQRSTUVWXYZ1234567890
PORTEZ CE VIEUX WHISKY AU JUGE BLOND QUI FUME.

Manito

Designer Garrett Boge
Nationality US
Date Designed 1990
Foundries Monotype Adobe
Number of weights 1

ABCDEFGHIJKLMNOPQRSTUVWXYZ
ABCDEFGHIJKLMNOPQRSTUVWXYZ1234567890
SIX BIG DEVILS FROM JAPAN QUICKLY FORGOT HOW TO WALTZ.

Shuriken Boy

Designer Joachim Müller-Lancé
Nationality DE
Date Designed 1996
Foundries Adobe
Number of weights 1

ABCDEFGHIJKLMNOPQRSTUVWXYZ
abcdefghijklmnopqrstuvwxyz1234567890
Quixotic Conservatives vat first key zero-growth jeremiad.

TF Guestcheck Heavy

Designer Joseph D Treacy
Nationality US
Date Designed 1990
Foundries Treacyfaces
Number of weights 1

ABCDEFGHIJKLMNO
PQRSTUVWXYZ
abcdefghijklmno
pqrstuvwxyz1234567890

Carmen

Designer Lutz Günther
Nationality DE
Date Designed 1996
Foundries Linotype
Number of weights 1

ABCDEFGHIJKLMNOPQRSTUVWXYZ
abcdefghijklmnopqrstuvwxyz1234567890
Jaded zombies acted quaintly but kept driving their oxen forward.

Overdose

Designer Donald Beekman
Nationality NL
Date Designed 1999
Foundries FontFont
Number of weights 1

ABCDEFGHIJKLMN
OPQRSTUVWXYZ
1234567890
FOR ONLY €49, JOLLY HOUSEWIVES.

Linotype Besque

Designer Rachel Ellaway
Nationality UK
Date Designed 1999
Foundries Linotype
Number of weights 1

ABCDEFGHDHLMNOPQRSTUVWXYZ
abcdefghijklmnopqrstuvwxyz
1234567890
Verbatim reports were quickly given.

Bandalero

Designer Richard Yeend
Nationality UK
Date Designed 2003
Foundries Linotype
Number of weights 1

ABCDEFGHIJKLMNOPQRSTUVWXYZ
abcdefghijklmnopqrstuvwxyz1234567890
Alike to no such aureate Earth are turn'd.

Adrielle

Designer Ad Vance Graphics
Nationality US
Date Designed 1983
Foundries Ad Vance Graphics
Number of weights 1

ABCDEFGHIJKLMNOPQRSTUVWXYZ
ABCDEFGHIJKLMNOPQRSTUVWXYZ1234567890
JAZZY SAXOPHONES BLEW OVER MICK'S TURGID QUIFF

Tsunami

Designer Donald Beekman
Nationality NL
Date Designed 1999
Foundries FontFont
Number of weights 1

ABCDEFGHIJKLMNOPQRSTUVWXYZ
ABCDEFGHIJKLMNOPQRSTUVWXYZ
1234567890
THE SEX LIFE OF THE WOODCHUCK IS PROVOCATIVE.

Delima

Designer	Monotype
Nationality	UK
Date Designed	1994
Foundries	Monotype
Number of weights	1

ABCDEFGHIJKLMNOPQRSTUVWXYZ

abcdefghijklmnopqrstuvwxyz1234567890

Jelly-like above the high wire, six quaking pachyderms kept the climax of the extravaganza in a dazzling state of flux.

Thornface

Designer	Jan Erasmus
Nationality	NL
Date Designed	1997
Foundries	Monotype
Number of weights	3

ABCDEFGHIJKLMNOPQRSTUVWXYZ

ABCDEFGHIJKLMNOPQRSTUVWXYZ1234567890

A MAD BOXER SHOT A QUICK, GLOVED JAB TO THE JAW OF HIS DIZZY OPPONENT.

Section

Designer	anon
Nationality	UK
Date Designed	1994
Foundries	Monotype
Number of weights	1

ABCDEFGHIJKLMNOPQRSTUVWXYZ

ABCDEFGHIJKLMNOPQRSTUVWXYZ1234567890

CRAZY FREDERICKA BOUGHT MANY VERY EXQUISITE OPAL JEWELS.

Trade 01

Designer	Fabrizio Schiavi
Nationality	IT
Date Designed	1994
Foundries	FontFont
Number of weights	1

ABKDEBBHIJKLMNOPQRSTUVWXYZ

abcdefghijklmnopqrstuvwxyz1234567890

Portez ce vieux whisky au juge blond qui fume.

Linotype Rory

Designer	Tad Biernot
Nationality	CA
Date Designed	1996
Foundries	Linotype
Number of weights	1

ABCDEFGHIJKLMNOPQRSTUVWXYZ

abcdefghijklmnopqrstuvwxyz1234567890

Jaded zombies acted quaintly but kept driving their oxen forward.

Aarcover

Designer	David Rakowski
Nationality	US
Date Designed	1991
Foundries	Typoasis
Number of weights	1

ABCDEFGHIJKLMNOPQRSTUVWXYZ
ABCDEFGHIJKLMNOPQRSTUVWXYZ1234567890
SPHINX OF BLACK QUARTZ JUDGE MY VOW.

New Yorker Type

Designer	Rea Irwin
Nationality	US
Date Designed	1923
Foundries	FontFont
Recut/Digitised by	Gerd Winscher, 1991
Number of weights	1

ABCDEFGHIJKLMNOPQRSTUVWXYZ
ABCDEFGHIJKLMNOPQRSTUVWXYZ1234567890
PROBABLY THE WORLD'S GREATEST MAGAZINE.

Craft

Designer	Peter Bilak
Nationality	SK
Date Designed	1994
Foundries	FontFont
Number of weights	1

ABCDEFGHIJKLMNOPQRSTUVWXYZ
abcdefghijklmnopqrstuvwxyz1234567890
Martin J. Hixeypozer quickly began his first word.

Vision

Designer	Dan-André Niemeyer
Nationality	DE
Date Designed	1997
Foundries	Linotype
Number of weights	1

ABCDEFGHIJKLMNOPQRSTUVWXYZ
abcdefghijklmnopqrstuvwxyz1234567890
Jail zesty vixen who grabbed pay from quack.

Jan LT

Designer	Michael Parson
Nationality	CH
Date Designed	2002
Foundries	Linotype
Number of weights	1

ABCDEFGHIJKLMNOPQRSTUVWXYZ
abcdefghijklmnopqrstuvwxyz1234567890
Which Jan is this?

Ashley Crawford

Designer	Ashley Havinden
Nationality	UK
Date Designed	1930
Foundries	Monotype
Number of weights	1

ABCDEFGHIJKLMNOPQRSTUVWXYZ
ABCDEFGHIJKLMNOPQRSTUVWXYZ1234567890
HOW RAZORBACK-JUMPING FROGS CAN LEVEL SIX
PIQUED GYMNASTS!

Xylo

Designer	Letraset Design Staff
Nationality	UK
Date Designed	1994
Foundries	Letraset Monotype ITC
Number of weights	1

ABCDEFGHIJKLMNOPQRSTUVWXYZ
abcdefghijklmnopqrstuvwxyz1234567890
A mad boxer shot a quick, gloved jab to the jaw of his
dizzy opponent.

Bees Knees

Designer	Dave Farey
Nationality	UK
Date Designed	1990
Foundries	ITC Adobe
Number of weights	1

ABCDEFGHIJKLMNOPQRSTUVWXYZ
ABCDEFGHIJKLMNOPQRSTUVWXYZ1234567890
MR. JOCK, TV QUIZ PH.D., BAGS FEW LYNX.

Knobcheese

Designer	Rian Hughes
Nationality	UK
Date Designed	1994
Foundries	FontFont
Number of weights	1

ABCDEFGHIJKLMNOPQRSTUVWXYZ
ABCDEFGHIJKLMNOPQRSTUVWXYZ1234567890
JACK AMAZED A FEW GIRLS BY DROPPING THE ANTIQUE
ONYX VASE!

F2F Tagliatelle Sugo

Designer	Alessio Leonardi
Nationality	IT
Date Designed	1995
Foundries	Linotype
Number of weights	1

ABCDEFGHIJKLMNOPQRSTUVWXYZ
abcdefghijklmnopqrstuvwxyz1234567890
Tagliatelle with sauce becomes round and fat.

Agfa Klash

Designer	Wildwood Creations
Nationality	UK
Date Designed	1997
Foundries	Monotype
Number of weights	1

ABCDEFGHIJKLMNOPQRSTUVWXYZ
abcdefghijklmnopqrstuvwxyz1234567890
A quick movement of the enemy will jeopardize six gunboats.

Quaint Roman

Designer	Gustav F Schroeder
Nationality	DE
Date Designed	1895
Foundries	Monotype
Number of weights	1

ABCDEFGHIJKLMNOPQRSTUVWXYZ
abcdefghijklmnopqrstuvwxyz1234567890
No kidding, Lorenzo called off his trip to visit Mexico City just because they told him the conquistadores were extinct.

Wac Wak Ooops

Designer	Carol Kemp
Nationality	US
Date Designed	1998
Foundries	Monotype CA
Number of weights	1

ABCDEFGHIJKLMNOPQRSTUVWXYZ
abcdefghijklmnopqrstuvwxyz1234567890
Puzzled women bequeath jerks very exotic gifts.

Cherie

Designer	Teri Kahan
Nationality	US
Date Designed	1997
Foundries	Linotype Monotype ITC
Number of weights	1

ABCDEFGHIJKLMNOPQRSTUVWXYZ
ABCDEFGHIJKLMNOPQRSTUVWXYZ1234567890
ASTRONAUT QUINCY B. ZACK DEFIES GRAVITY WITH SIX JET FUEL PUMPS.

Girlfriend

Designer	Adam Roe
Nationality	US
Date Designed	1993
Foundries	T-26
Number of weights	2

ABCDEFGHIJKLMNOPQRSTUVWXYZ
abcdefghijklmnopqrstuvwxyz1234567890
THE VISITOR EACH QUILE HAS GAZED UPON A BROWN FOX AND QUAIL.

TF Hotelmoderne Two

Designer Joseph D Treacy
Nationality US
Date Designed 1992
Foundries Treacyfaces
Number of weights 1

ABCDEFGHIJKLMNOPQRSTUVWXYZ

abcdefghijklmnopqrstuvwxyz1234567890

Just work for improved basic techniques to maximize your typing skill.

TF Hotelmoderne Three

Designer Joseph D Treacy
Nationality US
Date Designed 1992
Foundries Treacyfaces
Number of weights 1

ABCDEFGHIJKLMNOPQRSTUVWXYZ

abcdefghijklmnopqrstuvwxyz1234567890

A mad boxer shot a quick, gloved jab to the jaw of his dizzy opponent.

TF Hôtelmoderne Calligr

Designer Joseph D Treacy
Nationality US
Date Designed 1985
Foundries Treacyfaces
Number of weights 1

ABCDEFGHIJKLMNOPQRSTUVWXYZ

abcdefghijklmnopqrstuvwxyz1234567890

Sympathizing would fix Quaker objectives.

Marten

Designer Martin Wenzel
Nationality DE
Date Designed 1991
Foundries FontFont
Number of weights 1

ABCDEFGHIJKLMNOPQRSTUVWXYZ

abcdefghijklmnopqrstuvwxyz1234567890

My help squeezed back in again and joined the weavers after six.

Abaton

Designer Luis Siquot
Nationality AR
Date Designed 1997
Foundries ITC Linotype
Number of weights 1

ABCDEFGHIJKLMNOPQRSTUVWXYZ

ABCDEFGHIJKLMNOPQRSTUVWXYZ1234567890

QUICK WAFTING ZEPHYRS VEX BOLD JIM.

Cabaret

Designer	Letraset
Nationality	UK
Date Designed	1980
Foundries	Letraset Linotype ITC
Number of weights	1

ABCDEFGHIJKLMNOPQRSTUVWXYZ

abcdefghijklmnopqrstuvwxyz1234567890

Six big juicy steaks sizzled in a pan as five workmen left the quarry.

Ann Stone Initials

Designer	David Rakowski
Nationality	US
Date Designed	1991
Foundries	Font Diner
Number of weights	1

ABCDEFGHIJKLMNOPQRSTUVWXYZ

ABCDEFGHIJKLMNOPQRSTUVWXYZ

AS BURIED ONCE MEN WANT DUG UP AGAIN

Bangor

Designer	Richard Yeend
Nationality	UK
Date Designed	1995
Foundries	Monotype
Number of weights	1

ABCDEFGHIJKLMNOPQRSTUVWXYZ

abcdefghijklmnopqrstuvwxyz1234567890

Quick zephyrs blow, vexing daft Jim.

Arriba

Designer	Phill Grimshaw
Nationality	UK
Date Designed	1993
Foundries	ITC Letraset Monotype
Number of weights	1

ABCDEFGHIJKLMNOPQRSTUVWXYZ

abcdefghijklmnopqrstuvwxyz1234567890

Mix Zapf with Veljovic and get quirky Beziers.

Emphasis

Designer	Martin Wait
Nationality	UK
Date Designed	1989
Foundries	Letraset Linotype ITC
Number of weights	1

ABCDEFGHIJKLMNOPQRSTUVWXYZ

ABCDEFGHIJKLMNOPQRSTUVWXYZ1234567890

JUST WORK FOR IMPROVED BASIC TECHNIQUES TO MAXIMIZE YOUR TYPING SKILL.

Ragtime

Designer Alan Meeks
Nationality UK
Date Designed 1988
Foundries Letraset Monotype ITC
Number of weights 1

ABCDEFGHIJKLMNOPQRSTUVWXYZ

ABCDEFGHIJKLMNOPQRSTUVWXYZ1234567890

MOI, JE VEUX QUINZE CLUBS A GOLF ET DU WHISKY PUR.

Linotype Tiger

Designer Gerd Sebastian Jakob, Ewald
Meissner
Nationality DE
Date Designed 1996
Foundries Linotype
Number of weights 4

ABCDEFGHIJKLMNOPQRSTUVWXYZ

abcdefghijklmnopqrstuvwxyz1234567890

Breezily jangling £3,416,157,209 wise advertiser ambles to the bank,
his exchequer amplified.

Andreas

Designer Michael Harvey
Nationality UK
Date Designed 1988
Foundries Adobe
Number of weights 1

ABCDEFGHIJKLMNOPQRSTUVWXYZ

ABCDEFGHIJKLMNOPQRSTUVWXYZ1234567890

AN INSPIRED CALLIGRAPHER CAN CREATE PAGES OF BEAUTY USING STICK INK, QUILL, BRUSH,
PICK-AXE, BUZZ SAW, OR EVEN STRAWBERRY JAM.

Strumpf

Designer Mário Feliciano
Nationality PT
Date Designed 1994
Foundries Adobe Linotype
Number of weights 1

ABCDEFGHIJKLMNOPQRSTUVWXYZ

abcdefghijklmnopqrstuvwxyz1234567890

Fred specialized in the job of making very quaint wax toys.

Scratch T-26

Designer Greg Samata
Nationality US
Date Designed 1993
Foundries T-26
Number of weights 1

ABCDEFGHIJKLMNOPQRSTUVWXYZ

abcdefghijklmnopqrstuvwxyz1234567890

Zweedse ex-VIP, behoorlijk gek op quantumfysica.

Coriander

Designer	Timothy Donaldson
Nationality	UK
Date Designed	1995
Foundries	Adobe
Number of weights	1

ABCDEFGHIJKLMNOPQRSTUVWXYZ

ABCDEFGHIJKLMNOPQRSTUVWXYZ1234567890

Five wine experts jokingly quizzed sample chablis.

Letterine

Designer	Alessio Leonardi
Nationality	IT
Date Designed	1995
Foundries	FontFont
Number of weights	1

ABCDEFGHIJKLMNOPQRSTUVWXYZ

abcdefghijklmnopqrstuvwxyz1234567890

Letterine means tiny letters in Italian.

Aspect LT

Designer	Hans-Jürgen Ellenberger
Nationality	DE
Date Designed	1999
Foundries	Linotype
Number of weights	1

ABCDEFGHIJKLMNOPQRSTUVWXYZ

abcdefghijklmnopqrstuvwxyz1234567890

The sex life of the woodchuck is a provocative question for most vertebrate zoology majors.

Mega

Designer	Till F Teenck
Nationality	DE
Date Designed	1996
Foundries	Linotype
Number of weights	1

ABCDEFGHIJKLMNOPQRSTUVWXYZ

abcdefghijklmnopqrstuvwxyz1234567890

Will Major Douglas be expected to take this true-false quiz very soon?

Linotype Labyrinth

Designer	Frank Marciuliano
Nationality	US
Date Designed	2002
Foundries	Linotype
Number of weights	1

ABCDEFGHIJKLMNOPQRSTUVWXYZ

ABCDEFGHIJKLMNOPQRSTUVWXYZ1234567890

GRUMPY WIZARDS MAKE TOXIC BREW FOR THE EVIL QUEEN AND JACK

Linotype Lindy

Designer	Frank Marciuliano
Nationality	US
Date Designed	1997
Foundries	Linotype
Number of weights	1

ABCDEFGHIJKLMNOPQRSTUVWXYZ

abcdefghijklmnopqrstuvwxyz1234567890

We promptly judged antique ivory buckles for the next prize.

Automat

Designer	Frank Marciuliano
Nationality	US
Date Designed	2002
Foundries	Linotype
Number of weights	1

ABCDEFGHIJKLMNOPQRSTUVWXYZ

abcdefghijklmnopqrstuvwxyz1234567890

Change is inevitable. Except from an Automat.

Juanita Deco

Designer	Luis Siquot
Nationality	AR
Date Designed	1996
Foundries	ITC Linotype Monotype
Number of weights	1

ABCDEFGHIJKLMNOPQRSTUVWXYZ

ABCDEFGHIJKLMNOPQRSTUVWXYZ1234567890

HOW QUICKLY DAFT JUMPING ZEBRAS VEX.

Juanita Lino

Designer	Luis Siquot
Nationality	AR
Date Designed	1996
Foundries	ITC Linotype Monotype
Number of weights	1

ABCDEFGHIJKLMNOPQRSTUVWXYZ

ABCDEFGHIJKLMNOPQRSTUVWXYZ1234567890

WALTZ, NYMPH, FOR QUICK JIGS VEX BUD.

Juanita Xilo

Designer	Luis Siquot
Nationality	AR
Date Designed	1996
Foundries	ITC Linotype Monotype
Number of weights	1

ABCDEFGHIJKLMNOPQRSTUVWXYZ

ABCDEFGHIJKLMNOPQRSTUVWXYZ1234567890

THE FIVE BOXING WIZARDS JUMP QUICKLY.

Briem Gauntlet

Designer	Gunnlaugur S E Briem
Nationality	IS
Date Designed	2001
Foundries	Monotype
Number of weights	1

Scriba

Designer	Martin Wait
Nationality	UK
Date Designed	1992
Foundries	Letraset Monotype ITC
Number of weights	1

ABCDEFGHIJKLMNOPQRSTUVWXYZ
ABCDEFGHIJKLMNOPQRSTUVWXYZ1234567890
QUICK WAFTING ZEPHYRS VEX BOLD JIM.

Dummy

Designer	Tad Biernot
Nationality	CA
Date Designed	1996
Foundries	Linotype
Number of weights	1

ABCDEFGHIJKLMNOPQRSTUVWXYZ
abcdefghijklmnopqrstuvwxyz1234567890
A useful font if you plan to publish the works of M C Escher.

Linotype Henri Axis

Designer	Stefan Pott
Nationality	DE
Date Designed	1999
Foundries	Linotype
Number of weights	1

Linotype Henri Dimension

Designer	Stefan Pott
Nationality	DE
Date Designed	1999
Foundries	Linotype
Number of weights	1

ABCDEFGHIJKLMNOPQRSTUVWXYZ
abcdefghijklmnopqrstuvwxyz
1234567890
Pack my box with five dozen liquor jugs.

Archian

Designer	György Szönyei
Nationality	HU
Date Designed	1999
Foundries	FontFont
Number of weights	1

ABCDEFGHIJKLMNOPQRSTUVWXYZ
abcdefghijklmnopqrstuvwxyz1234567890
Exquisite farm wench gives body jolt to prize stinker.

Fiesta

Designer	Steve Miggas
Nationality	UK
Date Designed	1996
Foundries	Monotype
Number of weights	1

ABCDEFGHIJKLMNOPQRSTUVWXYZ
abcdefghijklmnopqrstuvwxyz1234567890
Jim just quit and packed extra bags for Liz Owen.

Kokoa

Designer	Jochen Schuss
Nationality	DE
Date Designed	1996
Foundries	Monotype ITC
Number of weights	1

ABCDEFGHIJKLMNOPQRSTUVWXYZ
ABCDEFGHIJKLMNOPQRSTUVWXYZ1234567890
Sympathizing would fix Quaker objectives.

Zambesi

Designer	Mecanorma
Nationality	FR
Date Designed	1991
Foundries	Mecanorma Monotype
Number of weights	1

ABCDEFGHIJKLMNOPQRSTUVWXYZ
ABCDEFGHIJKLMNOPQRSTUVWXYZ 1234567890
PORTEZ CE VIEUX WHISKY AU JUGE BLOND QUI FUME.

Shaman

Designer	Phill Grimshaw
Nationality	UK
Date Designed	1994
Foundries	Letraset LI
Number of weights	1

ABCDEFGHIJKLMNOPQRSTUVWXYZ
ABCDEFGHIJKLMNOPQRSTUVWXYZ1234567890
JAZZY SAXOPHONES BLEW OVER MICK'S TURGID QUIFF.

Zinjaro

Designer	Carol Kemp
Nationality	UK
Date Designed	1994
Foundries	Letraset ITC
Number of weights	1

ABCDEFGHIJKLMNOPQRSTUVWXYZ
ABCDEFGHIJKLMNOPQRSTUVWXYZ1234567890
ABOUT SIXTY CODFISH EGGS WILL MAKE A QUARTER POUND
OF VERY FIZZY JELLY.

Sassafras

Designer	Arthur Baker
Nationality	US
Date Designed	1990
Foundries	Monotype
Number of weights	1

ABCDEFGHIJKLMNOPQRSTUVWXYZ
abcdefghijklmnopqrstuvwxyz1234567890
Jim just quit and packed extra bags for Liz Owen.

Isis

Designer	Michael Gills
Nationality	UK
Date Designed	1990
Foundries	Letraset Monotype ITC
Number of weights	1

ABCDEFGHIJKLMNOPQRSTUVWXYZ
ABCDEFGHIJKLMNOPQRSTUVWXYZ1234567890
WALTZ, NYMPH, FOR QUICK JIGS VEX BUD.

Lingo

Designer	anon
Nationality	UK
Date Designed	1994
Foundries	ITC
Number of weights	1

ABCDEFGHIJKLMNOPQRSTUVWXYZ
abcdefghijklmnopqrstuvwxyz1234567890
Jeb quickly drove a few extra miles on the glazed pavement.

Oak Graphic

Designer	Arthur Baker
Nationality	US
Date Designed	1990
Foundries	Monotype Glyph Systems
Number of weights	1

ABCDEFGHIJKLMNOPQRSTUVWXYZ
abcdefghijklmnopqrstuvwxyz1234567890
Pack my box with five dozen liquor jugs.

Tangerine

Designer	Monotype
Nationality	UK
Date Designed	2000
Foundries	Monotype
Number of weights	1

ABCDEFGHIJKLMNOPQRSTUVWXYZ
1234567890
JIMMY AND ZACK, THE POLICE EXPLAINED, WERE
LAST SEEN DIVING INTO A FIELD.

CMC-7

Designer	Linotype
Nationality	DE
Date Designed	1994
Foundries	Linotype
Number of weights	1

ABCDEFGHIJKLMNOPQRSTUVWXYZ
ABCDEFGHIJKLMNOPQRSTUVWXYZ12
34567890
MIXZAPEWITHVELJJVICANDSETQUIRKY

Agfa Waddy 191

Designer	Aiko & Hideaki Wada
Nationality	JP
Date Designed	1999
Foundries	Monotype
Number of weights	1

ABCDEFGHIJKLMNOPQRSTUVWXYZ
ABCDEFGHIJKLMNOPQRSTUVWXYZ1234567890
NEW FARM HAND (PICKING JUST SIX QUINCES) PROVES
STRONG BUT LAZY.

Bernard Condensed

Designer	Lucian Bernhard
Nationality	AT
Date Designed	1926
Foundries	Monotype
Number of weights	1

ABCDEFGHIJKLMNOPQRSTUVWXYZ
abcdefghijklmnopqrstuvwxyz1234567890
Think, in this batter'd Caravanserai.

Goudy Extra Bold

Designer	Frederic W Goudy
Nationality	US
Date Designed	1926
Foundries	Monotype
Number of weights	1

ABCDEFGHIJKLMNOPQRSTUVWXYZ
abcdefghijklmnopqrstuvwxyz1234567890
Many-wived Jack laughs at probes of sex quiz.

University Roman

Designer	Letraset
Nationality	UK
Date Designed	1972
Foundries	Letraset
Number of weights	1

ABCDEFGHIJKLMNOPQRSTUVWXYZ
abcdefghijklmnopqrstuvwxyz1234567890
Whose Doorways are alternate Night and Day,

Rundfunk

Designer	Adolf Behrmann
Nationality	DE
Date Designed	1928
Foundries	Linotype
Number of weights	2

ABCDEFGHIJKLMNOPQRSTUVWXYZ
abcdefghijklmnopqrstuvwxyz1234567890
Pack my box with five dozen liquor jugs.

Adastra

Designer	Herbert Thannhaeuser
Nationality	DE
Date Designed	1928
Foundries	Stempel
Number of weights	1

ABCDEFGHIJKLMNOPQRSTUVWXYZ
abcdefghijklmnopqrstuvwxyz1234567890
The five boxing wizards jump quickly.

Torino

Designer	Alessandro Butti
Nationality	IT
Date Designed	1908
Foundries	Nebbiolo
Recut/Digitised by	Ed Benguiat
Number of weights	2

ABCDEFGHIJKLMNOPQRSTUVWXYZ
abcdefghijklmnopqrstuvwxyz1234567890
I can't believe Butti designed this aged 15.

Czykago Standard

Designer	Alexander Branczyk
Nationality	DE
Date Designed	1996
Foundries	Linotype
Number of weights	1

ABCDEFGHIJKLMNOPQRSTUVWXYZ
abcdefghijklmnopqrstuvwxyz1234567890
Like Chicago.

CzykagoTrans

Designer Alexander Branczyk
Nationality DE
Date Designed 1995
Foundries Linotype
Number of weights 1

ABCDEFGHIJKLMNOPQRSTUVWXYZ
abcdefghijklmnopqrstuvwxyz
1234567890
Was never deep in anything but wine.

Schachtelhalm

Designer Ilka Kwiatkowski (Ilka Preuss)
Nationality DE
Date Designed 1995
Foundries Linotype
Number of weights 1

ABCDEFGHIJKLMNOPQRSTUVWXYZ
ABCDEFGHIJKLMNOPQRSTUVWXYZ1234567890
QUICK ZEPHYRS BLOW, VEXING DAFT JIM.

Adamantium

Designer John Roshell
Nationality US
Date Designed 2001
Foundries ITC
Number of weights 1

ABCDEFGHIJKLMNOPQRSTUVWXYZ
abcdefghijklmnopqrstuvwxyz1234567890
A fictional alloy from Marvel Comics.

Vinyl

Designer J Keith Moore
Nationality US
Date Designed 1995
Foundries Linotype ITC Monotype
Number of weights 1

ABCDEFGHIJKLMNOPQRSTUVWXYZ
abcdefghijklmnopqrstuvwxyz1234567890
The sex life of the woodchuck is a provocative question for most vertebrate zoology majors.

Promdate

Designer Adam Roe
Nationality US
Date Designed 1993
Foundries CA Partners
Number of weights 2

ABCDEFGHIJKLMNOPQRSTUVWXYZ
ABCDEFGHIJKLMNOPQRSTUVWXYZ1234567890
Xavier, a wildly informal court jester, kept calling Queen Elizabeth 'Betty.'

Go Tekk

Designer	Critzler
Nationality	DE
Date Designed	1996
Foundries	Linotype
Number of weights	1

ABCDEFGHIJKLMNOPQRSTUVWXYZ
abcdefghijklmnopqrstuvwxyz1234567890

Forsaking monastic tradition, twelve jovial friars gave up their vocation for a questionable existence on the flying trapeze.

Flaco

Designer	Carlos Segura
Nationality	CU
Date Designed	1993
Foundries	Creative Alliance
Number of weights	1

ABCDEFGHIJKLMNOPQRSTUVWXYZ
ABCDEFGHIJKLMNOPQRSTUVWXYZ1234567890

FINE WINE IMPARTS JOININGLY GRIZZLED SIMPLE CHARMS.

Westwood

Designer	David Westwood
Nationality	UK
Date Designed	1991
Foundries	ITC
Number of weights	1

ABCDEFGHIJKLMNOPQRSTUVWXYZ
abcdefghijklmnopqrstuvwxyz1234567890

Hark! Toxic jungle water vipers quietly drop on zebras for meals!

Ponderosa

Designer	Kim Buker, Barbara Lind, Joy Redick
Nationality	US
Date Designed	1990
Foundries	Adobe
Recut/Digitised by	
Number of weights	1

ABCDEFGHIJKLMNOPQRSTUVWXYZ
ABCDEFGHIJKLMNOPQRSTUVWXYZ1234567890

I BELIEVE IN BEING IN STYLE.

Willow

Designer	Joy Redick
Nationality	US
Date Designed	1990
Foundries	Adobe
Number of weights	1

ABCDEFGHIJKLMNOPQRSTUVWXYZ
ABCDEFGHIJKLMNOPQRSTUVWXYZ1234567890

GIVE ME A HOME WHERE THE BUFFALOES USED TO ROAM.

Mesquite

Designer Kim Buker, Barbara Lind, Joy Redick

Nationality US

Date Designed 1990

Foundries Adobe

Number of weights 1

ABCDEFGHIJKLMNOPQRSTUVWXYZ

ABCDEFGHIJKLMNOPQRSTUVWXYZ1234567890

THOSE WIDE OPEN SPACES WITH NOTHING BUT MACDONALDS TO MARK THE MILES.

Pepperwood

Designer Kim Buker Chansler, Carl Crossgrove, Carol Twombly

Nationality US

Date Designed 1994

Foundries Adobe

Number of weights 1

ABCDEFGHIJKLMNOPQRSTUVWXYZ

ABCDEFGHIJKLMNOPQRSTUVWXYZ1234567890

ONE OF ADOBE'S GREAT WOOD WESTERN SERIES.

Italienne

Designer Richard Yeend

Nationality UK

Date Designed 2003

Foundries Linotype

Number of weights 1

ABCDEFGHIJKLMNOPQRSTUVWXYZ

abcdefghijklmnopqrstuvwxyz1234567890

Big Italian female presence in Rhyolite, then

Buffalo Gal

Designer Thomas A Rickner

Nationality US

Date Designed 1992

Foundries Monotype

Number of weights 1

ABCDEFGHIJKLMNOPQRSTUVWXYZ

abcdefghijklmnopqrstuvwxyz1234567890

Home, home on the range.

Birch

Designer Kim Buker, Barbara Lind, Joy Redick

Nationality US

Date Designed 1879

Foundries Adobe

Number of weights 1

ABCDEFGHIJKLMNOPQRSTUVWXYZ

abcdefghijklmnopqrstuvwxyz1234567890

Don't bring back the birch.

Old Town No 536

Designer	URW++
Nationality	DE
Date Designed	1990
Foundries	Linotype Stephenson Blake Elsner+Flake URW++
Recut/Digitised by	Elsner+Flake
Number of weights	2

ABCDEFGHIJKLMNOPQRSTUVWXYZ

abcdefghijklmnopqrstuvwxyz1234567890

Dumpy kibitzer jingles as exchequer overflows.

Zirkus

Designer	URW++
Nationality	DE
Date Designed	2001
Foundries	URW++
Number of weights	3

ABCDEFGHIJKLMNOPQRSTUVWXYZ

ABCDEFGHIJKLMNOPQRSTUVWXYZ1234567890

JELLY-LIKE ABOVE THE HIGH WIRE, SIX QUAKING PACHYDERMS KEPT THE CLIMAX OF THE EXTRAVAGANZA IN A DAZZLING STATE OF FLUX.

Ironwood

Designer	Kim Buker, Barbara Lind, Joy Redick
Nationality	US
Date Designed	1991
Foundries	Adobe Linotype Monotype
Number of weights	1

ABCDEFGHIJKLMNOPQRSTUVWXYZ

ABCDEFGHIJKLMNOPQRSTUVWXYZ1234567890

TREES?WHICH?FLOURISH?IN?HAWAI'I

Wanted

Designer	Letraset
Nationality	UK
Date Designed	1995
Foundries	Letraset Monotype ITC
Number of weights	1

ABCDEFGHIJKLMNOPQRSTUVWXYZ

abcdefghijklmnopqrstuvwxyz1234567890

Fred Nolan is the world's leading expert on Billy the Kid.

Figaro

Designer	Monotype
Nationality	UK
Date Designed	1939
Foundries	Monotype
Number of weights	1

ABCDEFGHIJKLMNOPQRSTUVWXYZ

abcdefghijklmnopqrstuvwxyz1234567890

A popular opera among cow hands.

Westside

Designer	Linotype
Nationality	DE
Date Designed	1993
Foundries	Linotype
Number of weights	1

ABCDEFGHIJKLMNOPQRSTUVWXYZ

abcdefghijklmnopqrstuvwxyz1234567890

New York Cowboys.

Branding Iron

Designer	Monotype
Nationality	UK
Date Designed	1950
Foundries	Monotype
Number of weights	1

ABCDEFGHIJKLMNOPQRSTUVWXYZ

abcdefghijklmnopqrstuvwxyz1234567890

This must hurt!

Poplar

Designer	Adobe Systems
Nationality	US
Date Designed	1830
Foundries	Adobe
Recut/Digitised by	Buker, Lind, Redick, 1990
Number of weights	1

ABCDEFGHIJKLMNOPQRSTUVWXYZ

abcdefghijklmnopqrstuvwxyz1234567890

Moi, je veux quinze clubs a golf et du whisky pur.

MN Circus

Designer	Mecanorma
Nationality	FR
Date Designed	1980
Foundries	Mecanorma Monotype
Number of weights	1

ABCDEFGHIJKLMNOPQRSTUVWXYZ

abcdefghijklmnopqrstuvwxyz1234567890

Western fonts are circus fonts as well.

Juniper

Designer	Kim Buker, Barbara Lind, Joy Redick
Nationality	US
Date Designed	1991
Foundries	Adobe Linotype Monotype
Number of weights	1

ABCDEFGHIJKLMNOPQRSTUVWXYZ

ABCDEFGHIJKLMNOPQRSTUVWXYZ1234567890

ABILENE, PRETTIEST TOWN I EVER SEEN.

Cottonwood

Designer Kim Buker, Barbara Lind, Joy Redick
Nationality US
Date Designed 1991
Foundries Adobe
Number of weights 1

ABCDEFGHIJKLMNOPQRSTUVWXYZ
ABCDEFGHIJKLMNOPQRSTUVWXYZ1234567890
YOU AIN'T SEEN MUCH THEN.

Steel Narrow

Designer Fabrizio Schiavi
Nationality IT
Date Designed 1995
Foundries CA Exclusives
Number of weights 1

ABCDEFGHIJKLMNOPQRSTUVWXYZ
abcdefghijklmnopqrstuvwxyz1234567890
Breezily jangling €3,416,857,209 wise advertiser ambles to the bank, his exchequer amplified.

Steel Moderne

Designer Fabrizio Schiavi
Nationality IT
Date Designed 1995
Foundries CA Exclusives
Number of weights 1

ABCDEFGHIJKLMNOPQRSTUVWXYZ
abcdefghijklmnopqrstuvwxyz1234567890
The sex life of the woodchuck is a provocative question for most vertebrate zoology majors.

PL Davison Americana

Designer M Davison
Nationality US
Date Designed 1950
Foundries Monotype
Number of weights 1

ABCDEFGHIJKLMNOPQRSTUVWXYZ
abcdefghijklmnopqrstuvwxyz1234567890
Farouk Engineer was a great Lancashire cricketer.

Buckeroo

Designer Rick Mueller
Nationality US
Date Designed 1997
Foundries Linotype ITC
Number of weights 1

ABCDEFGHIJKLMNOPQRSTUVWXYZ
ABCDEFGHIJKLMNOPQRSTUVWXYZ
1234567890
A BUCKEROO IS AN AUSTRALIAN DOLLAR, TOO.

Wide Latin

Designer	Stephenson Blake
Nationality	UK
Date Designed	1850
Foundries	Stephenson Blake
Number of weights	1

ABCDEFGHIJKLMN
OPQRSTUVWXYZ
abcdefghijklmnopqrstuvwxyz
1234567890

Zebrawood

Designer	Wells & Webb
Nationality	US
Date Designed	1854
Foundries	Adobe Monotype
Recut/Digitised by	Kim Buker Chansler, Carl Crossgrove, Carol Twombly, 1994
Number of weights	1

ABCDEFGHIJKLMNOPQRSTUVWXYZ
ABCDEFGHIJKLMNOPQRSTUVWXYZ1234567890
PRESUMABLY BLACK AND WHITE STRIPES.

Thunderbird

Designer	ATF Studio
Nationality	US
Date Designed	1925
Foundries	Bitstream Elsner+Flake URW++
Number of weights	2

ABCDEFGHIJKLMN
OPQRSTUVWXYZ
1234567890
PRIDE OF THE ALLEY.

Florinda

Designer	Rob Roy Kelly
Nationality	AR
Date Designed	1997
Foundries	Monotype ITC
Recut/Digitised by	Luis Siquot
Number of weights	1

ABCDEFGHIJKLMNOPQRSTUVWXYZ
ABCDEFGHIJKLMNOPQRSTUVWXYZ1234567890
WHAT WERE MR KELLY'S PARENTS THINKING?

Madrone

Designer	Barbara Lind
Nationality	US
Date Designed	1991
Foundries	Adobe
Number of weights	1

ABCDEFGHIJKLMN
OPQRSTUVWXYZ
abcdefghijklmnopqrst
uvwxyz1234567890

Façade Condensed

Designer	Julius Herriet Sr
Nationality	US
Date Designed	1994
Foundries	Creative Alliance
Recut/Digitised by	Steve Mattesen
Number of weights	1

ABCDEFGHIJKLMNOP
QRSTUVWXYZ
abcdefghijklmnop
qrstuvwxyz1234567890

Blackoak

Designer	Joy Redick
Nationality	US
Date Designed	1990
Foundries	Adobe Linotype
Number of weights	1

ABCDEFGHIJKLMN
OPQRSTUVWXYZ
abcdefghijklmnopqrst
uvwxyz1234567890

Folk

Designer	Ben Shahn
Nationality	US
Date Designed	1940
Foundries	FontFont
Recut/Digitised by	Maurizio Osti, 1995
Number of weights	1

ABCDEFGHIJKLMNOPQRSTUVWXYZ
ABCDEFGHIJKLMNOPQRSTUVWXYZ1234567890
GRUMPY WIZARDS MAKE TOXIC BREW FOR THE EVIL QUEEN
AND JACK.

Ad Lib

Designer	Freeman Craw
Nationality	US
Date Designed	1961
Foundries	ATF Bitstream Monotype
Number of weights	1

ABCDEFGHIJKLMNOPQRSTUVWXYZ
abcdefghijklmnopqrstuvwxyz1234567890
How Sultan after Sultan with his Pomp.

Lino Cut

Designer	Bob Anderton
Nationality	UK
Date Designed	1990
Foundries	Letraset Monotype ITC Linotype
Number of weights	1

ABCDEFGHIJKLMNOPQRSTUVWXYZ
abcdefghijklmnopqrstuvwxyz1234567890
Five wine experts jokingly quizzed sample chablis.

Grunge

Strobos

Designer	Vince Whitlock
Nationality	UK
Date Designed	1990
Foundries	Monotype ITC
Number of weights	1

ABCDEFGHIJKLMNOPQRSTUVWXYZ

ABCDEFGHIJKLMNOPQRSTUVWXYZ1234567890

BACK IN JUNE WE DELIVERED OXYGEN EQUIPMENT OF THE SAME SIZE.

Bitmax

Designer	Alan R Birch
Nationality	UK
Date Designed	1990
Foundries	Linotype ITC Letraset
Number of weights	1

ABCDEFGHIJKLMNOPQRSTUVWXYZ

ABCDEFGHIJKLMNOPQRSTUVWXYZ1234567890

THE JOB OF WAXING LINOLEUM FREQUENTLY PEEVES CHINTZY KIDS.

Fudoni

Designer	Max Kisman
Nationality	US
Date Designed	1991
Foundries	FontFont
Number of weights	1

ABCDEFGHIJKLMNOPQRSTUVWXYZ

abcdefghijklmnopqrstuvwxyz1234567890

Quick wafting zephyrs vex bold Jim.

Lavaman

Designer	Chank Diesel
Nationality	US
Date Designed	1992
Foundries	Chank Monotype
Number of weights	1

ABCDEFGHIJKLMNOPQRSTUVWXYZ

abcdefghijklmnopqrstuvwxyz1234567890

Mix Zapf with Veljovic and get quirky Beziers.

Stamp Gothic

Designer	Just van Rossum
Nationality	NL
Date Designed	1992
Foundries	FontFont
Number of weights	1

ABCDEFGHIJKLMNOPQRSTUVWXYZ

abcdefghijklmnopqrstuvwxyz1234567890

Six crazy kings vowed to abolish my quite pitiful jousts.

F2F Allineato

Designer	Alessio Leonardi
Nationality	IT
Date Designed	1992
Foundries	Linotype
Number of weights	1

ABCDEFGHIJKLMNOPQRSTUVWXYZ

abcdefghijklmnopqrstuvwxyz1234567890

If you read Allineato as one word, it means "put on a line"

Adolescence

Designer	Adam Roe
Nationality	US
Date Designed	1993
Foundries	Monotype
Number of weights	4

ABCDEFGHIJKLMNOPQRSTUVWXYZ

abcdefghijklmnopqrstuvwxyz1234567890

Mr. Jock, TV quiz Ph.D., bags few lynx.

Badoni

Designer	Chank Diesel
Nationality	US
Date Designed	1993
Foundries	Monotype
Number of weights	1

ABCDEFGHIJKLMNOPQRSTUVWXYZ

abcdefghijklmnopqrstuvwxyz1234567890

Xavier, a wildly informal court jester, kept calling Queen Elizabeth 'Betty.'

Riot

Designer	Mark Allen
Nationality	US
Date Designed	1993
Foundries	T-26
Number of weights	1

abcdwfghijklmnopqr@tuvw⊗yz123456789a

the quick brown fo⊗ jump@ over the lazy dog.

Handwrite Inkblot

Designer	Todd Brei
Nationality	US
Date Designed	1993
Foundries	T26
Number of weights	1

ABCDEFGHIJKLMNOPQRSTUVWXYZ

abcdefghijklmnopqrstuvwxyz1234567890

Portez ce vieux whisky au juge blond qui fume.

Variator

Designer	Jim Marcus
Nationality	US
Date Designed	1993
Foundries	T-26
Number of weights	1

ABCDEFGHIJKLMNOPQRSTUVWXYZ
ABCDEFGHIJKLMNOPQRSTUVWXYZ1234567890
WE PROMPTLY JUDGED ANTIQUE IVORY BUCKLES FOR THE NEXT PRIZE.

Harlem

Designer	Neville Brody
Nationality	UK
Date Designed	1993
Foundries	FontFont
Number of weights	1

ABCDEFGHIJKLMNOPQRSTUVWXYZ
abcdefghijklmnopqrstuvwxyz1234567890
The five boxing wizards jump quickly.

Nowwhat

Designer	Adam Roe
Nationality	US
Date Designed	1993
Foundries	Monotype
Number of weights	1

ABCDEFGHIJKLMNOPQRSTUVWXYZ
abcdefghijklmnopqrstuvwxyz1234567890
Jackdaws love my big sphinx of quartz.

F2F Al Retto

Designer	Alessio Leonardi
Nationality	IT
Date Designed	1993
Foundries	Linotype
Number of weights	1

ABCDEFGHIJKLMNOPQRSTUVWXYZ
abcdefghijklmnopqrstuvwxyz1234567890
Al stands for Alessio, Retto means straight line, and also
the end of the digestive system.

Epicure

Designer	Adam Roe
Nationality	US
Date Designed	1994
Foundries	T-26
Number of weights	2

ABCDEFGHIJKLMNOPQRSTUVWXYZ
ABCDEFGHIJKLMNOPQRSTUVWXYZ1234567890
JACKDAWS LOVE MY BIG SPHINX OF QUARTZ.

Facsimiled

Designer	Pete McCracken
Nationality	UK
Date Designed	1994
Foundries	Monotype
Number of weights	1

ABCDEFGHIJKLMNOPQRSTUVWXYZ
abcdefghijklmnopqrstuvwxyz1234567890
Dumpy kibitzer jingles as exchequer overflows.

Hatmaker

Designer	Jean Evans
Nationality	US
Date Designed	1994
Foundries	Monotype
Number of weights	1

ABCDEFGHiJKLMNOPQRSTUVWXYZ
ABCDEFGHIJKLMNOPQRSTUVWXYZ1234567890
NOW IS THE TIME FOR ALL BROWN DOGS TO JUMP OVER THE LAZY LYNX.

Morire

Designer	Hariette Gorn
Nationality	DE
Date Designed	1994
Foundries	Monotype
Number of weights	1

ABCDEFGHIJKLMNOPQRSTUVWXYZ
abcdefghijklmnopqrstuvwxyz1234567890
Jay visited back home and gazed upon a brown fox and quail.

Pink

Designer	Timothy Donaldson
Nationality	UK
Date Designed	1994
Foundries	ITC
Number of weights	1

ABCDEFGHIJKLMNOPQRSTUVWXYZ
abcdefghijklmnopqrstuvwxyz1234567890
No kidding, Lorenzo called off his trip to visit Mexico City just because they told him the
conquistadores were extinct.

Missive

Designer	Stephen Farrell
Nationality	US
Date Designed	1994
Foundries	T-26 Monotype
Number of weights	1

ABCDEFGHIJKLMNOPQRSTUVWXYZ
abcdefghijklmnopqrstuvwxyz1234567890
Breezily jangling $3,416,857,209,wise advertiser ambles to the bank, his
exchequer amplified.

Ekttor

Designer	Fabian Rottke
Nationality	DE
Date Designed	1994
Foundries	FontFont
Number of weights	3

ABCDEFGHIJKLMNOPQRSTUVWXYZ
ABCDEFGHIJKLMNOPQRSTUVWXYZ1234567890
NOW IS THE TIME FOR ALL BROWN DOGS TO JUMP OVER
THE LAZY LYNX.

Irregular

Designer	Markus Hanzer
Nationality	DE/GB
Date Designed	1994
Foundries	FontFont
Number of weights	1

ABCDEFGHIJKLMNOPQRSTUVWXYZ
abcdefghijklmnopqrstuvwxyz1234567890
Viewing quizzical abstracts mixed up hefty jocks.

Meta Plus Boiled

Designer	Erik Spiekermann, Neville Brody
Nationality	DE
Date Designed	1994
Foundries	FontFont
Number of weights	1

ABCDEFGHIJKLMNOPQRSTUVWXYZ
abcdefghijklmnopqrstuvwxyz1234567890
Verbatim reports were quickly given by Jim Fox to his amazed audience.

Metamorph

Designer	Markus Hanzer
Nationality	DE
Date Designed	1994
Foundries	FontFont
Number of weights	1

ABCDEFGHIJKLMNOPQRSTUVWXYZ
abcdefghijklmnopqrstuvwxyz1234567890
About sixty codfish eggs will make a quarter pound of very fizzy jelly.

Witches

Designer	Manfred Klein
Nationality	DE
Date Designed	1994
Foundries	FontFont
Number of weights	1

ABCDEFGHIJKLMNOPQRSTUVWXYZ
abcdefghijklmnopqrstuvwxyz1234567890
William Jex quickly caught five dozen Conservatives.

Zakk Globe

Designer	Thomas Nagel
Nationality	DE
Date Designed	1994
Foundries	Linotype
Number of weights	1

ABCDEFGHIJKLMNOPQRSTUVWXYZ
abcdefghijklmnopqrstuvwxyz 1234567890
Totally illegible.

Innercity

Designer	James Closs
Nationality	DE
Date Designed	1994
Foundries	FontFont
Number of weights	1

ABCDEFGHIJKLMNOPQRSTUVWXYZ
ABCDefGHIJKLMNOPQRSTuvwxy 1234567890
JAy vISITeD BACK HOMe AND GASeD uPON A BROwN fOx AND QuAIL

Schmelvetica

Designer	chester
Nationality	DE
Date Designed	1994
Foundries	FontFont
Number of weights	1

ABCDEFGHIJKLMNOPQRSTUVWXYZ
abcdefghijklmnopqrstuvwxyz1234567890
My grandfather picks up quartz and valuable onyx jewels.

Mulinex

Designer	Alessio Leonardi
Nationality	IT
Date Designed	1994
Foundries	FontFont
Number of weights	1

ABCDEFGHIJKLMNOPQRSTUVWXYZ
abcdefghijklmnopqrstuvwxyz1234567890
The movement of the machine has changed the forms of the letters.

Cavolfiore

Designer	Alessio Leonardi
Nationality	IT
Date Designed	1994
Foundries	FontFont
Number of weights	1

ABCDEFGHIJKLMNOPQRSTUVWXYZ
abcdefghijklmnopqrstuvwxyz1234567890
Italian for cauliflower. The font looks like a cauliflower.

Agfa Peppermint

Designer	Wildwood Creations
Nationality	UK
Date Designed	1997
Foundries	Monotype
Number of weights	1

ABCDEFGHIJKLMNOPQRSTUVWXYZ

abcdefghijklmnopqrstuvwxyz1234567890

The exodus of jazzy pigeons is craved by squeamish walkers.

Coltello

Designer	Alessio Leonardi
Nationality	IT
Date Designed	1994
Foundries	FontFont
Number of weights	2

ABCDEFGHIJKLMNOPQRSTUVWXYZ

ABCDEFGHIJKLMNOPQRSTUVWXYZ1234567890

Italian for knife. "In a good Pizzeria the knives never cut," adds
the designer mysteriously.

Baukasten

Designer	Alessio Leonardi
Nationality	IT
Date Designed	1995
Foundries	FontFont
Number of weights	10

ABCDEFGHIJKLMNOPQRSTUVWXYZ

abcdefghijklmnopqrstuvwxyz1234567890

Based on children's building blocks.

Carnival

Designer	Jim Marcus
Nationality	US
Date Designed	1995
Foundries	Monotype
Number of weights	1

ABCDEFGHIJKLMNOPQRSTUVWXYZ

ABCDEFGHIJKLMNOPQRSTUVWXYZ

JEB QUICKLY DROVE A FEW EXTRA MILES ON
THE GLAZED PAVEMENT.

Moonshine Murky

Designer	Chank Diesel
Nationality	US
Date Designed	1995
Foundries	Chank
Number of weights	1

ABCDEFGHIJKLMNOPQRSTUVWXYZ

abcdefghijklmnopqrstuvwxyz1234567890

Freight to me sixty dozen quart jars and twelve black pans.

Replicant

Designer	Adam Roe
Nationality	US
Date Designed	1995
Foundries	Monotype
Number of weights	1

ABCDEFGHIJKLMNOPQRSTUVWXYZ
abcdefghijklmnopqrstuvwxyz1234567890

Mr. Jock, TV quiz Ph.D., bags few lynx.

Smack

Designer	Jill Bell
Nationality	US
Date Designed	1995
Foundries	ITC
Number of weights	1

ABCDEFGHIJKLMNOPQRSTUVWXYZ
abcdefghijklmnopqrstuvwxyz1234567890

Ralph Steadman and Gerald Scarfe are two great British cartoonists

Time In Hell

Designer	Carlos Segura
Nationality	CU
Date Designed	1995
Foundries	T-26
Number of weights	1

ABCDEFGHIJKLMNOPQRSTUVWXYZ
abcdefghijklmnopqrstuvwxyz1234567890

Verbatim reports were quickly given by Jim Fox to his amazed audience.

Wet and Wilde

Designer	Marty Bee
Nationality	US
Date Designed	1995
Foundries	CA Partners
Number of weights	1

ABCDEFGHIJKLMNOPQRSTUVWXYZ
abcdefghijklmnopqrstuvwxyz1 2 3 4 5 6 7 8 9 0

Forsaking monastic tradition, twelve jovial friars gave up their vocation for a questionable existence on the flying trapeze.

Chipper

Designer	Andrew Smith
Nationality	UK
Date Designed	1995
Foundries	Linotype ITC
Number of weights	1

ABCDEFGHIJKLMNOPQRSTUVWXYZ
abcdefghijklmnopqrstuvwxyz1234567890

Jeb quickly drove a few extra miles on the glazed pavement.

Bludgeon

Designer Jon H Clinch
Nationality US
Date Designed 1995
Foundries Monotype
Number of weights 1

ABCDEFGHIJKLMNOPQRSTUVWXYZ

abcdefghijklmnopqrstuvwxyz1234567890

Portez ce vieux whisky au juge blond qui fume

Scratched Out

Designer Pierre di Sciullo
Nationality IT
Date Designed 1995
Foundries FontFont
Number of weights 1

ABCDEFGHIJKLMNOPQRSTUVWXYZ

abcdefghijklmnopqrstuvwxyz1234567890

Dumpy kibitzer jingles as exchequer overflows.

Singer

Designer Matthias Thiesen, Stefan Hägerling
Nationality DE
Date Designed 1995
Foundries FontFont
Number of weights 1

ABCDEFGHIJKLMNOPQRSTUVWXYZ

abcdefghijklmnopqrstuvwxyz1234567890

Exquisite farm wench gives body jolt to prize stinker.

Steel

Designer Fabrizio Schiavi
Nationality IT
Date Designed 1995
Foundries FontFont
Number of weights 1

ABCDEFGHIJKLMNOPQRSTUVWXYZ

ABCDEFGHIJKLMNOPQRSTUVWXYZ1234567890

JACK AMAZED A FEW GIRLS BY DROPPING THE ANTIQUE ONYX VASE!

Dirty Fax

Designer Fabian Rottke
Nationality DE
Date Designed 1995
Foundries FontFont
Number of weights 1

ABCDEFGHIJKLMNOPQRSTUVWXYZ

abcdefghijklmnopqrstuvwxyz1234567890

How do equal the fins record by solving six puzzles a week?

Motive

Designer	Stefan Hägerling
Nationality	DE
Date Designed	1995
Foundries	FontFont
Number of weights	1

ABCDEFGHIJKLVNCPQRSTUVWXYZ

abcdefghijklmnopqrstuvwxyz1234567890

Verbatim reports were quickly given by Jim Fox to his amazed audience.

Graffio

Designer	Alessio Leonardi
Nationality	IT
Date Designed	1995
Foundries	FontFont
Number of weights	3

ABCDEFGHIJKLMNOPQRSTUVWXYZ

abcdefghijklmnopqrstuvwxyz1234567890

Graffio means scratch. Look at the font.

INKy-black

Designer	Pete McCracken
Nationality	US
Date Designed	1995
Foundries	Monotype
Number of weights	1

ABCDEFGHIJKLMNOPQRSTUVWXYZ

abcdefghijklmnopqrstuvwxyz1234567890

Jazzy saxophones blew over Mick's turgid quiff.

Iodine

Designer	Stephan Müller
Nationality	DE
Date Designed	1995
Foundries	FontFont
Number of weights	3

ABCDEFGHIJKLMNOPQRSTUVWXYZ

abcdefghijklmnopqrstuvwxyz1234567890

Brawny gods just flocked up to quiz and vex him.

Littles

Designer	Simone Schöpp
Nationality	DE
Date Designed	1995
Foundries	FontFont
Number of weights	1

ABCDEFGHIJKLMNOPQRSTUVWXYZ

ABCDEFGHIJKLMNOPQRSTUVWXYZ1234567890

ALL QUESTIONS ASKED BY FIVE WATCH EXPERTS AMAZED THE JUDGE.

F2F MadZine Fear

Designer	Alexander Branczyk
Nationality	DE
Date Designed	1994
Foundries	Take Type 5
Number of weights	1

ABCDEFGHIJKLMNOPQRSTUVWXYZ

abcdefghijklmnopqrstuvwxyz1234567890

Back in June we delivered oxygen equipment of the same size.

Meta Plus Subnormal

Designer	Erik Spiekermann, Neville Brody
Nationality	DE/UK
Date Designed	1995
Foundries	FontFont
Number of weights	1

ABCDEFGHIJKLMNOPQRSTUVWXYZ

abcdefghijklmnopqrstuvwxyz1234567890

When we go back to Juarez, Mexico, do we fly over picturesque Arizona?

Persona

Designer	Franko Luin
Nationality	SL
Date Designed	1995
Foundries	Linotype
Number of weights	1

ABCDEFGHIJKLMNOPQRSTUVWXYZ

abcdefghijklmnopqrstuvwxyz1234567890

Exquisite farm wench gives body jolt to prize stinker.

Rufnu

Designer	Paul Bissex
Nationality	US
Date Designed	1995
Foundries	Monotype
Number of weights	1

ABCDEFGHIJKLMNOPQRSTUVWXYZ

abcdefghijklmnopqrstuvwxyz1234567890

The juke box music puzzled a gentle visitor from a quaint valley town.

Voodoo

Designer	Klaus Dieter Lettau
Nationality	DE
Date Designed	1995
Foundries	FontFont
Number of weights	1

ABCDEFGHIJKLMNOPQRSTUVWXYZ

abcdefghijklmnopqrstuvwxyz1234567890

Mix Zapf with Veljovic and get quirky Beziers.

F2F WhaleTree

Designer	Thomas Nagel
Nationality	DE
Date Designed	1995
Foundries	Linotype
Number of weights	1

ABCDEFGHIJKLMNOPQRSTUVWXYZ
abcdefghijklmnopqrstuvwxyz1234567890
Brawny gods just flocked up to quiz and vex him.

F2F Burnout Chaos

Designer	Alexander Branczyk
Nationality	DE
Date Designed	1993
Foundries	Linotype
Number of weights	1

ABCDEFGHIJKLMNOPQRSTUVWXYZ
abcdefghijklmnopqrstuvwxyz1234567890
The job of waxing linoleum frequently peeves chintzy kids.

F2F MadZine Script

Designer	Alexander Branczyk
Nationality	DE
Date Designed	1994
Foundries	Take Type 5
Number of weights	1

ABCDEFGHIJKLMNOPQRSTUVWXYZ
abcdefghijklmnopqrstuvwxyz1234567890
Back in June we delivered oxygen equipment of the same size.

F2F MadZine Wip

Designer	Alexander Branczyk
Nationality	DE
Date Designed	1994
Foundries	Take Type 5
Number of weights	1

ABCDEFGHIJKLMNOPQRSTUVWXYZ
abcdefghijklmnopqrstuvwxyz1234567890
Freight to me sixty dozen quart jars and twelve black pans.

F2F MadZine Dirt

Designer	Alexander Branczyk
Nationality	DE
Date Designed	1994
Foundries	Take Type 5
Number of weights	1

ABCDEFGHIJKLMNOPQRSTUVWXYZ
abcdefghijklmnopqrstuvwxyz1234567890
Questions of a zealous nature have become by degrees petty waxen jokes.

Carumba

Designer	Jill Bell
Nationality	US
Date Designed	1996
Foundries	Letraset ITC
Number of weights	2

ABCDEFGHIJKLMNOPQRSTUVWXYZ

abcdefghijklmnopqrstuvwxyz1234567890

The exodus of jazzy pigeons is craved by squeamish walkers.

Mediterraneo LT

Designer	Frank Marciuliano
Nationality	US
Date Designed	1996
Foundries	Linotype
Number of weights	1

ABCDEFGHIJKLMNOPQRSTUVWXYZ

abcdefghijklmnopqrstuvwxyz1234567890

My grandfather picks up quartz and valuable onyx jewels.

Orbital

Designer	Chank Diesel
Nationality	US
Date Designed	1996
Foundries	Chank
Number of weights	1

abcdefghijklmnopqrstuvwxyz

abcdefghijklmnopqrstuvwxyz1234567890

will major douglas be expected to take this true=false quiz very soon?

Orbus Multiserif

Designer	Chank Diesel
Nationality	US
Date Designed	1996
Foundries	Chank
Number of weights	1

ABCDEFGHIJKLMNOPQRSTUVWXYZ

abcdefghijklmnopqrstuvwxyz1234567890

Just work for improved basic techniques to maximize your typing skill.

Residoo

Designer	Roger Luteyn
Nationality	US
Date Designed	1996
Foundries	CA Partners
Number of weights	1

ABCDEFGHIJKLMNOPQRSTUVWXYZ

abcdefghijklmnopqrstuvwxyz1234567890

Pack my box with five dozen liquor jugs.

Schizoid

Designer	Frank Marciuliano
Nationality	US
Date Designed	1996
Foundries	ITC
Number of weights	1

ABCDEFGHIJKLMNOPQRSTUVWXYZ

abcdefghijklmnopqrstuvwxyz1234567890

Waltz, nymph, for quick jigs vex Bud.

Angst

Designer	Jürgen Hüber
Nationality	DE
Date Designed	1996
Foundries	FontFont
Number of weights	1

ABCDEFGHIJKLMNOPQRSTUVWXYZ

abcdefghijklmnopqrstuvwxyz1234567890

We promptly judged antique ivory buckles for the next prize.

Cadavre Exquis

Designer	Wiebke Höljes, Erik Faulhaber
Nationality	DE
Date Designed	1996
Foundries	Linotype
Number of weights	1

ABCDEFGHIJKLMNOPQRSTUVWXYZ

abcdefghijklmnopqrstuvwxyz1234567890

Moi, je veux quinze clubs a golf et du whisky pur.

Cerny

Designer	Mark Van Wageningen
Nationality	NL
Date Designed	1996
Foundries	Linotype
Number of weights	1

ABCDEFGHIJKLMNOPQRSTUVWXYZ

ABCDEFGHIJKLMNOPQRSTUVWXYZ1234567890

QUICK ZEPHYRS BLOW, VEXING DAFT JIM.

Dot

Designer	Lucy Davies
Nationality	UK
Date Designed	1996
Foundries	Linotype
Number of weights	1

ABCDEFGHIJKLMNOPQRSTUVWXYZ

abcdefghijklmnopqrstuvwxyz1234567890

Jay visited back home and gazed upon a brown fox and quail.

Dotty

Designer	Eva Walter, Ole Schäfer
Nationality	DE
Date Designed	1996
Foundries	FontFont
Number of weights	1

ABCDEFGHIJKLMNOPQRSTUVWXYZ
abcdefghijklmnopqrstuvwxyz1234567890
Job quickly drove a few extra miles on the glazed pavement.

Dutch Oven

Designer	Exploding
Nationality	US
Date Designed	1996
Foundries	CA Partners
Number of weights	1

ABCDEFGHIJKLTTNOPQRSTUVWXYZ
abcdefghijklmnopqrstuvwxyz1234567890
Breezily jangling $3,416,857,209, wise advertiser ambles to the bank,
his exchequer amplified.

Fresh Ewka

Designer	Dariusz Nowak-Nova
Nationality	PL
Date Designed	1996
Foundries	Linotype
Number of weights	1

ABCDEFGHIJKLMNOPQRSTUVWXYZ
abcdefghijklmnopqrstuvwxyz1234567890
Was there a quorum of able whizzkids gravely exciting the
jaded fish at ATug?

F2F Matto

Designer	Alessio Leonardi
Nationality	IT
Date Designed	1996
Foundries	FontFont
Number of weights	1

ABCDEFGHIJKLMNOPQRSTUVWXYZ
abcdefghijklmnopqrstuvwxyz1234567890
Matto means crazy. It is the first version of Leonardi's font Aposto, which
means OK? Matto and Aposto are brothers, but they don't like each other?

Not Painted

Designer	Robert Bucan
Nationality	DE
Date Designed	1996
Foundries	Linotype
Number of weights	1

ABCDEFGHIJKLMNOPQRSTUVWXYZ
ABCDEFGHIJKLMNOPQRSTUVWXYZ1234567890
WALTZ, NYMPH, FOR QUICK JIGS VEX BUD.

Russisch Brot

Designer	Markus Remscheid
Nationality	DE
Date Designed	1996
Foundries	Linotype
Number of weights	1

ABCDEFGHIJKLMNOPQRSTUVWXYZ

abcdefghijklmnopqrstuvwxyz1234567890

Verbatim reports were quickly given by Jim Fox to his amazed audience.

Red Babe

Designer	Moritz Majce
Nationality	AT
Date Designed	1996
Foundries	Linotype
Number of weights	1

ABCDEFGHIJKLMNOPQRSTUVWXYZ

abcdefghijklmnopqrstuvwxyz1234567890

Five or six big jet planes zoomed quickly by the tower.

Localiser Clones

Designer	Critzler
Nationality	DE
Date Designed	1996
Foundries	FontFont
Number of weights	1

ABCDEFGHIJKLMNOPQRSTUVWXYZ

abcdefghijklmnopqrstuvwxyz1234567890

Just keep examining every low bid quoted for zinc etchings.

Escalido

Designer	Jim Marcus
Nationality	US
Date Designed	1997
Foundries	T-26 Monotype
Number of weights	2

ABCDEFGHIJKLMNOPQRSTUVWXYZ

abcdefghijklmnopqrstuvwxyz1234567890

Questions of a zealous nature have become by degrees petty waxen jokes.

Bionic

Designer	Thomas Critzler Bierschenk
Nationality	DE
Date Designed	1997
Foundries	FontFont
Number of weights	1

ABCDEFGHIJKLMNOPQRSTUVWXYZ

abcdefghijklmnopqrstuvwxyz1234567890

Questions of a zealous nature have become by degrees petty waxen jokes.

Franklinstein

Designer	Fabian Rottke
Nationality	DE
Date Designed	1997
Foundries	FontFont
Number of weights	1

ABCDEFGHIJKLMN
OPQRSTUVWXYZ
1234567890
President Clinton.

Konflikt

Designer	Stefan Pott
Nationality	DE
Date Designed	1997
Foundries	Linotype
Number of weights	1

ABCDEFGHIJKLMNOPQRSTUVWXYZ
abcdefghijklmnopqrstuvwxyz1234567890
Hybrid bold sans and formal script.

Kropki

Designer	anon
Nationality	DE
Date Designed	1997
Foundries	Linotype
Number of weights	1

ABCDEFGHIJKLMNOPQRSTUVWXYZ
abcdefghijklmnopqrstuvwxyz1234567890
West quickly gave Bert large impromptu prizes for six juicy plums.

Pious Henry

Designer	Eric Stevens
Nationality	US
Date Designed	1997
Foundries	ITC
Number of weights	1

ABCDEFGHIJKLMNOPQRSTUVWXYZ
abcdefghijklmnopqrstuvwxyz1234567890
Crazy Fredericka bought many very exquisite opal jewels.

Linotype Pine

Designer	anon
Nationality	DE
Date Designed	1997
Foundries	Linotype
Number of weights	1

ABCDEFGHIJKLMNOPQRSTUVWXYZ
abcdefghijklmnopqrstuvwxyz1234567890
Alfredo just must bring very exciting news to the plaza quickly.

Jiggery Pokery

Designer	Carol Kemp
Nationality	UK
Date Designed	1998
Foundries	Monotype ITC Letraset
Number of weights	1

ABCDEFGHIJKLMNOPQRSTUVWXYZ
abcdefghijklmnopqrstuvwxyz1234567890

Forsaking monastic tradition, twelve jovial friars gave up their vocation for a questionable existence on the flying trapeze.

Kurt

Designer	Vivien Palloks
Nationality	DE
Date Designed	1998
Foundries	FontFont
Number of weights	3

ABCDEFGHIJKLMNOPQRSTUVWXYZ
abcdefghijklmnopqrstuvwxyz1234567890

Just keep examining every low bid quoted for zinc etchings.

Tremor

Designer	Alan Dempsey
Nationality	UK
Date Designed	1998
Foundries	ITC
Number of weights	1

ABCDEFGHIJKLMNOPQRSTUVWXYZ
abcdefghijklmnopqrstuvwxyz1234567890

Sexy qua lijf, doch bang voor het zwempak.

Fatsam

Designer	Stu's Font Diner
Nationality	US
Date Designed	1998
Foundries	Stu's Font Diner
Number of weights	1

ABCDEFGHIJKLMNOPQRSTUVWXYZ
ABCDEFGHIJKLMNOPQRSTUVWXYZ1234567890

WHEN WE GO BACK TO JUAREZ, MEXICO, DO WE FLY OVER PICTURESQUE ARIZONA?

Kentuckyfried

Designer	Stu's Font Diner
Nationality	US
Date Designed	1998
Foundries	Stu's Font Diner
Number of weights	1

ABCDEFGHIJKLMNOPQRSTUVWXYZ
abcdefghijklmnopqrstuvwxyz1234567890

Murky haze enveloped a city as jarring quakes broke forty-six windows.

Taylors

Designer	Stu's Font Diner
Nationality	US
Date Designed	1998
Foundries	Font Diner CA Exclusives
Number of weights	1

ABCDEFGHIJKLMNOPQRSTUVWXYZ
ABCDEFGHIJKLMNOPQRSTUVWXYZ1234567890
WILLIAM SAID THAT EVERYTHING ABOUT HIS JACKET WAS IN QUITE GOOD
CONDITION EXCEPT FOR THE ZIPPER.

Linotype Element

Designer	Jan Tomás
Nationality	CZ
Date Designed	1999
Foundries	Linotype
Number of weights	1

ABCDEFGHIJKLMNOPQRSTUVWXYZ
abcdefghijklmnopqrstuvwxyz1234567890
Jimmy and Zack, the police explained, were last
seen diving into a field of buttered quahogs.

Grassy

Designer	Inka Menne
Nationality	DE
Date Designed	1999
Foundries	Linotype
Number of weights	1

ABCDEFGHIJKLMNOPQRSTUVWXYZ
abcdefghijklmnopqrstuvwxyz1234567890
Sphinx of black quartz, judge my vow.

Linotype Barock

Designer	Jean-Jacques Tachdjian
Nationality	FR
Date Designed	2000
Foundries	Linotype
Number of weights	1

ABCDEFGHIJKLMNOPQRSTUVWXYZ
abcdefghijklmnopqrstuvwxyz1234567890
Six big juicy steaks sizzled in a pan as five workmen left the quarry.

Linotype Dropink

Designer	Christine Voigts
Nationality	DE
Date Designed	2000
Foundries	Linotype
Number of weights	1

ABCDEFGHIJKLMNOPQRSTUVWXYZ
ABCDEFGHIJKLMNOPQRSTUVWXYZ1234567890
The exodus of jazzy pigeons is craved by squeamish walkers.

Linotype Transis

Designer Kelvin Tan Tec Loong
Nationality CH
Date Designed 2000
Foundries Linotype
Number of weights 1

ABCDEFGHIJKLMNOPQRSTUVWXYZ
abcdefghijklmnopqrstuvwxyz1234567890
Zweedse ex-VIP, behoorlijk gek op quantumfysica.

Linotype Wildfont

Designer Meike Sander
Nationality DE
Date Designed 2000
Foundries Linotype
Number of weights 1

ABCDEFGHIJKLMNOPQRSTUVWXYZ
ABCDEFGHIJKLMNOPQRSTUVWXYZ1234567890
PLAYING JAZZ VIBE CHORDS QUICKLY EXCITES MY WIFE.

Don't Panic ITC

Designer Wayne Thompson
Nationality AU
Date Designed 2000
Foundries ITC
Number of weights 1

ABCDEFGHIJKLMNOPQRSTUVWXYZ
ABCDEFGHIJKLMNOPQRSTUVWXYZ1234567890
HOW QUICKLY DAFT JUMPING ZEBRAS VEX.

Merss ITC

Designer Eduardo Manso
Nationality ES
Date Designed 2000
Foundries ITC
Number of weights 1

ABCDEFGHIJKLMNOPQRSTUVWXYZ
abcdefghijklmnopqrstuvwxyz1234567890
Puzzled women bequeath jerks very exotic gifts.

Linotype Ordinar Double

Designer Lutz Baar
Nationality DE
Date Designed 1999
Foundries Linotype
Number of weights 1

ABCDEFGHIJKLMNOPQRSTUVWXYZ
abcdefghijklmnopqrstuvwxyz1234567890
Many big jackdaws quickly zipped over the fox pen.

Arty

Designer Barbara Mendelson
Nationality US
Date Designed 2001
Foundries Monotype
Number of weights 1

A⌂Jʔ JEFꟳᵒᵒiʊKLⓜMNMNR.RʃTUVMꝨꝨꝛ
ABCDEFGHIJKLMNOPQRSTUVWXYZ1234567890
JHACK IN MY QUAINT GARDEN JAUNTY ZINNIAS VIE WITH FLAUNTING PHLOX.

Blockade

Designer Hans Bacher
Nationality DE
Date Designed 2001
Foundries Monotype
Number of weights 1

ABCDEFGHIJKLMNOPQR.STUVWXYZ
ABCDEFGHIJKLMNOPQR.STUVWXYZ1234567890
THE JUKE BOX MUSIC PUZZLED A GENTLE VISITOR FROM A QUAINT VALLEY TOWN.

GitchHand

Designer Kenneth Gitschier
Nationality DE
Date Designed 2001
Foundries Monotype
Number of weights 1

ABCDEFGHIJKLMNOPQRSTUVWXYZ
abcdefghijklmnopqrstuvwxyz1234567890
Questions of a zedious nature have become by degrees petty woven jokes.

Ottofont

Designer Barbara Klunder
Nationality CA
Date Designed 2001
Foundries FontFont
Number of weights 5

ABCDEFGHIJKLMNOPQRSTUVWXYZ
abcdefghijklmnopqrstuvwxyz1234567890
A large fawn jumped quickly over white zinc boxes.

Assuri

Designer Fabian Rottke
Nationality DE
Date Designed 2002
Foundries FontFont
Number of weights 1

ABCDEFGHIJKLMNOPQRSTUVWXYZ
abcdefghijklmnopqrstuvwxyz1234567890
While waxing parquet decks, jaunty Suez sailors vomit abaft.

Linotype Leggodt

Designer	anon
Nationality	DE
Date Designed	2002
Foundries	Linotype
Number of weights	3

ABCDEFGHIJKLMNOPQRSTUVWXYZ

abcdefghijklmnopqrstuvwxyz1234567890

The exodus of jazzy pigeons is craved by squeamish walkers.

F2F Haakonsen

Designer	Stefan Hauser
Nationality	DE
Date Designed	1994
Foundries	Linotype
Number of weights	1

Achispado

Designer	Richard Yeend
Nationality	UK
Date Designed	2003
Foundries	Linotype
Number of weights	1

ABCDEFGHIJKLMNOPQRSTUVWXYZ

abcdefghijklmnopqrstuvwxyz1274567890

Sixty zippers were quickly picked from the woven jute bag.

F2F Styletti

Designer	Sibylle Schlaich
Nationality	DE
Date Designed	1996
Foundries	Linotype
Number of weights	1

ABCDEFGHIJKLMNOPQRSTUVWXYZ

abcdefghijklmnopqrstuvwxyz1234567890

West quickly gave Bert handsome prizes for six juicy plums.

Ice Age

Designer	URW++
Nationality	DE
Date Designed	2001
Foundries	URW++ Franklin Apple
Number of weights	1

ABCDEFGHIJKLMNOPQRSTUVWXYZ

abcdefghijklmnopqrstuvwxyz1234567890

Xavier, a wildly informal court jester, kept calling Queen Elizabeth 'Betty.'

Goodies

Designer	Anne Boskamp
Nationality	DE
Date Designed	2003
Foundries	Linotype
Number of weights	1

ABCDEFGHIJKLMNOPQRSTUVWXYZ
ABCDEFGHIJKLMNOPQRSTUVWXYZ1234567890
ABODE HIS HOUR OR TWO, AND WENT HIS WAY.

Hot Plate

Designer	Timo Brauchle, Nico Hensel
Nationality	DE
Date Designed	2003
Foundries	Linotype
Number of weights	1

ABCDEFGHIJ-KLMNOPQRSTUVWXYZ
abcdefghijklmnopqrstuvwxyz1234567890
They sly the Lion and the Lizard keep,

Raclette

Designer	Michael Parson
Nationality	CH
Date Designed	2003
Foundries	Linotype
Number of weights	1

ABCDEFGHIJKLMNOPQRSTUVWXYZ
abcdefghijklmnopqrstuvwxyz1234567890
The Courts where Jamshyd gloried and drank deep:

Shatter

Designer	Vic Carless
Nationality	UK
Date Designed	1973
Foundries	Letraset Monotype ITC
Number of weights	1

ABCDEFGHIJKLMNOPQRSTUVWXYZ
abcdefghijklmnopqrstuvwxyz1234567890
Two hardy boxing kangaroos jet from Sydney to Zanzibar on quicksilver pinions.

Blur

Designer	Neville Brody
Nationality	UK
Date Designed	1991
Foundries	FontFont
Number of weights	1

ABCDEFGHIJKLMNOPQRSTUVWXYZ
abcdefghijklmnopqrstuvwxyz1234567890
One of the most influential fonts of the 1990s.

F2F MekkasoTomanik

Designer	Alessio Leonardi
Nationality	IT
Date Designed	1992
Foundries	Linotype
Number of weights	1

ABCDEFGHIJKLMNOPQRSTUVWXYZ
abcdefghijklmnopqrstuvwxyz1234567890
A variation of MekkanikAmente done for Thomas Nagel.

Advert Rough

Designer	Just van Rossum
Nationality	NL
Date Designed	1992
Foundries	FontFont
Number of weights	5

ABCDEFGHIJKLMNOPQRSTUVWXYZ
abcdefghijklmnopqrstuvwxyz1234567890
Jeb quickly drove a few extra miles on the glazed pavement.

Outahere

Designer	Adam Roe
Nationality	US
Date Designed	1993
Foundries	Monotype
Number of weights	3

ABCDEFGHIJKLMNOPQRSTUVWXYZ?
abcdefghijklmnopqrstuvwxyz1234567890?
About sixty codfish eggs will make a quarter pound of very fizzy jelly.

F2F ZakkGlobe

Designer	Thomas Nagel
Nationality	DE
Date Designed	1993
Foundries	Linotype
Number of weights	1

ABCDEFGHIJKLMNOPQRSTUVWXYZ
abcdefghijklmnopqrstuvwxyz1234567890
Six big devils from Japan quickly forgot how to waltz.

Helix

Designer	Marius Renberg
Nationality	DE
Date Designed	1994
Foundries	T-26
Number of weights	1

ABCDEFGHIJKLMNOPQRSTUVWXYZ
abcdefghijklmnopqrstuvwxyz1234567890()
Alfredo just must bring very exciting news to the plaza quickly.

F2F Madame Butterfly

Designer Alessio Leonardi
Nationality IT
Date Designed 1994
Foundries Linotype
Number of weights 1

ABCDEFGHIJKLMNOPQRSTUVWXYZ
abcdefghijklmnopqrstuvwxyz1234567890
Leonardi likes the music and the name sounds good.

Atlanta

Designer Peter Bilak
Nationality SK
Date Designed 1995
Foundries FontFont
Number of weights 1

ABCDEFGHIJKLMNOPQRSTUVWXYZ
ABCDEFGHIJKLMNOPQRSTUVWXYZ1234567890
WE HAVE JUST QUOTED ON NINE DOZEN BOXES OF GRAY LAMP WICKS.

Bull

Designer John Critchley
Nationality UK
Date Designed 1995
Foundries FontFont
Number of weights 1

ABCDEFGHIJKLMNOPQRSTUVWXYZ
abcdefghijklmnopqrstuvwxyz1234567890
Back in my quaint garden jaunty zinnias vie with flaunting phlox.

Fur

Designer Paul Sahre
Nationality DE
Date Designed 1995
Foundries Creative Alliance
Number of weights 1

ABCDEFGHIJKLMNOPQRSTUVWXYZ
abcdefghijklmnopqrstuvwxyz1234567890
Five or six big jet planes zoomed quickly by the tower.

Orange

Designer Timothy Donaldson
Nationality UK
Date Designed 1995
Foundries Letraset Linotype ITC
Number of weights 1

ABCDEFGHIJKLMNOPQRSTUVWXYZ
abcdefghijklmnopqrstuvwxyz1234567890
Six big juicy steaks sizzled in a pan as five workmen left the quarry.

Siesta

Designer	Aerotype
Nationality	US
Date Designed	1995
Foundries	Monotype
Number of weights	1

ABCDEFGHIJKLMNOPQRSTUVWXYZ
abcdefghijklmnopqrstuvwxyz1234567890
How razorback-jumping frogs can level six piqued gymnasts!

Spooky

Designer	Timothy Donaldson
Nationality	UK
Date Designed	1995
Foundries	Monotype ITC Linotype Letraset
Number of weights	1

ABCDEFGHIJKLMNOPQRSTUVWXYZ
ABCDEFGHIJKLMNOPQRSTUVWXYZ1234567890
JAY VISITED BACK HOME AND GAZED UPON A BROWN FOX AND QUAIL.

Surrogate

Designer	Adam Roe
Nationality	US
Date Designed	1995
Foundries	Monotype
Number of weights	2

ABCDEFGHIJKLMNOPQRSTUVWXYZ
abcdefghijklmnopqrstuvwxyz1234567890
While waxing parquet decks, jaunty Suez sailors vomit abaft.

Moonbase Alpha

Designer	Cornel Windlin
Nationality	CH
Date Designed	1995
Foundries	FontFont
Number of weights	1

ABCDEFGHIJKLMNOPQRSTUVWXYZ
abcdefghijklmnopqrstuvwxyz1234567890
Moi, je veux quinze clubs a golf et du whisky pur.

Mutilated

Designer	Hannes Famira
Nationality	DE
Date Designed	1995
Foundries	FontFont
Number of weights	1

ABCDEFGHIJKLMNOPQRSTUVWXYZ
ABCDEFGHIJKLMNOPQRSTUVWXYZ1234567890
QUICK WAFTING ZEPHYRS VEX BOLD JIM.

F2F Twins

Designer Heike Nehl
Nationality DE
Date Designed 1995
Foundries Linotype
Number of weights 1

ABCDEFGHIJKLMNOPQRSTUVWXYZ
abcdefghijklmnopqrstuvwxyz1234567890
Waltz, nymph, for quick jigs vex Bud.

F2F Monako Stoned

Designer Heike Nehl
Nationality DE
Date Designed 1995
Foundries Linotype
Number of weights 1

ABCDEFGHIJKLMNOPQRSTUVWXYZ
abcdefghijklmnopqrstuvwxyz1234567890
Quick wafting zephyrs vex bold Jim.

Burokrat

Designer Matthias Rawald
Nationality DE
Date Designed 1996
Foundries FontFont
Number of weights 1

ABCDEFGHIJKLMNOPQRSTUVWXYZ
ABCDEFGHIJKLMNOPQRSTUVWXYZ
1234567890
HARK! TOXIC JUNGLE WATER VIPERS!

Schwennel

Designer Svenja Voss
Nationality DE
Date Designed 1996
Foundries Linotype
Number of weights 1

ABCDEFGHIJKLMNOPQRSTUVWXYZ
abcdefghijklmnopqrstuvwxyz1234567890
Mr. Jock, TV quiz Ph.D., bags few lynx.

F2F Lovegrid

Designer Heike Nehl
Nationality DE
Date Designed 1996
Foundries Linotype
Number of weights 1

ABCDEFGHIJKLMNOPQRSTUVWXYZ
abcdefghijklmnopqrstuvwxyz1234567890
Rorschach déja vû.

F2F ScreenScream

Designer Thomas Nagel
Nationality DE
Date Designed 1997
Foundries Linotype
Number of weights 1

ABCDEFGHIJKLMNOPQRSTUVWXYZ
abcdefghijklmnopqrstuvwxyz1234567890
Jazzy saxophones blew over Mick's turgid quiff.

F2F Shakkarakk

Designer Thomas Nagel
Nationality DE
Date Designed 1997
Foundries Linotype
Number of weights 1

ABCDEFGHIJKLMNOPQRSTUVWXYZ
abcdefghijklmnopqrstuvwxyz1234567890
Jim just quit and packed extra bags for Liz Owen.

F2F Tyrell Corp

Designer Thomas Nagel
Nationality DE
Date Designed 1997
Foundries Linotype
Number of weights 1

ABCDEFGHIJKLMNOPQRSTUVWXY
abcdefghijklmnopqrstuvwxyz1234567890
Pack my box with five dozen liquor jugs.

Fluxus

Designer Andreas Karl
Nationality DE
Date Designed 1997
Foundries Linotype
Number of weights 1

ABCDEFGHIJKLMNOPQRSTUVWXYZ
abcdefghijklmnopqrstuvwxyz1234567890
Quixotic Conservatives vet first key zero-growth jeremiad.

Zensur

Designer Gerald Alexandre
Nationality FR
Date Designed 1997
Foundries Linotype
Number of weights 1

ABCDEFGHIJKLMNOPQRSTUVWXYZ
abcdefghijklmnopqrstuvwxyz1234567890
Six crazy kings vowed to abolish my quite pitiful jousts.

Scribble

Designer	Ole Schäfer
Nationality	DE
Date Designed	1995
Foundries	FontFont
Number of weights	12

ABCDEFGHIJKLMNOPQRSTUVWXYZ

abcdefghijklmnopqrstuvwxyz1234567890

Brawny gods just flocked up to quiz and vex him.

Coventry

Designer	Brian Sooy
Nationality	US
Date Designed	1998
Foundries	ITC Linotype
Number of weights	1

ABCDEFGHIJKLMNOPQRSTUVWXYZ

abcdefghijklmnopqrstuvwxyz1234567890

William Jex quickly caught five dozen Conservatives.

Linotype Alphabat

Designer	Jan Tomáš
Nationality	CZ
Date Designed	2000
Foundries	Linotype
Number of weights	1

ABCDEFGHIJKLMNOPQRSTUVWXYZ

ABCDEFGHIJKLMNOPQRSTUVWXYZ1234567890

THE EXODUS OF JAZZY PIGEONS IS CRAVED BY SQUEAMISH WALKERS.

Boomshanker

Designer	John Siddle
Nationality	UK
Date Designed	2002
Foundries	FontFont
Number of weights	1

ABCDEFGHIJKLMNOPQRSTUVWXYZ

abcdefghijklmnopqrstuvwxyz1234567890

William said that everything about his jacket was in quite good condition except for the zipper.

Yokkmokk

Designer	Elke Herrnberger
Nationality	DE
Date Designed	1993
Foundries	FontFont
Number of weights	1

ABCDEFGHIJKLMNOPQRSTUVWXYZ

abcdefghijklmnopqrstuvwxyz1234567890

The outline version, yet more illegible, is called Yokkmokka.

Spacekid

Designer	Bo Berndal
Nationality	SE
Date Designed	1990
Foundries	Monotype
Number of weights	1

You Can Read Me

Designer	Phil Baines
Nationality	UK
Date Designed	1991
Foundries	FontFont
Number of weights	1

Art Gallery

Designer	Bo Berndal
Nationality	SE
Date Designed	1992
Foundries	Monotype
Number of weights	1

ABCDEFGHIJKLMNOPQRSTUVWXYZ
abcdefghijklmnopqrstuvwxyz1234567890
Six crazy kings vowed to abolish my quite pitiful jousts.

Flamingo

Designer	anon
Nationality	DE
Date Designed	1994
Foundries	Elsner+Flake
Number of weights	1

ABCDEFGHIJKLMNOPQRSTUVWXYZ
abcdefghijklmnopqrstuvwxyz1234567890
Questions of a zealous nature have become by degrees petty waxen jokes.

F2F HogRoach

Designer	Thomas Nagel
Nationality	DE
Date Designed	1995
Foundries	Linotype
Number of weights	1

ABCDEFGHIJKLMNOPQRSTUVWXYZ
abcdefghijklmnopqrstuvwxyz1234567890
Rorschach test.

F2F Shpeetz

Designer	Thomas Nagel
Nationality	DE
Date Designed	1996
Foundries	Linotype
Number of weights	1

★ℬℭⅅℰℱℊℋℐ ⱼℛℒℳℕℴℙℚℛℤ℘ⱴⱴℽℽⱼ

ℵℬℭⅆℯℱℊℏⅈℷℛℒℳℕℴℙℚℛ℘ⱴⱴⱱⱱⱼⱼ½¾$λ℘℘℘⅃

"Xavier, a wildly informal court jester, kept calling Queen Elizabeth ?Betty.?"

F2F Metamorfosi

Designer	Alessio Leonardi
Nationality	IT
Date Designed	1992
Foundries	Linotype
Number of weights	1

ΛΒ(ϽΕϜ(ℋℐℐℒℳℕℴℙℚℝℒⱤⱵℴⱴℽℽ×Ⲩⱬ

ə6ϲⅆεϜℊℏⅈℐℓℳℕℴℴⱺℳⱴⱺⱴⱴⱼⱬℐℤℨℨ⅘ℨℬⅆℐ℘ℴ

Λη εхⱣεⱤⅈℳεητɑℓ ⱳℴⱤℛ ℴη Ɽεⱥⅆɑ6ⅈℓⅈτⱴ ⱴℐⱼℊ Ɛ℠ⅈℛ SⱣⅈεℛεℳεⱤ's ℳετɑ.

Linotype Minos

Designer	Christian Götz
Nationality	DE
Date Designed	1996
Foundries	Linotype
Number of weights	1

ABCDEFGHIJKLMNOPQRSTUVWXYZ

ABCDEFGHIJKLMNOPQRSTUVWXYZ1234567890

HARDER TO DECIPHER THAN LINEAR B

Paint It

Designer	Jochen Schuss
Nationality	DE
Date Designed	1997
Foundries	Linotype
Number of weights	1

F2F Prototipa Multipla

Designer	Alessio Leonardi
Nationality	IT
Date Designed	1995
Foundries	Linotype
Number of weights	1

ABCDEFGHIJKLMNOPQRSTUVWXYZ

abcdefghijklmnopqrstuvwxyz

'"1234567890

Based on a copperplate scanned beforehand.

Linotype Submerge

Designer	Gary Tennant
Nationality	UK
Date Designed	2002
Foundries	Linotype
Number of weights	1

abcdefghijklmn
oopqrstuvwxyz
1234567890
sphinx of black quartz judge.

Classicus Titulus

Designer	Michael Parson
Nationality	CH
Date Designed	2003
Foundries	Linotype
Number of weights	1

ABCDEFGHIJKLMNOPQRSTUVWXYZ
abcdefghijklmnopqrstuvwxyz1234567890
And sphinx of black quartz judge Wok her.

Short Story

Designer	Jörg Herz
Nationality	DE
Date Designed	1997
Foundries	Linotype
Number of weights	1

Geäb Oil

Designer	Fabrizio Schiavi
Nationality	IT
Date Designed	1995
Foundries	FontFont
Number of weights	2

ABCDEFGHIJKLMNOPQRSTUVWXYZ
abcdefghijklmnopqrstuvwxyz1234567890
The sea life of the woodchuck is a provocative question for most
vertebrate zoology majors.

NineSixNilNil

Designer	Fabrizio Schiavi
Nationality	IT
Date Designed	1995
Foundries	FontFont
Number of weights	1

ABCDEFGHIJKLMNOPQRSTUVWXYZ
abcdefghijklmnopqrstuvwxyz1234567890
Oddly enough, this used to be my phone number.

F2F Entebbe

Designer	Alexander Branczyk
Nationality	DE
Date Designed	1995
Foundries	Linotype
Number of weights	1

aBcDEFGHiJKLMNOP Q rSTUVWXIZ
aBcDefg#ijK LMNOPorstNwXY21234567890
aLfreDO Just Must BrinG VerY exciting news tO
t#e PLaZa quiCKLY.

F2F Pixmix

Designer	Thomas Nagel
Nationality	DE
Date Designed	1995
Foundries	Linotype
Number of weights	1

ABCDEFGHIJKLMNOPQRSTUVWXYZ
abcdefghijklmnopqrstuvwxyz1234567890
My grandfather picks up quartz and valuable onyx jewels.

F2F PoisonFlowers

Designer	Alessio Leonardi
Nationality	IT
Date Designed	1992
Foundries	Linotype
Number of weights	1

ABCDEFGHI JKLMNOPQRSTUVWXYZ
ABCDEFGHI JKLMNOPQRSTUVWXYZ1234567890
THE NAME POISON FLOWERS COMES FROM A SONG BY THE POP GROUP.

F2F Provinciali

Designer	Alessio Leonardi
Nationality	IT
Date Designed	1992
Foundries	Linotype
Number of weights	1

ABCDEFGHIJKLMNOPQRSTUVWXYZ
abcdefghijklmnopqrstuvwxyz1234567890
My grandfather picks up quartz and valuable onyx jewels.

F2F TechLand

Designer	Alexander Branczyk
Nationality	DE
Date Designed	1995
Foundries	Linotype
Number of weights	1

ABCDEFGHIJKLMNOPQRSTUVWXYZ?
ABCDEFGHIJKLMNOPQRSTUVWXYZ1234567890?
PERHAPS PRESIDENT CLINTON'S AMAZING SAX SKILLS WILL BE
JUDGED QUITE FAVOURABLY.

F2F Mekanik Amente

Designer	Alessio Leonardi
Nationality	IT
Date Designed	1993
Foundries	Linotype
Number of weights	1

ABCDEFGHIJKLMNOPQRSTUVWXYZ

abcdefghijklmnopqrstuvwxyz1234567890

A playful word for done mechanically, machine generated.

F2F El Dee Cons

Designer	Thomas Nagel
Nationality	DE
Date Designed	1993
Foundries	Linotype
Number of weights	1

ABCDEFGHIJKLMNOPQRSTUVWXYZ

abcdefghijklmnopqrstuvwxyz1234567890

Best read at 6pt so you can take time to decipher it.

Hotel

Designer	NOT L Meuffels, that's another HOTEL
Nationality	US
Date Designed	1994
Foundries	Parkinson
Number of weights	1

ABCDEFGHIJKLMNOPQRSTUVWXYZ

ABCDEFGHIJKLMNOPQRSTUVWXYZ1234567890

WILL MAJOR DOUGLAS BE EXPECTED TO TAKE THIS
TRUE-FALSE QUIZ VERY SOON?

Linotype Bix

Designer	Victor Garcia
Nationality	AR
Date Designed	2003
Foundries	Linotype
Number of weights	1

ABCDEFGHIJKLMNOPQRSTUVWXYZ

ABCDEFGHIJKLMNOPQRSTUVWXYZ
1234567890

STAMPS O'ER HIS HEAD, AND HE LIES.

Funny Bones

Designer	Ingo Preuss
Nationality	DE
Date Designed	1997
Foundries	Linotype
Number of weights	1

ABCDEFGHIJKLMNOPQRSTUVWXYZ

ABCDEFGHIJKLMNOPQRSTUVWXYZ1234567890

EBENEZER UNEXPECTEDLY BAGGED TWO TRANQUIL AARDVARKS WITH HIS JIFFY VACUUM CLEANER.

Pleasure Bold Shaded

Designer Holger Seeling
Nationality UK
Date Designed 1987
Foundries ITC
Number of weights 1

ABCDEFGHIJKLMNOPQRSTUVWXYZ

ABCDEFGHIJKLMNOPQRSTUVWXYZ1234567890

THE JOB OF WAXING LINOLEUM FREQUENTLY PEEVES CHINTZY KIDS.

Philco

Designer Jasper Manchipp
Nationality UK
Date Designed 1994
Foundries Monotype
Number of weights 1

ABCDEFGHIJKLMNOPQRSTUVWXYZ

ABCDEFGHIJKLMNOPQRSTUVWXYZ1234567890

BREEZILY JANGLING $3,416,857,209, WISE ADVERTISER AMBLES TO THE BANK. HIS EXCHEQUER AMPLIFIED.

Grace

Designer Elisabeth Megnet
Nationality FR
Date Designed 1995
Foundries Linotype
Number of weights 1

ABCDEFGHIJKLMNOPQRSTUVWXYZ

abcdefghijklmnopqrstuvwxyz1234567890

Moi, je veux quinze clubs a golf et du whisky pur.

Slipstream

Designer Letraset
Nationality UK
Date Designed 1985
Foundries Letraset Franklin ITC
Number of weights 1

ABCDEFGHIJKLMNOPQRSTUVWXYZ

ABCDEFGHIJKLMNOPQRSTUVWXYZ1234567890

MARTIN J. HIXEYPOZER QUICKLY BEGAN HIS FIRST WORD.

Atomatic

Designer Johannes Plass
Nationality DE
Date Designed 1997
Foundries Linotype
Number of weights 1

ABCDEFGHIJKLMNOPQRSTUVWXYZ

abcdefghijklmnopqrstuvwxyz1234567890

Astronaut Quincy B. Zack defies gravity with six jet fuel pumps.

Deli Supreme

Designer	Jim Spiece
Nationality	US
Date Designed	1999
Foundries	ITC
Number of weights	1

ABCDEFGHIJKLMNOPQRSTUVWXYZ
abcdefghijklmnopqrstuvwxyz
1234567890
My grandfather picks up quartz.

Albafire

Designer	anon
Nationality	DE
Date Designed	1994
Foundries	Linotype
Number of weights	1

ABCDEFGHIJKLMNOPQRSTUVWXYZ
abcdefghijklmnopqrstuvwxyz1234567890
Murky haze enveloped a city as jarring quakes broke forty-six windows.

Albatross

Designer	anon
Nationality	DE
Date Designed	1994
Foundries	Linotype
Number of weights	1

ABCDEFGHIJKLMNOPQRSTUVWXYZ
abcdefghijklmnopqrstuvwxyz1234567890
King Alexander was partly overcome just after quizzing Diogenes in his tub.

Linotype Pegathlon

Designer	Hans-Jürgen Ellenberger
Nationality	DE
Date Designed	1999
Foundries	Linotype
Number of weights	1

ABCDEFGHIJKLMNOPQRSTUVWXYZ
abcdefghijklmnopqrstuvwxyz1234567890
An event yet to feature in the Olympics.

Beluga

Designer	Hans-Jürgen Ellenberger
Nationality	DE
Date Designed	1994
Foundries	Linotype
Number of weights	1

ABCDEFGHIJKLMNOPQRSTUVWXYZ
abcdefghijklmnopqrstuvwxyz1234567890
A mad boxer shot a quick, gloved jab to the jaw of his dizzy opponent.

Linotype Startec

Designer	Jan Tomás
Nationality	CZ
Date Designed	2000
Foundries	Linotype
Number of weights	1

ABCDEFGHIJKLMNOPQRSTUVWXYZ
ABCDEFGHIJKLMNOPQRSTUVWXYZ1234567890
SIXTY ZIPPERS WERE QUICKLY PICKED FROM THE WOVEN JUTE BAG.

Kismet

Designer	John F Cumming
Nationality	US
Date Designed	1879
Foundries	Linotype
Number of weights	1

ABCDEFGHIJKLMNOPQRSTUVWXYZ
abcdefghijklmnopqrstuvwxyz1234567890
Revived in the 1960s and still seen today.

Remedy

Designer	Frank Heine
Nationality	DE
Date Designed	1992
Foundries	Emigre
Number of weights	1

ABCDEFGHIJKLMNOPQRSTUVWXYZ
abcdefghijklmnopqrstuvwxyz1234567890
Architectural Follies in America

Mambo

Designer	Val Fullard
Nationality	CA
Date Designed	1992
Foundries	FontFont
Number of weights	1

ABCDEFGHIJKLMNOPQRSTUVWXYZ
abcdefghijklmnopqrstuvwxyz1234567890
While waxing parquet decks, jaunty Suez sailors vomit abaft.

Jokerman

Designer	Andrew Smith
Nationality	UK
Date Designed	1995
Foundries	Letraset Linotype
Number of weights	1

ABCDEFGHIJKLMNOPQRSTUVWXYZ
abcdefghijklmnopqrstuvwxyz1234567890
Breezily jangling $3,416,857,209,wise advertiser ambles to the bank, his exchequer amplified.

Curly

Buckethead

Designer	Chank Diesel
Nationality	US
Date Designed	1995
Foundries	chank
Number of weights	1

ABCDEFGHiJKLMNOPQRSTUVWXYZ
abcdefghijklmnopqrstuvwxyz1234567890
Jack amazed a few girls by dropping the antique onyx vase!

Swank

Designer	Jill Bell
Nationality	US
Date Designed	2000
Foundries	jillbell.com
Number of weights	2

ABCDEFGHIJKLMNOPQRSTUVWXYZ
abcdefghijklmnopqrstuvwxyz1234567890
Chichi, classy, deluxe, exclusive, expensive, fancy, fashionable, flamboyant, flashy, glamorous, grand

Gigi

Designer	Jill Bell
Nationality	US
Date Designed	1995
Foundries	Monotype ITC
Number of weights	1

ABCDEFGHIJKLMNOPQRSTUVWXYZ
abcdefghijklmnopqrstuvwxyz1234567890
May Jo equal the fine record by solving six puzzles a week?

Scruff

Designer	Timothy Donaldson
Nationality	UK
Date Designed	1995
Foundries	ITC
Number of weights	1

ABCDEFGHIJKLMNOPQRSTUVWXYZ
abcdefghijklmnopqrstuvwxyz1234567890
Dumpy kibitzer jingles as exchequer overflows.

Dancin

Designer	David Sagorski
Nationality	US
Date Designed	1995
Foundries	ITC
Number of weights	1

ABCDEFGHIJKLMNOPQRSTUVWXYZ
abcdefghijklmnopqrstuvwxyz1234567890
The sex life of the woodchuck is a provocative question for most vertebrate zoology majors.

Gramophone

Designer Serge Pichii
Nationality CA
Date Designed 1998
Foundries ITC Fontek Creative Alliance Monotype
Number of weights 1

ABCDEFGHIJKLMNOPQRSTUVWXYZ

abcdefghijklmnopqrstuvwxyz1234567890

We promptly judged antique ivory buckles for the next prize.

Uncle Stinky

Designer Chank Diesel
Nationality US
Date Designed 1997
Foundries T-26 CA Partners
Number of weights 1

ABCDEFGHIJKLMNOPQRSTUVWXYZ

abcdefghijklmnopqrstuvwxyz1234567890

Perhaps President Clinton's amazing sax skills will be judged quite favourably.

Bang

Designer David Sagorski
Nationality US
Date Designed 1993
Foundries Linotype ITC Letraset
Number of weights 1

ABCDEFGHIJKLMNOPQRSTUVWXYZ

ABCDEFGHIJKLMNOPQRSTUVWXYZ1234567890

MARTIN J. HIXEYPOZER QUICKLY BEGAN HIS FIRST WORD.

Zombie

Designer Christian Schwartz
Nationality US
Date Designed 1993
Foundries CHR
Number of weights 2

ABCDEFGHIJKLMNOPQRSTUVWXYZ

ABCDEFGhijKLMNOPQRSTUVWXYZ1234567890

KING ALEXANDER WAS PARTLY OVERCOME JUST AFTER QUIZZING DIOGENES IN HIS TUB.

Lambada

Designer David Quay
Nationality UK
Date Designed 1992
Foundries Linotype Letraset ITC
Number of weights 1

ABCDEFGHIJKLMNOPQRSTUVWXYZ

abcdefghijklmnopqrstuvwxyz1234567890

Six big devils from Japan quickly forget how to waltz.

Hollyweird

Designer	Jill Bell
Nationality	US
Date Designed	1995
Foundries	Monotype ITC
Number of weights	1

ABCDEFGHIJKLMNOPQRSTUVWXYZ

abcdefghijklmnopqrstuvwxyz1234567890

Hark! Toxic jungle water vipers quietly drop on zebras for meals!

Party

Designer	Carol Kemp
Nationality	UK
Date Designed	1998
Foundries	Letraset ITC
Number of weights	1

ABCDEFGHIJKLMNOPQRSTUVWXYZ

abcdefghijklmnopqrstuvwxyz1234567890

Ebenezer unexpectedly bagged two tranquil aardvarks with his jiffy vacuum cleaner.

Curlz

Designer	Steve Matteson, Carl Crossgrove
Nationality	US
Date Designed	2000
Foundries	Monotype
Number of weights	1

ABCDEFGHIJKLMNOPQRSTUVWXYZ

abcdefghijklmnopqrstuvwxyz1234567890

I sometimes think that never blows so red.

Mo' Funky Fresh

Designer	David Sagorski
Nationality	US
Date Designed	1993
Foundries	ITC
Number of weights	1

ABCDEFGHIJKLMNOPQRSTUVWXYZ

ABCDEFGHIJKLMNOPQRSTUVWXYZ1234567890

ALFREDO JUST MUST BRING VERY EXCITING NEWS TO THE PLAZA QUICKLY.

Christina

Designer	Andrew Smith
Nationality	UK
Date Designed	1998
Foundries	Monotype
Number of weights	1

ABCDEFGHIJKLMNOPQRSTUVWXYZ

abcdefghijklmnopqrstuvwxyz1234567890

Verbatim reports were quickly given by Jim Fox to his amazed audience.

Scorpio

Designer Jim Marcus
Nationality US
Date Designed 1993
Foundries T-26
Number of weights 1

ABCDEFGHIJKLMNOPQRSTUVWXYZ
ABCDEFGHIJKLMNOPQRSTUVWXYZ1234567890
PACK MY BOX WITH FIVE DOZEN LIQUOR JUGS.

Crumudgeon

Designer Mark Harris
Nationality US
Date Designed 1998
Foundries Monotype
Number of weights 1

ABCDEFGHIJKLMNOPQRSTUVWXYZ
abcdefghijklmnopqrstuvwxyz1234567890
A large fawn jumped quickly over white zinc boxes.

Jambalaya

Designer Frank Marciuliano
Nationality CA
Date Designed 1996
Foundries Creative Alliance ITC Fontek
Number of weights 1

ABCDEFGHIJKLMNOPQRSTUVWXYZ
abcdefghijklmnopqrstuvwxyz1234567890
William Jex quickly caught five dozen Conservatives.

Ziggy

Designer Bob Alonso
Nationality US
Date Designed 1997
Foundries ITC Monotype
Number of weights 1

ABCDEFGHIJKLMNOPQRSTUVWXYZ
abcdefghijklmnopqrstuvwxyz1234567890
The vixen jumped quickly on her foe barking with zeal.

MadZine

Designer Alexander Branczyk
Nationality DE
Date Designed 1994
Foundries Linotype
Number of weights 1

ABCDEFGHIJKLMNOPQRSTUVWXYZ
abcdefghijklmnopqrstuvwxyz1234567890
Now is the time for all brown dogs to jump over the lazy lynx.

Agfa Marbles and Strings

Designer	Wildwood Creations
Nationality	UK
Date Designed	1997
Foundries	Monotype
Number of weights	1

ABCDEFGHIJKLMNOPQRSTUVWXYZ

abcdefghijklmnopqrstuvwxyz1234567890

Jeb quickly drove a few extra miles on the glazed pavement.

La Bamba

Designer	David Quay
Nationality	UK
Date Designed	1992
Foundries	Linotype Letraset ITC
Number of weights	1

ABCDEFGHIJKLMNOPQRSTUVWXYZ

abcdefghijklmnopqrstuvwxyz1234567890

Exquisite farm wench gives body jolt to prize stinker.

Ironwork

Designer	Serge Pichii
Nationality	CA
Date Designed	1997
Foundries	ITC Linotype
Number of weights	1

ABCDEFGHIJKLMNOPQRSTUVWXYZ

abcdefghijklmnopqrstuvwxyz1234567890

Jaded reader with fabled roving eye seized by quickened impulse to expand budget.

Silver

Designer	anon
Nationality	DE
Date Designed	2000
Foundries	Linotype
Number of weights	1

ABCDEFGHIJKLMNOPQRSTUVWXYZ

ABCDEFGHIJKLMNOPQRSTUVWXYZ1234567890

MARTIN J. HIXEYPOZER QUICKLY BEGAN HIS FIRST WORD.

Substance

Designer	Adam Roe
Nationality	US
Date Designed	1995
Foundries	Monotype
Number of weights	1

ABCDEFGHIJKLMNOPQRSTUVWXYZ

abcdefghijklmnopqrstuvwxyz1234567890

Breezily jangling $3,416,857,209, wise advertiser ambles to the bank, his exchequer amplified.

Algologfont

Designer	Björn Hansen
Nationality	DE
Date Designed	1996
Foundries	Linotype
Number of weights	1

ABCDEFGHIJKLANOPQRSTUVWXYZ
ABCDEFGHIJKLANOPQRSTUVWXYZ1234567890
GRUMPY WIZARDS MAKE TOXIC BREW FOR THE EVIL QUEEN
AND JACK.

Laika

Designer	Mark van Wageningen
Nationality	NL
Date Designed	1997
Foundries	Linotype
Number of weights	1

ABCDEFGHIJKLMNOPQRSTUVWXYZ
abcdefghijklmnopqrstuvwxyz1234567890
Zweedse ex-VIP, behoorlijk gek op quantumfysica.

Water Flag

Designer	Mauro Carichini
Nationality	IT
Date Designed	2002
Foundries	Linotype
Number of weights	1

ABCDEFGHIJKLMNO
PQRSTUVWXYZ
abcdefghijklmno
pqrstuvwxyz1234567890

Glass Flag

Designer	Mauro Carichini
Nationality	IT
Date Designed	2002
Foundries	Linotype
Number of weights	1

ABCDEFGHIJKLMNO
PQRSTUVWXYZ
abcdefghijklmnopqrstuvw
xyz1234567890

Agfa Ghixma

Designer	Graphic Ecursions
Nationality	US
Date Designed	1997
Foundries	Monotype
Number of weights	1

ABCDEFGHIJKLMNOPQRSTUVWXYZ
abcdefghijklmnopqrstuvwxyz1234567890
Verily the dark ex-Jew quit Zionism, preferring the cabala.

Dig

Designer	Paul Sych
Nationality	CA
Date Designed	1991
Foundries	FontFont
Number of weights	1

ABCDEFGHIJKLMNOPQRSTUVWXYZ

ABCDEFGHIJKLMNOPQRSTUVWXYZ1234567890

THE JOB OF WAXING LINOLEUM FREQUENTLY PEEVES CHINTZY KIDS.

Montage

Designer	Alan Dempsey
Nationality	UK
Date Designed	1995
Foundries	Monotype ITC
Number of weights	1

ABCDEFGHIJKLMNOPQRSTUVWXYZ

ABCDEFGHIJKLMNOPQRSTUVWXYZ1234567890

JUST KEEP EXAMINING EVERY LOW BID QUOTED FOR ZINC ETCHINGS.

Digital Woodcuts Black ITC

Designer	Timothy Donaldson
Nationality	UK
Date Designed	1996
Foundries	Monotype ITC
Number of weights	1

ABCDEFGHIJKLMNOPQRSTUVWXYZ

ABCDEFGHIJKLMNOPQRSTUVWXYZ1234567890

WE HAVE JUST QUOTED ON NINE DOZEN BOXES OF GRAY LAMP WICKS.

Linotype Schere

Designer	Georg Kugler
Nationality	DE
Date Designed	1997
Foundries	Linotype
Number of weights	1

ABCDEFGHIJKLMNOPQRSTUVWXYZ

ABCDEFGHIJKLMNOPQRSTUVWXYZ

1234567890

HOW QUICKLY DAFT JUMPING ZEBRAS VEX.

Linotype Cutter

Designer	Georg Kugler
Nationality	DE
Date Designed	2000
Foundries	Linotype
Number of weights	1

ABCDEFGHIJKLMNOPQRSTUVWXYZ

ABCDEFGHIJKLMNOPQRSTUVWXYZ

1234567890

EXQUISITE FARM WENCH GIVES BODY JOLT !

Panic

Designer	Wayne Thompson
Nationality	US
Date Designed	2000
Foundries	ITC
Number of weights	1

ABCDEFGHIJKLMNOPQRSTUVWXYZ
ABCDEFGHIJKLMNOPQRSTUVWXYZ1234567890
QUICK WAFTING ZEPHYRS VEX BOLD JIM.

Amelia

Designer	Stanley Davis
Nationality	US
Date Designed	1965
Foundries	Bitstream Linotype
Number of weights	1

ABCDEFGHIJKLMNOPQRSTUVWXYZ
abcdefghijklmnopqrstuvwxyz1234567890
Makes you think of Jane Fonda as a sex object.

OCR-A

Designer	Adrian Frutiger
Nationality	CH
Date Designed	1966
Foundries	ATF Linotype Adobe Bitstream
Number of weights	5

ABCDEFGHIJKLMNOPQRSTUVWXYZ
abcdefghijklmnopqrstuvwxyz1234567890
Crazy Fredericka bought many very exquisite opal jewels.

OCR-B

Designer	Adrian Frutiger
Nationality	CH
Date Designed	1966
Foundries	Monotype Bitstream
Number of weights	5

ABCDEFGHIJKLMNOPQRSTUVWXYZ
abcdefghijklmnopqrstuvwxyz1234567890
My grandfather picks up quartz and valuable onyx jewels.

Computer

Designer	Monotype
Nationality	UK
Date Designed	1969
Foundries	Monotype
Number of weights	1

ABCDEFGHIJKLMNOPQRSTUVWXYZ
ABCDEFGHIJKLMNOPQRSTUVWXYZ1234567890
LAZY MOVERS QUIT HARD-PACKING OF PAPIER-MACHE JEWELLERY BOXES.

Data 70

Designer	Bob Newman
Nationality	UK
Date Designed	1970
Foundries	Letraset ITC
Number of weights	1

ABCDEFGHIJKLMNOPQRSTUVWXYZ

abcdefghijklmnopqrstuvwxyz1234567890

Quick wafting zephyrs vex bold Jim.

Quartz

Designer	Letraset
Nationality	UK
Date Designed	1972
Foundries	Elsner+Flake Linotype URW++
Number of weights	1

ABCDEFGHIJKLMNOPQRSTUVWXYZ

ABCDEFGHIJKLMNOPQRSTUVWXYZ1234567890

THE EXODUS OF JAZZY PIGEONS IS CRAVED BY SQUEAMISH WALKERS.

Synchro

Designer	Alan R Birch
Nationality	UK
Date Designed	1984
Foundries	Linotype ITC
Number of weights	2

ABCDEFGHIJKLMNOPQRSTUVWXYZ

ABCDEFGHIJKLMNOPQRSTUVWXYZ1234567890

MY HELP SQUEEZED BACK IN AGAIN AND JOINED THE WEAVERS AFTER SIX.

Network

Designer	Max Kisman
Nationality	US
Date Designed	1990
Foundries	FontFont
Number of weights	1

ABCDEFGHIJKLMNOPQRSTUVWXYZ

abcdefghijklmnopqrstuvwxyz1234567890

Grumpy wizards make toxic brew for the evil Queen and Jack.

LCD

Designer	Martin Wait
Nationality	UK
Date Designed	1991
Foundries	Letraset Linotype Elsner+Flake ITC Monotype URW++
Number of weights	1

ABCDEFGHIJKLMNOPQRSTUVWXYZ

ABCDEFGHIJKLMNOPQRSTUVWXYZ1234567890

LIQUID CRYSTAL DISPLAY

Diodes

Designer	Michel Bujardet
Nationality	FR
Date Designed	1992
Foundries	Match Software
Number of weights	1

ABCDEFGHIJKLMNOPQRSTUVWXYZ
abcdefghijklmnopqrstuvwxyz1234567890
Diodes are used as detector valves for radio signals.

Watch Outline

Designer	Mecanorma
Nationality	FR
Date Designed	1994
Foundries	Mecanorma Monotype
Number of weights	1

ABCDEFGHIJKLMNOPQRSTUVWXYZ
ABCDEFGHIJKLMNOPQRSTUVWXYZ1234567890
BREEZILY JANGLING £3,416,857,209, WISE ADVERTISER AMBLES TO THE
BANK, HIS EXCHEQUER AMPLIFIED.

Dot Matrix

Designer	Stefan Müller, Cornel Windlin
Nationality	DE
Date Designed	1994
Foundries	FontFont
Number of weights	1

ABCDEFGHIJKLMNOPQRSTUVWXYZ
abcdefghijklmnopqrstuvwxyz1234567890
A quick movement of the enemy will jeopardize six gunboats.

Cool Wool

Designer	Alessio Leonardi, Priska Wollein
Nationality	IT
Date Designed	1994
Foundries	Linotype
Number of weights	1

ABCDEFGHIJKLMNOPQRSTUVWXYZ
abcdefghijklmnopqrstuvwxyz1234567890
Designed to look like embroidered letters on textiles.

F2F OCRAlexczyk

Designer	Alexander Branczyk
Nationality	DE
Date Designed	1994
Foundries	Linotype
Number of weights	2

ABCDEFGHIJKLMNOPQRSTUVWXYZ
abcdefghijklmnopqrstuvwxyz1234567890
Five big quacking zephyrs jolt my wax bed.

Screen Matrix

Designer Stephan Müller, Cornel Windlin
Nationality DE
Date Designed 1995
Foundries FontFont
Number of weights 1

ABCDEFGHIJKLMNOPQRSTUVWXYZ
abcdefghijklmnopqrstuvwxyz1234567890
Puzzled women bequeath jerks very exotic gifts.

Airport

Designer Stephan Müller, Cornel Windlin
Nationality DE
Date Designed 1995
Foundries FontFont
Number of weights 1

ABCDEFGHIJKLMNOPQRSTUVWXYZ
abcdefghijklmnopqrstuvwxyz1234567890
Jail zesty vixen who grabbed pay from quack.

Murphy

Designer Fedor Hüneke
Nationality DE
Date Designed 1995
Foundries FontFont
Number of weights 1

ABCDEFGHIJKLMNOPQRSTUVWXYZ
abcdefghijklmnopqrstuvwxyz1234567890
Sexy qua lijf, doch bang voor het zwempak.

OCR-F

Designer Albert-Jan Pool
Nationality NL
Date Designed 1995
Foundries FontFont
Number of weights 7

ABCDEFGHIJKLMNOPQRSTUVWXYZ
abcdefghijklmnopqrstuvwxyz1234567890
Astronaut Quincy B. Zack defies gravity with six jet fuel pumps.

F2F OCRBczyk

Designer Alexander Branczyk
Nationality DE
Date Designed 1995
Foundries Linotype
Number of weights 2

ABCDEFGHIJKLMNOPQRSTUVWXYZ
abcdefghijklmnopqrstuvwxyz1234567890
The quick brown fox jumps over the lazy dog.

Facsimile

Designer	Jenny Luigs, Simon Wicker
Nationality	DE
Date Designed	1996
Foundries	Linotype
Number of weights	1

→←↑↓⊡FT«»◯◯◯◯◯◯◯◯◯◯◯❶❷❸❹❺❻❼❽❾❿

ABCDEFGHIJKLMNOPQRSTUVWXYZ1234567890

⊚HE JUKE BOX MUSIC PUZZLED A GENTLE VISITOR FROM A QUAINT VALLEY TOWN.

Union

Designer	Lewis Tsalis
Nationality	AU
Date Designed	1996
Foundries	T-26 Monotype
Number of weights	4

ABCDEFGHIJKLMNOPQRSTUVWXYZ

abcdefghijklmnopqrstuvwxyz1234567890

All questions asked by five watch experts amazed the judge.

Localiser

Designer	Critzler
Nationality	DE
Date Designed	1997
Foundries	FontFont
Number of weights	1

ABCDEFGHIJKLMNOPQRSTUVWXYZ

abcdefghijklmnopqrstuvwxyz1234567890

Lazy movers quit hard-packing of papier-mache jewellery boxes.

Chemo

Designer	Thomas Critzler Bierschenk
Nationality	DE
Date Designed	1997
Foundries	FontFont
Number of weights	1

ABCDEFGHIJKLMNOPQRSTUVWXYZ

abcdefghijklmnopqrstuvwxyz1234567890

Mr. Jock, TV quiz Ph.D., bags few lynx.

Xcreen

Designer	Steffen Sauerteig, Kai Vermehr
Nationality	DE
Date Designed	1998
Foundries	FontFont
Number of weights	3

ABCDEFGHIJKLMNOPQRSTUVWXYZ

abcdefghijklmnopqrstuvwxyz1234567890

May Jo equal the fine record by solving six puzzles a week?

SubVario / SubMono

Designer Steffen Sauerteig, Kai Vermehr
Nationality DE
Date Designed 1998
Foundries FontFont
Number of weights 1

ABCDEFGHIJKLMNOPQRSTUVWXYZ
abcdefghijklmnopqrstuvwxyz1234567890
3D layer colour.

Eboy

Designer Steffen Sauerteig, Kai Vermehr
Nationality DE
Date Designed 1998
Foundries FontFont
Number of weights 1

ABCDEFGHIJKLMNOPQRSTUVWXYZ
abcdefghijklmnopqrstuvwxyz1234567890
How vexing a fumble to drop a jolly zucchini in the quicksand.

TypeStar OCR

Designer Steffen Sauerteig
Nationality DE
Date Designed 1998
Foundries FontFont
Number of weights 2

ABCDEFGHIJKLMNOPQRSTUVWXYZ
abcdefghijklmnopqrstuvwxyz1234567890
Quick zephyrs blow, vexing daft Jim.

Droids

Designer Donald Beekman
Nationality NL
Date Designed 1999
Foundries FontFont
Number of weights 1

ABCDEFGHIJKLMN
OPQRSTUVWXYZ
1234567890
breezily jangling.

Papertape

Designer Matthias Jordan
Nationality DE
Date Designed 2000
Foundries FontFont
Number of weights 1

ABCDEFGHIJKLMNOPQRSTUVWXYZ
abcdefghijklmnopqrstuvwxyz1234567890
West quickly gave Bert handsome prizes for six juicy plums.

Linotype Punkt

Designer	Linotype
Nationality	DE
Date Designed	2000
Foundries	Linotype
Number of weights	1

abcdefghijklmnopqrstuvwxyz
abcdefghijklmnopqrstuvwxyz1234567890
grumpy wizards make toxic brew for the evil queen and jack.

Ticket

Designer	Daniel Frit
Nationality	FR
Date Designed	2000
Foundries	FontFont
Number of weights	1

abcdefghijklmnopqrstuvwxyz
abcdefghijklmnopqrstuvwxyz1234567890
Sexy times wex madly toted

Readout

Designer	Steffen Sauerteig
Nationality	DE
Date Designed	2001
Foundries	FontFont
Number of weights	1

AbCdEFGHIJkLANOPQrStuvwxyz
AbCdEFGhIJkLANOPQrStuvwxyz 1234567890
Layers to build up colour font

Linotype Pargrid

Designer	Michael Parson
Nationality	CH
Date Designed	2001
Foundries	Linotype
Number of weights	1

ABCDEFGHIJKLMNOPQRSTUVWXYZ
abcdefghijklmnopqrstuvwxyz
1234567890
Jaded zombies acted quaintly but kept.

Yardmaster

Designer	URW++
Nationality	DE
Date Designed	2001
Foundries	URW++
Number of weights	2

ABCDEFGHIJKLMNOPQRSTUVWXYZ
abcdefghijklmnopqrstuvwxyz1234567890
Exquisite farm wench gives body jolt to prize stinker.

Beadmap

Designer	David Crow, Ian Wright
Nationality	UK
Date Designed	2002
Foundries	FontFont
Number of weights	2

ABCDEFGHIJKLMNOPQRSTUVWXYZ

ABCDEFGHIJKLMNOPQRSTUVWXYZ1234567890

QUICK WAFTING ZEPHYRS VEX BOLD JIM.

Call

Designer	A Scheuerhorst, M Ignaszak, S Kister
Nationality	DE
Date Designed	2002
Foundries	FontFont
Number of weights	1

ABCDEFGHIJKLMNOPQRSTUVWXYZ

abcdefghijklmnopqrstuvwxyz1234567890

Xavier, a wildly informal court jester, kept calling Queen Elizabeth 'Betty.'

Screenstar

Designer	Steffen Sauerteig, Kai Vermehr, Svend Smital
Nationality	DE
Date Designed	2003
Foundries	FontFont
Number of weights	10

ABCDEFGHIJKLMNOPQRSTUVWXYZ

abcdefghijklmnopqrstuvwxyz1234567890

Lazy movers quit hard-packing of papier-mache jewellery boxes.

Lomo

Designer	Fidel Peugeot
Nationality	CH
Date Designed	2003
Foundries	Linotype
Number of weights	1

ABCDEFGHIJKLMNOPQRSTUVWXYZ

ABCDEFGHIJKLMNOPQRSTUVWXYZ

1234567890

THAT EVERY HYACINTH THE GARDEN.

Pistol Shot

Designer	Roselyne Besnard, Michel Besnard
Nationality	FR
Date Designed	2003
Foundries	Linotype
Number of weights	1

ABCDEFGHIJKLMNOPQRSTUVWXYZ

abcdefghijklmnopqrstuvwxyz1234567890

Moi, je veux quinze clubs a golf et du whisky pur.

BoneBlack

Designer	Peter Dako
Nationality	US
Date Designed	1991
Foundries	Microsoft
Number of weights	1

ABCDEFGHIJKLMNOPQRSTUVWXYZ
abcdefghijklmnopqrstuvwxyz1234567890
I think my bones are whitish.

Bizarro

Designer	David Rakowski
Nationality	US
Date Designed	1992
Foundries	Font Diner
Number of weights	1

ABCDEFGHIJKLMNOPQRSTUVXYZ
ABCDEFGHIJKLMNOPQRSTUVXYZ
DROPT IN ITS LAP FROM SOME ONCE LOVELY HEAD

Mastercard

Designer	John Hamon
Nationality	UK
Date Designed	1994
Foundries	Linotype ITC
Number of weights	1

ABCDEFGHIJKLMNOPQRSTUVWXYZ
ABCDEFGHIJKLMNOPQRSTUVWXYZ1234567890
ALL QUESTIONS ASKED BY FIVE WATCH EXPERTS AMAZED THE JUDGE!

Victorian Silhouette

Designer	Monotype
Nationality	UK
Date Designed	1994
Foundries	Monotype
Number of weights	1

ABCDEFGHIJKLMNOPQRSTUVWXYZ
ABCDEFGHIJKLMNOPQRSTUVWXYZ
WHILE WAXING PARQUET DECKS JAUNTY SUEZ SAILORS
VOMIT ABAFT

Frutiger Stones

Designer	Adrian Frutiger
Nationality	CH
Date Designed	1998
Foundries	Linotype
Number of weights	1

ABCDEFGHIJKLMNOPQRSTUVWXYZ
ABCDEFGHIJKLMNOPQRSTUVWXYZ
1234567890
THE FIVE BOXING WIZARDS JUMP QUICKLY.

MICMAC

Designer	Roselyne Besnard, Michel Besnard
Nationality	FR
Date Designed	1997
Foundries	Monotype
Number of weights	4

ABCDEFGHIJKLMNOPQRSTUVWXYZ

abcdefghijklmnopqrstuvwxyz1234567890

How razorback-jumping frogs can level six piqued gymnasts!

Pincers

Designer	Mark Harris
Nationality	US
Date Designed	1998
Foundries	Monotype
Number of weights	1

ABCDEFGHIJKLMNOPQRSTUVWXYZ

abcdefghijklmnopqrstuvwxyz1234567890

Jelly-like above the high wire, six quaking pachyderms kept the climax of the extravaganza in a dazzling state of flux.

Tommy's Type

Designer	Judith Sutcliffe
Nationality	US
Date Designed	1993
Foundries	Electric Typographer Monotype
Number of weights	1

ABCDEFGHIJKLMNOPQRSTUVWXYZ

JUST KEEP EXAMINING EVERY LOW BID QUOTED FOR ZINC ETCHINGS.

Toolbox

Designer	Adobe Systems
Nationality	US
Date Designed	1993
Foundries	Linotype
Number of weights	1

ABCDEFGHIJKLMNOPQRSTUVWXYZ

ABCDEFGHIJKLMNOPQRSTUVWXYZ1234567890

FREIGHT TO ME SIXTY DOZEN QUART JARS AND TWELVE BLACK PANS.

Party Time

Designer	Christo Velikov
Nationality	BL
Date Designed	1997
Foundries	Linotype
Number of weights	1

ABCDEFGHIJKLMNOPQRSTUVWXYZ

ABCDEFGHIJKLMNOPQRSTUVWXYZ1234567890

FOR ONLY $49, JOLLY HOUSEWIVES MADE INEXPENSIVE MEALS USING QUICK-FROZEN VEGETABLES.

Scrap

Designer	Ingo Preuss
Nationality	DE
Date Designed	1996
Foundries	Linotype
Number of weights	1

ABCDEFGHIJKLMNOPQRSTUVWXYZ

abcdefghijklmnopqrstuvwxyz1234567890

Many-wived Jack laughs at probes of sex quiz.

Stained Glass

Designer	Phill Grimshaw
Nationality	UK
Date Designed	1997
Foundries	ITC Linotype
Number of weights	1

ABCDEFGHIJKLMNOPQRSTUVWXYZ

SPHINX OF BLACK QUARTZ JUDGE MY VOW.

Identification

Designer	Rian Hughes
Nationality	UK
Date Designed	1993
Foundries	FontFont
Number of weights	1

ABCDEFGHIJKLMNOPQRSTUVWXYZ

ABCDEFGHIJKLMNOPQRSTUVWXYZ

1234567890

Barbed Wire

Designer	Andrew Smith
Nationality	UK
Date Designed	1995
Foundries	Monotype
Number of weights	1

ABCDEFGHIJKLMNOPQRSTUVWXYZ

abcdefghijklmnopqrstuvwxyz1234567890

Six big juicy steaks sizzled in a pan as five workmen left the quarry.

Migraph

Designer	Roselyne Besnard, Michel Besnard
Nationality	FR
Date Designed	1998
Foundries	ITC
Number of weights	1

ABCDEFGHIJKLMNOPQRSTUVWXYZ

abcdefghijklmnopqrstuvwxyz1234567890

King Alexander was partly overcome just after quizzing Diogenes in his tub.

Truckz

Designer Harry Giles-Thornbory
Nationality UK
Date Designed 1977
Foundries Linotype
Number of weights 1

ABCDEFGHIJKLMNOPQRSTUVWXYZ
ABCDEFGHIJKLMNOPQRSTUVWXYZ1234567890
BREEZILY JANGLING £73,416,857,209 WISE ADVERTISER
AMBLES TO THE BANK, HIS EXCHEQUER AMPLIFIED.

Freeway

Designer Ian Patterson
Nationality UK
Date Designed 1994
Foundries Creative Alliance
Number of weights 1

ABCDEFGHIJKLMNOPQRSTUVWXYZ
1234567890
THE VIXEN JUMPED QUICKLY ON HER FOE BARKING WITH ZEAL.

TF Finny

Designer Joseph D Treacy
Nationality US
Date Designed 1994
Foundries Treacyfaces Monotype
Number of weights 1

Hollywood

Designer Ian Patterson
Nationality UK
Date Designed 1995
Foundries Monotype
Number of weights 1

ABCDEFGHIJKLMNOPQRSTUVWXYZ
ABCDEFGHIJKLMNOPQRSTUVWXYZ1234567890
SHE DIED IN LESS THAN A MINUTE AND A HALF

Linotype Supatropic

Designer Isabell Laxa
Nationality DE
Date Designed 1996
Foundries Linotype
Number of weights 1

ABCDEFGHIJKLMNOPQRSTUVWXYZ
ABCDEFGHIJKLMNOPQRSTUVWXYZ1234567890
FREIGHT TO ME SIXTY DOZEN QUART JARS AND
TWELVE BLACK PANS.

Faithful Fly

Designer David Sagorski

Nationality US

Date Designed 1994

Foundries Monotype ITC

Number of weights 1

ABCDEFGHIJKLMNOPQRSTUVWXYZ
ABCDEFGHIJKLMNOPQRSTUVWXYZ1234567890
PUZZLED WOMEN BEQUEATH JERKS VERY EXOTIC GIFTS.

Cutout

Designer Max Kisman

Nationality US

Date Designed 1990

Foundries Display

Number of weights 1

ABCDEFGHIJKLMNOPQRSTUVWXYZ
ABCDEFGHIJKLMNOPQRSTUVWXYZ1234567890
JADED READER WITH FABLED ROVING EYE SEIZED BY
QUICKENED IMPULSE TO EXPAND BUDGET.

Rad

Designer John Ritter

Nationality US

Date Designed 1989

Foundries Adobe

Number of weights 1

ABCDEFGHIJKLMNOPQRSTUVWXYZ
ABCDEFGHIJKLMNOPQRSTUVWXYZ1234567890
A SKATEBOARD ALPHABET

Kiddo

Designer Tim Ryan

Nationality IE

Date Designed 1995

Foundries Monotype

Number of weights 1

ABCDEFGHIJKLMNOPQRSTUVWXYZ
ABCDEFGHIJKLMNOPQRSTUVWXYZ
QUICK ZEPHYRS BLOW VEXING DAFT JIM

Alligators

Designer Philip Bouwsma

Nationality US

Date Designed 1995

Foundries Monotype

Number of weights 1

ABCDEFGHIJKLMNOPQRSTUVWXYZ
ⵣ 1234567890
LOWER CASE IS SORTS

Animalia

Designer	Johannes Plass
Nationality	DE
Date Designed	1996
Foundries	Linotype
Number of weights	1

ABCDEFGHIJKLMNOPQRSTUVWXYZ
abcdefghijklmnopqrstuvwxyz1234567890
The risque gown marked a brazen exposure of very juicy flesh.

Catastrophe

Designer	Judith Sutcliffe
Nationality	US
Date Designed	1993
Foundries	Monotype
Number of weights	1

ABCDEFGHIJKLMNOPQRSTUVWXYZ
FREIGHT TO ME SIXTY DOZEN QUART JARS AND
TWELVE BLACK PANS.

Critter

Designer	Craig Frazier
Nationality	US
Date Designed	1996
Foundries	Adobe Linotype
Number of weights	1

ABCDEFGHIJKLMNOPQRSTUVWXYZ
ABCDEFGHIJKLMNOPQRSTUVWXYZ1234567890
WHILE WAXING PARQUET DECKS, JAUNTY SUEZ SAILORS
VOMIT ABAFT.

Osprey

Designer	Stephen Farrell
Nationality	US
Date Designed	1993
Foundries	T-26
Number of weights	1

ABCDEFGHIJKLMNOPQRSTUVWXYZ
ABCDEFGHIJKLMNOPQRSTUVWXYZ1234567890
QUESTIONS OF A ZEALOUS NATURE HAVE BECOME BY
DEGREES PETTY WAXEN JOKES.

Zootype

Designer	Victor Garcia
Nationality	AR
Date Designed	1999
Foundries	Linotype
Number of weights	1

ABCDEFGHIJKLMNOPQRSTUVWXYZ
ABCDEFGHIJKLMNOPQRSTUVWXYZ1234567890
BIRDS, ANIMALS AND FISH COMPRISE THE VARIETIES IN
THIS FONT.

Mythos

Designer Min Wang, Jim Wasco
Nationality US
Date Designed 1989
Foundries Adobe
Number of weights 1

ABCDEFGHIJKLMNOPQRSTUVWXYZ
ABCDEFGHIJKLMNOPQRSTUVWXYZ1234567890
SIX BIG JUICY STEAKS SIZZLED IN A PAN AS FIVE
WORKMEN LEFT THE QUARRY.

Ouch!

Designer Joachim Müller-Lancé
Nationality DE
Date Designed 1996
Foundries Adobe Linotype
Number of weights 1

ABCDEFGHIJKLMNOPQRSTUVWXYZ
ABCDEFGHIJKLMNOPQRSTUVWXYZ1234567890
HOSPITALISED FONT.

Mojo

Designer Jim Parkinson
Nationality US
Date Designed 1960
Foundries Adobe
Number of weights 1

ABCDEFGHIJKLMNOPQRSTUVWXYZ
ABCDEFGHIJKLMNOPQRSTUVWXYZ1234567890
IT JUST DON'T WORK ON YOU.

Peace

Designer Leslie Cabarga
Nationality US
Date Designed 1997
Foundries Monotype
Number of weights 3

ABCDEFGHIJKLMNOPQRSTUVWXYZ
ABCDEFGHIJKLMNOPQRSTUVWXYZ1234567890
HAIGHT-ASHBURY, SUMMER OF '67

Love

Designer Leslie Cabarga
Nationality US
Date Designed 1997
Foundries Monotype
Number of weights 3

ABCDEFGHIJKLMNOPQRSTUVWXYZ
ABCDEFGHIJKLMNOPQRSTUVWXYZ1234567890
FOREVER CHANGES

Psychedelic

Buxom

Designer	Facsimile Fonts
Nationality	UK
Date Designed	1967
Foundries	Elsner+Flake Linotype
Number of weights	1

ABCDEFGHIJKLMNOPQRSTUVWXYZ

ABCDEFGHIJKLMNOPQRSTUVWXYZ1234567890

FAT FRONTED GIRLS

Bottleneck

Designer	Tony Wenman
Nationality	UK
Date Designed	1972
Foundries	Letraset Linotype
Number of weights	1

ABCDEFGHIJKLMNOPQRSTUVWXYZ

abcdefghijklmnopqrstuvwxyz1234567890

Astronaut Quincy B. Zack defies gravity with six jet fuel pumps.

Jellybaby

Designer	Timothy Donaldson
Nationality	UK
Date Designed	1997
Foundries	Monotype ITC
Number of weights	1

ABCDEFGHIJKLMNOPQRSTUVWXYZ

abcdefghijklmnopqrstuvwxyz1234567890

Jelly-like above the high wire, six quaking pachyderms kept the climax of the extravaganza in a dazzling state of flux.

Stoned

Designer	Theo Nonnen
Nationality	DE
Date Designed	1996
Foundries	FontFont
Number of weights	6

ABCDEFGHIJKLMNOPQRSTUVWXYZ

ABCDEFGHIJKLMNOPQRSTUVWXYZ1234567890

FAR GON AND SOLID MAN

Pierrot

Designer	Linotype
Nationality	DE
Date Designed	1996
Foundries	Linotype
Number of weights	1

ABCDEFGHIJKLMNOPQRSTUVWXYZ

abcdefghijklmnopqrstuvwxyz1234567890

Exquisite farm wench gives body jolt to prize stinker.

INDEX OF FONTS

INDEX OF FONTOGRAPHERS

Volta

Bayer Corporation

Central

CG Symphony

Highscript

Bean, Russell

Eumundi

Washington

Becker, Alf R

Modern Poster

Modern Roman

Bee, Marty

Wet and Wilde

Beekman, Donald

Automatic

Beekman

Breeze

Droids

Flava

Imperial

Manga

Noni Wan

Overdose

Stargate

Totem

Tsunami

Behrmann, Adolf

Rundfunk

Bell, Jill

Bruno

Caribbean

Carumba

Clover

Gigi

Hollyweird

Smack

Stranger

Swank

Belshaw, Nick; Meeks, Alan

Frankfurter

Belwe, Georg

Belwe

Belwe, Georg; Meeks, Alan

Belwe Mono

Benguiat, Ed

Benguiat

Edwardian Script

Panache

PL Benguiat Frisky

Barcelona

Bauhaus

Century Handtooled

Benson, John

Alexa

Balzano

Caliban

Benton, Morris Fuller

Alternate Gothic

Broadway

Broadway Poster

Century Expanded

Century Old Style

Century Schoolbook

Clearface

Clearface Gothic

Commercial Script

Empire

Franklin Gothic

Goudy Catalogue

Greeting Monotone

Hobo

Lightline Gothic

LinoScript

Linotext

Modernique

New Century Schoolbook

News Gothic

Old English Text

Parisian

Phenix American

PL Tower Condensed

Riviera Script

Silhouette

Souvenir

Stymie

TC Broadway

Wedding Text

Benton, Morris Fuller; Goodhue, Bertram

Cheltenham Handtooled

Cheltenham Old Style

Berd, Fryda

Quake

Bergquist, Lars

Monteverdi

Pavane

Whitenights

Berlow, David

Throhand

Berndal, Bo

Art Gallery

Belltrap

Benedikt

Berndal

Boberia

Boscribe

Bosis

Brigida

Buccardi

Carl Beck

Esseltube

Euclides

Exlibris

Gianpoggio

Golota

Grafilone

Grantofte

Jerrywi

Johabu

Läckö

Lebensjoy

Linotype Zurpreis

Logoform

Magellan

Maricava

Moorbacka

Naniara

Nordik

Olaus Bandus

Olaus Magnus

Palekin

Pocketype

Promemoria

Sabellicus

Siseriff

Spacekid

Swingbill

Trotzkopf

Unotype

Vadstenakursive

Bernhard, Lucian

Berlinsans

Bernard Condensed

Bernhard Antique

Bernhard Bold Condensed

Bernhard Fashion

Bernhard Modern

Bernhard Modern Roman

CG Bernhardt

Berranger, Eric de

Berranger Hand

Maxime

Mosquito

Mosquito Formal

Octone

Berthold

AG Old Face

Akzidenz-Grotesk

Basic Commercial LT

Englische Schreibschrift

Besley, R

Clarendon

Besnard, Roselyne; Besnard, Michel

MICMAC

Migraph

Odyssée

Pistol Shot

Typados

Biernot, Tad

Dummy

Linotype Rory

Bierschenk, Thomas Critzler

Bionic

Chemo

Bigelow, Charles; Holmes, Kris

Lucida

Bilak, Peter

Atlanta

Craft

Eureka

Masterpiece

Bilz, W; Simoncini, F

Life

Birch, Alan R

Bitmax

Rubber Stamp

Synchro

Birkenbach, Johannes

Jeunesse

Jocelyn

Palazzo

Perrywood MT

Ulissa

Bissex, Paul

Rufnu

Bitstream

Engravers' Old English

Blackman, Alan

Galahad

Blake, Stephenson

Britannic

C

Cabarga, Leslie
  Angle
  Central Station
  Haarlem
  Kobalt
  Love
  Ojaio
  Peace
Cabarga, Leslie;
    Cabarga, Demetrio R
  Cabarga Cursiva
Caflisch, Max
  Columna
Calvert, Margaret
  Calvert
Carichini, Mauro
  Arab Stroke
  Glass Flag
Carless, Vic
  Shatter
Carnase, Tom
  Manhattan
Carnase, Tom; Onder, Ronnie
  Machine
Carpenter, Ron
  Calisto
  Cantoria
Carter, Douglas
  Revolution
Carter, Matthew
  Bell Centennial
  Cascade Script
  Charter
  Galliard
  Georgia
  Olympian
  Shelley Script
  Snell Roundhand
  Tahoma
  Verdana
Carter, Matthew; Berlow, David
  Skia
Carter, Will
  Klang
Carter, Will; Kindersley, David
  Octavian
Carvalha, Patricia
  Cethubala

Caslon
  Doric 12
Caslon, William
  Caslon
Cassandre, A M
  Matra
  Peignot
Cavazos, Rodrigo Xavier
  Peregrine
Cerasoli, Genevieve
  Arnova
CG
  Hollandse
Chansler, Kim Buker; Crossgrove, Carl;
    Twombly, Carol
  Pepperwood
  Rosewood
Chappell, Warren
  CG Lisbon
  Lydian
  Trajanus
Chekoulaev, Alexei
  Linotype Bariton
Chester
  Schmelvetica
Chiadmi, Bachir Soussi
  Bousni Carré & Ronde
Chippindale, John
  Avenida
Cho, Hyun; Choi, Sung Min
  Tronic
Churchward, Joseph
  Churchward Brush
Chwast, Seymour
  Chwast Buffalo
Clarke, Paul
  One Stroke Script
Clinch, Jon H
  Bludgeon
  Howl
Closs, James
  Innercity
Connare, Vincent
  Trebuchet
  Wildstyle
Connell, Peter; Jones, Dick;
    Whitlock, Vince
  Crillee
Cooke, Nick
  Dartangnon ITC

  Penguin
Cooper, Oswald B
  Cooper Black
  Cooper Stencil
Costello, Chris
  Papyrus
Craw, Freeman
  Ad Lib
Critchley, John
  Bull
  Child's Play
Critchley, John;
    Raven, Darren
  Bokka
Critzler
  Down Town
  Go Tekk
  Linotype Mindline
  Localiser Clones
  Localiser
  TradeMarker
Crome, Paul; Lyons, Tony
  Buzzer Three
Crook, J H
  Ortem
Crossgrove, Carl
  Minska
  Origami
Crous-Vidal, Enric
  French Flash
Crow, David; Wright, Ian
  Beadmap
Cruz, Ray
  Bandolero Bandolera
  Cantina
  Cruz Swinger
  Elegante
  Romantica Condensed
Cuaz, Jean-Renaud
  Augustal Cursiva
  Cerigo
  Ellipse
  Galena
  Peplum
  Stancia
Cumming, John F
  Binner
  Kismet
  Skjald
  Virile

Currie, Leonard
  Impakt
Curtis, Nick
  Atelier
  Cuppajoe ITC
  Jeepers ITC
  Mister Chuckles
  Mustang Sally
  Photoplay ITC
  Scram Gravy ITC
  Tugboat Annie
  Woodley Park
Cushing, J Stearns
  Cushing
Cusick, Rick
  Nyx
Cuttle, Howard
  Inkspot

D

Dair, Carl
  Cartier
Dako, Peter
  BoneBlack
D'Amico, Dee Densmore
  Deelirious
Darnell, Kathryn
  Sweeney MT
Davies, Lucy
  Dot
  Linotype Dot
Davis, Stanley
  Amelia
Davison, M
  PL Davison Americana
  PL Davison Zip Bold
Dawson, Richard
  Gabardine
Decker, Joel
  Inkling
Dempsey, Alan
  Montage
  Tremor
Design, DS
  Kid TYPE
Deutsche Industrie Normal
  DIN
  DIN 1451
  DIN Mittelschrift

Didot, Firmin
  Didot
Diedrich, Yvonne
  Dyadis
Diesel, Chank
  Badoni
  Bonehead
  Buckethead
  Chauncy
  Cosmic
  Jawbox
  Lavaman
  Mister Frisky
  Moonshine Murky
  Orbital
  Orbus Multiserif
  Uncle Stinky
Dijk, Jan van
  Demian
  Squash
  Underscript
DiSpigna, Antonio; Benguiat, Edward
  Korinna
DiSpigna, Antonio; Lubalin, Herb
  Serif Gothic
Dom, Pete
  Dom Casual
Donaldson, Timothy
  Banshee
  Coriander
  Cult
  Cyberkugel
  Digital Woodcuts Black ITC
  Etruscan
  FancyWriting
  Farmhaus
  Flight
  Green
  Humana Sans ITC
  Humana Script ITC
  Humana Serif ITC
  Immi 505
  Jellybaby
  John Handy
  Klee
  Musclehead
  Neo Neo
  Orange
  Pink
  Pneuma

  Postino
  Riptide
  Ru'ach
  Scruff
  Spooky
  Talking Drum
  Telegram
  Trackpad
  Twang
  Ulysses
  Airstream
  Angry Hog
Dovey, M
  Kino
Drescher, Arno
  Antiqua
Dresscher, J
  MN Art World
DTF
  Bamberg
Dulkinys, Susanna
  Letter Gothic Slang
Duman, Ferdinay
  BlackWhite
Dupré, Xavier
  Angkoon
  Jambono
  Parango
  Reminga
  Tartine Script
Dwiggins, W A
  Caledonia
  CG Gothic
  CG Gothic No 1
  CG Gothic No 3
  CG Gothic No 4
  Elante
  Electra
  Metro #2
  New Caledonia
  Stuyvesant

E

Eckmann, Otto
  Eckmann
Edelstein, Ronny
  Linotype Mineru
Ehmcke, F H
  Carlton

Ehrhardt
  Ehrhardt
Ellaway, Rachel
  Linotype Besque
Ellenberger, Hans-Jürgen
  Cajoun
  Albawing
  Aspect LT
  Linotype Inagur
  Rana
  Beluga
  Carlin Script
  Linotype Pegathlon
  Escript LL
  Linotype Colibri
  Mateo
  Aspectintro LT
Elstrom, Per
  Coolman
Emcke, F H
  Carlton
  Ehmcke
Erasmus, Jan
  Thornface
Erbar, Jakob
  Erbar
  Koloss
  Candida
  Phosphor
**Erler, Johannes;
  Design, Factor**
  Pullman
Errico, Giuseppe
  Ludwig ITC
Estudio Mariscali
  Mundo Sans
Evans, Jean
  Hatmaker
Excoffon, Roger
  Antique Olive
  Banco
  Choc
  Mistral
Exploding
  Dutch Oven

F

Fahrenwaldt, M
  Minister

Fahrni, Peter
  Quadrus
Famira, Hannes
  Blocker
  Mutilated
Farey, Dave
  Bees Knees
  Cachet
  Font
  Greyhound Script
  Highlander
  Maigret
  Ozwald
  Revolution Normal
  Virgin Roman
Farmer, A D
  Scotch Roman MT
Farrell, Stephen
  Commonworld
  Entropy
  Flexure
  Missive
  Osprey
Fehrle, Erich
  Fehrle Display
Feliciano, Felice
  Felix
Feliciano, Mario
  Strumpf
Fenocchio, Umberto
  Brio
Ferrand, Louis
  Civilité
Finke, Thomas
  Bergell
Fontek
  Static
FontFont
  Bambus Initials
Fonts, Facsimile
  Buxom
Forsberg, Karl-Erik
  Berling
Forster, Tony
  Tiranti Solid
  Willow Plain
FotoStar
  Blippo
Foundry
  Bastarda

Fournier, P S
Fournier
Franosch, Max
Franosch
Frazier, Craig
Critter
Frere-Jones, Tobias
Dolores
Freytag, Arne
Freytag
Frit, Daniel
Ticket
Friz, Ernst
Friz Quadrata
Frutiger, Adrian
Apollo
Avenir
Breughel
Centennial
Egyptienne
Frutiger
Frutiger Stones
Glypha
Herculanum
Icone
Meridien
OCR-A
OCR-B
Ondine
Pompeijana
Rusticana
Serifa
Univers
Vectora
Versailles
Fullard, Val
Mambo
Science Regular
Fumarolo, L
MN Fumo DropShadow

G

Galapagos
Musica
Galiad Computers
Thorndale
Gallo, Gerald
Embossed
Gallo Serif

Ganeau, François
Vendôme
Garamond, Claude
Adobe Garamond
CG Garamond No. 3
Garamond
Garamond 3
Garamond Adobe
Garamond Classico
Garamond Handtooled
Garamond ITC
Granjon
Simoncini Garamond
Stempel Garamond
Garcia, Victor
Linotype Bix
Zootype
Garland, F Scott
Enviro
Garrett, Malcolm
Stealth
Gassner, Christof
Leopard
Geddes, Tony
Capone Light
CG Musketeer
Flamenco
Spotlight
Genzsch & Heyse
Alte Schwabacher
Gerlach, Verena
Karbid
Pide Nashi
Giles-Thornbory, Harry
Truckz
Gill, Eric
Gill Facia
Gill Floriated Caps MT
Gill Kayo Condensed
Gill Sans
Golden Cockerel Type
Joanna
Perpetua
Perpetua Titling
Pilgrim
Madame
Gillies, William S
Gillies Gothic
Gillies Gothic
Ex Bd Shaded

Gills, Michael
Charlotte
Charlotte Sans
Elysium
Fling
Forkbeard
Frances Uncial
Gilgamesh
Hand Drawn
Isis
Katfish
Prague
Gimeno, Pepe
Pepe
Gitschier, Kenneth
GitchHand
Glenn, Calvin
Jacoby
Tekno
Godfrey, Rachel
Clascon
Goede, Julius de
Augusta
Gaius
Julius Primary
Uncia
Goede, Julius de;
Veen, Fiel van der
Amadeo
Goldsmith, Hollly
Vintage
Havergal
Goodhue, Bertram G
Cheltenham
Gorn, Hariette
Morire
Götz, Christian
Linotype Minos
Goudy, Frederic W
Berkeley Oldstyle
Copperplate Gothic
Goudy
Goudy Extra Bold
Goudy Handtooled
Goudy Heavyface
Goudy Modern MT
Goudy Old Style
Goudy Sans
Goudy Text
Hadriano

Scripps College Old Style MT
Truesdell
Goudy, Frederic W; Marder, Clarence
Copperplate
Goulsbra, Roland John
Agrafie
Alexie
Granjon, Robert
News Plantin
Plantin
Plantin Schoolbook
Plantin Titling
Graphic Excursions
Agfa Ghixma
Greene, Alan
Atma
Grey, Gregory
Matisse
Griffith, Chauncey H
Bell Gothic
Corona
Excelsior
Ionic
Griffo, Francesco
Bembo
Bembo Titling
Griffo Classico
Poliphilus
Grimshaw, Phill
Arriba
Bendigo
Braganza
Gravura
Grimshaw Hand
Hazel
Kallos
Kendo
Klepto
Noovo
Obelisk ITC
Oberon
Pristina
Regallia
Rennie Mackintosh
Samuel
Scriptease
Shaman
Stained Glass
Stoclet
Tempus

Tempus Sans
Zaragoza
Zennor
Grinbergs, Gustav Andrejs
Gneisenauette
Linotype Brewery
Rowena
Groot, Lucas de
Transit
Günther, Lutz
Carmen
Gürtler, André
AT Basilia
Basilia
Egyptian 505

H

Haaparaanta, Tomi
Teebrush Paint
Teethreedee
Twinkle
Haas
Anzeigen Grotesk
Hägerling, Stefan
Motive
Ham, Marianne van
Double Dutch
Hammer, Victor
American Uncial
Hammer Uncial
Neue Hammer Unziale
Hamon, John
Mastercard
Hansen, Björn
Algologfont
Hansson, Lennart
Crane
Dex Gothic
Renasci
Runa Serif
ZiP
Hanzer, Markus
Irregular
Metamorph
Harling, Robert
Tea Chest
Harris, David
Becka Script
Chromium One

Harris, James L
Andesite
Harris, Mark
Crumudgeon
Pincers
Scrawlz
TwoVooDoo
Harvey, Michael
Andreas
Ellington
Strayhorn
Studz
Hashim, P M
Indus
Haus, Reinhard
Guardi
Haus, Reinhard; Gürtler, André
LinoLetter
Hauser, Stefan
F2F Haakonsen
Havinden, Ashley
Ashley Crawford
Ashley Script
Hüber, Jürgen
Ginger
Heidelberger
Modified Gothic
Heine, Frank
Amplifier
Chelsea FF
Contrivance
Cutamond
Instanter
Remedy
Hell Design Studio
Olympia Light
Hell, Dr Rudolf
Digi Antiqua
Digi Grotesk
Hemker, Jorg
Zwo
Herrnberger, Elke
Yokkmokk
Herz, Jörg
Short Story
Hess, Sol
Twentieth Century MT
Hesse, Gudrun Zapf von
Alcuin
Ariadne

Smaragd
Diotima
Hickson, Pat
Studio Script
Hickson, Paul
Wade Sans
Hitchen, Jonathan
Snafu
Hoefer, Karlgeorg
Bigband
Notre Dame
Omnia
Saltino
Salto
San Marco
Sho
Hoefler, Jonathan
Hoefler Text
Hoffman, H
Block
Hofman, Thomas
HoTom
Höljes, Wiebke; Faulhaber, Erik
Cadavre Exquis
Holland, Hollis
CG Holland Seminar
Holland Title
Hollandsworth, Cynthia
Agfa Wile Roman
Hiroshige
Hiroshige Sans
Hiroshige Serif
**Hollandsworth, Cynthia;
 Baker, Arthur**
Tiepolo
Holmes, Kris
Isadora
Lucida Blackletter
Lucida Calligraphy
Holmes, Kris; Prescott, Janice
Shannon
Howell, Robert J
Roughedge
Hüber, Jürgen
Angst
Plus Sans
Hudson, John
Aeneas
Hughes, Charles
Indy Italic

Hughes, Rian
CrashBangWallop
Identification
Knobcheese
Outlander
Revolver
Hullinger, Andy
Decco Modern
Hulst, Léon
ReadMyHand
Hüneke, Fedor
Murphy
Huschka, Karin
Linotype Authentic Sans
Linotype Authentic Serif
Linotype Authentic Small Serif
Linotype Authentic Stencil
Huschka, Peter
Sinah
Huxley, Walter
Aldous Vertical

I

Ihlenburg, Herman
Isabella
Iontef, Yanek
Cartonnage
Irwin, Rea
New Yorker Type
Isbell, Richard
Americana
Isbell, Richard; Campbell, Jerry
Isbell
ITC
Winchester New ITC
Ivir, Milo Dominik
Gotharda

J

Jackaman, Steve
Dungeon RR
Jackson, William F
Raphael
Jacquet, B
Jackson
Jaeger, Gustav
Beckett

Jagodzinski, Martin
   Tetria
Jakob, Gerd Sebastian; Meissner,
   Ewald
   Dharma
   Linotype Tiger
Jalleau, Franck
   Oxalis
   Virgile
Jamra, Mark
   Jamille
   Latienne
Janiszewski, Julian
   Tabula ITC
Jedding, Jan
   Friday, Saturday, Sunday
Jensen, Dick
   Serpentine
   Serpentine Serif
Jenson, Nicolas; Arrighi, L de
   Jenson Classico
Johnson, Michael
   Zeitgeist
Johnston, Edward
   Johnston's Railway Type
Jones, John
   Taut
Jordan, Matthias
   Papertape
Jordan, Mott
   Hornpype
   Verkehr
Jordan, Smiths & Mackellan
   Tiffany
Jörgensen, Helga
   Dinitials
Jørgensen, Per Baasch
   Bagel
   Falafel
Jost, Heinrich
   Beton
Jung, Andreas
   Trombo

K

Kadan, Joel; Stan, Tony
   American Typewriter
   Kaeser, Silvan

Seebad
   Kahan, Teri
   Cherie
   Surfboard
Kalscheuer, Christopher
   Maverick
Kare, Susan
   Chicago
   Geneva
Karl, Andreas
   Fluxus
   Linotype Mailbox
Kaufmann, Max R
   Balloon
   Kaufmann
   Swing
Kelly, Philip
   Zipper
   Algerian
Kelly, Rob Roy
   Florinda
Kemp, Carol
   Jiggery Pokery
   Party
   Wac Wak Ooops
   Zinjaro
Kettler, Howard
   Courier
Kim, Albert J
   Adagio
Kim, Julius
   Blizzard
King, Patty
   Blaze
   Kick
   Skylark
   Spirit
Kingsley
   Railroad Gothic
Kipp, Claudia
   Kipp
Kirchner, Robert
   Isonorm
Kis, Nicholas
   Janson
   Janson Text
   Kis Classico
Kisman, Max
   Cutout
   Fudoni

Jacque
   Network
   Rosetta
   Scratch FF
   Vortex
Klassen, Tony
   Tattoo
Klein, Manfred
   Carolus Magnus
   Johannes G
   Koberger
   Quill
   Schoensperger
   Spontan
   Witches
Kloos-Rau, Rosemarie
   Wiesbaden Swing
Klumpp, E J
   Mahogany Script
Klunder, Barbara
   Klunder Script
   Ottofont
Kobayashi, Akira
   Acanthus
   Linotype Conrad
   Luna
   Magnifico Daytime
   Scarborough
   Silvermoon
   Skid Row
   Vineyard
   Woodland
   Clifford Eighteen
Koch, Andreas
   Linotype Projekt
Koch, Erwin
   Dalcora HE
Koch, Rudolf
   Ambrose
   Kabel
   Koch Antiqua
   Koch Original
   Locarno
   Neuland
   Othello
   Wilhelm Klingspor Gotisch
Kolben, Robert
   Venezia
Kolodziejzyk, Greg
   Signature

König, Heinz
   Falstaff
Kortemaeki, Sami
   Nelio
Krátky, Andrej
   Bradlo
   Bradlo Slab
Kramer, Dale R
   Harvey
Krimpen, Jan van
   Haarlemmer
   Spectrum
Krimpen, Jan van; Dijck, Christoffel Van
   Van Dijck
Kugler, Georg
   Linotype Cutter
   Linotype Schere
Kulik, Carol
   Monaco
Kurz, Dieter
   Matthia
   Sketch
Kwiatkowski, Ilka
   Schachtelhalm

L

Laan, Paul van der
   Linotype Rezident
Lambert, Fred
   Compacta
Lang, Paul
   Langer
Lange, Günther Gerhard
   Boulevard
Laubinger, Gabriele
   Linotype Sangue
Lautenbach, E
   Monotype Script Bold
Lavrow, Dmitri
   Hardcase
Laxa, Isabell
   Linotype Supatropic
Lee, Geoffrey
   Impact
   Impact
Lehnhoff, Joern
   Linotype Ego
Lemoine, Louis
   Linotype Spacera

Lemon, David
  Copal
Leonardi, Alessio
  Baukasten
  Cavolfiore
  Coltello
  F2F Al Retto
  F2F Allineato
  F2F Madame Butterfly
  F2F Matto
  F2F Mekanik Amente
  F2F MekkasoTomanik
  F2F Metamorfosi
  F2F PoisonFlowers
  F2F Prototipa Multipla
  F2F Provinciali
  F2F Tagliatelle Sugo
  Graffio
  HaManga Irregular LL
  Handwriter
  Letterine
  Mulinex
  Priska Serif
Leonardi, Alessio; Wollein, Priska
  Cool Wool
Leonhard, Michael
  Linotype Flamingo
Lester, Sebastian
  Scene
Letraset
  Aachen
  Cabaret
  Einhorn
  Iris
  Plaza
  Premier Lightline
  Premier Shaded
  Princetown
  Pump
  Quartz
  Revue
  Rialto
  Romic
  Slipstream
  University Roman
  Victorian
  Wanted
  Rundfunk Antiqua
  Rundfunk Grotesk
  Xylo

Lettau, Klaus Dieter
  Voodoo
Leu, Olaf
  Compatil Exquisit
  Compatil Fact
  Compatil Letter
  Compatil Text
Leuschke, Rob
  Arid
Lich, Ingrid
  Clair
  Liant
Lillie, Patricia
  Cinderella ITC
  Delilah
  Tickle
Lind, Barbara
  Madrone
Linotype
  Buckingham Fraktur
  Cartoon Script
  Case Study No. 1
  Clairvaux
  CMC-7
  Dala LT
  Flyer
  Forbes
  Grafiko
  Jiffy
  Kursivschrift
  Linotype Kaliber
  Linotype Punkt
  Linotype Puritas
  Linotype Richmond
  Luthersche Fraktur
  Macbeth
  Pierrot
  Serlio
  Spartan Classified
  Textur Gotisch
  Textur Lombardic
  Westside
  Woodstock
  Roemisch
Loane, Trevor
  Citation
Lochu, Jean
  Loire
  Selune

Lomba, Luiz Da
  Le Chat Noir Toulouse Lautrec
  Le Petit Trottin Toulouse Lautrec
  Moulin Rouge Toulouse Lautrec
  Pierre Bonnard Toulouse Lautrec
  Theatre Antoine Toulouse Lautrec
Loon, Chew
  Accolade
Loong, Kelvin Tan Tec
  Linotype Transis
Lopetz, Gianfredo
  Linotype Aroma
Lubac, André Michel
  Le Griffe
Lubalin, Herb
  Lubalin Graph
Lubalin, Herb; Carnase, Tom
  Avant Garde Gothic
  Busorama
Lubbers, Marc
  Impacta
  LuMarc
Ludlow
  Bookman Old Style
Luigs, Jenny; Wicker, Simon
  Facsimile
Luin, Franko
  Ad Hoc
  Birka
  Carniola
  Devin
  Dialog
  Emona
  Esperanto
  Fortuna
  Isolde
  Jesper
  Jonatan
  Kalix
  Kasper
  Marco Polo
  Memento
  Miramar
  Norma
  Nyfors
  Odense
  Omnibus
  Pax
  Pax #2
  Persona

  Ragnar
  Res Publica
  Rustika
  Saga
  Semper
  Transport
  Vega
Luteyn, Roger
  Residoo
  Tiffany

M

Maehler, H
  Salut
Majce, Moritz
  Red Babe
Majoor, Martin
  Scala
  Seria
**Malin, Charles;
  Peignot, Georges**
  Cochin
Manchipp, Jasper
  Aikiko
  Philco
Mannella, Roberto
  Linotype Sicula
Manso, Eduardo
  Merss ITC
Marciuliano, Frank
  Automat
  Isilda
  Jaft
  Jambalaya
  Linotype Constitution
  Linotype Labyrinth
  Linotype Lindy
  Mediterraneo LT
  Schizoid
Marcus, Jim
  Albany Telegram
  Carnival
  Django T-26
  Escalido
  Integral
  Scorpio
  Skreech
  Slide
  Variator

Mardersteig, Giovanni
  Dante
Marecki, Thomas
  Tag Team 1 Marker Skinny
Mariscalchi, Gérard
  Baylac
  Comic Strip
  Evita
  Lineale
  Link
  Marnie
  Toots
  Iona
  Redonda
Marshall, David
  Biffo
Martin, Phil
  Adroit
  CG Heldustry
Martin, William
  Bulmer
Mastandrea, Maryanne
  Cirrus
Matheis, Helmut
  Charme
  Slogan
Matteson, Steve
  Andale Mono
  Andy
  Blueprint MT
  Fineprint
Matteson, Steve; Crossgrove, Carl
  Curlz
Mayers, Anthony
  Monolith
McAuley, Lee Martin
  Heliotype
McCallion, Marcus
  Linotype Marcu San
McCracken, Pete
  Facsimiled
  INKy-black
McFadden, Steve; Diesel, Chank
  Skippy Sharp
McGrath, Bob
  Elefont
  Roman Script
  Springfield
McGregor, Chris
  Epaulet

Mecanorma
  Gothique
  Milton Demibold
  MN Circus
  Organda
  Swaak Centennial
  Watch Outline
  Zambesi
Mediavilla, Claude
  Galba
Meeks, Alan
  Bertie
  Bickley Script
  Bramley
  Burlington
  Campaign
  Cancellaresca Script
  Champers
  Chesterfield
  Claude Sans
  Fashion Compressed
  Fashion Engraved
  Follies
  Glastonbury
  Inscription
  Jazz
  Lightnin
  Limehouse Script
  Malibu
  Ragtime
  Regatta Condensed
  Savoye
  Tannhäuser
  Varga
  Waterloo
Meerbeeck, D van
  DuChirico
  DuDuchamp
  DuGauguin
  DuMathieu
  DuMifu
  DuMoore
  DuTurner
Meester, Anthony de
  Vienna Extended
Megnet, Elisabeth
  Grace
Mehallo, Steve
  Alta California
  Chandler 42

  Martini At Joes
Meier, Hans Eduard
  Barbedor
  Linotype Syntax
  Linotype Syntax Lapidar
  Syndor
Mendelson, Barbara
  Arty
Mendoza, José
  Mendoza
  Sully Jonquières
Menhart, Oldrich
  Figural
Menne, Inka
  Grassy
Merlaut, Alexis
  Equilibre Gauche
  Esquisse
Meuffels, L
  Dextor
  Hotel
Middleton, R Hunter
  Cloister Open Face
  Coronet
  Delphian Open Titling
  Eden
  Florentine Script II
  PL Radiant Bold
    Extra Condensed
  Stellar
  Stencil
  Umbra
  Tempo
  Cloister
Miedinger, Max
  Helvetica
  Helvetica Inserat
  Neue Helvetica
Miggas, Stephen
  Khaki
  Mission
  Fiesta
Miladinov, Slobodan
  Coconino
  Freemouse
Milano, G de
  Neon Extra Condensed
Miles Inc
  PL Brazilia 3 & 7
  Uncial

Miller, Anistatia
  Metronome Gothic
Miller & Richard
  Old Style 7
Mills, Ross
  Plantagenet
Minott, Louis
  Davida
Müller, Stefan; Windlin, Cornel
  Dot Matrix
Modelhart, Herbert O
  Linotype Reducta
Möllenstadt, Bernd
  Formata
Monotype
  Artisan Roman
  Century Gothic
  Clarion
  Colmcille
  Delima
  Derek
  Egyptian 72
  Engravure
  Figaro
  Footlight
  Gloucester Old Style MT
  Goudy Ornate MT
  Grotesque MT
  Headline MT
  Horley Old Style
  Imprint
  Italian Old Style
  Mahsuri Sans
  Monotype Modern
  Modern No. 20
  Modern No. 216
  Monoline Script
  New Clarendon
  Old English
  Palace Script
  Rockwell
  Runic
  Sackers Solid Antique Roman
  Victoria Titling
  Victorian Silhouette
  Wittenberger Fraktur
  Floridian Script
  Poster Gothic
Montalbano, James
  Freddo

Hollywood
Pegoraro, Paul
Ginko
Pelavin, Daniel
Anna
Kulukundis
Peter, John
Peter's Miro
Peters, Fritz
Vivaldi
Peters, John
Castellar
Petrick, Robert
Boink
Pettit, Trevor
Pablo
Peugeot, Fidel
Lomo
Pfannkuchen, Bernd
Linotype Lichtwerk
Phemister, Alexander
Bookman
Monotype Old Style MT
Old Style Bold Outline
Phinney, Joseph W
Globe Gothic
Photo-Lettering
AT Brazilia Seven
Barclay Open
Flatiron
PL Brazilia Three
PL Fiorello Condensed
PL Latin
Westerveldt
Pichii, Serge
Drycut
Gramophone
Ironwork
Pinggera, Albert
Letter Gothic Text
Strada
Pischner, C W
Neuzeit S
DIN Neuzeit
Planet, Mat
Planet Informal
Planet Sans Book
Planet Serif
Plass, Johannes
Animalia

Atomatic
Auferstehung
Poget, Grégoire
Linotype Sansara
Pool, Albert-Jan
Imperial URW
OCR-F
Porchez, Jean-François
Angie
Pott, Gottfried
Arioso
Carolina
Duc de Berry
Ruling Script Two
Pott, Stefan
Konflikt
Linotype Henri Axis
Linotype Henri Dimension
Powell, Gerry
Arsis
Onyx
Preuss, Ingo
Funny Bones
Scrap
Psychoglyph
Claude
Puyfoulhoux, Thierry
Alinea Incise
Alinea Roman
Alinea Sans
Bebop
Cicero
Korigan

Q

Quay, David
Agincourt
Aquinas
Arta
Blackmoor
Bordeaux
Bordeaux Script
Bronx
Coptek
Digitek
La Bamba
Lambada
Latino Elongated

Marguerita
Mekanik
Milano
Quay Sans
Robotik
Santa Fé
Scriptek
Teknik
Vegas

R

Rafique, Themina
Araby Rafique
Rakowski, David
Aarcover
Adine Kirnberg
Ann Stone Initials
Bizarro
Diner
Dobkin
Ramsey-Passmore, René
Renee Display
Rawald, Matthias
Burokrat
Redick, Joy
Blackoak
Willow
Redon, Michel; Demriane, Denis
Patouillard
Bibracte
Rees, Dudley
Black Tulip
Reichel, Hans
Dax
Sari
Schmalhans
Reiner, Imre
Matura
Mercurius Script Bold
Pepita
Reiners, Norbert
Eirinn
Octane
Tarquinius
Reissberger, Carl
Forte
Remscheid, Marcus
MhaiThaipe
Russisch Brot

Renberg, Marius
Helix
Renner, Paul
Futura
Futura Black
PL Futura MaxiBook
Plak
Retzko, Armin
Quasaria
Reuss, Achaz
Compress
Type Revivals
School Script
Reyes, Mauricio
Binary
Rühl, Alexander
Lennox
Rickner, Thomas A
Buffalo Gal
Amanda
Ritter, John
Rad
Ritzel, Arthur
Rotation
Robertson, Roger
Letter Gothic
Rocha, Claudia
Gema
Underscript
Roe, Adam
Adolescence
Alexander
Blind Date
Category
Epicure
Girlfriend
Malaise
Nowwhat
Outahere
Percolator
Promdate
Replicant
Solace
Substance
Surrogate
Technique
Rogers, Bruce
Centaur
Rolands, Tim
Orlando AT

Ronaldson, Binny
Binny Old Style
Ronen, E-lan
Aura
Roos, S H De
Hollandse Mediaevel
Simplex
Roshell, John
Achtung Baby
Adamantium
Rossum, Just van
Advert
Advert Rough
Brokenscript
Confidential
Dynamoe
Flightcase
Justlefthand
Karton
Schulbuch Bayern
Schulbuch Nord
Schulbuch Süd
Schulschrift
Stamp Gothic
Rothschild, Noah
Balance
Rottke, Fabian
Assuri
Dirty Fax
Ekttor
Franklinstein
Atelier de Rouen
ROM
Rückel, Siegfried
Alega
Russell, John
Russell Square
Ruzicka, Rudolph
Fairfield
Lake Informal
Ruzicka Freehand
Ryan, George
Adderville ITC
Eborg ITC
Kristen Normal
Migrate
Ryan, Tim
Boomerang
Kiddo
Mod

S

Sachse, Christina
Boundaround
Sack, Freda
Ignatius
Orlando ITC
Vermont
Safeyev, Tagir
Stenberg
Sagorski, David
Bang
Bluntz
Dancin
Faithful Fly
Juice
Mo' Funky Fresh
Snap
Tag
Sahre, Paul
Fur
Sallwey, Friedrich Karl
Present
Roundy
Sallwey Script
Salzmann, Max
Dolmen
Samata, Greg
Mata
Ramiz
Scratch T-26
Sander, Meike
Linotype Wildfont
Sassoon, Rosemary
Sassoon Infant
Sassoon Primary
Sassoon San Slope
Sassoon Sans
Sauerteig, Steffen
Jigger
Readout
TypeStar
TypeStar OCR
Sauerteig, Steffen; Vermehr, Kai
Eboy
SubVario / SubMono
Xcreen
Screenstar
Sauerteig, Steffen; Wagenbreth, Henning

Prater Block
Prater Sans
Prater Script
Prater Serif
Saunders, Patricia
Columbus
Monotype Corsiva
Sayer, Manfred
Sayer Interview
Sayer Script
Schaar, Edwin W
Imperial
Schaarschmidt, Hartmut
Veto
Schäfer, Ole
Fago Monospaced
Fago Office Sans
Turmino
Scribble
Zine
Schäfer, Ole; Spiekermann, Erik
Govan
Schelter & Giesecke
Flamme
Schenk, Robert
Double Back
Scheuerhorst, A; Ignaszak, M; Kister, S
Call
Schiavi, Fabrizio
Geäb Oil
NineSixNilNil
Steel
Steel Moderne
Steel Narrow
Trade 01
Schikorski, Martina
Linotype Mild
Schlaich, Sibylle
F2F Styletti
Schlesinger, Stefan; Dooijes, Dick
Rondo
Venus
Schmitt, Maria Martina
Airam
Schnäbele, Thomas
Inky Script
Linotype Method
Schneidler, F H E
Schneidler Amalthea

Schneidler CG
Schneidler Mediaeval
Schneidler Stempel
Scholing, Alex
Engine
Roice
Schöpp, Simone
A Lazy Day
Littles
Schraubstädter, William
French Script
Schroeder, Gustav F
Eccentric
McCollough
Quaint Roman
Schumann, Heinz
Stentor
Schuss, Jochen
Kokoa
Out of the Fridge
Paint It
Schuss Hand
Vino Bianco
Whiskey
Schwartz, Christian
Bau
Elroy
Hairspray
Morticia
Twist
Zombie
Schwekendiek, Gerhard
Greyton Script
Schwerdtner, W
Metropolis
Sciullo, Pierre di
Minimum
Scratched Out
Scobie, Trevor
Quantum
Sedore, Vaughan
Techno Outline
Typeface 6 & 7
Seeling, Holger
Pleasure Bold Shaded
Segura, Carlos
Flaco
Neo Bold
Square 40
Time In Hell

Sehmi, Satwinder
  Simran ITC
Semmad, Taouffik
  Atmosphere
Shaar, Edwin W
  Gazette
  Nuptial Script
  Flash
Shahn, Ben
  Folk
Shaw, Paul
  Göteborg
  Kolo
  Old Claude
Shaw, Paul; Boge, Garrett
  Stockholm
  Uppsala
Shinde, Nagesh
  Seven T-26
Shinn, Nick
  Fontesque
  Merlin FF
  Oneleigh
  Paradigm
Siddle, John
  Boomshanker
Siegel, David
  Eaglefeather Formal
  Eaglefeather Informal
  Graphite
Siegel, David; Wasco, Jim;
  Ching, Francis
  Tekton
Simon, H A
  Market
Simoncini, Francesco
  New Aster
Simonson, Mark
  Kandal
Simpson, Kevin
  Aitos
Siquot, Luis
  Abaton
  Juanita
  Juanita Deco
  Juanita Lino
  Juanita Xilo
  Portago
Slimbach, Robert
  Giovanni

Minion
Poetica
Slimbach
Utopia
Slimbach, Robert; Twombly, Carol
  Myriad Headline
Smeijers, Fred
  Quadraat
Smit, Leonard H D
  Orator
Smital, Svend
  SuperGrotesk
Smith, Andrew
  Barbed Wire
  Chiller
  Chipper
  Christina
  Jokerman
  Scratch ITC
  Smudger
Smith, Clayton
  Prestige Elite
Smith, Robert E
  Brush Script
  Park Avenue
Smith, Scott
  Scotty
  Scotty Normal
Sniffin, Willard T
  Liberty
  CG Chaplin
  Hardwood
Snyder, Pat
  Marker Felt
Søgren, Poul
  Jante Antiqua
Solo, Dan X
  Boul Mich
  Clyde
  Grock
  Xerxes
Solt-Bittner, Viktor
  Ballerino
  Danubia
  Johann Sparkling
  Voluta Script
Sommer, K
  Dynamo
Søndergaard, Ole
  Signa

Sooy, Brian
  Coventry
SourceNet
  School Oblique
Spemann, Rudo
  Gavotte
Spiece, Jim
  Blair
  Deli Deluxe
  Deli Supreme
  Kingsbury Condensed SG
  Tweed
Spiekermann, Erik
  Meta
Spiekermann, Erik; Brody, Neville
  Meta Plus
Spiekermann, Erik; Schäfer, Ole
  Info
  Officina
Spiekermann, Erik;
  Schwartz, Christian
  Unit
Herriet, Julius
  Façade Condensed
Stacey, Michael
  True Grit
  Wisteria
Stan, Tony
  Pasquale
Stanczyk, Mark
  Linotype Typo American
Stempel
  Stempel Schneidler
Stephenson Blake
  Britannic
  PL Britannia Bold
  Thorowgood
  Wide Latin
  Windsor
Stevens, Donald
  Aristocrat
Stevens, Eric
  Kumquat
  Lintball
  Pious Henry
  Tapioca
Stojadinovic, Olivera
  Aspera
  Hedera ITC
  Rastko ITC

Stone, Sumner
  Arepo
  Silica
  Stone Informal
  Stone Print
  Stone Sans
  Stone Serif
Storm, Frantisek
  Biblon
  Malstock
  Zeppelin
Storm, Nina Lee
  Storm Sans
Strassburger, Michael
  Imperfect
Strockis, Mindaugas
  Elementa
Struller, Michael
  Salamander
Stu's Font Diner
  Fatsam
  Kentuckyfried
  Linotype Belle
  Taylors
Stutz, Isabelle
  Taylors
Sutcliffe, Judith
  Arabia Felix
  Catastrophe
  Daly Hand
  Daly Text
  Daylilies
  Hibiscus
  Kiilani
  Tommy's Type
Sych, Paul
  Dig
  Dog
  Hip
Szönyei, György
  Archian
Szujewska, Laurie
  Giddyup

T

Tachdjian, Jean-Jacques
  Linotype Barock
  Alex